A Century of Service

A Century of Service

LIBRARIANSHIP IN THE UNITED STATES AND CANADA

Edited by
SIDNEY L. JACKSON
Kent State University

ELEANOR B. HERLING
University of Houston Libraries

E. J. JOSEY
New York State Education Department

WITHDRAWN

AMERICAN LIBRARY ASSOCIATION
Chicago 1976

Library of Congress Cataloging in Publication Data
Main entry under title:

A Century of service.

    Includes bibliographical references.
    1. Libraries—United States—History—Addresses, essays, lectures. 2. Libraries—Canada—History—Addresses, essays, lectures. I Jackson, Sidney Louis, 1914– II. Herling, Eleanor B. III. Josey, E. J., 1924–
Z731.C425   021′.0097   76-41815
ISBN 0-8389-0220-0

Copyright © 1976 by the American Library Association

All rights reserved. No part of this publication may be reproduced in any form without permission in writing from the publisher, except by a reviewer who may quote brief passages in a review.

Printed in the United States of America

Contents

Preface   vii

PART ONE
Clienteles

CHAPTER 1   Service to the Urban Rank and File   1
Hardy R. Franklin

2   Service to Urban Children   20
Clara O. Jackson

3   Service to Ethnic Minorities Other than Afro-Americans and American Indians   42
Haynes McMullen

4   Service to Afro-Americans   62
A. P. Marshall

5   Service to Academia   79
Samuel Rothstein

6   Service to Special Clienteles   110
Angelina Martinez

PART TWO
Personnel

CHAPTER 7	A Century of Personnel Concerns in Libraries David Kaser and Ruth Jackson	129
8	Women in Librarianship Dee Garrison	146

PART THREE
Facilities

9	Reference Services and Technology Budd L. Gambee and Ruth R. Gambee	169
10	Technical Services and Technology: The Bibliographical Imperative Suzanne Massonneau	192
11	Technical Services and Technology: Technological Advance Ann H. Schabas	208
12	Library Buildings A. Robert Rogers	221

PART FOUR
Environment

13	The National Libraries of the United States and Canada John Y. Cole	243
14	The Principal Library Associations Peter Conmy and Caroline M. Coughlin	260
15	The Library World and the Book Trade Grant T. Skelley	281
16	Image of Librarianship in the Media Neal L. Edgar	303
17	Services to Library Life Abroad Vivian D. Hewitt	321
18	Research Sidney L. Jackson	341

Preface

"Essays in Honor of" are customarily written to celebrate the labors and influence of an individual. They are frequently timed to coincide with the honoree's retirement or round-number birthday. The contributions traditionally include a sketch of his or her life, bibliography by and about the individual, and a number of scholarly essays by associates which on the whole relate to their common interests.

The present volume is different. It honors a profession and those who practice it, by reviewing broadly, facet by facet, the advances, failures, and present prospects of libraries and librarianship in the United States and Canada. Any time is a good time to do that. An especially good moment is the completion of a century of organized professional life, and it was with such sense of occasion that an ad hoc committee of library historians commissioned this work at the Midwinter meeting of the American Library Association in January 1973.

In considering the totality of the essays we observe that certain concerns are given prominence. The outstanding demographic feature of the past century in the United States and Canada is the concentration of population in urban areas. It is fitting, therefore, that our first two chapters should be devoted to the efforts of librarians to serve the urban rank and file. In the case of the adults this meant essentially the public libraries; in the case of the children, both public and school libraries. A very important component in the smaller communities as well as the metropolitan areas, developing a variety of facets during the course of the century, are the immigrants and their posterity. Chapter 3 addresses the port-of-entry phase of that story; the factory and mining town phases remain for some future investigator. Our concern with equal rights for disadvantaged minorities is reflected in chapter 4.

Second in importance only to the library service rendered are those who rendered it, how they fared, and the concerns that developed within a professional group functioning as an instrument of education not fully recognized. This is the subject of chapter 7. Chapter 8 analyzes the effect on an emerging profession of the predominance of women among library troops led primarily by male officers. The tools and techniques these persons created are considered in the sphere of reference work, then in the sphere of the technical services. The physical surroundings in relation to architectural possibilities are treated in chapter 11. All three reveal in one way or another the interpenetration of knowledge, imagination, technical advance, vested interest, and encrusted habit.

The broader organizational environment is examined in chapters on the national libraries of the United States and Canada, and on the American Library Association. Relations with the book trade, the image of librarianship in the "outside" world's media, and the give and take with thinking abroad, detail the interaction with institutions in the background.

The standing of a profession depends not only on the service it renders and the images it has earned. To develop scientifically grounded literature and standards for training and performance presupposes ability to conceptualize aims and organize meaningful scientific research in pursuit thereof. The relation between goals and research as an instrument for approaching them is explored in the last chapter. Indications of what has been accomplished in research are given.

To obtain competent contributors was not so easy a matter as might be supposed. There were, of course, many persons able to undertake the preparation of the chapters; but other obligations precluded some of them from participating. We could have overlooked some appropriate individuals simply because we were not aware of them. The selection of writers was also shaped by a policy commitment, to acknowledge the high significance in 1976 of an equal share in professional leadership for women, and an appropriate share for our principal minorities and our good neighbors in Canada.

The drafts submitted were examined by all three editors, and in nearly every instance were revised by their authors. We believe that the profession will find in the following pages a reasonable measure of the sort of satisfactions and challenges thinking people want.

Thanks are due the American Library History Round Table, all contributors, and our publisher.

PART ONE

Clienteles

1

Service to the Urban Rank and File

HARDY R. FRANKLIN
District of Columbia Public Library

The public library, it is often said, has been dedicated from its earliest days to the economic and cultural improvement of the common man. The library movement was born in a social period illumined by what Sidney Ditzion has called "the bright light of exuberant democracy" and was raised on the nineteenth-century belief that education was the key to social advancement.[1]

A recent study observes that the use of libraries by blue-collar workers has never been closely scrutinized and that public libraries have made little concentrated effort to reach this group of non- or, at best, light users.[2] Nevertheless, throughout the first hundred years of the American Library Association, our sense of professional obligation to the urban rank and file, that segment of the population which labors with its hands, has remained constant—even if we have not always known what to do about it. Especially in industrial cities has it been the inspiration, periodically, for experimental services aimed at bridging the gulf between a concerned but largely middle-class profession and a usually reluctant, or at least indifferent, less affluent, and less educated clientele. "Outreach" is the most recent label we have found for such activities, and during the past ten years the urban public libraries throughout the country have indeed reached out in an astonishing variety of ways. Despite the air of novelty about many of these activities, however, the tradition, the inspiration, and even some of the techniques have been with us since our professional beginnings.

EARLY VOCATIONAL LIBRARIES

Libraries for the working class was a notion of some currency even before the Civil War. As early as 1849, H. Stevens, Yale College librarian, testified before the British Committee on Public Libraries that mechanics' institutes were many and flourishing in all the large towns in America, offering not only free access to books but also other cultural activities including debating societies, lyceums, and lectures. Patriotic fervor may have accounted for Stevens's additional statement that he had never seen "an American born who could not read and write, above eight years of age." He was, furthermore, surprised in coming to England "to see how little reading there is among the labouring and business classes."[3]

The mechanics' libraries which flourished in the early nineteenth century were established with two purposes in view. They provided, first, the pragmatic, utilitarian opportunity for the improvement of skills needed in a time of growing industrialization; hence, for the employee, a hoped-for opportunity for economic advancement. Second, at least in the hopes of the employer, they provided a constructive recreational outlet for underprivileged laborers who had newly migrated from Europe or the local rural life and who were all too easily led, it was feared, into the moral delinquency of the saloon and the bawdy house. To its social superiors, the working class very early carried with it the threat of disruption of the peace and the social order. Later, with the growth of the unions, the mistrust was mutual.

After a brief period of enthusiasm, interest in the vocational library turned to disillusionment, for "reading failed to produce a marked increase in either skills or income."[4] A more pessimistic view ascribes the decline of such libraries to the boredom and indifference of the patrons when faced with the heavy and patronizing doses of cultural uplift that the lyceums and lecture programs prescribed. As these libraries were privately supported, they generally perished as a consequence.[5] Although a few hardy and well-endowed specimens of the vocational library endured into the twentieth century, most faded rapidly; many of them were literally absorbed by the new wave of tax-supported public libraries. Their significance for us lies in the twin goals they bequeathed to the public library: vocational improvement and recreation. Librarians discuss their relative merits to this day.

EARLY DAYS OF THE PUBLIC LIBRARY

Given the economic as well as intellectual ferment of the later years of the century, it is not surprising that the public librarians, like the humanitarians of the time, were concerned with the welfare of the working man. The need for educational opportunities intensified as the evils of industrialism and exploitation became apparent in the social deterioration of slums, poverty, and delinquency. Fired by the belief that education was the key not only to economic advancement but also to the understanding and preservation of democracy, the humanitarians, educators, and librarians of this period saw that their work was cut out for them. The advocates of free public education envisioned the free public library as the capstone of the educational system: the interdependency of the public schools and the public libraries is a vital issue to us still. What good was it, they said, to teach everyone to read, if we did not provide a source of materials to be read? Librarians, for their part, "placed the library alongside sanitation, street lighting, public parks, and hospitals as minimum social services which a democratic society owed itself."[6] They were not quite so sure, perhaps, about how to convey these social services to the laboring class in a time marked by strikes and bloody battles of labor and employer, a time of class alienation and profound distrust on the part of the working man of all social and philanthropic institutions.

There were in addition, at the end of the nineteenth century, other social attitudes and economic truths common to such industrialized cities as Baltimore, Cleveland, and Detroit, that seriously impeded the use of the public library by the laboring classes in the manner envisioned by many zealous and idealistic librarians of the period. The goal of unlocking the cultural treasure trove for the masses of laboring men and women supposedly hungry for knowledge and educational guidance was praiseworthy indeed, but not often capable of fulfillment.

The Enoch Pratt Free Library, for example, was opened in Baltimore in 1886 during a business depression. With unemployment high, one might have expected a significant amount of interest in the library on the part of the laboring class. In actuality, few of this class were able to utilize library resources to a significant degree because of lack of a basic education: at that time, only one-third of the public school children reached the fourth grade and only 6 percent finished elementary school. "Considering the fact that the parents ... were even more poorly educated, the simple lack of reading ability barred many from the benefits of the library."[7]

Working conditions in the Baltimore sweatshops and canneries of that period were probably typical of industry elsewhere: thousands of women and children going to work before dawn to labor for twelve hours at mass production lines in filthy, badly ventilated workrooms or factories, for a daily wage of one dollar. Returning in a state of fatigue to a crowded tenement late at night, few indeed could be expected to summon the energy or enthusiasm for a trip to the library. Those who did occasionally faced social intimidation as well, which reflected the uneasy gulf separating librarians and laborers. While the Pratt library of the 1890s announced that its reading room was filled with representatives of every class, from elegant young ladies to shabbily dressed workingmen, in another part of town, James Duncan, president of the Baltimore Federation of Labor, charged in the press that he had been sneered at in the Peabody Library for appearing in his working clothes. The case, known locally as Duncan's Clothes, underlines the social predicament of group attitudes which surfaces at intervals throughout the history of public library service.

Special efforts to reach the working class took various forms. In 1885 the library commissioners of Detroit suggested that the library be open on Sundays for the benefit of the working man. Violation of the Sabbath was not a new idea, but it was still a sensitive issue, and the clergy responded with eloquence. The commissioners were charged with setting into motion forces which would endanger civil advancement. Opening libraries would lead to the opening of other institutions, such as saloons; Sunday books would lead to Sunday beer. Those who felt that the library should indeed be open "to the honest laboring man who only wishes to enrich his mind" ultimately prevailed, and on the first Sunday, three-fourths of the men and boys present in the reading room were said to be of the working classes, "neatly dressed and well ordered."[8]

At the same period, libraries in cities such as Chicago, Boston, and Milwaukee experimented with neighborhood stations where public library books could be ordered and returned at a local candy, book, or drug store—one of the first forms of outreach. In 1905 at the suggestion of a Burroughs Adding Machine employee, Detroit opened the first of many deposit stations in factories and settlement houses. Local industries were interested and the program soon included cigar and motor car factories, among others, selected for their "superior class of skilled labor." While factories with transient employees failed to respond, others where there was "a class of employees of fair intelligence and education" showed interest in books and "all the mental uplift and widened horizon which books must mean to such persons."[9] In Baltimore in the same period, deposit outlets included police and fire-engine houses and three reformatories.[10]

Soon, too, and with particular enthusiasm, the champions of books and reading for the working-class children arose. As early as 1880 in Boston, small home libraries for children were deposited in tenements, with the children responsible for circulating the books. There were, in addition, weekly book discussions by visiting volunteers of the Children's Aid Society.[11] Home libraries for working-class children were also to be found in Cleveland, where all aspects of service to children were vigorously championed by Effie L. Power. Over fifty home libraries existed by 1911.[12]

The lot of the children of the poor was truly frightful. A settlement house librarian described it this way in 1900:

> They have no athletics, no real games, no music, no art. The changing seasons mean little more to them than the transition from winter's cold to the sweltering heat of summer. They know nothing of nature. Wild flowers! They rarely see them. They never see the stars, though the sky is above them—the street lamps blind their eyes. . . . Their hours are divided into those

spent at home in a hot, crowded, unsanitary tenement, those spent in the street or candy saloon, and those spent in the dark, overcrowded school. Their home life few can know; it is often destroyed by privation and ignorance; their street life, he who has eyes and a heart may read.[13]

The public libraries soon took up their cause, and with the introduction of special children's rooms and services to children, the public library made one of its most enduring contributions to American society. William Brett, the far-sighted librarian of the Cleveland Public Library, was the first to establish a branch library exclusively for children, in an industrial area dominated by box and casket factories, iron foundries, a laundry, and numerous saloons. Opened in 1908, Perkins House was an early cooperative venture in community involvement, in which the librarians joined with social workers of the settlement house and staff of the Day Nursery and Free Kindergarten Association.[14] Often, as later librarians everywhere felt the need to establish a more active and aggressive role in community service, it was the children's librarians who set the example of innovation and outreach. (Further developed in chapter 2.—Ed.)

The rapid growth of the laboring class brought with it a burgeoning of political and organizational power. Mingled now with the more idealistic goals of intellectual and vocational improvement as expounded by the progressive spokesmen of the day, we discern more than a faint note of alarmed concern for the preservation of the social structure, from those classes who had derived the most comforts from it. Specters of strikes and communism, anarchy and populism arose as the labor unions for the first time showed their muscle. Patriotism and self-interest merged in new educational efforts directed toward the common man, for "Unless correct books were put into the hands of the people, they would be easy prey for such false and foreign philosophies as were destructive of the foundations of our republic."[15]

CULTURAL PLURALISM: THE IMMIGRANTS

Civic education, especially in the cities of the Northeast, became a subject of consuming interest as the labor force grew with wave upon wave of European immigrants. The cultural vitality, the ambition, and the earnestness with which the immigrant masses embraced "Americanization" was nowhere more apparent than in the ghettos of Manhattan, during the first two decades of the twentieth century; and here the public library found ample work to do.

Phyllis Dain has given a vivid and detailed picture of this new immigration of "people alien to the dominant Nordic stock and Anglo-Saxon culture of the United States . . . the dark-skinned, dark-haired Slavs, Italians, and Jews, with their odd clothes, exotic foods, strange languages, and peculiar customs." By 1910 41 percent of the city was for-

6 / *Clienteles*

eign born and, significantly, "ever-shifting" for "they moved as soon as they earned enough to leave the slums."[16]

New York was neither the only city to be faced with the assimilation of the immigrant, nor the only one to plan library branches in the centers of foreign population, offering special programs and collections of foreign language materials to a working class highly motivated to acquire education and advancement. In a life devoid of books or other luxuries, the public library became truly a haven offering genteel peace and order to the many bent on self-improvement and social advancement, and this was true in Baltimore, Cleveland, Detroit, Chicago, Boston, and elsewhere. Nearly 70,000 foreign born lived in Baltimore in 1900. A station deposit attendant in the heart of the foreign colony who was fortunately able to speak German, Russian, Yiddish, and Hebrew was regularly required to do so.[17] Perkins House in Cleveland knew foreign-born children from Germany, Russia, Italy, Austria, Hungary, Romania, England, and Poland.[18] In Detroit it was stated that 75 percent of the children using the Utley Branch Library came from homes with foreign-born and often non-English-speaking parents.[19]

Today, in viewing all the humanitarian activities of libraries, churches, and settlement houses, we may be struck by a somewhat disaffecting note of condescension. So much emphasis on the virtuous elevation of the lower classes and the assimilation of "American" ways sounds much like self-congratulation or at least sentimentality. Yet, these were the intellectual currents of the progressive era, a period of needed social reform, and the librarians and social workers were, after all, part of their age. The education and assimilation of vast numbers of immigrants in search of the "American" dream were real; and the dedicated public librarians of the time played a significant part in bringing it about.

More recently, the popular notion of the melting pot has been questioned by Leonard Borman, who has shown that immigrant groups preserve a strong sense of individual tradition, and that their choice of an individual life-style represents significant rights and deserves our respect.[20] The outreach librarian of today would do well to remember this, and the point was not entirely lost on the earlier generations:

> Though neither reformers nor social workers, librarians in some of the branches had close ties with the humanitarian settlement house workers and can be classed with them in the liberal faction of Americanizers, concerned for the welfare of the immigrant as well as that of American culture. Like the social workers, too, the librarians in contact with the realities of immigrant life and adjustment gradually acquired a respect and even affection for cultural diversity and a wish to preserve it. They seem to have adopted the approach later called cultural pluralism rather than the popular melting pot theory. . . .[21]

Liberal, middle-class products of their time, librarians in New York, Cleveland, Chicago, Boston, and other centers of the foreign born nevertheless, pioneered successfully in many of the techniques of community involvement which we now take for granted: foreign language collections, exhibits, tutoring, deposits, classes, meetings, conferences, and entertainment. (Further discussed in chapter 3.—Ed.)

THE ACTIVIST LIBRARIAN

The atmosphere of middle-class respectability which from the beginning clung to the public library undoubtedly alienated many members of the working class. The incident of Duncan's Clothes must have had its counterpart in many another library. Yet metropolitan libraries very soon found themselves in a new relationship to working-class communities. As branch networks began to expand the library presence in the city, a new awareness of the library's potential for community involvement began to suffuse the professional thinking of the day. An early herald of the new spirit was Sam Walter Foss, poet and librarian of the Somerville Public Library in Massachusetts, who in 1899 complained about "the sepulchral gloom, the graveyard silence" prevailing in libraries and suggested that librarians should learn from barrooms, where there are no signs invoking silence and no one walking on tiptoe, but where rather an atmosphere of hearty cordiality and friendliness prevailed. Foss hailed the passing of the dignified, old-time librarian who frightened children and had a face so long it dragged on the floor, and called instead for a librarian who could be agreeable to men, women, children, and dogs. Such a librarian, in his eyes, through personal intercourse and intellectual zest, could become a powerful, educative influence in the community.[22]

In 1904 President Angell of the University of Michigan pleaded for more personal involvement on the part of the librarian with the patrons and their reading needs, specifically for reader guidance from the librarian based on knowledge of the reader's personal aptitudes. "Personal suggestions to meet particular needs" should be joined with judicious book selection, especially "to procure books attractive and useful . . . to artisans, mechanics, and common laborers," so that the library would be known as the place where they could find "something to bring new brightness into their monotonous lives."[23]

Practical, everyday working people had a very limited time for reading and no particular interest in the library, according to the librarian of the Minneapolis Public Library in 1905. Yet they could be attracted to the library to satisfy their social instincts, and once brought there by their desire for pleasure, could be held by the library provided the building were "managed in the broadest spirit of hospitality" and made the setting for "social intercourse and amusement." The writer urged her fellow librarians to attract community groups. "If there are social or study clubs, organized labor guilds or missionary societies, or any other organization, encourage them to meet at the library, so that the library can enter more vitally into their lives."[24]

With the growth of branch libraries, opportunities for the library to become socially active multiplied. By 1917 St. Louis libraries had become so involved in what was termed *social work* that a branch librarian was able to report that several libraries had to turn away numbers of clubs applying for use of the library meeting rooms, even though full complements of "community halls, churches, saloons, Turnvereins, settlements, club houses, Masonic Temples, and public schools" were also available in the neighborhood for public gatherings. Early experiences with program planning soon taught this librarian a lesson which we have had, periodically, to relearn: The day was past when the library could reform or uplift the public; many programs "conceived in the finest spirit of service" withered and died when they did not embody the spontaneous expression of the particular community's needs. The example is given of a suffragist lecturer, highly successful in one part of town, who was greeted in a neighborhood of illiterate foreign women by an audience of "one deaf old lady and fifty Jewish children under twelve who had heard that candy was to be given away."[25]

The librarian's activist role was extended to a variety of personal and group services generally gathered under the banner of Adult Education. Although recreational reading was condoned as the first step in arousing intellectual curiosity, the librarian tried to see that reading did not stagnate at that level. When movies and radio began to supply a share of the public's recreational needs in the 1920s, librarians sought a more active role in the interpretation of, and guidance in, reading materials, especially for the patron interested in self-education. Readers' advisors and reading plans were the result.

Cleveland, Detroit, Chicago, and Milwaukee were among the earliest to establish readers' advisory departments, and Washington, D.C., was the first to create the readers' advisor as a branch position. Reading plans, tailored to the individual or produced by the ALA's Reading with a Purpose program, were especially popular during the next decade, as many people cast adrift by the depression turned to libraries for both intellectual consolation and vocational improvement. Reading programs ranged from literacy training in Cincinnati to Great Books seminars in Chicago.[26]

Also at this time libraries awoke to the possibilities of catering to the specialized interests of community groups. Ernestine Rose, writing in 1952 when the concept of group involvement was no longer new, observed that "The library social programs have now come a long way toward maturity . . . the library has learned to think in terms of groups and group relationships. . . . These relationships and the social program which has grown from them have been established partly on the basis of subject interests and resources and partly as the result of contact with the institutional life of the community."[27]

"Forums; discussion groups; lecture courses; classes in all sorts of subjects: art, music, and theatre groups" are some of the new activities given as examples. Praiseworthy and enriching activities, to be sure, but they have, somehow a faint air of middle-class cultural adornment, rather than social necessity. One is reminded, too, of the lyceums of the nineteenth century, when uplift was at its most earnest.

When the lean years of the depression brought new challenges to libraries, there was a considerable change in the public's reading habits. "People turned to the free libraries for non-recreational and cultural materials to improve their educational qualifications and skills, in the hope of achieving economic security," says Jesse Shera.[28] We might ask who these library users were. A study quoted by Douglas Waples in 1932, the depth of the depression, revealed a by-now familiar occupational pattern among library registrants in one large metropolitan area: students, housewives, white-collar workers, and professionals predominated. Skilled trades supplied only 6 percent of the registrants and unskilled labor, 1.6 percent.[29] In 1939 a foreign observer, Wilhelm Munthe of Oslo, visited the United States and was somewhat dismayed to report that perhaps 25 or 30 percent of the population "in an ordinary good library town" were card holders, but 50 percent of them were children. Of the adult group, 50 percent were high school students and 21 percent were housewives. Skilled and unskilled labor each made up only 5 percent of the adult card holders, which he considered "amazingly low." Munthe, interested in the vanishing male patron, decided that the great mass of men were hard to reach; although they might use the library's resources as they did during the depression to help find work, once employed they had no time for reading.[30]

In the same year an executive of the Standard Oil Company gave the ALA Conference an unblinking description of what the average public library looked like to the company's industrial workers. Though his embellishments were different, the theme was remarkably familiar: in many cities libraries were not conveniently located for industrial workers; the hushed atmosphere suggested city hall or a bank, making the worker feel uncomfortably in need of a clean collar, close shave, and shined shoes; the borrowers were mostly children, women, and old men; and a discouraging air of feminine fastidiousness hung over all. Standard Oil had a more than casual interest in public libraries at that time, for the industry was actively concerned with obsolescence in industrial processes and with the need to retain industrial workers. Reading and independent study would speed the process of learning new skills; hence, any encouragement of the reading habit would indirectly benefit their training program. "We set out to get employees to read, not just for the sake of reading books, but to use them as one means of self-training." Experiments with reading programs foundered; too many of the recommended titles were not readily available at the local library. More disheartening still was the conclusion of the company training representatives: Only in a very few cases has the library "been recast in a modern and active role of helping men to live happier and more successful lives."

The harshest criticism from these managerial specialists was the observation that the "capable and competent librarian, who could render so much guidance and inspiration, spends most of her time stamping books."[31]

In essence then, according to this industry, too many libraries that might have played a legitimate and practical role in the lives of industrial workers were not, in the postdepression period. To complete the picture, a company survey revealed that only 1 to 2½ percent of all Standard Oil personnel used libraries with any regularity, and all but a negligible number of books borrowed were for escape reading.

Louis Adamic, himself an immigrant with an intense interest in the social issues of the working class, had a checkered political and literary career which brought him in contact with workers in industrial centers throughout the country. His interest in the proletarian literature of the thirties led him to examine the reading habits of the working class in some detail. In 1934 he concluded that "The overwhelming majority of the American working class does not read books and serious, purposeful magazines. In fact, the American working class hardly reads anything apart from the . . . newspapers and an occasional copy of *Liberty, True Stories, Wild West Tales,* or *Screen Romances.*" Consequently, the audience for the serious radical literature of the period he estimated to be "less than one-half of one percent of the proletarian population."[32]

Although the public appetite for romance and the wild west is now largely satisfied by television, Lowell Martin has shown that the reading of magazines to meet special subject or hobby interests continues unabated.[33] The activity, however, has remained only peripheral to library services, since much of this popular material is readily available in neighborhood outlets such as newsstands and drug stores.

THE UNIONS

With service to community groups a well-established form of library outreach, it is not surprising that a new effort to reach the working class was about to begin; or, more accurately, had already begun, with the pioneer work of Miriam Tompkins in Milwaukee. Mathew S. Dudgeon, librarian at the time, described how it started:

> Possibly the typical member of labor groups is not characteristically a library patron. . . . He may not be likely to become a regular reader. Our experience, however, has demonstrated that this typical worker is nevertheless a potential patron . . . and responds more readily to a presentation of what the library has for him.
>
> . . . there were two approaches: one was through the employers and the industries in order to enlist their general cooperation in placing book collections on the premises where the workers worked; the second approach was a direct appeal to the em-

ployees themselves in order to challenge their individual interest."[34]

Establishing bonds of faith and mutual interest with union organizations was not easy, for labor had a long-standing distrust of middle-class institutions, especially those known for their support by rich philanthropists such as Andrew Carnegie, whose name was not hallowed in the memory of the working class. Detroit's early solicitation of Carnegie funds to launch their branch building program, for example, provoked a rhetorical storm of opposition from labor at the turn of the century, and the reaction was similar in other industrial areas. More than one voice suggested that Carnegie give his "blood money" back to the workingmen in the Detroit steel mills, since they were the ones who made his fortune possible.[35]

Labor had meanwhile gone a long way toward organizing its own educational resources and programs in the postdepression; this proved to be the library's opportunity. In Milwaukee, "the Trades Council started the Milwaukee Labor College, a school devoted to the teaching of economics, labor history, parliamentary law, public speaking, social psychology, and other subjects of particular importance and interest to union members."[36]

The pioneering Tompkins was elected a trustee of the college and saw to it that the library supplied books to the classes, which conveniently met in the library. She also received permission "to attend all meetings of the Trades Council with a collection of books to be issued to the delegates"[37] and to visit trade unions and local meetings. Deposit stations in both union offices and factories resulted, as well as regular contributions to union publications.

Service to labor groups grew slowly. In 1940 Elsa Posell of the Cleveland Public Library published a list of seventeen ways an aggressive librarian might serve labor and, in those days of low budgets, observed with some asperity: "So often we hear from librarians that they have no books, they have no facilities, they haven't sufficient staff. None of these reasons is in itself valid enough to excuse a librarian from making an attempt to develop this work." The most needed element was "an understanding and sympathetic and well-informed staff" with "imaginanation and ingenuity adequate to make use of available material, to find out what is needed and to fill that need as efficiently as possible with the available material by calling attention to it and proving the utility of it."[38]

Interestingly, the cry for staff involvement, identified as the crucial element, recalls the earliest advocates of the activist librarian, whom we have already noted, and will be heard again whenever libraries engage in self-evaluation. Hiatt, for example, in 1962 considered staff involvement one of the elements contributing to the successful program of Baltimore's inner-city Pennsylvania Avenue Branch: "The approach to service is one of broad coverage . . . flexibility and even experimentation . . . there is a continual effort to approach and offer assistance to each in-library patron."[39] Martin, in the fourth Deiches Fund study in 1974, calls for a revitalization of services through the intensification of reader guidance on a person-to-person basis, in which the professional will come to know his client as an aspiring human being.[40]

Faced with a second world holocaust and the urgency of the war effort, some urban libraries continued to seek cooperative activities with labor, to offer support to educational and training programs, and even to plan for the postwar years. In 1944 Carl H. Milam, then executive secretary of ALA, wrote to R. J. Thomas, president of United Auto Workers, to enlist support for the expansion of "materials and advisory service for adult education . . . [and continuation of] the war information services developed in recent years, especially for the benefit of discharged servicemen and dislocated war workers."[41] Thomas replied that the union was "most interested in doing everything possible to see that such services are extended to all groups of people with special regard for industrial workers who are in the shop. . . . We would also . . . be quite willing to discuss the possibilities of using our influence in calling for larger appropriations for extension of larger library facilities."[42] This was a change in attitude indeed, and ALA continued to work for a firmer relationship. In 1948 the Joint Committee on Library Service to Labor was formed, and this committee in turn issued the quarterly *Library Service to Labor Newsletter*.

Notable among the cities developing services to labor in the forties were Newark, Akron, New York, and Milwaukee. For most it was an uphill struggle, given the reserve of labor officials and the indifference of the workers. The effort, however, went in several directions. In order to focus service on organized labor in the same way that service had been developed for the business community, libraries had to build their reference resources in the technology, history, and economic issues of labor. Materials on legislation, collective bargaining, and industrial relations were needed as well as the many publications of the labor unions themselves. In this way it was hoped to serve the specialized needs of trade union officials and other personnel.

Another effort was directed toward labor education programs. With the formation of the Congress of Industrial Organizations (CIO) in 1935 by three education-conscious unions, especially the International Ladies' Garment Workers Union (ILGWU), union support of educational agencies such as the Workers' Education Bureau had advanced rapidly. By 1937 the ILGWU alone had 20,000 students enrolled in 553 classes around the country, with a mass education program involving lectures, moving pictures, musical, dramatic, and radio programs.[43] Since unions had developed worker-education programs of their own, it was an appropriate adult education function for the library to assist in setting up classes, institutes, and other courses, or to supply exhibits, lists, and materials. Typical educational groups meeting in the Des Moines Public Library in 1939 included a CIO local of hosiery workers studying current events, an American Federation of Labor (AFL) research project, an AFL Women's Bureau group studying home decoration, and a Workers' Alliance unit of the Works Progress Administration (WPA) workers and pensioners studying low-cost housing. The librarian attended meetings, offered to register the participants, and gave tours of the library.[44]

Finally, a renewed effort was made to reach workers at the personal level, through deposits in factories, union headquarters, and other meeting rooms; through factory bookmobile stops, and book tables and displays at union meetings.

In 1953 a Detroit UAW-CIO librarian observed that there were two types of library service needs to be met: the research needs of union officers and staff, and the educational and recreational needs of the members. While the former could be met by labor information centers in public libraries, the latter were more difficult to attain, for "the workers, despite all the wooing through films, discussion groups, Great Books classes, bright book jackets, entertainment for their children, and visits to their union halls have remained relatively unenthusiastic."[45] The problem, it was admitted, had not been entirely solved by union education directors either. The by-now familiar problems were mentioned once again: Workers did not feel free to go to the library in their working clothes; they were too tired; the library was too far away; or they did not know how to express their wants.

To Gilbert Cohen in 1959 it appeared that progress had been, after all, only relative:

> On the surface . . . this area of librarianship is a relatively minor one to be filed under "Reader Services" and discussed seriously and at length by only those few zealots who . . . practice what some of the founding fathers of the public library professed as one of its most lofty goals: the cultural, social, and economic uplifting of the working man.

He nevertheless urges continuation of the effort, for "the organized working man is an articulate force in the community who needs the resources of the library as much as the library needs his support."[46] Davies, however, is more pessimistic and dismisses the blue-collar worker with the observation that working men delight in their homes, workshops, and gardens, enjoy a few convivial beers at the local tavern, and visit with friends and relatives, but have never had any inclination to become involved in community improvement groups or organizations such as libraries.[47] Sylvia Goodstein in 1967 came to a similar conclusion: The union man had by now a comfortable income, had moved to the suburbs, watched TV, worked on his car, fished, and had no great interest in cultural improvement. Although in many cases he had moved into the middle-class environment, he did not especially assimilate middle-class intellectual pursuits, though it was probable that his children would.[48]

ANOTHER MIGRATION

The blue-collar worker has not been the only citizen to experience change, as all of us know who experienced or were products of the postwar years. We have seen the pace accelerate with technological advance; new jobs are created and old ones perish, and in all walks of life the need to adjust, to absorb new information, and to gain the skill to manipulate new technologies—or just to be literate in their vocabularies —requires a greater effort than ever before. For the unskilled and undereducated the hurdles are now still higher.

In 1967 Dan Lacy, for the National Advisory Commission on Libraries, drew a perceptive picture of what the last twenty years of technology and social change have meant for, among others, the unskilled worker:

> There have been massive movements in the post-war decades from rural and small town areas to metropolitan areas, from core cities to suburbs. . . . a tragically important part of the migration consisted of unskilled and semiliterate agricultural laborers, mostly Negro, Puerto Rican, or Mexican, made useless by the introduction of new machinery and chemical weedkillers and pesticides. . . .
>
> . . . the human reality existed in the stark despair of the millions made useless on the farms and in the mines, who were driven to cold and indifferent cities and there set apart by race and by peasant ignorance of city ways and city jobs. They drifted into crowded and ill-served ghettos and were reduced to anarchy by the shattering of the network of personal, family, church, and occupational ties.[49]
>
> Schools and libraries . . . need to be instruments to transform the whole class itself, since society no longer has a need or a role for unskilled labor. . . . these institutions themselves, on a massive scale, must enter into the lives and relate to the values of the whole population that has hitherto lived beyond their scope.[50]

This is a staggering challenge indeed, and, in reviewing the activities of the past ten years, we cannot begin to count the many and varied ways that urban libraries took up the challenge and fought the war against poverty. Recalling the outstanding work with immigrants which many libraries performed in the early days of the century, the postwar migrations might at first glance seem to have been history repeating itself, but in actuality there were crucial differences. The new immigrants to urban areas had not brought with them the same expectations of success through educational opportunity. Alienation and frustration have been greater, expressed in outbursts of social disorder destructive to the cities at the very time the cities' economic resources have been diluted by industrial growth in the suburbs and the gravitation to the suburbs of the more educated, mobile, and younger elements of the city population. The resulting vacuum has been filled by those "less educated, in poorer health . . . and obliged by skin color or economic contingency to take substandard housing."[51] Conant observes that "the physical ghetto has created a psychological ghetto characterized by fear, suspicion, antagonism . . . and mutual ignorance of life styles . . . a barrier to opportunity and mainstream acculturation."[52]

Estimates of the level of reading ability among deprived adults have varied. A 1970 Harvard study quoted by Cramer, rather apprehensively, estimates that half of the United States's adults appear to be unable to cope with newspapers, job applications, driving manuals, or "the simplest exposition."[53] Cleveland's Reading Centers project, an experiment with adult literacy diagnosis and guidance, was one library's approach to the problem. Martin, in his study of the Pratt Library, is more sanguine about the prevalence of adult reading as well as the inner-city adult's faith in education, if not in the existing structure of schools and libraries. Martin maintains that "reading of newspapers has remained a regular activity of approximately 90 percent of the adult population, while magazine reading has increased significantly from some 60 percent of adults in the 1940s to 80 percent in the 1960s"; furthermore, "It would be inaccurate to say that all or most of the book readers have moved to the suburbs. . . ."[54] Meanwhile, a recent study by the National Assessment of Educational Progress, in which some 5,000 seventeen-year-old students were tested, reports that 89 percent were functionally literate, a 2 percent increase over 1971. Cautious optimism in this case might be tempered by the realization that school dropouts are not included in the study, and that functional literacy is defined as the very basic skills essential for reading daily newspapers, job applications, instructions, and driver's license tests, "a functional definition different from school achievement and grade level equivalent."[55]

The obligation to meet urgent human needs in the inner city and to assist in peaceful social change is more pressing than ever; but for many libraries, the search for a meaningful and sustained role in the life of the inner city continues. We are, perhaps, wiser and sadder by the discovery that many of our traditional techniques have not turned the tide. Fern Long, in describing Cleveland's Reading Centers project, after three years in helping functionally illiterate adults improve their reading ability, came to a conclusion that many librarians will recognize: "We learned what has been learned by all who labor in this particular vineyard, and that is the smallness of result in proportion to the magnitude of effort."[56]

While the educational wants of the underprivileged may not encompass the kind of cultural or intellectual aspirations frequently ascribed to the middle class, there is wide recognition that education can lead to vocational opportunities which in turn bring within reach the much advertised material benefits and financial security enjoyed by the middle class, if not for oneself, at least for one's children. Becker considered that the popularity of trade schools in urban areas indicated a desire for technical training among lower-class youth and a willingness to do something about it.[57] Moreover, the ghetto resident is interested in the printed word for pragmatic reasons such as the news, the weather, sports, For Sale ads, or job opportunities. He will not be much inclined to visit his branch library if the library clings to the traditional concept of a balanced collection representing a cultural storehouse, with an even distribution over all aspects of literature and learning, most of which has little relevance to his existence. Martin, for this reason, urges that we stress localized interests and needs in planning inner-city services, if we are ever to succeed in bridging the gap.

Meanwhile, the relative significance of library service to workers in one urban area was discouragingly evident from a 1968 study of Baltimore and the adjacent Maryland counties: employed adults were 25.9 percent of all library users, but of that figure, only 7.5 percent were craftsmen, foremen, or kindred workers, 2.7 percent were service workers, 1.4 percent were operatives, and .5 percent were laborers. For craftsmen, foremen, and kindred workers, the need for greater library specialization was particularly evident; they were the lowest of the employed groups using the library for general reading, next to the highest in using the library for information, and the highest in using reference tools and periodical indexes. They were also the most dissatisfied because the library did not have the book they wanted, they couldn't locate material, or the material was out-of-date. It was concluded that "it is unfortunate if it should prove to be true that the craftsmen, the group most dependent on their local library, are getting insufficient attention."[58]

In Baltimore itself, where the Enoch Pratt Library had early taken an active approach to inner-city problems, some basic truths were soon discovered. An inner-city librarian, after a door-to-door survey of her neighborhood, was forced to conclude that "a large number of people did not regard reading books as a 'pleasurable experience'." A Young Adult librarian in the new Pennsylvania Avenue Branch observed that the branch's low-income population believed that their new library "had two major functions; to answer school assignments, and to furnish information needed to secure better jobs."[59]

If, as this evidence suggests, informational, pragmatic service is most relevant to the everyday vocational, economic, and educational needs of the working classes, then a considerable revision of library collections and library programming are called for before we can establish contact with this major adult community group. Up to now the blue-collar worker has had little use for libraries and smaller satisfaction from them. If we are to believe the experts, the uneducated, underemployed worker of the future may be even more isolated, more unprepared to compete in a world of technological complexity, and more in need of assistance than ever before. In addition to developing specialized information resources, we will continue to need human resources of a special kind. Beyond the routine dispensation of requested information, there must be a willing personal involvement and commitment to assistance on the part of librarians; an identification with the patron's needs in relation to the broader social exigencies of his life. This alone can result in the knowledgeable interpretation of his often poorly expressed demands. Activist librarians have a long and honorable history of service, whether in the settlement house, union hall, or, more recently, neighborhood cruiser. But they will need still greater skills, they will need to empathize more with differing life-styles, experiment more radically, and command more complex and novel information and instructional resources if the library is to make a real contribution to the welfare of these working groups now largely isolated and excluded by their lacks in education and training. We have seen some notable if sporadic forays in the past, but the true battle has hardly been joined, much less won.

NOTES

1. Sidney H. Ditzion, "Mechanics and Mercantile Libraries," *Library Quarterly* 10:206 (Apr. 1940).
2. System Development Corporation, *The Public Library and Federal Policy* (Westport, Conn.: Greenwood, 1974), p. 123.
3. James H. Wellard, "Popular Reading and the Origins of the Public Library in America," *Library Journal* 60:185 (Mar. 1, 1935).
4. Jesse H. Shera, "Causal Factors in Public Library Development," in Michael H. Harris, ed., *Reader in American Library History* (Washington, D.C.: NCR Microcard Editions, 1971), p. 155.
5. D. W. Davies, *Public Libraries as Culture and Social Centers* (Metuchen, N.J.: Scarecrow, 1974), p. 123.
6. Sidney H. Ditzion, *Arsenals of a Democratic Culture* (Chicago: American Library Assn., 1947), p. 72.
7. Philip Arthur Kalisch, *The Enoch Pratt Free Library: A Social History* (Metuchen, N.J.: Scarecrow, 1969), pp. 71–72.
8. Frank B. Woodford, *Parnassus on Main Street* (Detroit: Wayne State Univ. Pr., 1965), p. 144.
9. Ibid., p. 171.
10. Kalisch, p. 85.
11. Harriet G. Long, *Public Library Service to Children: Foundation and Development* (Metuchen, N.J.: Scarecrow, 1969), p. 86.
12. C. H. Cramer, *Open Shelves and Open Minds* (Cleveland: Pr. of Case Western Reserve, 1972), p. 68.
13. Quoted in Long, p. 87.
14. Cramer, p. 69.
15. Ditzion, *Arsenals of a Democratic Culture*, p. 65.

18 / *Clienteles*

16. Phyllis Dain, *New York Public Library* (New York: The Library, 1972), p. 288.
17. Kalisch, p. 89.
18. Cramer, p. 69.
19. Woodford, p. 201.
20. Leonard D. Borman, "Melting Pots, Vanishing Americans, and Other Myths," *Library Trends* 20:210–22 (Oct. 1971).
21. Dain, pp. 291–92.
22. Sam Walter Foss, "The Library as an Inspirational Force," in Arthur F. Bostwick, ed., *The Library and Society* (New York: Wilson, 1920), p. 421.
23. James Burrill Angell, "The Use of the Public Library," in Bostwick, p. 426.
24. Gratia Alta Countryman, "The Library as a Social Centre," in Bostwick, p. 437.
25. Margaret Closey Quigley, "Where Neighbors Meet," in Bostwick, pp. 443–44.
26. System Development Corporation, p. 11.
27. Ernestine Rose, *Public Library in American Life* (New York: Columbia Univ. Pr., 1954), p. 103.
28. Jesse Shera, "Information Storage and Retrieval: Libraries," in *International Encyclopedia of the Social Sciences* 7:315 (New York: Macmillan and Free Pr., 1970).
29. Douglas Waples, "Social Implications of the Popular Library," in *Encyclopedia of the Social Sciences* 12:664 (New York: Macmillan, 1934).
30. Wilhelm Munthe, *American Librarianship from a European Angle* (Chicago: American Library Assn., 1939), pp. 45–48.
31. C. C. Camp, "The Great Library Misery," *ALA Bulletin* 33:485–90 (July 1939).
32. Louis Adamic, "What the Proletariat Reads," *Saturday Review of Literature* (Dec. 1, 1934), p. 321.
33. Lowell A. Martin, *Adults and the Pratt Library* (Baltimore: Enoch Pratt Free Lib., 1974), pp. 17–18.
34. Matthew S. Dudgeon, "Extramural Service to Labor Groups," in John Chancellor, ed., *Helping Adults to Learn* (Chicago: American Library Assn., 1939), p. 57.
35. Woodford, p. 184.
36. Ruth Shapiro, "Reaching Labor," *Wilson Library Bulletin* 15:436 (Jan. 1941).
37. Ibid.
38. Elsa Posell, "Reaching Labor," *Wilson Library Bulletin* 15:216 (Nov. 1940).
39. Peter Hiatt, *Public Library Branch Services for Adults of Low Education* (Ann Arbor, Mich.: University Microfilms, 1964), p. 113.
40. Martin, p. 80.
41. "Organized Labor and the ALA," *ALA Bulletin* 35:252 (July 1944).
42. Ibid., pp. 252–53.
43. "Educating the Workers," *New Republic* (Dec. 22, 1937), p. 185.
44. Forrest B. Spaulding, "Workers' Education Classes," *Library Journal* 64:524 (July 1939).
45. Patricia Humphrey, "Toward Library-Labor Cooperation," in Dorothy K. Oko, ed., *Library Service to Labor* (Metuchen, N.J.: Scarecrow, 1963), p. 35.
46. Gilbert Cohen, "Library Service to Labor: Historical Roots and Current Needs," in Oko, pp. 51–52.
47. Davies, p. 69.
48. Sylvia Goodstein, "Labor and Libraries," in Mary Lee Bundy, ed., *The Library's Public Revisited* (College Park: Univ. of Maryland, 1967), pp. 46–59.
49. Dan Lacy, "Social Change and the Library: 1945–1980," in Douglas M. Knight and E. Shepley Nourse, eds., *Libraries at Large* (New York: Bowker, 1969), pp. 4–5.

50. Ibid., p. 20.
51. John T. Eastlick and Theodore A. Schmidt, "The Impact of Serving the Unserved on Public Library Budgets," *Library Trends* 23:605 (Apr. 1975).
52. Ralph W. Conant, "The Metropolitan Library and the Educational Revolution: Some Implications for Research," in Ralph W. Conant and Kathleen Molz, eds., *The Metropolitan Library* (Cambridge, Mass.: MIT Pr., 1972), p. 22.
53. Cramer, p. 218.
54. Martin, p. 16.
55. "17-Year-Olds Gain in Basic Reading Skills, Functional Literacy Study Shows," *NAEP Newsletter*, Oct. 1975, p. 1.
56. Fern Long, *Reading Centers Project, Final Report*, ERIC Reports, ED 023 430; LI 001 030 (Bethesda, Md.: ERIC Documents Reproduction Service, 1967).
57. Howard S. Becker, quoted in Judith D. Guthman, *Metropolitan Libraries, The Public Library Reporter*, no. 15 (Chicago: American Library Assn., 1969), p. 20.
58. Mary Lee Bundy, *Metropolitan Public Library Users* (College Park: Univ. of Maryland, 1968), pp. 71–72.
59. Kalisch, p. 203.

2
Service to Urban Children

CLARA O. JACKSON
Kent State University

Among the questions posed by William I. Fletcher in his chapter, "Public Libraries and the Young," in the 1876 landmark report, *Public Libraries in the United States*, were these:

> What shall the public library do for the young, and how? . . . Who shall presume to set the age at which a child may first be stirred with the beginnings of a healthy intellectual appetite on getting a taste of the strong meat of good literature? . . . What are good juvenile books? . . . What shall the library furnish to this class in order to meet its wants?[1]

In the intervening century there have been multitudinous approaches and responses to these questions, reflecting changing emphases in our society, in attitudes towards children's needs and potentials, in professional understandings and goals of librarians, in the metamorphosis of cities, and in the transformation of school programs.

The definition of *children* adopted in this chapter is that used by Clifton Fadiman in his recent comprehensive article on children's literature: "All potential or actual young literates, from the instant they can with joy leaf through a picture book or listen to a story read aloud, to the age of perhaps 14 or 15. . . ."[2] In this rich presentation Fadiman credits Comenius with the view of the child as a child and commends his *Orbis Pictus* (1658) for understanding "of a special order" and innovative use of material. Both continue to be reflected variously in modern library services to children.[3]

FROM 1876 TO THE CENTURY'S END

Before 1876 most public libraries closed their doors to children below the age of twelve. Contemporary situations and services are described in *Public Library Service to Children*,[4] in which Harriet Long intertwines recognition of the child as a worthy member of society, the movement toward free public education in the United States, and many social considerations and understandings. Gwendolen Ree's carefully prepared fifty-year-old history of libraries for children, including the United States, remains useful, and the more recent *The World of Children's Literature*, assembled by Anne Pellowski, includes developments in both Canada and the United States in its worldwide picture through commentary and bibliographic notations.[5] The path of public school library development is condensed in *Libraries at Large*,[6] and the opening chapter of *Creating a School Media Program*.[7]

The U.S. Bureau of Education's report on public libraries is voluminous, but its index lacks a single entry under "child" or "children." We are nevertheless indebted to it not only for Fletcher's chapter just mentioned, but also for the short section by S. R. Warren and S. N. Clark on "Common School Libraries," which provides a historical sketch of school libraries in the United States and Canada.[8] Both chapters leave us with impressions and descriptions which can help us appreciate a century's progress, revealing links between the past and present.

After the Civil War, industrial expansion, the spread of railroads, increased immigration, the growth of compulsory schooling—all contributed to the quickening of the pace and spirit of free education. The growing need for an educated citizenry was reflected in the emerging state system of free schools, publicly controlled and supported. The larger world represented in the school gradually spread to the library. Thwarted earlier by problems of support and administration, the free public library movement came to benefit from growing secularization and more uniform, economical, and efficient methods of administration which were developed. The vista of patrons embraced every grade, kind, age, race, and condition of citizens—and, eventually, children. They had become the focus of more sympathetic and humanizing cultivation, and numerous social welfare efforts were directed at lifting some of the burdens of childhood from them, especially in the cities.

The caliber and variety of library service to children that began to flourish is discernible in the pioneer work of many individuals, including Minerva Sanders ("Auntie Sanders"). In 1877 she created a children's section at Pawtucket (R.I.) Public Library, which provided low tables and chairs for some seventy children. Cramer considers her

> The first public librarian to do something for children who were roaming the streets. . . . She was something of a "radical" who believed in a people's library; she had introduced open shelves, had encouraged workingmen to come to her institution, and was

most interested in children at a time when they were considered noisy nuisances.[9]

After its faltering beginnings in the 1830s and 1840s, the movement to establish school libraries independent of public libraries had been revived in the 1860s and 1870s, especially in secondary schools. The year 1879 marked a promising beginning of healthy cooperation, when the Worcester (Mass.) Public Library worked closely with teachers representing their students' needs, described in Charles F. Adams's "The Public Library and the Public Schools."[10] In contrast, the annual report of Irad L. Beardsley, librarian of Cleveland Public Library, for the same year expressed concern about the effect of sensational books on the young, "restricted drawings on the part of those attending school, to once a week," and prohibited the "lingering" of children in the building.[11]

School library services to children in the 1880s arose from cooperation with public libraries. W. E. Foster described Providence Public Library's teacher loan collection and student reference use,[12] and Samuel S. Green the many-faceted cooperative plan between the Worcester library and schools.[13] At the Boston Public Library, Jenkins emphasized reading guidance rather than random selection from the catalog; Quincy (Mass.) Public Library prepared booklists, and Rochester (N.Y.) Public Library provided a variety of reading matter for area school children.

In 1882 when her reading guide, *Books for the Young*, appeared, Caroline M. Hewins, long-time librarian of the Hartford (Conn.) library, started a practice later continued by others. Based on questionnaires, a national survey of library services to children was reported periodically at library conferences. Two years later William Howard Brett started his service as librarian of the Cleveland Public Library urging "immediate attention to children and their needs." Work with teachers began, necessitating the enrichment of the book stock he personally supervised; reportedly, he was acquainted with every juvenile volume on the shelves, and in time came to be regarded as "the greatest children's librarian."[14]

Service to youth in "alcoves or rooms or other facilities of public institutions," first appeared in 1885, the initial one credited to Emily Hanaway, principal of the primary department of Grammar School No. 28 in New York City.[15] Also in that year St. Louis Public Library distributed free tickets for summer use, and Pawtucket Public Library displayed a notebook containing articles about crimes committed after the reading of trashy dime novels. In 1887 Boston librarians became involved with the Children's Home Library movement, pioneered by the Children's Aid Society, which deposited books in homes for neighborhood children to which volunteers came. The same year Detroit Public Library began its work with schools. Two years later the Children's Library Association in New York started a library solely for children to elevate their reading and "keep them off the streets." They possessed one visual aid, a stereoscope. By the end of the decade the Cleveland Public Library began to issue books to pupils through their teachers.

Whatever the impact of the depression and subsequent recovery, the 1890s saw the growth of the central city library, often including a museum, and the formal beginnings of recognized library service to children. Among the basic patterns established was the first separate children's room (1890), in the Brookline (Mass.) library's basement, accommodating some thirty children. Hartford and Philadelphia followed, and soon afterwards Cleveland had deposits of from 30 to 50 volumes in seven grammar schools; by 1891 more than 3,000 volumes were placed in sixty-one schools which eventually grew into small branch libraries.

Between 1890 and 1895 the nation's high school libraries increased from some 2,500 to about 4,000, some dependent on and others independent of public libraries. In 1892 the New York State Library Law of 1839, which had offered—but not assured—matching funds to school districts for libraries, was supplanted by another authorizing state funds to be used solely to provide "suitable" books for children. Included in the 1892/93 *Report of the Commissioner of Education* was a summary of library work with children and a significant paper by Caroline Hewins, "Reading of the Young," which was based on responses to some eleven questions gathered from 152 libraries.[16] The next year Minneapolis Public Library provided a corridor for children. In 1897 innovator John Cotton Dana, first director of the Denver Public Library, opened the first "Children's Library," with some 3,000 books and periodicals, and also introduced the practice of lending book sets to schools. Dana summarized his views:

> Children can hardly begin too soon to ramble about among books. They need guidance first, and most needed is that which will take them into the wilderness of books. Once within, guides will not be hard to find.[17]

During the first year and a half of operation, 90,000 volumes were circulated, and hundreds of children, allowed free access to the shelves, used the room for both reference and recreational purposes.

The day of the children's room had dawned. The Cambridge (Mass.) and Minneapolis public libraries opened their children's rooms. In 1895 Boston Public Library's new building included a children's room, and San Francisco became the first library in the West to have one. Anne Carroll Moore had begun the story-telling tradition without a children's room, however. In 1879 she began inviting children to come to the library at Pratt Institute.[18] In 1897 Cleveland Public Library established the Children Library League, an idea of Effie L. Power and Linda Eastman. Its motto was "Clean Hearts, Clean Hands, and Clean Books!" Compliance was encouraged through the use of devices like "red-letter honor cards and badges of white metal for which the wearer was charged three cents." Books were distributed widely, with suggested readings and admonitions; one read, "Help me to keep fresh and clean and I will help you to be happy!"[19]

In 1898 the children's departments of Philadelphia and the Pittsburgh Carnegie libraries were organized. The same year William Brett opened Cleveland's first improvised children's room, supervised by Effie L. Power. This juvenile alcove functioned by the rule "to select the book, draw it, and depart." One user recalls:

> What thrills have been mine as I stood perched on one leg like a stork half way up a ladder, utterly oblivious of time and space, drinking in equal parts of Jules Verne and the dust of the Central Library which Euclid Avenue knows no more.[20]

The greater recognition of children as part of the public needing their own quarters, their own book collections, and a special, trained staff is plain in several papers read at the second International Library Conference, held in London, July 13–16, 1897. Caroline Hewins presented "Books That Children Like," with telling comments by boys and girls, an approach suggested to her by R. R. Bowker. John Cotton Dana, Melvil Dewey, Samuel Green, Herbert Putnam, and Katherine L. Sharp were represented in the discussion, affirming that to establish the reading habit "the free public library, in its educational work, must be . . . the library for the very young."[21] In 1898 Pratt Institute introduced courses for the training of children's librarians,[22] and in the last year of the century a Joint Committee of Teachers and Librarians representing the National Education Association and the American Library Association suggested methods for increased cooperation between librarians and schools, the first of many significant joint ventures.

THE TWENTIETH CENTURY: THE FIRST TWENTY YEARS

With the help of Andrew Carnegie, library buildings multiplied rapidly during these years with improved facilities for children, and increased support for service to children. By 1900 Pittsburgh was responding even to summer playground needs. The Montreal conference of the Canadian Library Association which established a Council of Children's Librarians prompted the American Library Association to replace its Children's Librarians Club with a Section for Children in 1901. The same year Cleveland Public Library opened a bona fide children's room. The vitality of heightened professional concern for service to children resulted also from the combined imagination and concerted efforts of pioneers like Caroline Burnite, Linda Eastman, Alice I. Hazeltine, Caroline Hewins, Clara W. Hunt, Anne Carroll Moore, and Francis Jenkins Olcott, all of whom wrote about aspects of children's work. Notable for considering children's interests were Olcott's *The Children's Reading* (1912) and Hunt's *What Shall We Read to the Children?* (1915).

Adding vigor to the discussion of cooperation between the library and school was *The Relationship between the Library and the Public Schools: Reprints of Papers and Addresses* (1914), with notes by Arthur E. Bostwick, the first in the series, Classics of American Librarianship. Perhaps the most accepted view was the following:

> The library must have the school to stir the craving for knowledge, awaken, and train the reading habit. The school needs the library to illustrate, enlarge, and complete its work, not only through the period of school days, but for the lifetime that follows.[23]

Besides, librarians as well as teachers were being challenged by new immigrant children in the cities whose service needs were complicated by the problems of adjusting to a strange culture. One of several related studies praised eastern European Jewish children as studious and eager, while children of Italian background were labeled "volatile," and Irish children a "marked contrast." Though tending to the stereotype, this study nevertheless indicated the tremendous interest taken in children's reading; it specifically emphasized the need for civics books and English grammars, and the children's preference for fairy tales.[24] Incidentally, in those years children often read aloud to their immigrant parents.

Meanwhile native-born black children were barely considered. Conspicuous was the opening of the Colored Branch of Louisville Free Public Library in 1905, with Rachel D. Harris in charge of children's services. Doubts that blacks were a "reading people" proved unfounded when the children made heavy use of the library: from 150 to 180 appeared each week just for story hours. The library maintained an active program and established twenty-one deposit stations and thirty-five classroom collections.[25] That year also youngsters under seventeen borrowed 40 percent of the books loaned from the St. Louis Public Library.[26]

The bulk of the new libraries built during this period, in Buffalo, Cincinnati, Milwaukee, and Toledo, had separate children's rooms. In 1902 the first children's library in Canada opened in St. Thomas, Ontario, and in 1903 the Ontario school library law provided a new beginning for Canadian school libraries. Clara W. Hunt became head of Children's Services in the Brooklyn Public Library in the same year. On New Year's Day 1906, the Central Children's Room of the New York Public Library began operations at Fifth Avenue and 42nd Street, where it was to remain until May 1970, with Anne Carroll Moore as its head until 1941. New York's Carnegie Hudson Park Branch comes alive in Mary D. Pretlow's description of some 500 children eagerly waiting for books.[27] In 1908 Cleveland established Perkins House, the first branch library in the United States devoted to children, in a congested, multi-national neighborhood. Children's rooms were opened in Toronto in 1909 and in St. Louis in 1910.

In large cities where children lived in cramped tenement quarters, children's rooms provided pleasant contrasts: spacious attractive areas, pic-

26 / *Clienteles*

tures on the walls, scaled-down furniture, and rubber-tiled floors to muffle noise. Bulletin boards, reading clubs, school visits, and story hours were program essentials. The latter quickly caught the attention of young children; through the librarian's personal contact, storytelling came to be viewed as an effective way to plant in the young child's mind the seeds of interest in books. Since so many children attended story hours, maintaining order sometimes required a policeman, to the vexation of many librarians. Said one of the latter:

> I should be very sorry to have a children's room as perfectly noiseless as a reading room for adults. It is so unnatural for a roomful of healthy boys and girls to be absolutely quiet for long periods that if I found such a state of affairs I should be sure something was wrong—that all spontaneity was being repressed.[28]

Extremely popular with children who felt too old for story hours were reading clubs. Hewins's report is an exact chronicle of the careful preparations needed to maintain them.[29] Cleveland Public Library had one of the most successful programs; by 1910 about sixty clubs flourished with a volunteer force of attorneys, businesspeople, and students from Western Reserve University. Both aesthetic and utilitarian, bulletin boards, or picture bulletins, offered outlets for creativity. One questionnaire sent to librarians about the most popular ones revealed that exhibits ranged from Queen Victoria, Robert Louis Stevenson, and Changes of the Last Century, to Life in Puerto Rico, and Nature.

To make the library's collections accessible to the greatest number of children, deposit stations were set up in schools for books and other illustrative material. Librarians often held story hours in schools and taught catalog use. New York Public Library established some 5,830 classroom libraries, with 321,921 volumes producing a circulation rate of 1,849,345. The Traveling Library Office had deposit stations in 55 places including neighborhood homes. Playgrounds and other recreational areas were also sites for book deposits as well as story hour programs. Well aware of the realities of tenement life, big-city libraries left books in juvenile courts as well as in settlement houses.[30]

Ideas of Victorian morality remained conspicuous in book selection; many librarians felt that only books with strong moral precepts were suitable for impressionable children in order to prevent them from indulging in "riotous living in the streets or reading of yellow fiction." Children's librarians berated the moral ambiguities of dime novels. Theaters and comics were likewise viewed with alarm; children were like clay, and it was the librarian's duty to select only the best books, usually the classics, to shape them.[31]

One early censorship incident worth noting was a children's librarian's banning as undesirable *Huckleberry Finn.* Her position was upheld by the editor of *Library Journal,* who believed that boys were little savages easily led to evil paths by such exposure.[32] A more liberal librarian, who had several scholars testify to the book's literary merit, declared that it was nonsensical to believe that criminals were stirred to action by what they had read, expressing the conviction that boys needed some romance and adventure in their lives as well as "disregard for smug respectability."[33] Although it is difficult to ascertain how many librarians supported this ban, their opposition to the light fiction of the day and their solemn supervision of children's reading were apparent. In contrast, Caroline Hewins protested that too much guidance stifled children's creativity and imagination and pleaded for greater freedom of choice for them.[34]

The emphasis on children's services prompted at least one librarian to protest that adults were being neglected. Criticism was also heaped on some of the methods used and services rendered. A survey undertaken by Arabelle H. Jackson of the Pittsburgh Carnegie Library in 1906 indicated great need for improvement.[35]

By now there was broad recognition of the need for separate and more adequate facilities and programs for children. Local activity was stressed in J. W. Emery's *The Library, the School, and the Child* (1917). It was generally agreed that the public library should not compete with the school library, but librarians were urged to work closely with teachers to ascertain children's abilities and reading needs. In some cases strict guidance by the teacher was suggested to select and restrict reading. Former librarian Sophy H. Powell quoted an expert who went so far as to discourage any reading before the age of ten because it was said to be bad for the eyes, and many children could not understand the words.[36] The author stressed the need for facts to balance the prevalence of opinions.

Public librarians were urged to go into the schools to teach the use of reference tools, to present book talks, and to arrange special consultations with teachers, cooperating with them in guiding reading, in lesson preparation, reading or telling stories, and furnishing the school with supplementary materials. Some school librarians actually spent thirty minutes each week with individual students in special literature sessions. The theme was cooperation: the public library, in keeping a close watch on classes and special developments, would help create for children a bridge with the school, and the school, users for the public library.

Based on community surveys, numerous new programs were introduced. One extended service hours into the evening to give access to reading matter to children forced to work during the day. Collections of books continued to be placed in bath houses, juvenile courts, playgrounds, social settlements, and even department stores and telegraph offices, where young workers and messenger boys occasionally had time to spare for reading.

Created to bring books to children unable to reach the library, the Home Library Department was described by Jessie M. Carson as follows:

28 / *Clienteles*

> It penetrates into the most sordid parts of the city and puts its small cases of forty or fifty books in the homes of these poverty-stricken people, and sends a friendly visitor once a week to circulate books, read or tell stories, and play games with the children.[37]

There was also a strong movement to involve libraries with Boy Scouts and Campfire Girls, units of which often adopted the name of the sponsoring library.

Children's rooms tended to be crowded after school, frequently with long lines at the entrance and checkout desk. In contrast, housed in its own beautiful building, which opened in 1914—with a grinning face on the doorhandle—the Brownsville Children's Branch of the Brooklyn Public Library was an example of a library planned to provide a flow of books to youth. It catered to children's demands for twenty years in a community of eastern European immigrants.

Notable is the range of activity and services reflected in Alice I. Hazeltine's assemblage of papers and addresses representing forty years of growth, from reference work to special methods and types of work in different settings.[38] In some libraries maps, models, pictures, puzzles, and small circuses were available; lectures illustrated with lantern slides and motion pictures were common. Story hours were frequent, with classics and fairy tales librarians' favorite choices. In Toronto during 1915 many stories involving Canadian historical characters were told for the benefit of immigrant children. Librarians were urged not to choose stories about the devil or hobgoblins and malicious animals because "the purpose of the library in its relations with children should be to train the imagination wholesomely rather than to merely amuse...."[39]

One California library sponsored a hiker's club whose maps, records, and specimens were displayed. Other activities included reading aloud, distribution of catalogs and booklists, demonstration of indexes, and talks on the use of books. The establishment in 1916 of the Bookshop for Boys and Girls in Boston by Bertha Mahony (later Miller), under the auspices of the Women's Educational Industrial Union, is important for its focus on the world of children's books.

Both selection and other aspects of service to children were affected by the European War. To some extent librarians felt that "good war stories enlarge the child's world, setting forth the development of courage, endurance, perseverance, honesty, and chivalry, showing these qualities at their best."[40] By 1917 the overcrowding in the children's rooms in Toronto was an item in the public library's annual report. In the same year the Public Library Commission sent qualified people into the schools to classify and arrange school libraries at no charge. Cleveland had long set the pace in that sphere. At William Brett's death in 1918, the public library included among its units "17 libraries in high and grade schools, . . .487 classroom libraries, . . . [and] 7 children's stations...."[41] The 1918–19 influenza epidemic created a preoccupation with clean books and facilities: books could not be circulated or made available to children with any type of contagious disease. The year 1919 also marked the beginning of National Children's Book Week and New York Public Library's appointment of a superintendent of work with schools whose significant duties included the training in each branch library of an adult staff member to aid young people in their reading and reference work—eventually to become characteristic of such service.

1920s AND 1930s

In the twenties, the decade of the car, jazz, Prohibition, the Harlem Renaissance and a blossoming of class-commentary literature, "Prosperity," and the onset of the Great Depression, even larger-scale service to children developed. In 1921 "Films and Books for Children" were discussed in *Library Journal*,[42] the Madison (Wisc.) Free Library issued a booklet for school libraries, Della McGregor wrote about the Youngstown Plan to encourage home reading by children, the Detroit Board of Education issued its *Standards for School Libraries*, Effie L. Power described reference work with children in "The Peterkin Family and the Project Method,"[43] and Los Angeles held a Hans Andersen Festival.

In 1922 Toronto purchased an old house, remodeled it for $25,000, and opened it two years later as the Boys and Girls House which served as a club, had lending facilities, and reading and story hour rooms. In 1927 a Little Theatre was added for performing plays ranging from puppetry to Shakespeare. "The first library building on the continent devoted entirely to children's work" has served throughout as a model for children's collection building and programming.[44]

The influential *Horn Book Magazine* was founded in 1924 by Bertha Mahony and Elinor Whitney. In 1925 appeared the first library room devoted entirely to youth, Cleveland's Robert Louis Stevenson Room, matching its Lewis Carroll Room for children; the holdings were primarily recreational books built around the interests of young people and a reference collection for school assignments. The following year Effie L. Power introduced the first book caravan, and a young people's department was organized on the second floor of Brooklyn's heavily used Brownsville Public Library. The five numbers of the *School Library Yearbook* (published by the ALA Committee on School Libraries, 1927–32), and the four numbers of the *Children's Library Yearbook* (published by ALA's Section on Library Work with Children, 1929–32) offer insights into the progress of companion library programs for children.

Among library services enjoyed by children in this decade were programs emphasizing biography, poetry, and travel. Others included a

30 / Clienteles

community survey done by children, festivals, hospital service, pageants, the playground book wagon, and weekly talks with mothers about children's books. Library maps featured adventure and fairyland, and reading clubs covered tràvel, vacations, and woodcraft. Classes visited the public library, which in turn provided classroom libraries and school visits by librarians. There was a title catalog with annotations by children, exhibits of books and children's projects, little theaters using a puppet stage set up on a section of bookshelves with scenes arranged by children, and widespread reference service.[45]

Despite the span of time in Effie L. Power's "A Century of Progress in Library Work with Children," and Ralph Munn's fundamental questions and mature understanding in "The Social Significance of Library Work with Children," neither article touches the impact of the depression.[46] Its effects were seriously felt as funds were cut back, and many libraries were forced to reduce their services. The depression also deepened public library involvement in school library services. Often youth service was curtailed so that adult services could continue, although the presence of children's rooms made their retention easier. Mary R. Lucas, children's librarian of Providence, offered this representative advice:

> Cut back on services to large groups (story-hours, book clubs), but give more individual attention. Offer the child something to alleviate the tense environment—father out of work, etc. Don't buy many new books, but be extra selective. Work through parents and teachers.[47]

Programs conducted included Berkeley Library Day, where students and teachers impersonated characters from history or fiction, book clubs, library day for hospital children, reading clubs, Saturday picture hours. Book wagons were retained, a lending "library" of toys was functioning, and a few libraries offered special services to young adults, including separate reading rooms, discussion groups, and readers' advisory service. It is interesting to note that in the thirties two children's library systems operated in Montreal, one in English, the other in French. Travel by way of books, the most popular summer activity for children, undoubtedly a reaction to the inhibiting atmosphere created by the depression, was used by many different libraries.

Nineteen thirty-six brought the demise of the Bookshop for Boys and Girls in Boston, and the establishment of the Library Services Branch in the U.S. Office of Education. In 1937 Augusta Baker came to work at New York Public Library's 135th Street Branch. From 1938 on she compiled editions of *Books about Negro Life for Children*, an expanding list of works about black life experiences suitable for the children whose background and heritage she helped cultivate.

In the latter half of the decade, perhaps because economic conditions eased, extension services were renewed, including services to children's hospitals. Radio programs became common: Denver Public Library had a "Once-upon-a-Time" show; New York's broadcasts combined music and storytelling, and Julia L. Sauer of Rochester (N.Y.) broadcast book talks.

1940s AND 1950s

During World War II the library developed further its role of educator, instilling intellectual and social values in response to the war's threats.[48] Functioning in addition as a social welfare agency, the library became something of an emotional factor in the lives of many children, both because of librarians' human support, and the comfort children's rooms afforded. The civilizing influences of the Newark Public Library on a ten-year-old during the forties were recalled by writer Philip Roth in an article in the *New York Times* of March 1, 1969.

Patriotism permeated much of the literature of the early forties; the very concepts of "enemies" and "allies" gave rise to uncertainties and many questions from children. In this spirit, during the summer of 1940, Dallas Public Library's Boys and Girls Room planned a reading program about the United States, to add roots for children in the culture, geography, and history of the United States. Children's home lives were upset by fathers' joining the military and by mothers' taking jobs. Responding with new awareness, many libraries, in cooperation with the Children's Bureau and related units, offered parents information on child welfare through books, pamphlets, and group discussion. Librarians assisted many organizations in program planning, helped train child care volunteers, and established reading corners and story hours in schools and child care centers.[49]

While concentrating on the confused or upset child, libraries also sought future directions. In 1943 ALA's Committee on Postwar Planning established minimum standards for service, "aware that we possess a powerful force for the international rehabilitation of children after the war."[50]

Fortunately, this heightened social consciousness also found expression in publications. In 1942 Paul Hazard's *Books, Children, and Men* was published by *Horn Book*, emphasizing that "smilingly the pleasant books of childhood cross all frontiers," and offering an illuminating defense of childhood, not in one country, but in the world.[50] The year 1943 brought *Work with Children in Public Libraries*, by Effie L. Power,

> to convey to beginning workers a sense of the joy that comes from a close association with children and their books as well as to assist them in solving the daily problems which arise on organizing and administering libraries serving to meet children's interests and needs.[52]

The 1940s also saw the opening of a pioneer unit exclusively for youth: the Nathan Straus Branch of the New York Public Library. In

1941 the ALA Division of Libraries for Children and Young People was established to attain greater standardization of service nationally. The year 1944 brought the organization of the Children's Book Council, with links between publishers, libraries, and related organizations. In 1945 ALA presented national standards in *School Libraries for Today and Tomorrow*.[53] Edited by Mary T. Peacock Douglas, and formulated by key figures in the U.S. school library movement, this statement served as a blueprint for postwar planning.

Although most service to children was concentrated in a particular library's neighborhood, urban systems tried to reach outlying areas also. The Enoch Pratt Free Library sent a horsedrawn wagon into areas of Baltimore which lacked branch service; Kern County (Calif.) Library attempted to serve many children who lived in remote rural areas.

Following World War II the establishment of school libraries increased. In Pittsburgh nearly one-third of all books lent for home reading were from school libraries. On its twenty-first birthday in 1946, Cleveland's Robert Louis Stevenson Room added a Browsing Alcove with comfortable furniture, reflecting the new trend of informality. The reaffirmation of the purpose of children's services surfaced with an acknowledgment that good service should be defined more as searching and working to find answers rather than assuming the answers.

In 1947 the University of Chicago Graduate School of Library Science hosted a library institute devoted wholly to consideration of service to children and young people. A group of impressive papers, entitled *Youth, Communication, and Libraries*, edited by Frances Henne, Alice Brooks, and Ruth Ersted,[54] were published. Together they contributed much information about the contemporary library scene, describing meaningful, recent developments with valuable background facts, posing specific goals, and pointing toward new directions and vistas of library work with youth.

The 1950s brought the cold war, McCarthyism, the antisegregation decision in the Brown case, and the spread of television. From 1949 to 1952 the Public Library Inquiry was conducted to study the activities of public libraries across the nation and to suggest improvements. Although it was generally acknowledged as a "classic success," study of children's services was omitted, a lack keenly felt by both practitioners and library science teachers. One of the latter, Elizabeth Gross, sought funds for such a study, and in 1958 received $16,000 from the Old Dominion Foundation. A publication resulted,[55] but the need for a thorough current study remains.

After the report of the Public Library Inquiry was issued,[56] many regional meetings were arranged to study various aspects of children's services for possible change and upgrading. One such meeting held in 1953 by the California Library Association's Standards Workshop discussed the growing need for written policy and selection standards. A number of suggested guidelines were adopted by other states, including the recognition of the growing importance of media and the need for audiovisual collections, children's access rights, and the continued need for cooperation between school and public libraries.

Following a "School Libraries" column in *Library Journal*, edited from 1948 to 1952 by Frances Henne and Ruth Ersted, *School Libraries* was started in 1952; by 1954 interest in library service to children and young adults had become strongly rooted, and *School Library Journal* (first called *Junior Libraries*) was begun with specialized feature articles and news sections. In 1955 New York City opened its Donnell Library across the street from the Museum of Modern Art, including a well-stocked children's room on the mezzanine, and on the second floor a teen-age library, open daily from noon to 10 P.M., extending the pioneering services begun by the unique Nathan Straus Branch, since demolished to make room for public housing.

Many services noted above continued, but new programs emerged, especially those for preschool children. British librarian Vyvien Newton spent the year 1954–55 on the staff on the Brooklyn Public Library and in the *Library Association Record* the following year wrote "activities involved work with pre-school groups, story sessions in parks, service to immigrants, specialized work with teen-agers, and an extensive programme of staff training."[57]

Further expansion made use of television and other media: variegated story hours and radio book reviews; Margaret Scoggins's program with teen-agers at the New York Public Library was a lively example. With greater recognition of the need for a variety of approaches to learning, libraries reshaped their collections with many multimedia items and developed programs utilizing more of these motley resources.

Service was extended to children shut in by illness or handicaps; both Cincinnati and New York public libraries developed services for exceptional children, guided by sensitive specialists. Increased services to ghetto children, though rooted in past decades, were discussed by Augusta Baker of the New York Public Library, who encouraged new methods of library minority aid. Although this service did not peak until the sixties, greater concern for minority children was gradually shown, in both materials gathered and individual programs extended.[58]

The launching of Sputnik by the Soviet Union in 1957 set off a reaction felt in libraries across the country. The decade ended with interest mounting in developing science and math collections for youth in school and public libraries, as reflected by the National Defense Education Act and a growing concern about educational change and its counterparts in library service.

THE BUSTLING 1960s

During these years our country experienced continued population shifts, assassinations of public figures, urban riots, heightened minority consciousness, the Elementary and Secondary Education Act, the burst of activities stimulated by the Great Society programs, the repercussions of the Vietnam War involvement, and student unrest. Aspects of many of these happenings seeped into library services to children.

With emphasis on professional standards, library service to children became fully developed and sophisticated, but basic questions persisted. Many formerly convenient central children's rooms in large public libraries were no longer easily accessible to urban children, and with shifting populations it became imperative to alter services to reach the disadvantaged. Federal funds were used to initiate many such programs; after 1964 approximately $10 million was expended under Title I of the Library Services and Construction Act (LSCA).

Among the innovative ideas and projects, and the spending institutions, were these:

> The Alley Library, Washington, D.C. where an after school program was established
> Bilingual story programs (e.g., Pura Belpré White's in South Bronx in Spanish and English)
> Library-Go-Round put into operation by the Queens Borough Public Library whose Langston Hughes Community Branch became a model unit for collection development and programming
> Madison (Wisc.) Project Head Start—based on "involvement with restrained warmth, rather than zealous enthusiasm," with carefully concentrated service
> Neighborhood library service by way of an old green car to Milwaukee's inner city with books, films, fun and games, and teenage volunteers
> Preschool programs in day care centers (Brooklyn Public)
> School Book Fairs (Kansas City) reflecting more observable cooperation between library and school
> Sidewalk service by autovan by Brooklyn Public Library coordinators to meet the needs of persons who never visited a library and didn't know such services were free.

Two special contemporary issues of *Library Trends* reveal much about the central concerns of more traditional service. "Public Library Service to Children," edited by Winifred C. Ladley, touched the origins of service, the collection, standards of services operating under systems organization, storytelling and the story hour, service to the exceptional child, utilization of nonbook activities and materials, services to adults working with children, and the relation to the state library agency in the United States.[59] The counterpart issue for October 1968, devoted to "Young Adult Service in the Public Library," was edited by Audrey Biel, and reflected her rich experience in the Detroit Public Library.[60] Covered were: understanding the adolescent reader, young adult service on the public library organizational chart, the Young Adult librarian and training needs, the collection's choice and location, the relationship to the school library, programming, young adult service in Canada, and in the state, regional, and county systems.

Although attention to teens had increased after World War II, this field stirred varying controversy, and many libraries found excuses of space, staff, and so forth to dispense with their related units. The appearance in 1969 of Margaret A. Edwards's *The Fair Garden and the Swarm of Beasts* with her humanistic view of the interplay between the librarian and young people confronts one with much of the personal, educational, and social impact of such losses.[61]

Throughout the decade came more evidence of library links to child-centered programs. There was greater sensitivity to the contents of minority materials in trade books and media and public response to end the overwhelming Anglo-Saxon and middle-class emphasis in such materials. The U.S. pavilion at the New York World's Fair of 1965 in its library area presented newer aspects of changing library environments: the Children's World Theatre in the round, lighting variety, creative programming with media, dial-reviews, and computer printouts of popular subject bibliographies.

Despite these advances, two years after the publication of *Standards for School Library Programs*,[62] slightly more than 50 percent of all schools in the 50 states and Washington, D.C. still lacked central school libraries. Although such resources were available in more than 90 percent of all secondary schools, partly because of accreditation demands, about two-thirds of all elementary schools had none. *Better Libraries Make Better Schools*, collected by Charles L. Trinker, describes many existing situations.[63]

By the end of the decade the Elementary and Secondary Education Act had brought drastic changes in many forms to schools and school libraries. Through its first three titles, this pioneering sweeping legislation stimulated the expansion of school library collections and services, especially at the elementary level. So momentous were these developments, so rich in accomplishments despite the lack of matching support for professional personnel, that literally every pupil was touched. An important article to absorb is "Evaluation of Media Services to Children and Young People in Schools," by Mary Helen Mahar, education program officer, Bureau of Libraries and Library Resources, U.S. Office of Education.[64] The supporting literature about the School Library Development Project, the Knapp School Library Project, 1963–68 (summarized in Peggy Sullivan's *Realization*),[65] and the Knapp School Library Manpower Project initiated in 1968 represents attempts to share "demonstration" school library situations and efforts to experiment with background training for the more complicated school libraries envisioned.

The demonstration value of the Encyclopaedia Britannica-sponsored Project Discovery and its School Library (later School Media) awards programs was also significant. The vast changes in perspective and attack during this decade are reflected in the 1969 *Standards for School Media Programs*.[66] Yet in many communities the greater school library development set off rivalry between public and school libraries serving children, the latter catching up breathlessly and the former straining to preserve its basic services.

In this examination of library service to youth, one question recurs: which unit can best serve today's library-media needs? In earlier decades the school alone was insufficient; later the public library's servicing of the school proved inadequate. The school library grew within the framework of the school's individual program with varying and unequal resources and professional support, achieved sometimes with local funds and sometimes aided by foundation or federal government sources. During the late sixties, when such developments escalated, children's services lagged in many large city libraries despite their attempts to catch up through LSCA and other funds. It is ironic that it was in New York State, where the system-wide public library service to children had reached a peak of professionalism and where school libraries were beginning to redevelop their services, that controversy flared in the regents' request to give the elementary school library the basic role of responding to children's media needs. Because the pilot study that was to be the basis for the final decision has not yet been funded, the situation remains unresolved,[67] and its shock waves moved into the 1970s.

HALFWAY INTO THE 1970S

The 1970s opened with growing evidences of "future shock" in our society, the nightmares of Nixon and Watergate, bankrupt cities surrounded by urban sprawl, amidst calls for accountability. Nevertheless, there were striking attempts to maintain some of the gains of the sixties. Legacy of the late James Allen, long New York's commissioner of education, the Right to Read efforts were slow to be launched, but came to be woven into many of the activities which both school and public libraries assumed.

The following checklist offered by Binnie L. Tate in "On Beyond 999Z"[68] contains many of the types of creative programming designed for the active participation of children that children's librarians developed through funded experiments or on their own:

> Book programs (chain reading games, free and swap, and reading improvement)
> Poetry and creative writing, including read-ins
> Provision for ethnic materials (including cultural fairs, ethnic language games and quizzes, and spotlighting special birthdays and holidays)
> Storytelling (including stories with bilingual ethnic themes in dance, stories in a tent, and tell it on tape)
> Visuals and audiovisuals: film making, record listening posts, rock bands, TV viewing centers

Working with community and community agencies (bookmobile programs, career conferences, day care, grooming and modeling services, Head Start).

Many of these involved cross-age-group emphasis. There was also a growing awareness of the needs of exceptional children. Some large city libraries started mobile van programs of many types to stimulate activities like these:

Atlanta Public Library's Project Enlarge, which taught photography to young people
Buffalo and Erie County Public Library's RAM Van (Readily Accessible Materials)
Cincinnati and Hamilton County's Playmobile project which circulated play equipment
Dallas Public Library's Showmobile with its mini stage for puppet shows
Kansas City Public Library's Instant Movies at the Curbstone
Woodlawn (Chicago) Public Library's camera club.

Outgrowths of the impact of the National Endowment for the Arts, programs associated with the arts were popular: Greenwich, Connecticut held a multimedia festival; Brooklyn's Bushwick Branch featured kitemaking. Programs emphasizing reading and other projects representing cooperation between the schools and public libraries have emerged. Especially interesting because it is operated by community residents as well as library and education professionals is the Philadelphia Student Library Resources project. This action library, an inner-city learning center, was recently threatened with extinction when government funds ran out. Many programs have involved both children and adults, among them the Early Start program in New England, the Good Start program, offering reading readiness in Glassboro (N.J.) Public Library, and the Multi-Media Center for Preschoolers innovative for both its variety of materials and programs, recently incorporated into the Erie (Pa.) Metropolitan Library.[69]

With illustrations of both slight and significant changes which have altered school library settings and services, the *Wilson Library Bulletin* for January 1975 included a grassroots description of "School Libraries/Media Center—1975" around the country. Whether they can hold their own in the face of slashed budgets is a ringing question.

The Educational Amendments of 1974 (Public Law 93–380) extended the range of established programs, created some new ones, and called for a number of important "reforms" which will force media specialists to articulate and actively negotiate their needs. No longer will Title II, ESEA and Title III, NDEA be earmarked for school media programs alone. Together with guidance and testing, they were consolidated into Title IV, part B of the law cited. Future funding of media programs will be at the discretion of local administrations and school boards.

38 / Clienteles

CONCLUSIONS

A century of shared inspiration and sustained effort, work by a tremendous number and variety of individuals and their staffs, has contributed to youth's delight, growth, and informational needs. But as critically severe problems faced by cities translate into shrinking budgets, there is a continual threat of further reduction and even elimination of service.

During the American Library Association Conference in New York, July 1974, Spencer Shaw, incoming president of the Children's Services Division, who had chaired the Public Library Association's Standing Committee on Library Services to Children, reported what *Library Journal* called chilling news:

> Conditions found included: a steady elimination of coordinators of children's services throughout the country; the downgrading of children's specialists on the library administration organization charts; the closing of rooms in central libraries; incipient transfers of children's public library programs to schools, and lack of published rationales to justify these actions from trustees and library directors.[70]

During the Midwinter meeting in Chicago in January 1975, the first copies of *Media Programs: District and School* were released. Developed jointly by the American Association of School Librarians and the Association for Educational Communications and Technology to supersede the 1969 *Standards*, the "partnership of the media program and classroom instruction is conveyed by a careful characterization of staff functions and media services at the local and district level."[71]

But what of the personal needs of the child within the school day? And what of the library/media services outside the school? How will the later seventies muster support to maintain them on an optimal level and reach for a balance that will cater to the needs of the whole child and youth?

Looking back with the perspective of a century, it is perhaps most appropriate to conclude with the opening statement of the 1973 Children's Task Force paper:

> Children are creative, inquiring individuals with unique capacities for intellectual and emotional growth. . . . As an integral part of the community, libraries should serve as active partners in planning and working with other agencies and individuals seeking to meet the needs of children.[72]

What Anne Carroll Moore referred to as the "re-creation of childhood" and what Alice Hazeltine called the "vision of library work with children as an integral part of library work as a whole and as an educational movement" are still essential for the adults providing library service to children.[73] Yet with the coming tide of a new century and distinct evolving needs, we feel the pull of planning and priorities recorded by Diane G. Farrell in her "Library and Information Needs of Young Children."[74] which retains the best of the past century and anticipates deepened and branched services to come.

NOTES

1. U.S. Bureau of Education, *Public Libraries in the United States of America: Their History, Condition, and Management*, Special Report (Washington, D.C.: Govt. Print. Off., 1876), pp. 412, 414, 415, 416.
2. *Macropaedia* 4:228 in *The New Encyclopaedia Britannica*, 15th ed. (Chicago: Encyclopaedia Britannica, 1974).
3. The research that laid the detailed basis for these summaries was contributed in part by the following graduate students in the writer's class, "Library Service to Children and Young People," given at the Kent State University School of Library Science during the spring of 1974: Kenneth Cromer, Arlene Dunbar Willoughby, Jane Faires, Barbara Hawkins, Deborah Herdman, Cynthia Meisner, Wendy Jann Pierce, Krista Sawyckyj, Sherry Sims, Rebecca Thomas, and Linda Young.
4. Harriet G. Long, *Public Library Service to Children: Foundation and Development* (Metuchen, N.J.: Scarecrow, 1969).
5. Gwendolen Rees, *Libraries for Children: A History and a Bibliography* (London: Grafton, 1924); Anne Pellowski, *The World of Children's Literature* (New York: Bowker, 1968).
6. *Libraries at Large*, Douglas M. Knight and E. Shepley Nourse, eds. (New York: Bowker, 1969), pp. 89–91.
7. John Thomas Gillespie and Diana L. Spirt, *Creating a School Media Program* (New York: Bowker, 1973), pp. 4–15. See also Lillian Shapiro, *Serving Youth* (New York: Bowker, 1975), pp. 34–39.
8. U.S. Bureau of Education, pp. 38–58.
9. Clarence H. Cramer, *Open Shelves and Open Minds: A History of the Cleveland Public Library* (Cleveland and London: Pr. of Case Western Reserve Univ., 1972), p. 62.
10. Charles Francis Adams, "The Public Library and the Public Schools," in Arthur E. Bostwick, ed., *The Relationship between the Library and the Public Schools* . . . (White Plains, N.Y.: Wilson, 1914), pp. 23–32.
11. Cramer, p. 61, quoting the annual report.
12. In Bostwick, pp. 33–34.
13. Ibid., pp. 45–62.
14. Cramer, p. 61.
15. Ibid., p. 62.
16. *Report of the Commissioner of Education* vol. 1, pt. 2, 1892–93 (Washington, D.C.: Govt. Print. Off., 1895), pp. 944–49.
17. *Denver Public Library News*, no. 4 (undated).
18. Margo Sassi, "The Children's Librarian in America," *School Library Journal* 86:23 (Jan. 1961).
19. Cramer, p. 66.
20. Ibid., p. 64.
21. J. C. Dana, quoted in International Library Conference, 2d, London, July 13–16, 1897, *Transactions and Proceedings* . . . (Edinburgh, Morrison & Gibb, 1898).
22. Anne Carroll Moore, "Special Training for Children's Librarians," *Library Journal* 23:80–82, 134 (Conference No., 1898).
23. W. R. Eastman, "The Public Library and the Public School," in Bostwick, p. 96.

40 / Clienteles

24. Charlotte H. Meade, "Noted on Children's Reading," *Library Journal* 29:476 (Sept. 1904).
25. Rachel D. Harris, "Work with Children at the Colored Branch of the Louisville Free Public Library," *Library Journal* 35:160–61 (Apr. 1910).
26. "St. Louis, Missouri Public Library," *Library Journal* 30:239 (Apr. 1905).
27. Mary Denson Pretlow, "The Opening of a Public Library," *Charities and the Commons* 15:888–89 (Mar. 1906).
28. Clara Whitehill Hunt, "Maintaining Order in the Children's Room," in *Library Work with Children*, ed. by Alice I. Hazeltine (White Plains, N.Y.: Wilson, 1917), p. 234.
29. Caroline Marie Hewins, "Reading Clubs for Older Boys and Girls," in *Library Work with Children*, pp. 317–23.
30. Edwin White Gaillard, "An Experiment in School-Library Work," *Library Journal* 30:201–3 (Apr. 1905).
31. Grace Thompson, "On the Selecting of Books for Children," *Library Journal* 32:427–31 (Oct. 1907).
32. Editorial, *Library Journal* 32:302 (July 1907).
33. E. L. Pearson, "The Children's Librarian vs. Huck Finn: A Brief for the Defense," *Library Journal* 32:312 (July 1907).
34. For her views reflecting her knowledge of children and her broad interests, see especially her introductory remarks as well as her interspersed criticism in her *Books for Boys and Girls* (Chicago: ALA Publishing Board, 1897); 2d ed., 1904; 3rd rev. ed., 1915.
35. Arabelle H. Jackson, "Report on Library Work with Children," *Library Journal* 31:89–97 (Aug. 1906).
36. Sophy Powell, *The Children's Library: A Dynamic Factor in Education* (New York: Wilson, 1917), p. 9. Includes an extensive bibliography, pp. 341–456.
37. Jessie M. Carson, "The Children's Share in a Public Library," *Library Journal* 36:254 (May 1912). See also Martha Pond, "Evening Work with Children," *Library Journal* 39:892 (Dec. 1914).
38. Alice I. Hazeltine, *Library Work with Children* (White Plains, N.Y.: Wilson, 1917).
39. *Library Journal* 38:386 (July 1913).
40. "General Libraries," *Library Journal* 40:923 (Dec. 1915).
41. Cramer, p. 74.
42. *Library Journal* 46:902 (1921).
43. Effie L. Power, "The Peterkin Family and the Project Method," *Public Libraries* 26:572–73 (Nov. 1921).
44. Pellowski, p. 383.
45. See especially Arthur E. Bostwick, "The Library and the Child," *ALA Bulletin* 20:281–87 (Oct. 1926).
46. Effie L. Power, "A Century of Progress in Library Work with Children," *Library Journal* 58:822–25 (Oct. 15, 1933); Ralph Munn, "The Social Significance of Work with Children," *Library Journal* 55:638–40 (Aug. 1930).
47. Mary R. Lucas, "The Children's Librarian Takes Stock," *Library Journal* 58:342 (Apr. 15, 1933). The thoughts are further developed in her "Young People and Some Books on Present Day Problems," *Library Journal* 59:200–202 (Mar. 1, 1934), and "Library Service for Youth: The Primary Activities," *Library Journal* 60:831–33 (Nov. 1, 1935).
48. Julia Sauer, "Library Services to Children in a World at War," in Pan-American Child Congress, 8th, Washington, 1942. *Proceedings . . .* Publication 2847, Conference Series 100 (Washington, D.C.: Dept. of State, 1948), pp. 417–25.
49. Katherine Lenroot, "The Significance of the Children's Charter in Wartime," *ALA Bulletin* 36:610–19 (Oct. 1, 1942); Julia Sauer, "Making the World Safe for the Janey Larkins," *Library Journal* 66:49–53 (Jan. 1, 1941).

50. American Library Association, Committee on Postwar Planning, *Minimum Standards for Service* (Chicago: The Association, 1943). Other publications by this committee are pertinent also.
51. Bostwick, p. 147.
52. Effie L. Power, *Work with Children in Public Libraries* (Chicago: American Library Assn., 1943), p. xi.
53. American Library Association, *School Libraries for Today and Tomorrow*, Planning for Libraries, 5 (Chicago: The Association, 1945).
54. Frances Henne, Alice Brooks, and Ruth Ersted, eds., *Youth, Communications, and Libraries* (Chicago: American Library Assn., 1949).
55. Elizabeth H. Gross and Gene I. Namovicz, *Children's Service in Public Libraries: Organization and Administration* (Chicago: American Library Assn., 1963).
56. Robert Leigh, *The Public Library in the United States: The General Report of the Public Library Inquiry* (New York: Columbia Univ. Pr., 1950).
57. Vyvien V. Newton, "A Year with the Children's Department at Brooklyn," *Library Association Record* 58: 64–67 (Feb. 1956).
58. See for instance Emerson Greenaway's "What About Tomorrow's Children," *Library Journal* 75:656–59 (Apr. 15, 1950); and "St. Petersburg Provides Library Service to Negro Community," *Library Journal* 75:468 (Mar. 15, 1950).
59. *Library Trends* 12, no. 1:3–118 (July 1963).
60. *Library Trends* 17, no. 2:115–220 (Oct. 1968).
61. Margaret A. Edwards, *The Fair Garden and the Swarm of Beasts* (New York: Hawthorne, 1969).
62. American Association of School Librarians, *Standards for School Library Programs* (Chicago: American Library Assn., 1960).
63. Charles L. Trinkner, ed., *Better Libraries Make Better Schools* (Hamden, Conn.: Shoe String, 1962).
64. Mary Helen Mahar, "Evaluation of Media Services to Children and Young People in Schools," *Library Trends* 22, no. 3:377–86 (Jan. 1974). See also the counterpart article by Pauline Winnick, "Evaluation of Public Library Services to Children," ibid., pp. 361–75.
65. Peggy Sullivan, *Realization* (Chicago: American Library Assn., 1968).
66. American Association of School Librarians, *Standards for School Media Programs*, ed. by the Department of Audio-Visual Instruction, National Education Association (Chicago: American Library Assn., 1969).
67. For background and analysis, see J. Gordon Burke and Gerald R. Shields, eds., *Children's Library Service: School or Public?* (Metuchen, N.J.: Scarecrow, 1974).
68. Binnie L. Tate, "On Beyond 999Z: Patterns of Library Service to Children of the Poor," in *Advances in Librarianship*, ed. by Melvin J. Voigt, 3:7–9 (New York: Seminar Pr., 1972).
69. See for instance Donald B. Pierson and Mary J. H. Yurchak, "Brookline Early Education Project," *Top of the News* 31:41–45 (Nov. 1974).
70. Quoted from report in *Library Journal* 99:2218–19 (Sept. 15, 1974).
71. American Association of School Librarians and Association for Educational Communications and Technology, *Media Programs: District and School* (Chicago: American Library Assn., 1975).
72. Quoted by Phyllis M. Wilson, "Planning for Children," *American Libraries* 6, no. 1:7 (Jan. 1975).
73. Alice I. Hazeltine, "What Is a Children's Librarian?" *Public Libraries* 26:513 (Nov. 1921).
74. Diane G. Farrell, "Library and Information Needs of Young Children," in Conference on the Needs of Occupational, Ethnic, and Other Groups in the United States, *Library and Information Service Needs of the Nation* . . . (Washington, D.C.: Govt. Print. Off., 1974), pp. 143–54.

3

Service to Ethnic Minorities Other than Afro-Americans and American Indians

HAYNES McMULLEN
University of North Carolina, Chapel Hill

When the librarians of the United States and Canada began to serve ethnic minorities, they became involved in one of the greatest movements of peoples in the history of the world; in the years from 1876 through 1973, about 37 million people have come to the United States and about 10 million have come to Canada.

The primary concern of the librarians has been to help the newcomers to adjust to life in North America but a secondary concern has been to help the native born to understand and sympathize with the immigrants. One authority, writing about the Americanization movement as it existed in the United States in the early twentieth century, has said, "The impulse of fear and the impulse of love ran throughout its whole course, clashing in principle though in practice sometimes strangely blended."[1] The librarians considered themselves a part of the movement and definitely had the impulse of love, even though they sometimes worked side-by-side with those who feared.

Most of the librarians in Canada and the United States who have been at the forefront in service to immigrants have not been the "leaders" in the profession; they have been branch librarians in large public libraries or have been the head librarians of smaller libraries. Those who have urged greater attention to this kind of work have been women (not often men) who practiced what they preached—true missionaries who went far beyond the call of duty. The record shows that they were often happy to help bewildered strangers by translating letters, explaining official American documents, and even, at times, accompanying women to doctors to help explain their symptoms. Some of the librarians must have had truly magnetic personalities. One of them advocated going into the homes to collect fines; she had found, she said, that such visits provided excellent opportunities for making friends for the library.

The changes in the amount and kind of concern for the foreign born have been so gradual that its history cannot be divided into neat periods. No continuing attempt to measure this kind of service has ever been made; one cannot say exactly when it increased or improved. Furthermore, none of the limited number of surveys and partial histories, written by librarians or others, has ever claimed that there were any sudden changes in the nature of these services.

In Canada the history of service to ethnic minorities has been quite different from that in the United States. The earliest libraries were established by the French, who later became a minority. However, in many communities in Quebec, the English-speaking persons continue to be an ethnic minority. Over the years the tendency in Canada has been for each of the two groups to take care of its own needs as it has seen them.

The pattern of immigration into the two countries has been quite different. The great influx from Europe into the United States in the latter part of the nineteenth century was not matched in Canada where there were more emigrants than immigrants in every decade from 1860s through the 1890s. For both countries there was little immigration during the Great Depression and the duration of the Second World War; both saw an increase after that war but Canada's increase was much greater; more than a third of its immigration for the last century has occurred since 1945.

Only since the Second World War has there been much concern in Canada for service to minorities other than the French and English. Because most library activity directed by a majority toward a minority has occurred during the last hundred years in the United States, this paper is mainly concerned with trends and events which occurred in that country.

In the United States, as we shall see, the concern of librarians for ethnic minorities was quite definitely increasing up to about the time of the First World War; by the 1930s a decrease was beginning. It will be convenient to divide the period into four parts: first, the years before 1904, when these services seem to have been quite limited in most libraries; second, the years from 1904 to 1918 when librarians in the United States became much more aware of the problems of the immigrants and became much more eager to serve them; third, the years from 1919 to 1935 when the librarians' efforts became better organized and then began to decline; and last, the years since 1935, when activity and interest in the United States seem to have been mainly concerned with service to three groups: European refugees from totalitarian states, a small number of Orientals, and, most recently, a large number of Spanish-speaking persons.

The rise and decline of the librarians' concern for immigrants has been closely related to changes in North American life and to trends in other aspects of librarianship. The most obvious change has been in two aspects of immigration itself: the number of immigrants coming into either the United States or Canada and the kinds of persons who were coming in. In the United States, this occurred during the late nineteenth century and the early twentieth; in Canada, in the 1950s.

The need for services did not change abruptly when immigration increased or decreased. It was, for the most part, related to difficulty in using English, varying with the age of the immigrant, with his or her occupation in this country, and, sometimes, with his or her nationality. Librarians observed that children adapted very quickly, that adult males in the work force were perhaps slower, and that females, especially if they were homemakers, were even slower; the elderly continued to need foreign language materials the longest.

The relationship between the attitudes of librarians and the attitudes of the general public toward immigrants is noteworthy. In years such as those around the beginning of the First World War, when many in the United States were alarmed at the number of foreigners who were not citizens and could not speak English, an article by a librarian might start by echoing this alarm, and then quickly switch to a more soothing note, demonstrating a deep sympathy and affection for the newcomers. Almost without exception, and through all the years, the librarians agreed with those liberal-minded, enlightened fellow-citizens who wanted to make the transition to the new society as easy and pleasant as possible. They favored the gradual assimilation of the new groups, but they also wanted to help these people in their efforts to preserve an interest in the cultural heritage of the old country.

The attitudes of librarians toward service to the foreign born have also been related to the general attitude of public librarians and library trustees in the United States regarding the mission of the library. In both the United States and Canada, service to immigrants has expanded at times when service to other groups was increasing—service to children and to the blind, for example. The idea of special services for special groups of users was prevalent in the thinking of many members of the library profession. Immigrants constituted a clearly defined group with easily identified needs.

The amount and kind of services to minorities have of course been affected over the years by the economic well-being of the libraries themselves. During the Great Depression of the 1930s, these services, like all others, had to be curtailed; for other years, however, it is often difficult to determine the importance of financial considerations.

BEFORE 1904

No one knows when the first immigrants began to use libraries in the United States or Canada. There is little evidence that special services were offered to them in libraries in operation before the twentieth century; in the United States a few of the newcomers from Germany began to establish their own libraries as early as the eighteenth century. The Germans were by far the most active, particularly after the failure of the revolution of 1848 caused many of the more cultural and liberal-minded to come to the United States. Records have been found concerning sixty-five libraries established in the United States by German immigrants before 1876 and of only two established by persons of any other national origin.[2]

Access to a library founded by a native-born U.S. citizen had great influence on one immigrant boy before 1876 and, through him, on many libraries in the United States and elsewhere. In the early 1850s Andrew Carnegie was allowed to use the private collection of a retired businessman, James Anderson, of Allegheny, Pennsylvania. Soon after Carnegie began to read in the collection, the owner set it up as an apprentices' library under a board of trustees; the young Carnegie continued to use it, becoming convinced of the value of such a library for persons who wished to educate themselves.

For the years between 1876 and 1904, only a few writers mention the use of U.S. or Canadian libraries by the foreign born. The great encyclopedic Bureau of Education report of 1876 on the libraries of the United States is silent about service to immigrants, even though newcomers to this country had surely been using many of the libraries it describes. The *Report of the Commissioner of Education* for 1887–88 refers to a statement by the superintendent of schools of Minnesota that in counties populated largely by Scandinavians, children were reading books from school libraries and, as a result, were becoming interested in American literature and history.[3]

A French publisher, writing about printing and bookselling in connection with the World's Columbian Exposition of 1893, commented on the great number of German books to be found in American public libraries; he noted that the Chicago Public Library contained sixty-five German periodicals and twenty-one German newspapers, compared with twenty-one French periodicals and two French newspapers. He attributed the greater number of German publications to the greater number of German immigrants and to their interest in keeping alive in their children a knowledge of the German language.[4]

One early attempt to serve a minority occurred in Ontario. In 1900 apparently because of the concern of one man, Alfred Fitzpatrick, small collections of French and English books and periodicals were placed in a number of logging camps. The work was still in progress in 1904.[5]

One of the central issues in service to immigrants has been whether libraries in the host country should supply books in the native languages of the newcomers. It is clear that by the 1890s some librarians in the United States were deliberately acquiring foreign-language books that were intended primarily to meet the needs of persons who were not comfortable with the use of English. The issue was brought into the open through an unsigned editorial in the October 1894 issue of *Library Journal* opposing the practice. The writer felt that a proposal to publish a list of Swedish books "raises a somewhat interesting question of library ethic." The preparation of such a list was "a further development of the rather recent tendency to consider the supplying of books in foreign languages as one of the functions of a public library." The main thrust of the editor's argument was this:

> There can be no argument against these collections, so long as they represent the best works of the chief European languages and are mainly designed as an aid to the study of those languages; but when the circulation of foreign books among foreign-speaking readers becomes of noteworthy importance in a library, and when the foreign collection is extended to cover works in comparatively little-known tongues, we are brought fairly to the question whether it is desirable thus to keep up language divisions among a population which, by virtue of residence and assumption of citizenship at least, should be wholly American.[6]

The passage above is worthy of quotation because it seems to be the only statement in the library press of either the United States or Canada printed during the last hundred years in opposition to the acquisition of these materials. Not one librarian among the authors of some 250 later articles about the public library and the immigrant argues against the purchase of books in foreign languages.

This editorial brought forth two direct replies: one, in the next issue of *Library Journal*, by Aksel G. S. Josephson, the source of the original proposal to buy Swedish books; Josephson was then a cataloger at the Lenox Library. He argued that readers of books about their native countries would later read about their new country.[7] The other reply, more detailed and more convincing, was written by Gratia Countryman, the head librarian at the Minneapolis Public Library. She said that she had originally agreed with the writer of the editorial but that her experiences in Minneapolis—particularly in seeing the delight which French books brought to the French Canadians—had convinced her that the library must attract readers before it could "Americanize" them.[8]

Elsewhere in the Middle West, other efforts were being made to serve the newcomers from northern Europe. A handbook issued jointly by the library commissions of Minnesota, Iowa, and Wisconsin, published in 1902, pointed out that some librarians had had long experience in ordering books in foreign languages. The readers being served, according to the authors of the handbook, "are usually adults, and many of them are taxpayers. It is both just and politic to please them by providing books in their native languages."[9] The Wisconsin Library Commission began a traveling library service with eleven collections of German books, bought with money donated by several German settlers. By 1905 the commission had seventy-nine German collections in circulation, sixteen in Scandinavian languages, and a few other collections that included Polish and Czech volumes. The provision of these libraries was the most popular service which the commission offered.[10]

1904–1918

In the years after 1904, librarians in the United States began to report with greater frequency and greater conviction about their experience in serving the foreign born. Activity continued in the Middle West: the Minnesota Library Commission could not meet the heavy demand for its traveling libraries in 1905; in 1906 it was sending out books in Norwegian, Swedish, German, French, and Finnish.[11] Activity was also increasing in large and medium-sized public libraries in the East. In 1906 James H. Canfield, the librarian at Columbia University, not himself directly involved, nevertheless spoke of work with the foreign population as "what may very properly be called a new movement in the public library world of this country."[12]

One librarian of a smaller library, J. Maud Campbell, head of the Passaic (N.J.) Public Library, deeply engaged in service to immigrants, began in 1904 to write a series of eloquent articles, telling of her experiences and urging other librarians to participate. In her first article she noted that almost four of every ten of the Passaic population were foreign born; one branch needed books in eleven languages.[13] A later contribution of hers brought warm endorsement in an editorial in the July 1908 issue of *New York Libraries*. The editor added that "reports from large city libraries almost invariably show in their statistics of circulation that it is in the centers where the foreign-born population is the largest that the percentage of current fiction read is the lowest and the percentage of history, science, and the arts called for is highest." Experience had "uniformly shown" the value of circulating books in foreign languages.[14]

Campbell's articles brought Aksel G. S. Josephson back into print. Supposing that librarians might like help in purchasing Swedish books, he described in the December 1908 issue of *Library Journal* some low-priced series of standard works available from publishers in Sweden.[15] Other librarians, perhaps because they were in closer touch with the needs of the newcomers, advocated the acquisition of lighter literature, books about the United States, and current periodicals and newspapers; they were concerned about ways to select popular material wisely and to order it without too much difficulty.

In these years librarians began to write about the special attitudes and needs of different nationalities; the Jews from Russia, the Poles, the Czechs, and the Italians; they even wrote about the differences between the immigrants from northern and southern Italy. Librarians were aware of the diffidence and distrust on the part of the foreigners and the problems occasioned when a shifting population caused the needs in any neighborhood to change rapidly.

Occasionally, librarians who were recognized leaders in the profession wrote or spoke about service to immigrants. Henry E. Legler, librarian of the Chicago Public Library, spoke at some length of the needs of the foreign born in his address as president of ALA in 1913. He cited the startling census report, just issued that year, showing that native whites of native parentage made up more than 50 percent of the population in only fourteen of the fifty cities with population above 100,000 in 1910. He reviewed the recent trends in immigration and pointed out the great challenge to libraries in the cities. He did not offer detailed suggestions but mentioned the importance of providing information in foreign languages about the United States and of serving immigrant children.[16]

In the years just before the war, the librarians were, quite naturally, most eager to help the "new immigrants" from southern and eastern Europe who had come in increasing numbers since the 1880s. Only rarely was service to other groups considered; in 1913 the writer of the article "What of the Black and Yellow Races?" praised the Japanese users of libraries and reported that "as a class of patrons they are not only inoffensive but desirable."[17]

These efforts soon began to attract the attention of the general public. The *Delineator* in January 1911 carried an article, "The Library's Part in Making Americans," mentioning work done in several libraries and recounting several touching anecdotes. It was illustrated with an artist's sketches which, incidentally, depicted the librarians as young and beautiful.[18] Articles with similar purposes, but limited to New York City, apeared in the *Independent* on January 23, 1913[19] and in the *World's Work* in May of the same year.[20]

At about the same time that outsiders were being informed of the good work of librarians, one outsider began a career of prodding librarians to greater efforts. John Foster Carr, who had founded the nonprofit Immigrant Publication Society, speaking before the Massachusetts Library Club in May 1913, urged the librarians of Massachusetts to make greater efforts.[21] Later he was to write and speak many more times about the need for serving the foreign born.

Soon after the beginning of the war, many persons in the United States were alarmed to discover that about a fourth of the male population old enough to vote was born abroad and that fewer than half of these foreign-born men had become citizens. All sorts of organizations, including libraries, set about "Americanizing" the foreign population. The word, *Americanize*, had been in the language for a long time but took on a new, aggressive meaning about 1915. Various organizations and leaders had somewhat varying conceptions as to its meaning but they agreed that it meant, at least, insuring the loyalty of the foreign-born population through the teaching of English and citizenship. There was general agreement that libraries, already engaged in a form of Americanization, were appropriate agencies to aid in the work.

During the early years of the war, the number of immigrants coming into the United States dropped sharply; after this country entered the conflict in 1917, the number dropped again. The interest of librarians in serving immigrants and in Americanization seems to have continued, as strong as ever: editorials in library periodicals urged support for Americanization.[22] But those librarians actually working with foreigners seemed more concerned with encouraging tolerance and understanding on the part of native-born librarians. The only new emphasis seems to have been on the identification and acquisition of easy books in English for beginning adult readers.

During the war an important step was taken toward the encouragement of library service to ethnic minorities, the establishment of the ALA Committee on Work with the Foreign Born. In 1916 the Executive Board of the association considered but tabled the matter. The next year, it "Resolved that a committee of five on work with the foreign-born be appointed to collect from libraries and supply them information on the desirable methods of assisting in the education of the foreign-born in American ideals and customs and the English language."[23] The committee was appointed by February 1918 with John Foster Carr of the Immigrant Publication Society as its chairman.[24]

1919–1935

Most librarians continued to support the idea of Americanization for several years after the war; they continued to supply materials for use in Americanization classes, and, sometimes, space where the classes could meet. They often obtained the help of naturalization officers and judges in order to make sure that all persons applying for naturalization should learn about services available to them at the libraries.[25]

In the United States the years just after the war also brought a strong drive, for various reasons, toward forced Americanization and severe restrictions on future immigration. The Emergency Quota Act of 1921 was the first immigration law to set limits on the number of persons coming in, country-by-country, in order to drastically reduce the numbers entering the United States from southern and eastern Europe.

There were a few librarians who by 1920 were becoming disenchanted with Americanization. In March of that year *Library Journal* published a short, bitter article by Della R. Prescott who was in charge of work with the foreign born in the Newark Free Library. She started by saying "'Americanization,' has failed,—in spirit, methods, and results."

Later in the article she wrote: "However well concealed, the insistent note in Americanization is, either force,—learn English or get out; or, a virtuous note of paternalism which sings the personal pleasure of doing 'something nice for the poor foreigner.'" She did not attack librarians but rather the Americanization movement and the deportation of "undesirable" aliens after unfair trials.[26] It is true that many in the United States were almost hysterically afraid of "radical" thinkers among the immigrants and were determined to limit immigration or to stop it altogether. A few months before the Prescott article appeared, the army transport *Buford* had departed from American shores, carrying 249 deportees; the immigration commissioner in New York believed that 10 million Europeans were waiting to come in this direction.[27]

There seems to be nothing in print to indicate that librarians shared this fear of the immigrants. They saw the foreign born as people who needed more than the help ordinarily given by libraries. The continued development of this service was one of a half-dozen aims of the Enlarged Program, proposed by the Executive Board of the American Library Association in 1920. The association had been quite successful in its efforts to serve the members of the armed services during the war; the library had proved an effective means for adult education.[28] After the war librarians had become inspired to expand their services to Americans in general, and particularly to those who had been neglected, such as the blind, the foreign born, and persons in institutions. A budget was established for work with immigrants, $60,000 for three years, to support a person at ALA headquarters and an office to collect and disseminate information about libraries' needs (especially, materials for the use of the foreign born) and about library services available to the immigrants.[29] Unfortunately, the Enlarged Program had to be abandoned in the same year it was launched, because of the association's lack of ability to obtain the necessary funds.[30] However, interest in all of its elements apparently continued; there is no conspicuous evidence to indicate that the librarians' concern for the immigrant decreased in the next few years.

The main agency that performed the kinds of services envisioned in the Enlarged Program was the ALA Committee on Work with the Foreign Born. In its annual reports, which appeared in the *ALA Bulletin* for almost all of the committee's thirty-year life (1918–48), its members pleaded eloquently for improved public library service to immigrants and gave very practical advice to other librarians as to how to render this service.

The committee was quite active in the 1920s; perhaps its most valuable contribution was the publication of articles in library and other periodicals about library services for immigrants. The committee also prepared several pamphlets, each focused on the immigrants from a particular country and written by a librarian familiar with their needs. Typically, the pamphlet gave some information about the customs and recent history of the country, followed by a short list of readings about the country for the use of native-born clients. Then came the main bibliography, a list of books and periodicals which the immigrants liked to read. At least four such pamphlets were issued: *The Polish Immigrant and His Reading* appeared in 1924; parallel titles appeared on the Italian in 1925, the Greek in 1926, and the German in 1929.

The committee not only disseminated information, it also provided a means for librarians to exchange ideas. From the early 1920s on, the committee was involved almost every year in organizing a program at the ALA Annual Conference for the Round Table on Work with the Foreign Born. These programs usually consisted of talks by practicing librarians or others interested in the welfare of immigrants, followed by discussion from the floor.[31]

The help given to librarians was often very direct and personal: in 1924 the coordinator reported that during the year the committee had assisted other librarians (apparently public librarians), through correspondence, in the acquisition of materials in fifteen languages.[32] In her next annual report she mentioned having written 150 letters[33] and, in the next, more than 100.[34] Sometimes, a letter was passed on to a librarian who was familiar with the literature of a particular country.

In the process of disseminating information to the users of libraries, the committee worked for several years after the First World War with an organization which had originated as part of the propaganda effort of the federal government during the war, the Foreign Language Information Service, originally operated by the Committee on Public Information under George Creel. Initially, the main function of the service was to distribute news and other governmental information, prepared in foreign languages, to the immigrant press in the United States. Later it also distributed other useful information; its officers were always glad to disseminate booklists and other materials prepared by librarians. Its work was so much appreciated by its users that, when government support was withdrawn soon after the war, public-spirited citizens came to its aid; the service was still in existence when the Second World War broke out.[35]

The Committee on Work with the Foreign Born was fortunate in its leadership. John Foster Carr, who has already been mentioned, held the office only a few years. During the first part of the 1920s it was chaired by Eleanor E. Ledbetter, who was for many years the librarian of the Broadway Branch of the Cleveland Public Library. For her unselfish service to the Polish people of Cleveland, she was awarded the Haller's Cross by the Polish government; she was one of the librarians who took the trouble to learn the native language of her patrons. From 1927 into the early 1930s, Edna Phillips chaired the committee; she had been the supervisor of work with racial groups of the Massachusetts Division of Public Libraries since 1923 and often wrote and spoke about library service to the foreign born.

52 / *Clienteles*

Many of the bibliographies of foreign-language books which began to appear in 1919 in the ALA *Booklist* must have been mainly useful with English-speaking readers. An examination of the issues from 1919 to 1938 indicates a respectable total of seventy-seven bibliographies; however, French titles were the most frequently represented, appearing on twenty-nine bibliographies through 1938. Unfortunately, the French language is not known to have been familiar to many of the foreign-born users of the libraries in the United States. The bibliographies may have been used by French Canadians, but the attitude of the religious and political authorities in Quebec towards public libraries and much modern literature is likely to have limited the usefulness of the bibliographies there too.[36]

Italian titles were the second most frequently listed, appearing in fifteen bibliographies; Italian was spoken by many immigrants in the United States. German titles appeared on nine bibliographies; German was also spoken by a considerable number; however, no bibliography of German books appeared before 1925. The need was great before that date; one wonders if anti-German sentiment right after the war could have deterred the *Booklist* editors.

Librarians would have obtained almost no help from *Booklist* in providing books in some languages widely spoken by immigrants, and the few foreign language lists that did appear often were published after the greatest need had passed: three Polish lists were issued, the earliest in 1933; two Russian lists appeared, one in 1935 and and one in 1937. One list only was issued for each of the following groups, none of them before 1936: Bulgarian, Czech, Hungarian, Serbian and Croatian, and Yiddish. By 1936 immigration of these persons had been sharply restricted for at least fifteen years.

Service to refugees from Germany and other central European countries drew the attention of librarians in the 1920s, increased in the 1930s and 1940s, but died out after that. The authors of some articles expressed concern about the scarcity of books for adults in simple English, but several librarians reported that these new readers handled English easily, especially in their own vocational fields. The librarians agreed that these well-educated foreigners needed books about the United States which could supplement or correct the impressions they had received from their reading in Europe. The refugees were often amazed at the freedom of access to libraries in the United States, the diversity of viewpoints in the reading matter available to them, and the eagerness of librarians to help.[37]

It is difficult to determine the actual extent of work with ethnic minorities which was being carried on in libraries in the United States and Canada between 1918 and 1936. The committee which prepared the budget in 1920 for work with the foreign born as part of the Enlarged Program estimated that 300 libraries were engaged in the work and that libraries in 500 more towns and cities were "interested" in it, presumably ready to take part if they were encouraged and aided. Very likely, most or all of these were in the United States. But the major survey of library service in the United States produced in the years between 1918 and 1936, the one published by the American Library Association in 1926 and 1927, contained information from only a few librarians. Although approximately 1,200 public libraries responded to the survey, the section dealing with service to the foreign born seems to be based on fewer than 50 replies. However, almost all of the libraries which had been leaders in this work are represented; we can assume that the replies give a fair picture of the situation around the year 1925 in the cities where the best work was being done.

The librarians who filled out the ALA questionnaire late in 1924 or in 1925 were resourceful in determining the need for this service and in attempting to meet it. They maintained contacts with a variety of immigrant organizations, welfare groups, and knowledgeable individuals in the foreign communities; the librarians were as imaginative as ever in the kinds of services they offered.

Twenty-eight of the libraries reported holdings in thirty-three foreign languages. They included: French, 224,000; German, 210,000; Italian, 45,000; Yiddish, 37,000; Spanish, 35,000; and Polish, 28,000. There were almost the same number of Czech and Russian books: 25,000 Czech and 24,000 Russian; in no other language were there more than 18,000 volumes.

Nineteen of the libraries reported circulation for part or all of their language collections. In 1931 a professor at the Graduate Library School of the University of Chicago, William M. Randall, published an article analyzing most of these statistics, comparing holdings and the relative amount of use of foreign- and English-language books in order to determine whether libraries were giving sufficient attention to the selection of books in foreign languages. He found that in these libraries the ratio of foreign-language books to English-language books was far lower than the ratio of foreign-born persons to the native born. He also found that, for English-language books, the greater number of books the higher the annual circulation per book, whereas for foreign books, there was no positive relationship between the number per capita and the circulation per book.

Yet he discovered that, when books in each language were considered separately, the rate of use, as measured by the circulation per volume, varied widely. He then argued that because any one nationality was not likely to vary widely from city to city in their attitudes towards reading, the various libraries must have varied widely in the attractiveness of their offerings. His statistical analysis raised the question whether some of the libraries might not be failing to provide reading matter for their foreign-born users that was as popular and attractive in nature as the fare which they were providing in the English language.[39]

No very precise idea can be drawn from the ALA *Survey* on the importance which public librarians in the United States attached to service to immigrants in contrast to service to other groups. The space allotted within the *Survey* itself may, however, give a rough indication: 100 pages on service to children, 40 pages on service to the foreign born, and 12 pages on service to the blind.

In the United States in the years between 1925 and 1936, there was little new in services to immigrants. In the first place the law of 1924 caused a drastic reduction in the number of new immigrants; there were fewer and fewer persons who needed a kind of service different from that given to the native born. Then, the advent of the Great Depression cut the number of newcomers even more drastically by removing the economic incentive and the wherewithal for coming to the United States.

The articles written by librarians and the discussions at the annual meetings of the Round Table on Work with the Foreign Born indicate this somewhat subdued level of activity. The total number of articles per year is lower than at any time since the beginning of the First World War and few new ideas are advanced about the needs of immigrants or ways of meeting them.

However, new attitudes may have been developing which are not apparent in publications of those days. One thoughtful librarian, Elsa Z. Posell, experienced in serving the foreign born, wrote during the 1940s about the 1920s and 1930s. In the years before the mid-1920s, she suggested, librarians had usually helped in the education of immigrants only up to the point of attainment of citizenship; about 1928 librarians had become more aware of the continuing needs of individuals and particular groups. On the whole, she felt that librarians in the United States had failed to encourage full participation in U.S. life on the part of the immigrants and their children.[40]

If librarians in the United States really did show more concern for the continuing welfare of immigrants during the latter half of the decade of the 1920s, one reason may have been the insights gained from contacts with persons in the adult education movement, which blossomed in the mid-1920s. Public libraries and their predecessors had exhibited varying amounts of interest in the education of adults at least since the early nineteenth-century days when the lyceum movement had spread across the eastern United States. One student of the history of adult education work in libraries has cited services to the foreign born as one of the few successful attempts at library adult education made before the First World War.[41] There is some evidence in the articles by librarians that in the 1920s, as the public schools began to accept the provision of classes in citizenship and English as their responsibility, libraries began to play a less direct role, less often supplying classrooms and teachers. In the 1920s classes for immigrants became very well known; a writer on the adult education movement complained in 1935 that, in the years since 1915, it had been "difficult to convince the American, relatively well-educated in contrast to the European masses, that adult education could be anything that applied to other than those definitely handicapped by alien birth or lack of basic training."[42] The same writer praised the intelligence and cooperativeness shown by librarians since about the mid-1920s, as they had been participating in the general movement.

In Canada in the fifteen to twenty years following the First World War, concern increased over the needs of the English-speaking minority in Quebec and the French-speaking minority in Ontario. Canadian librarians were not so quick to report their struggles and triumphs in the published literature as were their colleagues to the south; the record is far from complete. The most useful statement about conditions in Canadian libraries during these years is the report, *Libraries in Canada: A Study of Library Conditions and Needs*, by the Commission of Enquiry. Members of the commission visited all parts of Canada during 1930; their findings and recommendations were published in 1933.[43]

The commission's main finding was that four-fifths of all Canadians did not have public library service. In discussing the reasons for this situation, linguistic problems were noted but in describing existing services, few instances of work with ethnic minorities were mentioned.

Because the problems varied so much in different parts of the country, the public library section of the report was presented in chapters, one for each province. Beginning with the maritime provinces, the commission noted that in New Brunswick, in certain sections, nothing but French was spoken; this situation would need to be taken into consideration in future library planning. In Quebec the English-speaking minority of approximately 15 percent was being poorly served, but the French majority was not much better off; the commission found that the only public library "that functions in any way comparable to the good city libraries of the rest of Canada" was the one in Westmount, an English-speaking suburb of Montreal. Moving westward into Ontario, the commission praised the bilingual library in Ottawa where a third of the population was French-speaking; a second bilingual library was found in Kitchener, serving a German minority. Moving farther west, the commission noted that in Manitoba and Saskatchewan, only about half of the population was of British or Canadian origin; it did not report on any efforts to give special services to groups from other countries. Other sources of information for these years before the middle thirties corroborate the findings of the commission.

AFTER 1937

In the years since 1937, three main changes have taken place in the service which libraries in the United States and Canada have given to ethnic minorities.

1. In Canada a large increase in immigration after the Second World War caused a marked increase in the need for services to ethnic minorities. The cities, especially in Ontario, received immigrants from several European countries (it was estimated that a third of the population of Toronto in 1961 had come from Europe since 1945).

2. In recent years the increased immigration from Cuba, Mexico, and elsewhere into the United States has caused the need for greatly expanded services to Spanish-speaking persons.

3. In the United States the apparent need for services to non-Spanish-speaking immigrants has declined; many of the refugees from Germany and other parts of central Europe who came just before and after the war seem to have adjusted rather quickly to U.S. life.

The improvement in library service in Canada since the war has been related not only to the increase in the number of immigrants but also to the development of a national consciousness, a determination not to be culturally dependent on the United States, which has brought support for various educational activities of a formal and informal nature. Part of the "multiculturalism" program inaugurated by the Canadian government in 1971 was intended to aid in the production and dissemination of printed and audiovisual materials in a number of languages. Responsibility for implementation, as in the United States, is decentralized to the provinces and their subdivisions.

Library agencies in Canada which were already aware of the needs of minorities have greatly expanded their services in recent years; an example is the Toronto Public Library, long one of the better public libraries on the North American continent.[44]

In the United States since World War II the problems of serving Spanish-speaking persons have been in some ways like those encountered in Canada in serving the French and English minorities; however, they have been, in other ways, like the problems encountered with a variety of minorities in the first half of this century. Librarians in the United States are slowly coming to see that in several parts of the country, Spanish is just as much a permanent second language as French is in Canada, that bilingual collections and staff will continue to be needed.

As in Canada, some older, larger libraries have expanded their services. By 1960 the Spanish-speaking population of New York City had reached 1.6 million; in the 1960s Spanish language materials and services in the New York Public Library had to be reorganized and expanded. That library's best-known effort was the federally funded South Bronx project designed to improve service in eight branches.[45] The Miami Public Library had to increase its Spanish materials and Spanish-speaking staff after refugees from Cuba came in the 1960s.[46]

However, most libraries which tried to help the Spanish-speaking were in the Southwest and in California. One (El Paso) is so close to the border that some of its borrowers actually live in Mexico.[47]

Just as in the past, some librarians have had difficulty in understanding and meeting the needs of minority users; on occasion it has been hard to find staff who speak Spanish fluently and are also competent librarians. One difference from the past is that the users, at least in the Southwest, have had some spokesmen who have not hesitated to tell librarians about their failures.[48]

The problems connected with new services to the Spanish-speaking were like the problems with speakers of other languages fifty years earlier, in that librarians found it hard to obtain attractive materials, particularly for children. The format of Latin American books was often dull and unimaginative; the Spanish in some materials, hastily prepared to take advantage of the market, was poor. Therefore, project LEER was started in 1967 to provide librarians with selected lists of materials and to make sure that copies were available for purchase. The title of the project, the Spanish word *to read,* was a clever acronym based on the words *Libros Elementales, Educativos y Recreativos.*[49]

The growth in service to the Spanish-speaking is easy to document. The decline in the amount of service given to the foreign born other than the Spanish-speaking since the 1930s is not—library chroniclers are not fond of describing declines. It is difficult to be certain about the reasons for the decreased emphasis on this kind of service, but it is easy to speculate about them: First, although the amount of immigration has increased since 1936, it has not approached the level of the early years of the century, and the most noticeable increase has been in immigration from Spanish-speaking countries. Immigration from the Americas apart from Canada made up 10 to 15 percent of the total in the early 1950s, then rose to about 40 percent by the early 1960s; the act of 1965, which became effective in 1968, has preserved that ratio by limiting the annual number from the Western Hemisphere to about 120,000 and the number from elsewhere to about 170,000. For the smaller number of relatively better educated individuals arriving currently from Europe, the machinery set up by libraries to serve the earlier immigrants may be quite adequate. Furthermore, the reduction in the amount of library literature about services to immigrants owes something to changes in the general attitude of the U.S. public toward the foreign born. The immigrant was no longer considered a threat to the "American way of life"; his Americanization was no longer considered necessary for the national health.[50]

The nature of the decline of services to European ethnic groups is worthy of examination. Was it a matter of decreasing need or of flagging enthusiasm on the part of librarians? There are indications that it was some of both.

In 1940 a writer in the *Library Journal* noted that the Providence (R.I.) Public Library had "discontinued its time-honored and seemingly indispensable Foreign Department with no appreciable loss of custom."[51] The authors of several articles implied that service of this

58 / *Clienteles*

nature had decreased, although they urged that it not be abandoned; the title of one article, published in 1945, expresses their sentiment: "There's Still Work to Be Done with the Foreign Born."[52]

One aspect of the earlier forms of service remained: the effort to encourage the foreign born to retain the cultural values of their homelands. Librarians had always organized exhibits of handicrafts and programs of folksongs and dance. But in the 1940s, even these attempts were not always successful. In 1945 the Cleveland Public Library, whose service over the years had been much appreciated by the people of foreign birth, opened an Intercultural Library. It was closed the next year for lack of interest. At about the same time, Cleveland's Norwood Branch tried foreign language programs; there was little response and they were discontinued.[53]

The fate of the ALA Committee on Work with the Foreign Born is perhaps symptomatic. By 1947 members of the committee were convinced that, because of changing conditions, the committee should be reorganized under a new name, Committee on Intercultural Relations."[54] The ALA's Committee on Boards and Committees recommended to Council that the new name be the Committee on Intercultural Action. It was to have four purposes: (1) to further mutual understanding among cultural groups; (2) to emphasize the unity of all mankind, with particular concern for the individual rather than race; (3) to spread understanding of the United Nations and UNESCO; and (4) to disseminate information that would help to curb violence in racial friction.[55] No record of the activity of the new committee has been found among the published reports of other ALA committees.

The low priority given to service for immigrants in the late 1940s is reflected in the volumes published by the Public Library Inquiry. Neither the volume on service to the public, *The Library's Public* (1949), nor the general report, *The Public Library in the United States* (1950), has any reference to work with the foreign born.

Since the beginning of the Second World War, several California librarians have written about service to users of Oriental background;[56] if there has been a general improvement in such services in that state, its dimensions should be explored in print.

CONCLUSION

In Canada and the United States, since 1876, two kinds of ethnic minorities have needed library services. The greatest need, the most obvious, has been that of persons from European countries who were in the process of being assimilated into the general population. These immigrants came to the United States in great numbers before the 1930s; in Canada a notable influx has occurred since the Second World War. The second kind of need has been felt by continuing minorities, the French-speaking in Canada outside Quebec, the English-speaking in Quebec, and the Spanish-speaking in the United States.

Librarians have been slow in meeting the needs of these minorities; until the twentieth century, service even to majorities was badly in need of improvement; service to any kind of a minority, ethnic or otherwise, was rare. But when librarians in the United States did begin to concern themselves about immigrants in the early twentieth century, they tried very hard to understand their foreign-born patrons and to make transition to American ways easier. Some librarians also recognized two other needs: they encouraged the immigrants and their children to remain in contact with their ancestral culture and they encouraged the native born to understand the newcomers and their way of life.

NOTES

1. John Higham, *Strangers in the Land: Patterns of American Nativism, 1860–1925* (New York: Atheneum, 1971), p. 237.
2. Information gathered by the author of this chapter from many sources as a basis for a study, not yet published, on the prevalence of various kinds of libraries in the United States before 1876.
3. U.S. Office of Education, *Report of the Commissioner of Education for the Year 1887–88* (Washington, D.C.: Govt. Print. Off., 1889), p. 165.
4. Henri le Soudier, "Chicago Exposition: Printing and the Book Trade," in U.S. Office of Education, *Report of the Commissioner of Education for the Year 1892–93* (Washington, D.C.: Govt. Print. Off., 1895), p. 596.
5. "Libraries in Canadian Lumber Camps," *Library Journal* 26:141 (Mar. 1901); and Alfred Fitzpatrick, "Camp Libraries in Ontario," *Public Libraries* 9:201–3 (May 1904).
6. Editorial, *Library Journal* 19:328 (Oct. 1894).
7. Aksel G. S. Josephson, "Foreign Books in American Libraries," *Library Journal* 19:364 (Nov. 1894).
8. Gratia Countryman, "Shall Public Libraries Buy Foreign Literature for the Benefit of the Foreign Population?" *Library Journal* 23:229–31 (June 1898).
9. *Handbook of Library Organization*, comp. by the Library Commissions of Minnesota, Iowa, and Wisconsin (Minneapolis: Minnesota Library Commission, 1902), p. 29.
10. "Traveling Libraries of Foreign Books," *Wisconsin Library Bulletin* 1:74–75 (Sept. 1905).
11. Karen M. Jacobson, "What Minnesota Does for Its Foreign Citizens," *Minnesota Public Library Commission Library Notes and News* 1:31–32 (Dec. 1906).
12. James Hulme Canfield, "The Library in Relation to Special Classes of Readers: Books for the Foreign Population," *Library Journal* 31:65 (Conference of Librarians, 1906).
13. J. Maud Campbell, "Supplying Books in Foreign Languages in Public Libraries," *Library Journal* 29:65–67 (Feb. 1904).
14. "Books for Immigrants," *New York Libraries* 1:98 (July 1908).
15. Aksel G. S. Josephson, "Books for the Immigrants, I. Swedish," *Library Journal* 33:505 (Dec. 1908).

16. Henry E. Legler, "President's Address: The World of Print and the World's Work," *Bulletin of the American Library Association* 7:73–82 (July 1913).

17. William F. Yust, "What of the Black and Yellow Races?" *Bulletin of the American Library Association* 7:159–67 (July 1913).

18. Mabel Potter Daggett, "The Library's Part in Making Americans: Free Books Are Helping Our Foreign-Born Citizens to a Bigger and Better Patriotism," *Delineator* 77:17–18 (Jan. 1911).

19. Carl W. Ackerman, "The Book-Worms of New York: How the Public Libraries Satisfy the Immigrant's Thirst for Knowledge," *Independent* 74:199–201 (Jan. 1913).

20. Sarah Comstock, "Eight Million Books a Year," *World's Work* 26:100–108 (May 1913).

21. John Foster Carr, "What the Library Can Do for Our Foreign-Born," *Library Journal* 38:566–68 (Oct. 1913).

22. For example, "The Library's Part in Making Americans," *New York Libraries* 4:235–36 (Aug. 1915) and "What One Library Is Doing in the Making of Americans," ibid. 5:110 (May 1916).

23. "Committee on Work with the Foreign Born," *Bulletin of the American Library Association* 11:336 (July 1917).

24. "American Library Association," *Library Journal* 43:120 (Feb. 1918).

25. Many librarians reported various techniques for reaching immigrants through immigration officers. An example is described in "Americanization Work in Seattle Public Library," *Public Libraries* 25:448–49 (Oct. 1920).

26. Della R. Prescott, "What Americanization Is Not," *Library Journal* 45:218 (Mar. 1, 1920).

27. George M. Stephenson, *A History of American Immigration, 1820–1924* (New York: Ginn, 1926), pp. 174–76.

28. Robert Ellis Lee, *Continuing Education for Adults through the American Public Library, 1833–1964* (Chicago: American Library Assn., 1966), pp. 43–44.

29. "Work with the Foreign Born and Preparation for Citizenship," *Bulletin of the American Library Association* 14:299–300 (June 1920).

30. Lee, p. 46.

31. Such a meeting is described in "Work with the Foreign Born," *Bulletin of the American Library Association* 20:562–63 (Oct. 1926).

32. "Work with the Foreign Born," *Bulletin of the American Library Association* 18:249 (Aug. 1924).

33. "Work with the Foreign Born," *Bulletin of the American Library Association* 19:220 (July 1925).

34. "Work with the Foreign Born," *Bulletin of the American Library Association* 20:399 (Oct. 1926).

35. John Palmer Gavit, "Through Neighbors' Doorways," *Survey Graphic* 29:471–72 (Sept. 1940).

36. Commission of Enquiry, *Libraries in Canada: A Study of Library Conditions and Needs* (Toronto: Ryerson Pr. and Chicago: American Library Assn., 1933) pp. 38–39. Also, Jean-Charles Bonenfant, "Progrès des Bibliothèques au Canada Français," in *Librarianship in Canada, 1946 to 1967, Essays in Honour of Elizabeth Homer Morton*, ed. by Bruce Peel (Victoria, British Columbia: Canadian Library Assn., 1968), pp. 95, 100.

37. This situation is reported in several articles such as Ilse Bry, "Reading for Refugees," *Library Journal* 65:903–6 (Nov. 1, 1940). See also the statements made by Josephine Butkowska Bernhard, in charge of Polish work in the Tompkins Square Branch of the New York Public Library in an article, "Suitable Books for Foreign-Born Readers," *Booklist* 31:149–52 (Jan. 1935), and the discussions at the round table meeting held by the Committee on Work with the Foreign Born during the ALA Conference of 1938: "Work with the Foreign-Born Round Table," *Bulletin of the American Library Association* 32:984–85 (Oct. 15, 1938).

38. American Library Association, *A Survey of Libraries in the United States*, 4 vols. (Chicago: The Association, 1926–27). The section on public library work with the foreign born is in vol. 3, pp. 218–59.
39. William M. Randall, "What Can the Foreigner Find to Read in the Public Library?" *Library Quarterly* 1:79–88 (Jan. 1931).
40. Elsa Z. Posell, "The Librarian Works with the Foreign Born," *ALA Bulletin* 35:424–26 (July 1941).
41. Lee, p. 43.
42. Morse Adams Cartwright, *Ten Years of Adult Education* (New York: Macmillan, 1935), p. 136.
43. Commission of Enquiry, *Libraries in Canada*.
44. H. C. Campbell, "Multi-lingual Library," *Wilson Library Bulletin* 38:68–69, 79 (Sept. 1963); Leonard Wertheimer, "Language Studies in Public Libraries," ibid. 62:985–92 (Sept. 1968).
45. Joseph A. Rosenthal, *Special Services for the Spanish-speaking Public Served by the Branch Libraries of the New York Public Library*, Twelfth Seminar on the Acquisition of Latin American Library Materials, SALALM, University of California, Los Angeles, June 22–24, 1967, Working Paper no. 11 (Washington, D.C.: Pan American Union, 1967).
46. Helga H. Eason, "More than Money," *Wilson Library Bulletin* 36:825–28 (June 1962).
47. See Robert P. Haro, "Libraries on the Border," *California Librarian* 34:10 (Jan. 1973).
48. For example, Robert P. Haro in "How Mexican-Americans View Libraries: A One-Man Survey," *Wilson Library Bulletin* 44:736–42 (Mar. 1970) and Nelly Fernandez in "Outreach Program for Chicanos," *California Librarian* 34:14–17 (Jan. 1973).
49. Marietta Daniels Shepard, "Reading Resources and Project LEER," *Wilson Library Bulletin* 44:748–50 (Mar. 1970).
50. Oscar Handlin, *Race and Nationality in American Life* (Boston: Little, Brown, 1957), pp. 177–87.
51. Karl Brown, "What Sells the Library," *Library Journal* 65:748–49 (Sept. 15, 1940).
52. Mary B. McClellan, "There's Still Work to Be Done with the Foreign Born," *Library Journal* 70:676–77 (Aug. 1945).
53. Virginia S. Phillips, "Fifty-six Years of Service to the Foreign-Born by the Cleveland Public Library" (Master's thesis, Western Reserve Univ., 1957), p. 31.
54. "Work with the Foreign Born," *ALA Bulletin* 41:401-2 (Oct. 15, 1947).
55. "Committee on Work with the Foreign Born," *ALA Bulletin* 42:69 (Sept. 15, 1948).
56. For example, Mabel R. Gillis, "Library Service to Japanese Assembly and Relocation Centers," *California Library Association Bulletin* 4:16–17 (Sept. 1942) and Keum Chu Halpin, "The Hinomoto Library of Los Angeles," *California Librarian* 33:216–19 (Oct. 1972).

4

Service to Afro-Americans

A. P. MARSHALL
Eastern Michigan University

1865–1876: PRELUDE

Eleven years elapsed between the end of the Civil War and the founding of the American Library Association in 1876, years in which some rapid changes took place for Afro-Americans. On the one hand there were large numbers of former bondsmen who faced adjustments to freedom and self-dependency. On the other there were large numbers of persons who had secured their freedom even before the war and who could now exercise liberties previously denied them. Society itself was divided; some of the population, out of their own frustrations, threatened, intimidated, and even murdered Afro-Americans. The labor movement was divided; some unions were willing to either absorb Afro-American laborers or form separate unions to accommodate them; others stood strongly against them as a threat to their own existence.

Persons of Afro-American descent were already making history with their achievements. Alexander Graham Bell recognized the talents of Lewis Howard Latimer, who translated ideas into blueprints and prepared patent applications preliminary to the introducing of the telephone. Hiram S. Maxim secured many patents in the field of electrical energy, a great boon for Thomas A. Edison. In 1872 Charlotte E. Ray became the first woman to receive a law degree, setting new sights for all women. Justin Holland's publication, *Comprehensive Method for Guitar*, provided the standard work in that instrument for years to come. In 1876 Edward Bouchett, a student at Yale, became the first

American of African descent to receive the doctor of philosophy degree; at that time there were 314 Afro-Americans who held degrees from regional colleges.

With 571,506 Afro-American children enrolled in public schools in 1876, the die was cast for a greater role for this formerly outcast group in the development of America's economy, culture, and social life. A kind of second Chautauqua movement had been developed, bringing Frederick Douglass and other Afro-American speakers and artists to cities and towns throughout the North and the South. Several colleges and universities were already in operation, including Fisk University in Tennessee, Howard University in Washington, D.C., Lincoln University in Pennsylvania, Virginia Union, Lincoln University in Missouri, Talladega College in Alabama, and Hampton Institute in Virginia. For years to come the graduates of these schools played key roles in reducing illiteracy rates, building racial pride, and even establishing libraries. From meager beginnings, Afro-Americans would become well-qualified to achieve self-fulfilling positions in society. It was against this background that the American Library Association was formed on October 6, 1876.

1876–1900: THE ADOLESCENT PERIOD OF AMERICA'S GROWTH

The last quarter of the nineteenth century was a period of "growing up" for the United States. During that twenty-five-year period the nation developed insights and traditions which determined its destiny for the next century. Many mistakes were made, some growing out of earlier miscalculations of the U.S. spirit; others were caused by the rather rapid industrialization process which ignored some of the rural and old-world traditions.

Afro-Americans, Mexican Americans, native Americans, and some immigrants from Europe were already realizing that the promises of the American Dream as enunciated in the Declaration of Independence and the Constitution were considered by many idle words to be ignored. Those of African and Asiatic backgrounds knew that their distinguishing characteristics would relegate them to a second-class citizenship for some time to come. Others placed their hopes in their children, who merely had to absorb the ways of the United States in order to be accepted. But for the moment all had to bide their time while tying their hopes to one great panacea, education.

As the idea of education moved with the expanding frontier, the need for libraries gradually entered the consciousness of educational and political leaders. The first foothold for libraries was in the schools, where teachers recognized the value of additional books to supplement texts. A report by the U.S. commissioner of education in 1876 showed a majority of the thirty-eight states with state libraries, and many of the larger cities reported some type of circulating library for their citizens.[1] Three universities reported 100,000 volumes or more in their collections.[2] The segregated patterns of the South decreed that most minorities, particularly those with marked physical characteristics such as Afro-Americans, native Americans, and Orientals, could be legally denied the use of public libraries although their taxes helped to support them.

In 1865 only one in twenty Afro-Americans was literate. By 1880 the percentage had increased to 30 percent. Throughout the South, particularly in the larger cities, there was a need for opportunities of continuing education. There was a growing professional class; often they organized themselves into literary and civic clubs and, recognizing the need for reading materials for the young literates of their communities, opened reading rooms where books could be borrowed or read on the premises. Settlement houses, reform schools, orphanages, and other philanthropic agencies often boasted small collections of books and magazines available to their charges. Sometimes they organized classes to help the nonliterates learn the art of reading and writing. The Excelsior Club of Guthrie, Oklahoma, supported a small reading room for a number of years before the city government saw fit to provide some funds for its support.[3] The Sojourner Truth Club was established to support a library in Montgomery, Alabama.[4] A small library was in existence in Dallas before the turn of the century, supported by Afro-American club women.[5]

The librarian of the Charleston (S.C.) Society, Arthur Mazyck, reflected a growing concern by many people of the South when he wrote in 1876:

> We must say with regret that notwithstanding the occasional instances of favorable progress . . . a view of the condition of public libraries in the Southern States presents after all but a barren prospect. In proportion to the population their number is exceedingly small, they are poorly supported, are conducted on no general or fixed system, and are confined usually to the large cities, while the smaller communities in these States are, for the most part, absolutely destitute of this most necessary means of education and refinement.[6]

The U.S. commissioner of education emphasized reasons for Mazyck's concern when he reported state library collections as follows: Alabama, 14,000 volumes; Georgia, 20,000; Mississippi, 16,000; North Carolina, 40,000; Tennessee, 20,000; Virginia, 35,000. The only southern states to report public libraries were: Kentucky (Louisville, 50,000 volumes); South Carolina (Charleston, 15,000); Texas (Galveston, 10,000).[7] It was not until after the turn of the century that these states and cities made serious efforts to serve the minority populations of their environs.

The philosophy regarding libraries which prevailed at the end of the last century was to make books available to those who could use them to the best advantage. Afro-Americans, particularly in the South, were too often considered incapable of using books. As a result they were left to their own devices, resulting in subscription and private library collections which were made available to members, and on occasion, to others in the community. It was during the next century that the whole philosophy began to change as more books became available and increasing literacy made the library an important entity in society, especially for the minorities who were demonstrating their own desires for social and intellectual development.

1900–1925: "WALK TOGETHER CHILDREN"

The idea of libraries supported from public funds spread rapidly during the first quarter of the twentieth century. Encouraged by gifts from Andrew Carnegie, many cities boasted magnificent public library structures, although the book collections and services were not always adequate. In areas where the number of Afro-Americans was small, particularly in Ohio, Nebraska, Iowa, and northern states, the idea that public meant everybody was accepted. In other states, however, like North Carolina, Mississippi, Alabama, Florida, and Georgia, basic grants from Carnegie did not always take into consideration the separate nature of societies in those areas. W. E. B. DuBois wrote in 1909: "Most of the public libraries of the South exclude Negroes, even though they pay taxes."[8] He reported that although public taxation supported the Carnegie Public Library of Atlanta, Georgia, Afro-Americans were excluded.[9]

Depending upon local circumstances, Afro-Americans challenged exclusionary tactics in three ways. In some cities like Montgomery, Alabama, the Sojourner Truth Club organized a subscription library which was open to members six hours daily. It contained about 500 volumes which were circulated.[10] In Jacksonville, Florida, the Public Library Board acquiesced to pressure and supported a "colored department," which circulated 7,182 books in 1907 and 1908 to 234 registered borrowers.[11] A Colored Branch of the Louisville Public Library opened on September 23, 1905 in temporary quarters. Property was acquired, on which a Carnegie Branch to serve Afro-Americans was opened on October 29, 1908.[12] This branch proved so popular that a second branch was opened in May 1909. In other cities little or nothing was done, though several instances of continuous pressure upon civic leaders prevented the issue from dying.

In Charlotte, North Carolina, an act of the legislature in 1903 established the Charlotte Public Library for Colored People.[13] The same act stipulated that $2,500 be turned over to the library trustees annually for the operation of both libraries. For several years the average received by the Charlotte Public Library for Colored People was $400. Donations supplied the bulk of operating expenses and acquisitions.

66 / Clienteles

A reorganization came in 1917 and support improved, but branch status did not come until 1929.[14]

Louis R. Wilson wrote in 1922 that there were sixty-four public and seven private libraries in towns and cities of 2,000 to 48,000 population in North Carolina serving whites, but only three serving Afro-Americans. For the "750,000 or more Negroes" in the state (approximately one-third of the total population), five public libraries provided only 15,000 books. About 30,000 volumes were provided by twenty-four colleges and training schools.[15]

In Muskogee, Oklahoma, a Colored Public Library was organized in 1913 by Lois R. Perdue, an Afro-American teacher and civic leader. To help support the venture she organized the Frances Harper Club. A group of Afro-American businessmen eventually formed a board to assist the women in their efforts. Later, the Federation of Women's Clubs decided to assist with the project. In addition to support from membership dues, funds were raised through public dinners, from church and individual contributions, and various other projects. The Muskogee Public Library Board was induced to pay the salary of a librarian in 1916, but full responsibility was not assumed until 1929, when it became a branch library.[16]

In Guthrie, Oklahoma, where the Excelsior Club had long supported a subscription library, the city contributed $2,000 toward the $3,000 needed to purchase a building, and in 1906, this library operated as a partly public-supported service to Afro-Americans.[17] In Oklahoma City a Dunbar Branch was established in 1921, as a result of the efforts of Mabel H. Peacock, librarian of the Carnegie Public Library.[18] Okmulgee erected an $18,000 building in 1923, supported completely by tax funds. Tulsa opened a branch of the public library in 1924. Boley, an all Afro-American town, supported a subscription library as early as 1910, organized by the Industrial Club.[19]

Carnegie provided funds for the establishment of libraries to serve Afro-Americans when genuine public interest could be demonstrated. Mound Bayou and Meridian, Mississippi, were approved for grants in 1910 and 1913, respectively, but evidently Mound Bayou, an all Afro-American town, was unable to raise matching funds and the library was never built. Meridian built a $38,000 building as a branch of the public library and this building was still being used in 1972.[20]

The concept of a publicly supported traveling library emerged early in the century when the Kentucky Library Commission circulated two collections of fifty volumes each among minority groups. In 1910 James S. Gregory of Marblehead, Massachusetts asked G. S. Dickerman of Hampton Institute to supply the names of schools in the South so that he could give their graduates "certain character forming books." Dickerman suggested a plan for traveling libraries, and collections of forty-eight titles were eventually made available through the Atlanta University Library. They circulated to any individual or institution who would accept responsibility for them.

Although most colleges established reading rooms or "libraries" early in their development, a 1917 study showed that "out of 653 private and public schools established especially for the training of Afro-American youth, only 27 were known to have a collection of books that on the most liberal interpretation could be called a library." Only 11 of the 27 were known to have a fair collection of books, arranged and managed to contribute to the education of the pupils.[21] A few of the colleges, however, had recognized the value of libraries and not only had spent fairly substantial sums for books and materials, but had also employed able personnel to manage the collections. Howard University lured Edward C. Williams from a District of Columbia public high school in 1916 to become the first Afro-American professional to head its library. Williams had also served as the first Afro-American director of the library at Western Reserve University, and had studied at the Albany (N.Y.) Library School from 1899 to 1900.[22]

School libraries were becoming less rare during this period, and such states as North Carolina, Tennessee, Georgia, and South Carolina were making modest efforts to provide books to supplement classroom instruction. In North Carolina they had been promoted as early as 1900. Through combined efforts of many persons who were dedicated to education, the literacy rate for Afro-Americans was 55.5 percent by 1900.[23] More than 2,000 Afro-Americans now held college degrees, and there were 21,267 Afro-American teachers to instruct 1.5 million school children. The census of that year reported the following number of Afro-Americans in professions: 1,734 doctors, 212 dentists, 310 journalists, 728 lawyers, 236 artists, sculptors, and art teachers, 3,915 musicians and music teachers, 247 photographers, and 52 architects, designers, draftsmen, and inventors.[24]

On June 28, 1922 a group of librarians met at the Detroit Public Library to explore problems related to providing library service to Afro-Americans. This Round Table on Work with Negroes was informed about the training programs already in operation in the Louisville Public Library through which eleven "colored assistants from other southern cities" had been trained to work in libraries. At this meeting it was announced that there were plans to establish a library school in connection with the Louisville Public Library's Colored Department. A study on library service to Afro-Americans was conducted by the group and tabulated by Marion P. Watson of the 135th Street Branch of the New York Public Library; out of 122 libraries polled, 98 responded. "It is evident," the report concluded, "that the demand for properly trained colored librarians is increasing, and that this demand will have to be met with well-qualified professional workers."[25]

The persons who attended that meeting were harbingers of changes to come. Within a few years there would be "color" gracing the classes of the most prestigious library schools of the country. Hampton Institute would establish a library school, supported by the Rosenwald Fund, for the special purpose of training Afro-American librarians.

68 / *Clienteles*

Thus it might be said that the first quarter of the twentieth century was a period in which Afro-Americans were being prepared for transformation into an entity with which the United States would have to deal on a respectable level. The transformational concept from *Negro* to *black* or *Afro-American* was beginning to evolve, concurrent with the important period later known as the Harlem Renaissance. It was not only the musical and artistic talents that were being awakened in this sleeping giant but there was also the feeling of individual worth bursting from this "cocoon" of a dying system. Only the future would reveal the extent of this change.

1925–1950: THE SLEEPING GIANT AWAKENS

The second quarter of the twentieth century reflected a continuous awakening of minorities in general and Afro-Americans in particular to the necessity of demanding rights of citizenship. Advances in the availability of education resulted in 83.7 percent literacy among Afro-Americans by 1930.[26] The role of libraries in the total educational program of the country was now being realized and efforts were underway to expand them to the reach of all citizens. There were still areas where such efforts needed to be accelerated, and another twenty-five years passed before such services would be viewed as a right of citizens rather than a privilege.

In response to a questionnaire circulated by Louis Shores in 1930, several cities with sizable Afro-American populations indicated that they provided no library services to this minority group. Among them were: Alexandria, Louisiana (5,834); Columbus, Georgia (9,093); Dallas, Texas (24,023); Jackson, Mississippi (9,936); Miami, Florida (9,270); Mobile, Alabama (23,906); Monroe, Louisiana (6,540); Raleigh, North Carolina (8,544); Shreveport, Louisiana (17,485); Witchita Falls, Texas (2,717).[27]

The survey showed that many libraries made their services available to all citizens in all branches, although some were located where they were more accessible to certain minorities. Baltimore, Maryland, for example, reported that several branches were located in predominantly Negro communities; but because of the library's efforts to carry out the "spirit and intention of Enoch Pratt, who established the library in 1882, specifying that no distinction should ever be made in service to the public," no branch was designated Negro.[28] Several other cities reported that their policies required serving all citizens equally, among which were: Bartlesville, Oklahoma; Chicago, Illinois; Pittsburgh, Pennsylvania; Cincinnati, Ohio; Detroit, Michigan; Boston, Massachusetts; Brooklyn, New York; Cleveland, Ohio; El Paso, Texas; Milwaukee, Wisconsin; Minneapolis, Minnesota; Newark, New Jersey; San Francisco, California; and Seattle, Washington.[29]

The availability of Julius Rosenwald Fund money for improving library services in the southern states stimulated many improvements. The Southeastern Library Association resolved "that library service to Negroes should be a part of every library program." The association also indicated that "there is every reason to believe that the demand for trained workers in the next few years will exceed the supply furnished by present training facilities."[30]

A report of a survey of Florida libraries in 1935 showed that there were "431,828 Negroes living in the state," and that 65,167 of them were illiterate, most of the latter living in rural areas. Branch libraries for Afro-Americans were reportedly located in Jacksonville, Orlando, Eustis, Lakeland, Ormond, Palatka, St. Petersburg, and Tampa.[31]

The state of North Carolina was among the "leaders" in library development for Afro-Americans during this period. In the fall of 1926 the city of Asheville employed Irene O. Hendrick as librarian of the Colored Branch. Her specific assignment was to organize a library to serve those who had made several organized requests for such services. It was not until 1951, however, that this library became a part of the city system and was named the Market-Eagle Branch.[32]

Bookmobile service was provided Afro-American citizens after 1939, with Durham and Wake counties providing joint service to both races. Five additional counties provided service on a part-time basis, although white librarians did the serving.[33]

Despite recognition of the need to provide services to Afro-Americans in other parts of the state, the city of Raleigh provided library services to whites only as late as 1935. Limited use of the state library was permitted, but reluctantly. Responding to demands, library officials lured Mollie H. Lee from her position as librarian of Shaw University to establish a library for Afro-Americans. Lee had received a degree in library science from Columbia University in 1934.[34]

A survey of library services was conducted by Eliza Atkins Gleason in 1939–40, as a part of her requirements for the doctor of philosophy degree from the University of Chicago. Entitled *The Southern Negro and the Public Library*, it was published in 1941.[35] This study showed the extent of discrimination and segregation practiced in the thirteen southern states. One of Gleason's conclusions was that "Approximately one-fifth of the Negro population of the thirteen southern states . . . are provided with public library service. Of the 8,805,635 Negroes in the South in 1930, only 1,883,125 receive library service, which is provided by 99 of the 744 public libraries in the South."[36]

Gleason's study revealed that, in various state libraries, there were differences in provisions for use, based on race. In North Carolina, for example, the state librarian was "directed to fit up and maintain a separate place for the use of the colored people who may come to the library for the purpose of reading books and periodicals."[37] Texas state library laws provided that "Any white person of such county may use the county free library under rules and regulations prescribed by the Commissioners' Court and may be entitled to all privileges thereof. Said Court shall make proper provision for the Negroes of said county to be served through a separate branch or branches of the county free library, which should be administered by a custodian of the Negro race under the supervision of the county librarian."[38]

Several states provided package and traveling library services from the state libraries; Arkansas provided service for whites only. Again, availability of service was frequently dependent upon race. Florida reported that because "one good-sized collection" had been kept overtime and mistreated, the practice of serving minorities had been discontinued. Georgia provided traveling and package libraries to whites only, on account of inadequate staff and collection. Kentucky provided no such service from the state library for minorities, while Mississippi reported service in a few cases only. Traveling libraries were available to blacks from the state library in North Carolina, and Oklahoma imposed no restrictions on the use of its traveling library collections. The extension library of Texas was operated for the "white residents of Texas." Virginia made all of its state library services available to any citizen. Tennessee had no such service from the state agency, but did provide traveling library service through the state department of education, available to all schools.[39]

In 1937 Delta Sigma Theta, a public service sorority, developed a program that had a catalytic effect on both Afro-American citizens and public libraries in several southern communities.[40]

At the sorority's convention in Cleveland, Ohio in 1937 attention was called to the inadequacy of books in southern schools. Under the direction of Anne E. Duncan of Washington, D.C., the national organization solicited funds from local chapters, and two librarians, Mollie Huston Lee of Raleigh, North Carolina and Virginia Lacy Jones of Atlanta University, helped formulate a plan. The project was initiated in Franklin County, North Carolina in 1945, after being delayed by World War II. Book baskets with appropriate selections were placed in 17 one-teacher schools, 11 two-teacher schools, 7 three-teacher schools, and 3 five-or-more-teacher schools.

After four years of operation the people of Louisburg in Franklin County financed the construction of a library center. The dedication on April 11, 1949 proved the value of demonstration projects in a rural community.

The Delta Sigma Theta project moved its efforts to western Georgia. Although initial library programs were begun earlier under the auspices of Georgia State Department of Education, "there was a clear need for improvement in terms of wider service and more and better equipment." A bookmobile, purchased by the sorority, was moved to Carrollton, Georgia.[41] The sorority equipped the vehicle with books, a movie projector, and a record player. The librarians' arrival in a rural community signaled a response to those accorded the traveling vendors of an earlier period in American history. Leroy Childs, a professional, would give a brief lecture on such subjects as "Superstition and Science," and even people who could not read were provided with sewing patterns and other samples of new knowledge from the outside world. The bookmobile was described by a sorority representative as being "a symbol of something vital in their lives."

A similar project at Saint Helena Island, South Carolina resulted in the creation of nine library outposts in the community. By this time rapid progress was being made in extending library services throughout the country: the Delta Sigma Theta library program was terminated in favor of more demanding social welfare programs.

Nonetheless, when, in August 1939, five young Afro-American men sought service in the Alexandria (Va.) Public Library, they were ordered to leave by the librarian and by policemen who had been hastily summoned to enforce the order. Failing to leave, they were charged with disorderly conduct.[42] The court found that the young men in question had failed to follow stated procedures of filling out a request for a library card, including the listing of persons to properly vouch for them.

In summary this period saw the beginning of accelerated demands for an equal share in the American dream. The National Association for the Advancement of Colored People (NAACP) intensified its activities in the courts for equal access to higher education, resulting in a concomitant attention to library services. The events of the period of World War II heightened these concerns, resulting in the opening of several previously closed avenues of education. This growing militancy by Afro-American minorities brought into focus the need for library services to all citizens. By 1950 there were signs of change on the horizon which would result in unprecedented progress during the next twenty-five years.

1950–1975: THE RESPONSIVE PERIOD

On January 1, 1950 Gretchen Knief Schenk reflected on library progress of the last 50 years, then pointed out:

> There are still 35 million lacking library service in this country, and many more millions who have only a token service. In thousands of schools, teachers and children still lack the tools which others take for granted; in scores of colleges and universities professors and students are handicapped at every turn for want of bibliographical background and research materials.[43]

A large proportion of those citizens still denied library services were living in the South, but the North was beginning to awaken to the

72 / Clienteles

fact that library services to the poor, the disadvantaged, and minorities were even then nothing to brag about. Lillie K. Daly made a cursory survey which showed that some progress was being made in the South although there was still a long way to go. "Five Southern States," she pointed out, "have established positions for Negro library supervisors attached to the offices of the state library agency."[44]

The pattern at this point in history was to provide library service to Afro-Americans in keeping with local customs. Southern libraries willing to serve all citizens of the community were usually accorded special recognition by those who sought to promote equality; such instances were still rare. The Louisville Public Library, under the directorship of Clarence R. Graham, was one of the pioneers in the integration of its staff as well as its services. In Charlotte, North Carolina Hoyt Galvin was moving gradually toward open access even in the late forties. Cities with library directors and/or boards who were attuned to the changing times and were welcoming all patrons became more numerous after World War II. Most southern librarians, however, were willing to resist any changes in practices, falling back upon local or state statutes and/or customs.

Dorothy McAllister surveyed the libraries of Mississippi and published a summary of her findings in early 1955.[45] She found some improvements over past years. The range of support for library service to Afro-Americans was from a low of $6,517 at Pascagoula to $76,612 at Jackson. Most were spending upwards of $20,000 a year on services to the minority group. "On the dark side is the fact that of the 50 communities which provide library service only 12 provide this service for Negro citizens." In 1939 there were only two cities in the state, Meridian and Clarksdale, "with public library service for Negroes." The decision in *Brown* vs. *Board of Education of Topeka, Kansas* (1954), which struck down the *Plessy* vs. *Ferguson* "separate but equal" doctrine of 1896, signaled changes in library services as well. Most border states began a reexamination of the legal bases for segregation and libraries in several of these areas opened their doors to all citizens. There were many libraries, however, particularly in the deep South, which chose to await court challenges before acquiescing to new constitutional interpretations.

It was only natural that problems affecting school desegregation should infiltrate library meetings. Application of the Library Bill of Rights to all libraries was a focal point from which minorities launched their fight in the American Library Association, not only for desegregation of services, but also for the integration of staffs. As the challenge to the discriminatory mores and customs of the South grew in intensity, there were increased charges that other types of discrimination were prevalent in the North. These concerns finally led to the formulation of a plan to determine the extent of progress toward desegregation throughout the country. In 1960 a survey was approved by the American Library Association to document this lack of access by citizens to library services.

International Research Associates (IRA) was engaged to "examine the scope and extent of limited access to public libraries throughout the United States with particular reference to the problem of racial segregation in Southern libraries." The major focus of the study was "upon the restrictions based on race. This means, primarily, the restrictions leveled against the Negro in the South."[46]

For the purposes of the study, discrimination was described as direct and indirect. Direct discrimination was used to describe those libraries that deprived members of one racial group of "enjoying the resources of a particular library, or, alternatively, when utilization of these resources is permitted only within certain limitations that are applied with particular force to one group." Indirect discrimination was described as in effect "when its branches are so located and the resources of these branches are so differentiated in terms of quantity and quality, that one group is more limited in its access to the library resources of the community than another."[47]

The focus of this report was significant in that, previously, little attention had been given to the indirect discrimination resulting from the location of branches. It was also significant that this study was conducted in the epoch of the reversal of the *Plessy* vs. *Ferguson* decision of 1896. The repudiation of the "separate but equal" doctrine was followed by similar decisions regarding municipally operated golf courses, city parks and recreational facilities, and, eventually, libraries. Subsequent cases continued to make it clear that racial discrimination in any governmental facilities clearly violated the equal protection clause of the Fourteenth Amendment to the Constitution of the United States.

One of the first tests of the new interpretation of the Constitution came in *Gilves* vs. *Library Advisory Committee of Danville, Virginia*. The city of Danville operated two public libraries, one for whites and another for Afro-Americans. When members of the deprived group sought use of the library designated for whites, the facility was ordered closed by the city manager. The city council subsequently ordered the library reopened, but only to those who presently held library cards, offering the reason that it was "overtaxed by the demands of its patrons." The federal district court, responding to a suit by deprived citizens, issued a preliminary injunction which ordered the city to allow citizens holding library cards in either unit to use the services of both units.[48]

In most public library facilities voluntary desegregation followed the demands of citizen groups. There were a few instances of "sit-ins," where a large number of Afro-Americans, often accompanied by sympathetic whites, would occupy the facility until their demands for desegregation were met. A suit was filed in Memphis, Tennessee by an Afro-American resident to force the discontinuation of racial desegregation in the city and county public libraries. Before the court had an opportunity to move, the municipal government announced that "all public library units and facilities," both in the city and county, would be available to all qualified persons regardless of race or color.[49]

The increased demands for libraries supported by public funds to open their facilities and services caused various responses from public officials:

1. Certain libraries desegregated voluntarily. For example, the Greensboro (N.C.) Public Library responded to persistent demands and requests of the Afro-American citizenry and prevented open conflict. The government and the prospective litigants were also spared the expenses of a court case.

2. Some libraries refused to capitulate, insisting upon orders from a federal court. Reasoning for such actions rested on such arguments as buying time for the people to get used to the idea, or protecting officials from prosecution for having failed to support local and/or state ordinances or laws.

3. Pressure from Afro-Americans, in some cases, found staunch resistance from officials until suits were filed. Several cities followed the example of Memphis, Tennessee, in 1960 and Savannah, Georgia, in 1962 and instead of waiting for cases to be heard, at considerable cost to the taxpayers, moved to open all library facilities without regard to race or color.

4. Surprisingly, a few libraries actually took the route of closing library facilities for some period of time. One library in southern Missouri closed for a few days, reopening after having removed all the chairs from the reading areas. This type of action was similar to that characterized by Harry Golden as "stand-up integration."

One of the findings of the access study evoked intense objections from some large public libraries. They were charged with practicing indirect discrimination. Philadelphia, Detroit, and New York, along with six large southern library systems, were accused of indirect discrimination by locating branches in areas not likely to be utilized by minorities. "In Philadelphia, a heavily white neighborhood is six times as likely to possess a branch as a predominantly non-white section. In Detroit, twice as many branches are located in heavily white neighborhoods and these branches contain more than one and one-half times as many books as those in predominantly non-white areas."[50]

The IRA study emerged as a unique contribution to the desegregation of public libraries in the United States.[51] It also laid the foundation for the development of library services for the underserved throughout the country, both in segregated and unsegregated areas. Once attention was called to the practice, other cities began examining their library services to the poor, the aged, the minorities, the handicapped, and the foreign born. Information centers began to spread, and the measurement of services no longer was based solely upon the number of books circulated but upon the impact in the lives of people.

On June 2, 1965 several Afro-Americans "opened a proposed three-month civil rights campaign in Bessemer, Alabama by desegregating the city's white public library." The population of Bessemer was 30,000, with about 19,000 being Afro-Americans. The leader of the group, though not a city resident, was duly registered, and after paying a $2 nonresident fee, was allowed to withdraw a book.[52]

Many challenges against discriminatory practices in the South emerged out of the civil rights movement. In 1965 Frederick W. Heinze called attention to library conditions in Mississippi and related the impact of freedom libraries on a "closed society."[53] Through a project by the Council of Federated Organizations (COFO) long closed "windows" to the outside world were opened.

> Every COFO project has a library operating as a most important part of the project, serving as a public library for adults, a school library for students. It is often the only facility available to Negroes in the area, and is usually superior to the Negro, and even white, school libraries.[54]

Heinze referred to Mississippi as a police state in which by plan new ideas were systematically prevented from crossing its borders. He points out that book stores were absent in most instances, that reading matter such as the *New York Times*, the *New Republic*, and the *Nation* were unavailable at newstands, and that when certain magazines carried articles which officials considered to be inciting, they were banned. Heinze also alleged considerable harassment from officials as "windows" were being opened to Afro-Americans who were anxious to learn anything, even foreign languages.

The resultant outreach focus of libraries was labeled with varied names. Many libraries responded to the dictates of the rapidly accelerating militancy of Afro-American organizations and individuals. Ralph W. Conant suggested in 1968:

> The white institutions of the central city (prominent among which are public libraries) that aspire to serve central city clientele must adopt organizational behavior patterns similar to any organization that wants to attract new clientele.[55]

Various kinds of outreach programs were developed and attracted sufficient notice from editors to deserve recognition. Charles W. Crosby reported in 1969 on a community relations program in Providence, Rhode Island, in which book deposits in out of the way places, such as churches, stores, clubs, coffee houses, and service organizations were establishing contacts with people previously ignored.[56] Alex Ladenson reported on Chicago's concentration over a two-year period on "programs designed to reach the residents of underprivileged areas of the city, with particular stress on the black communities."[57] Other cities established similar programs tailored to the peculiar needs of their communities, notable examples being Detroit, St. Louis, Washington, D.C., Cleveland, and San Francisco. Where branches were not considered feasible, bookmobile stops were established to call attention to local library services.

POSTLUDE: THE DREAM NO LONGER DEFERRED

At age one hundred, the American Library Association is a strong advocate of free access to all public libraries. The organization has used its strength and influence to help in the attainment of library services for all members of the U.S. public. That this strength was not exercised until ALA was well over age 50 may be considered a discredit, but a credit when it is recognized that the challenge was met when the time seemed ripe.

Even at this writing there must be some small library in some hamlet of the United States which bans Afro-Americans from using its collections and services. This is possible because while moving to this stage in our total development there have always been obstacles preventing full development. It is still true that when one is deprived of knowledge and learning, one is enslaved, though the victim may not know it. The officials of Bessemer, Alabama enslaved most of their citizens, including whites, by controlling access to outside ideas. Now that these walls have been penetrated, it will take time for the minds behind those walls to absorb the knowledge denied them for so long, and then to mature in the use of that knowledge.

The second century of ALA will be entwined with problems of society as a whole but with libraries playing a significant part. There are still cancerous hatreds and malcontentedness in existence which only time and continued vigilance on the part of Afro-Americans can ease. Recognition of Americans of African descent as complete citizens who contribute to the quality of life in these United States is still a major problem. Knowledge of Afro-Americans' accomplishments and contributions, once purged from our books, must be spread widely.

William Howard Day, when he was a librarian of the Cleveland Public Library in the 1850s, must have felt the frustration of supplying books to readers which distorted the Afro-American contribution.[56] This is perhaps why he later published the *Aliened American*. Today's Afro-American librarians still face the uncompleted task. It is not only a problem of bringing to the Afro-American child a record of past accomplishments of his people and their contributions to U.S. life; it is also a challenge to bring to all in the United States the knowledge that one's color has nothing to do with the quality of the person inside.

E. J. Josey, writing in the *Library Scene*, pointed out that the "black press" must still be relied upon to provide the in-depth news of how the Afro-American thinks and what he does.[58] Libraries in new communities should provide resources for whites to use to gain some understanding not only of the great heritage of black people but also their contributions to world culture. He goes on to say that "most of our public libraries, including the large metropolitan libraries, provide their readers only materials to mirror the white community. In short, black experience is invisible in most library collections."

This is the challenge of the second century. It took one hundred years for the Afro-American to become visible. The second century should make the color invisible by absorbing the Afro-American into the mainstream of U.S. life and allowing release of the pent-up abilities and emotions, exploding "the dream, no longer deferred."

NOTES

1. *An American Almanac and Treasury of Facts . . . for the Year 1878*, ed. by Ainsworth R. Spofford (New York: American News, 1878), pp. 83–84.
2. Ibid.
3. *Atlanta University Publications . . .* no. 14 (Atlanta: Atlanta Univ. Pr., 1909), p. 118.
4. Ibid., p. 117.
5. Ibid., p. 118.
6. U.S. Bureau of Education, *Public Libraries in the United States* (Washington, D.C.: Govt. Print. Off., 1876), p. 1890.
7. *An American Almanac . . . 1878*, pp. 83–84.
8. *Atlanta University Publications . . .* , p. 117.
9. Ibid.
10. Ibid.
11. Ibid., p. 118.
12. Ibid., p. 117.
13. Eliza Atkins Gleason, *The Southern Negro and the Public Library* (Chicago: Univ. of Chicago Pr., 1941), p. 20.
14. Ibid., p. 21.
15. Louis R. Wilson, "The Use of Books and Libraries in North Carolina," *Journal of Social Forces*, n. p. (Jan. 1923).
16. *Muskogee (Okla.) Sunday Phoenix and Times Democrat*, Apr. 9, 1972.
17. *Oklahoma Libraries, 1900–1937: A History and Handbook* (Oklahoma City: Oklahoma Library Commission, 1937), p. 167.
18. Ibid., p. 168.
19. Ibid.
20. Willie D. Halsell, "Eleven Libraries in Ten Communities in Eight Years: Carnegie's Contribution to State," *Mississippi Library News*, Dec. 1972, p. 212–15.
21. Perepa Watson, "The Development of the Negro College Library in North Carolina," *North Carolina Libraries* 3:8 (May 1944).
22. E. J. Josey, "Edward Christopher Williams: A Librarian's Librarian," *Journal of Library History* 4:106–28 (Apr. 1969).
23. Peter M. Bergman, *Chronological History of the Negro in America* (New York: Harper, 1969), p. 329.
24. Ibid.
25. "Work with Negroes Roundtable," *ALA Conference Proceedings*, in *ALA Bulletin* 16:361–66 (July 1922).
26. Bergman, p. 448.

78 / *Clienteles*

27. Louis Shores, "Public Library Service to Negroes," *Library Journal* 55: 150–54 (Feb. 1930).
28. Ibid., p. 153.
29. Ibid., p. 154.
30. Ibid.
31. Helen Virginia Stelle, "Florida Library Survey, 1935: A Report Prepared for the Florida Library Association," 1937.
32. *Asheville City Times*, July 17, 1966.
33. Mollie Huston Lee, "Development of Negro Libraries in North Carolina," *North Carolina Libraries* 3, no. 2: 3 (May 1944).
34. Columbia Civic Library Association. *A Directory of Negro Graduates of Accredited Library Schools, 1900–1936* (Washington, D.C.: The Association, 1937), pp. 26–31.
35. Gleason, p. 20.
36. Ibid., p. 108.
37. Ibid., pp. 54–55.
38. Ibid.
39. Ibid.
40. Mary Elizabeth Vroman, *Shaped to Its Purpose: Delta Sigma Theta—The First Fifty Years* (New York: Random, 1965), pp. 45–53.
41. The sorority originally purchased the bookmobile for use in Franklin County, North Carolina. However, the state moved to provide this service from state funds.
42. Gleason, p. 64.
43. Gretchen Knief Schenk, "Our Libraries Can Keep Last 50 Years' Promises," *Library Journal* 75:7–9+ (Jan. 1950).
44. Lillie K. Daly, "Progress Is Noted in Negro Libraries," *Library Journal* 75:147–49 (Feb. 1, 1950).
45. Dorothy McAllister, "Library Service in Mississippi," *Library Journal* 80:536–39 (Feb. 1, 1950).
46. *Access to Public Libraries, a Research Project*, Prepared for the Library Administration Division, American Library Association, by International Research Associates, Inc. (Chicago: American Library Assn., 1963).
47. Ibid., p. xx.
48. Ibid., p. 139.
49. Ibid., p. 140.
50. Ibid., p. 59.
51. While the IRA study contributed to desegregation of public libraries to a small degree, there were complaints about the shortcomings of the study. See E. J. Josey, "A Mouthful of Civil Rights and an Empty Stomach," *Library Journal* 90:202–5 (Jan. 15, 1965).
52. "Alabama Civil Rights Campaigners Start with Public Library," *Library Journal* 90:2992 (July 1965).
53. Frederick W. Heinze, "The Freedom Libraries: A Wedge in the Closed Society," *Library Journal* 90:1991 (Apr. 15, 1965).
54. Ibid.
55. Ralph W. Conant, "Black Power in Urban America," *Library Journal* 93:1963 (May 15, 1968).
56. Charles W. Crosby, "Providence: A Community Relations Program," *Wilson Library Bulletin* 43:892–93 (May 1969).
57. Alex Ladenson, "Chicago: The Public Library Reaches Out," *Wilson Library Bulletin* 43:875–81 (May 1969).
58. E. J. Josey, "Libraries, Reading, and the Liberation of Black People," *Library Scene* 1:4–8 (Winter 1972).

5

Service to Academia

SAMUEL ROTHSTEIN
University of British Columbia

The year 1876 is a very good starting point for more than ceremonial reasons. Although American academic libraries had their formal commencement as far back as 1636 with the foundation of Harvard College, their true beginnings as an effective and meaningful service can be more appropriately dated from the establishment of Johns Hopkins University in 1876. For the salient fact about academic libraries before 1876 is that they were, as in one university president's incisive characterization, "an aside in education, to be almost entirely omitted without making a serious change in the sense."[1]

The point is easily demonstrated by a single statistic. In 1876 the Boston Public Library, founded only twenty-four years before, exceeded in number of volumes the holdings of Brown, California, Cornell, Columbia, Michigan, Pennsylvania, and Princeton put together.[2] Moreover, if the comparison could have been made on a qualitative rather than a quantitative basis, the disparity might have been even more marked. Where the Boston Public Library had sizable annual book funds and a carefully selected stock, the academic libraries generally had neither. Their collections were pretty much what had drifted in—a happenstance accumulation of gifts, often the residue of the settlement of estates.

Such ragtag collections could not have been expected to attract much use and what use they might have had was stifled by narrowly conceived and rigorously applied regulations which made the books all but untouchable. In 1875 the historian, Henry Adams, complained to the Harvard Corporation about the existing policy of keeping books all but locked up. Having cast aside the textbook method in favor of having his students go directly to the original sources, he demanded greater accessibility to library materials.

1876–1900: FROM MUSEUM TO WORKSHOP

Gradually the idea of the greater use of the library took on symbolic power. It became common, especially on ceremonial occasions, to refer to the library as the institution's "workshop" or "laboratory," especially for the humanities and social sciences. By the time that Benjamin Ide Wheeler became president of the University of California at the turn of the century, he could announce grandly: "Give me a library and I'll build a university around it."[3] The rhetoric was compelling. Even though the actual use of the library by undergraduates may still have been mainly for "assigned reading," referring to the library as "the heart of the university" meant for it greater prestige, interest, and funds.

If for the undergraduate students the change was perhaps more show than substance, for a new breed of faculty members the library's role was beginning to be very substantially altered indeed. Once again, the process had its roots outside the library, in the scholarly world itself. Arthur Bestor has described the transformation of American scholarship that took place in the latter half of the nineteenth century as an "intellectual revolution."[4] He points out two central and related facts. The first is that up to then research activity was insignificant and indeed little esteemed. The second is that there were scarcely any organized arrangements for the promotion, training, and support of scholarship. The scholar was usually a gifted amateur, a Prescott or Parkman who worked on his own, with no institutional connections or support. Research was not yet a profession.

Perhaps the most potent influence for change came from without in the form of ideas and methods imported from the German university. In the early nineteenth century the German universities had become world centers for advanced scholarship, attracting many students from America. From Germany they brought back home new teaching techniques such as the use of the seminar, vastly enlarged expectations of what facilities such as laboratories and libraries ought to be provided and, above all, the conviction that research was the highest function and responsibility of the university. Indeed it might be said that they brought back the idea of the university itself, an institution which would offer graduate and professional studies as well as the liberal arts and which would give the extension of knowledge an even higher priority than its transmission.

The ideas imported from Germany, reinforced and assimilated by indigenous influences, found their fullest realization in the Johns

Hopkins University, established in 1876. Daniel Coit Gilman, the founding president of Johns Hopkins, described his new institution as having "research as the center, the heart, of the whole organism."[5] The example of Johns Hopkins, at least in what it represented if not necessarily for what it directly brought about, was in its turn a major force in making graduate work and research standard features in the pattern of American higher education.

By accepting research as one of its basic functions, the university in effect institutionalized and professionalized scholarship. Where U.S. scholars had previously worked independently, relying on their own resources, the university now undertook to assure its scholars appropriate institutional arrangements for their work. The U.S. college of 1850 made room only for teachers and of a very few subjects at that; the U.S. university of 1900 made a place for the scholar and in an ever-growing number of specializations.

With the conversion from college to university came a fundamental reorientation of the faculty's attitudes to their library. The basic conditions of professionalized scholarship are that it is cumulative (building on previous knowledge) and original (not duplicating previous research). It must also be constant; the professional scholar must go on plying his scholarship. All three conditions imply the availability of massive amounts of library materials—theoretically, at least, all publications pertinent to the subject, especially the "original sources."

Inevitably, then, the scholars' necessity forced the wholesale growth of academic libraries. The pressure for expansion became the dominant theme of almost every annual report. Justin Winsor, librarian at Harvard, observed in 1883 that no single American library had yet come close to satisfying the specialist's book requirements in any given field and felt that the only hope lay in almost indiscriminate collecting.[6] Raymond Davis in 1906 characterized his whole career as librarian at the University of Michigan as having been simply "A struggle for books."[7]

The result was a sharp, almost dramatic, increase in the size of American university libraries. In the fifteen years from 1876 to 1891, the Brown University Library's holdings went from roughly 45,000 volumes to 71,000, California's from 14,000 to 42,000, Cornell's from 10,000 to 111,000, Columbia's from 34,000 to 135,000, Harvard's from 228,000 to 292,000, Michigan's from 28,000 to 78,000, Pennsylvania's from 25,000 to 100,000, Princeton's from 41,000 to 84,000, and Yale's from 114,000 to 185,000. The New World university libraries, whose collections had been insignificant in comparison with those of their European counterparts, were beginning to rival the Old World in extent of resources if not in value.[8]

In building up their collections, the librarians also brought in a brand-new factor in scholarly library development, themselves. The expansion of libraries brought a need for purposeful thinking about them. Just as had occurred with scholarship itself, the new element of growth converted library work from an amateur or clerical occupation to one calling for specialized knowledge, a profession. Collections which were small and little used could almost arrange themselves. A collection of thousands of volumes, serving a large and varied clientele, required detailed and careful classification. Similarly, larger collections created the need for rules of entry and such other paraphernalia of cataloging as lists of subject headings, authority files, and shelflists. In short growth forced the development of a whole range of organizational methodology, the so-called technical services, which became the hallmark of the professionally administered library.

Even more important, the professionalization of librarianship brought a new spirit into library work—the goal of service and the idea that the librarians themselves should become a significant factor in the educational experience. This emphasis on service and involvement in the educational process was, it should be pointed out, by no means the invention of the university librarians. The concept was undoubtedly borrowed from the public librarians, who played the major part in the creation of a professional library "philosophy." Created almost de novo about the middle of the nineteenth century, American public libraries had not been fettered by the restrictive custodial tradition which had been inherited by the academic library. On the contrary, faced from the outset with the necessity of justifying the expenditure of public funds, the librarians of the new public libraries had every incentive to look for ways to increase public support by promoting greater use and developing reader services. Melvil Dewey, describing the Brooklyn Public Library in 1885, proudly called it "the modern library idea":

> So came into prominence what we fondly term the "modern library idea." The old school librarian was a jailer who guarded his books, often from being read. . . . The modern librarian is active, not passive. He is as glad to welcome a reader as the earnest merchant a customer. . . . He magnifies his office, and recognizes in his profession an opportunity for usefulness to his fellows inferior to none.[9]

And then Dewey, who was at the time librarian of Columbia College, significantly added: "We are trying to work out the modern library idea in a university library."

As worked out in Dewey's own institution, the "modern library idea" meant, most visibly, vastly increased hours of opening. The Columbia College Library gave twelve hours of service a week in 1876; in 1888 it was fourteen hours a day.[10] Access to materials was much freer than before. And there was now too, a new form of "aid to readers . . . the aid of someone fully acquainted with the resources of the library . . . at hand to impart the desired help."[11] This "desired help" was not merely a matter of courtesy and occasional personal assistance. It was an organized service, staffed by two full-time librarians, who constituted the "reference department."[12]

With his characteristic élan, Dewey was going well ahead of his academic contemporaries in offering patrons so well defined and fully developed a form of reference service. The usual progress was much more modest. The overriding priority given to acquisitions, the persistence of the custodial tradition, some doubts about the propriety of "doing students' work for them" acted as a braking force, preventing the reference service in university libraries from achieving, by the turn of the century, the full-fledged departmental status which it enjoyed in the larger public libraries of the time. Even so, the recognition that personal assistance was part of an academic library's responsibility and that it called for the assignment of professional personnel with special training in reference work was a very significant step forward. "Reader services" were now being offered alongside of the "technical" departments. The academic library had become a service as well as a facility.

By around 1900 the academic library, at least in the universities and elite colleges, bore little resemblance to the educational nonentities of the generation or two before. Symbolically it had become, if not quite the "heart of the university" described in commencement addresses, at least an important "workshop" for the campus. Administratively, the academic library had taken the significant step of coming under the management of professionally trained librarians. Operationally, the library now had a service orientation and was not just a source of books. When one considers that almost nowhere in the world before that time had college and university libraries gained such status, the American library of 1900 represented a noteworthy beginning.

1900–1950: STANDARD PRACTICES AND PERSISTENT PROBLEMS

Although the fifty years following the turn of the century encompassed two world wars and a Great Depression, the major themes of American academic library history during this period derived from professional rather than political considerations; in short, the academic library was well enough established to be proof against abrupt change by "outside" events. Keyes Metcalf, who as the longtime librarian of Harvard was an unofficial spokesman for his profession, analyzed these major themes. In a book which appeared at the precise mid-century point, Metcalf looked backwards and forwards. He identified the persistent problems of university libraries as follows: book selection policy, the search for economy in technical services, accessibility and the encouragement of use, accommodation to match a geometric rate of growth in collections, financing, and staffing. These were indeed both the functions and the continuing concerns of academic libraries from 1900 to 1950.[13]

84 / *Clienteles*

Metcalf preferred to speak primarily in terms of problems rather than of achievements but the achievements were actually considerable, notably with respect to growth of collections. "Viewed in the setting of world cultural history," contends Robert Vosper, the American university library was "indeed a phenomenal institution" and "a marvel to many foreign observers."[19] J. Periam Danton's detailed comparisons between German and American universities offer convincing statistical evidence for this point. In 1900 the German university libraries averaged holdings of 300,000 volumes and an annual book fund of some $24,000 as against the corresponding average for the thirty largest American institutions of 88,000 volumes and $10,000. By 1920 the German libraries stood at 486,000 volumes and $9,000 as against the American 300,000 volumes and $27,000. By 1940 the American libraries had achieved larger holdings (774,000 volumes vs. 745,000) and triple the book funds ($79,000 vs. $24,000).[15]

This remarkable pace was the result of an almost rapacious approach to collection building on the part of both the librarians and the scholars whom they served. Where the German librarians stressed *selection*, involving a precise evaluation of the intrinsic merits of each publication considered for purchase, the American style was "gross and accumulative," stressing wholesale *collection*.[16] Buying up private libraries was, in fact, a favored method of building up resources,[17] and even more welcome were the frequent acquisitions of famous collections through the benefactions of carefully cultivated "friends of the library."

The motivations behind this aggressive policy were well mixed. Undoubtedly there was a long-standing tendency in the United States to equate quality and importance of holdings with their sheer magnitude. As long ago as 1876 the U.S. Bureau of Education's special report on public libraries had noted the prevailing habit of indiscriminately increasing "the number of volumes which are placed upon the library shelves" because "libraries are usually rated by their numerical contents."[18] Joseph Green Cogswell had already given the classical disparagement of this numerical basis of rating when he stated "I would as soon tell you how many tons the library weighs as how many books it contains."[19] But Cogswell's criticism was little heeded, then or later. The size of the library continued to count for many points in the contest for academic prestige and the availability of relatively ample funds kept the rivalry burning.

Other reasons were less crass. The universities themselves were growing apace, with a constant addition to the range of subjects taught and researched. There was a genuine belief in the importance of the library, especially for humanistic research, and legitimate doubts about the ability to predict just what materials might be in demand by the researcher of the future. What is more, every U.S. university library bore the responsibility of making those predictions on its own. Under the tradition of local control and local autonomy in higher education, each university library was operating more or less independently of the others, seeking to provide by its own efforts and on its own premises the materials that its scholars then or later might need.

Inevitably, then, this uncoordinated approach led to a good deal of duplication and wastefulness, a situation compounded by the fact that the libraries normally left most of the decisions about book selection to the faculty members. The usual division of book funds put a good 80 percent of the money into "departmental allocations," over which the librarians had relatively little control. The assumption was that the scholars knew best what was needed but, as Danton has tellingly demonstrated, the disadvantages and deficiencies of faculty selection were actually numerous. Quite aside from the philosophical objections to the librarians' abdication of a primary responsibility, faculty members could not be counted on to work at selection systematically and objectively, and effective coordination was all but impossible.[20]

Danton's study was not published until 1963 and represented a retrospective view which was not widely shared in the earlier period itself. Until the second half of the century, the continuing and major concern regarding collections development was not over responsibility for selection or even the quality of the materials acquired but over their sheer number. The university libraries were still unanimously committed to a policy of vigorous acquisitions, but the consequences of continuing growth were beginning to attract serious attention.

The point was powerfully made in what is probably the most dramatic book ever published regarding American academic librarianship. In his *Scholar and the Future of the Research Library* (1944) Fremont Rider, the librarian of Wesleyan University, reviewed 300 years of American library history. He presented data indicating that over that period American university libraries had been doubling the size of their collections on the average of every sixteen years.[21] The percentage of increase was consistent and seemingly inevitable; Rider more or less suggested that the libraries were committed to an endless process of exponential growth at this staggering rate. Thus, unless some drastic change occurred, the Yale University Library would, a hundred years hence, have 200 million books and 6,000 miles of shelving.[22]

Some needed correctives were soon applied to Rider's paradigm of library growth. It was pointed out that the percentage of increase was not constant; it diminished considerably as the library "matured" or attained a certain size. By and large, however, Rider's professional colleagues accepted his basic thesis and shared his alarm over the prospects of indefinite expansion. In addition to the obvious problem of finding additional storage space, continued expansion meant greater complexity of administration and higher "per unit" costs for technical services. Indeed, almost every one of the basic research library problems identified by Metcalf derived from or was closely affected by the phenomenon of growth.

Rider could foresee no drastic change in the demand for materials but he did propose an imaginatively sweeping solution for their accommodation. The *microcard* would, by photographic reduction, house the text of a given publication on the catalog card itself, thereby eliminating the need for book storage space.[23] And Rider, like his mentor Dewey, a doer as well as a seer, went on to provide actual examples of such microcards through a foundation which he established.

Despite the impressiveness of this demonstration, Rider's solution gained far less acceptance than his analysis. The hopes for the microcard did not materialize. Photoreproduction of texts, even at considerable reductions, was too expensive in relation to the value of the space saved. Except for very bulky materials such as newspapers and, to a lesser extent, periodicals, micropublication was seen primarily as a means of making more materials available rather than compacting those already held. Other techniques for "compact storage," pioneered once again by Rider,[24] were more successful, but at best the savings were inconsiderable.

The real prospect for significant improvement lay in the movement which had been slowly gathering support for a century, cooperation. Greatly spurred by the establishment of the Association of Research Libraries in 1932, the cooperative movement rested on one compelling observation: no library, however large, could possibly be self-sufficient; it had to look to others to supplement its own capacities. The idea was translatable into two different though interrelated forms. It could be seen as a means of *extending existing resources* by making the materials of many libraries available or more accessible to each. Hence the development of interlibrary lending, union catalogs and union lists, bibliographic centers, and cooperative photographic projects such as microfilming manuscript holdings. The other main form of cooperation was prompted primarily by the desire to eliminate unnecessary costs—duplication in collecting, cataloging, and storage. This motive of *economy* was to be seen in the various ventures for centralized cataloging, division of fields in acquisitions, and the establishment of joint storage centers.

The trouble was that cooperation seemed to work best in the extension of resources, where it was little noticed, and worked worst in the drive for economy, where the chief pressures existed. Through the development of interlibrary lending codes (from 1917 on) and the provision of union lists and catalogs, almost any publication held in the country could be located and secured for borrowing—a truly notable contribution to scholarship which was too often taken for granted. On the other hand, the economy measures, while successful enough, simply did not amount to much. The various agreements to divide up fields of collecting[25] normally affected only materials of marginal interest, and the joint storage centers, such as the New England Deposit Library and the Hampshire Inter-Library Center, produced minimum savings.[26]

The greatest disappointment was felt regarding cooperative or centralized cataloging. Librarians since Charles Coffin Jewett had noted the wastefulness implied in many libraries separately cataloging the same title. A huge potential economy existed in the availability of cataloging copy from the Library of Congress through the purchase of its printed cards—provided that the Library of Congress had indeed already acquired and cataloged that particular title and that the LC cataloging copy was acceptable without much modification. Unfortunately, neither condition could be met easily. A university library which ranged fairly widely in its scope of acquisitions could count on the Library of Congress's supplying copy for less than half of its titles, especially for publications in foreign languages. Even more vexing for library administrators was the fact that they often could not take full advantage of such LC cards that were available, either because their libraries were still saddled with an outmoded classification scheme or because their catalogers insisted on making extensive and expensive revisions in the LC copy.

It appeared, in fact, that there had been developing something of an undeclared war between the chief librarians and their technical services staff. What the latter, and a good many reference librarians as well, regarded as merely the appropriate detail and accuracy necessary for scholarly cataloging was seen by the administrators as perfectionism. When the draft of the new edition of the *ALA Cataloging Rules*, issued in 1940, called for even more meticulousness and complexity in bibliographic description, it provoked the angry criticism typified in Andrew Osborn's bellwether article, "The Crisis in Cataloging."[27] The protests brought a reexamination of the *Rules* and eventually considerable simplification, but the cost of cataloging, justified or not, continued to be a sore point. Classification, on the other hand, appeared by then to be a safely dead issue. As Maurice Tauber rather resignedly explained in 1949, "the classifications in use now have been found to be unsatisfactory" but reorganization seemed to be justified "only when necessary to clarify a chaotic situation on the shelves."[28]

On the public service side, there was less quarrelling and a greater sense of progress. Reference work, which at the turn of the century had been pretty much confined to guidance in the use of the library, had gradually become accepted as a central responsibility of the academic library, requiring its own full-time staff. At the same time the limitations on the degree and kind of assistance accorded began to be lifted. The main issue was whether the reference staff was to supply the information itself or only help in finding it. The "conservative" policy was represented by libraries such as Harvard, which as late as the 1940s still "did not believe in doing reference work" for students,[29] presumably for fear of "spoonfeeding" them. Most libraries by then had adopted the "moderate" position,[30] being willing, for some types of question ("factual") and in some circumstances, to supply the information outright. The steady movement to subject specialization in the reference service during the 1920s and 1930s was a particularly significant advance in that it made possible an informed assistance for the researcher. Indeed, some department, professional school, and institute libraries, particularly after 1940, came to offer the kind of "liberal" or extensive service characteristic of special libraries,[31] while the main library continued to espouse a conservative or moderate policy.

Such marked variations in the nature and extent of services offered at different points on the same campus brought home the important fact that the university library was no longer a simple administrative unit. In the larger universities the library might well have consisted of thirty or forty departments; in addition there were likely to be a number of reading rooms and professional school libraries which were right outside the main library system. In fact, the organization, administration, and control of the library were themselves seen as constituting one of the basic problems of academic librarianship.

The problems of organization grew with size and therefore came more sharply into consciousness after the 1920s, by which time a good hundred American universities had acquired collections of over 200,000 volumes. Until then the usual approach had been laissez faire; such teaching departments (usually in the sciences) and professional schools as had the will and the means to develop their own reading rooms and libraries were allowed to do so without much dispute. In Germany the same process had eventually led to the existence of numerous and large "institute" libraries, wholly independent of the main library and each other, duplicating resources wastefully and almost unusable except by the "members" of the institute. In U.S. and Canadian universities, whose structure was modeled more closely on the business corporation, departmental autonomy was not allowed to go unchecked; indeed, the issue of library centralization versus decentralization attracted close attention from the university presidents as well from the librarians. In general the librarians and presidents favored centralized control on the grounds of diminishing needless duplication and increasing coordination. Faculty members tended to think that their need for convenience, speed of service, and attention to their own special circumstances warranted separate control and funding. In the resulting push-pull of campus politics, no uniform pattern developed for the handling of departmental, school, and laboratory libraries, but the tendency was definitely toward increasing centralization, particularly when new library buildings could be erected.

Within the library system itself the problems of control and coordination could be almost as onerous, if not quite so acrimonious. Up to the end of the 1930s, the average large university library was organized along departmental lines. Work was divided among departments based on "function" (such as reference, cataloging, circulation, etc.), "form" (e.g., serials, government publications, rare books), or "subject" (education, commerce, etc.). The heads of these departments all reported to the chief librarian and required his direct supervision. The "span of control" was thus becoming impossibly large for the chief librarian and by the forties a process of reorganization was generally under way. The changeover was to a form of divisional organization whereby the departments of the library were grouped into two to four major subdivisions, each headed by an assistant administrator. The most frequent form of division was simply into public (or readers') services and technical services. In the new style the chief librarian generally became known as the "director of the library" or, if he or she had won the struggle for centralized administration, "director of libraries." Her or his span of control was now limited to the handful of "assistant or associate directors," plus perhaps an "administrative assistant" or two to help with budget work, accounting, and building maintenance.

In a number of medium-sized libraries the movement toward reorganization along divisional lines was based on grouping by subject rather than by function. As so often happens, the initial cue came from changes in the curriculum itself. As a reaction to the fragmentation produced by the free elective system, some universities in the thirties began to stress subject interrelationships. There was also a tendency, for reasons of administrative convenience, to bring similar departments together into larger divisions—most commonly the humanities, natural sciences, and social sciences. At Brown University in 1938 librarian Van Hoesen "planned a divisional arrangement corresponding to a projected regrouping in the course of study" and produced an integration of eighteen departmental libraries into four subject divisions.[32] Almost simultaneously a similar approach was taken by Ralph Ellsworth at the University of Colorado, in connection with the new library building which he planned there. At Nebraska Frank Lundy carried the idea one step further by making the divisional staff responsible not just for the public service functions but also for the acquisitions and cataloging relating to their materials.[33]

Under the subject divisional plan, the general reference department was usually discontinued, the reference work being divided among the subject divisions, where it was assumed that the professional would have had advanced training in the subject field as well as in librarianship. This would afford enquirers a degree of expertise in service which could not have been available from a general reference department or from a small departmental library. The trouble was that staff of such qualifications were difficult to obtain and were seldom in such numbers as to staff reference desks for more than a few hours a day. Other difficulties encountered included readers and questions which did not fit neatly into one of the subject divisions and the necessity for a good deal of duplication of reference books and records.[34]

The subject divisional plan was essentially a compromise designed to realize some of the benefits of centralization while allowing readers and staff to achieve some of the familiarity with materials and sense of "belonging somewhere" which the good departmental library offered. No very large university library adopted it but by the end of the forties it was well established among the medium-sized universities.

Very few such organizational considerations beset the smaller institutions. Even long-established libraries, such as those serving the prestigious liberal arts colleges of the Northeast, seldom had as many as half-a-dozen professional staff before World War II. Teachers' colleges, junior colleges, Negro colleges, and the great majority of the denominational colleges were markedly worse off; as often as not, they had no more than one trained librarian. Such departmentation as existed therefore was normally along functional lines: cataloging and acquisitions (combined); circulation and reference (combined); administration.

The relatively small staffs were indicative of the fact that the college libraries by and large grew at a very modest pace over the half century since 1900. Without the university's commitment to research and especially to the requirements of future historians, the college libraries concentrated on immediate needs. The professed ideal was to limit the collection to the "active" books and they stressed that good selection meant systematic discarding as well as accumulation.[35] In practice, however, few college libraries reached a ceiling. Expectations as to how many volumes constituted an adequate collection somehow kept steadily rising. In any case enthusiasm for the work of acquisitions always exceeded that for discarding.

College libraries tended thus to gauge their progress by impact rather than size. Three stages could easily be distinguished. Some libraries had scarcely moved into the twentieth century, serving largely as a central study hall for students reading their own textbooks. At a second level of service, the library was called upon to supply a good deal of reading material but chiefly from a limited stock of "reserve books." The optimum level equated the library with the laboratory; in this case not only would students make effective use of the library for a wide array of reading but also the library staff would take an active part in prompting and guiding such use.

A landmark study by Harvie Branscomb showed just where the facts lay.[36] In his *Teaching with Books* (1940), Branscomb proved conclusively that most college libraries of the time were operating at no better than the second level. His data on the use of the library indicated that the mean number of books borrowed per student per year was only twelve; that most of these titles were "assigned reading"; that many students, and not necessarily those with low grades, borrowed no books at all from the college library; that there was in fact seemingly no correlation between students' grades and their use of library materials. Branscomb concluded that, as matters stood in most of the colleges surveyed, the students had really little need or incentive to use the library.

Branscomb laid the chief blame for this situation at the door of the faculty members, charging that most of them simply did not make wide use of the library an important requirement of their courses. But he also indicated that the librarians could do much more themselves. A great variety of means was at their disposal: exhibits, attractive quarters, browsing rooms, readers' advisory services, dormitory libraries, book talks, instruction in library methods, audiovisual services. All of these depended in turn on the availability of functional buildings and a library staff of real academic caliber. Unfortunately, few colleges before the Second World War had either, let alone both.

For the college library then, as well as for the university library, the mood of the thirties and forties was hardly buoyant. The problems all seemed to be of the "continuing" kind, while the sense of progress, so heady in the earlier years, was not. Seen retrospectively, the half century was a period of necessary consolidation—converting the previous period's innovations into standard practice, identifying and beginning to attack the persistent problems of academic librarianship. At the time, however, the situation of the academic library may well have appeared more static than promising. Few could foresee the sweep and scope of the changes just ahead.

1950–1970: THE ACADEMIC LIBRARY IN "EXPLOSION"

The favorite clichés used to describe developments in academe in the 1950s and 1960s all carried connotations of sharp, even violent change. Thus one heard much of the "student explosion," the "information explosion," the "building boom," the "computer revolution," "future shock," and so forth. Even after due discount is made for the extravagance of the imagery, it remains true that the U.S. college and university, and therefore its library, underwent far more thoroughgoing transformation in the last quarter-century than in the fifty years before.

The dimensions of the change in academic libraries are discernible in a few representative statistics selected by William Dix. In 1952 the average total expenditure for the fifty-eight members of the Association of Research Libraries was $478,980; in 1969 these libraries averaged an annual expenditure of $2,866,922, some six times as much. The holdings of these same libraries, which had averaged 928,052 volumes in 1952, came to a mean of 1,893,511 volumes in 1969. Only fifteen university libraries in the United States had collections of over a million volumes in 1952; by 1972 there were at least sixty-six "library millionaires." Dix, who as librarian of Princeton University had witnessed and participated in the whole process of development, seemed himself in some awe of the outcome: "Never in history in any country have there been academic library resources of the magnitude of those which developed in the United States in the 1950s and 1960s."[37]

As usual, the library growth reflected factors of both supply and demand in the universities themselves. The percentage of total institutional expenditures allotted to the library did not go up, but in a period of unparalleled affluence for higher education that percentage yielded vastly greater sums than ever before. And quite apart from their parent institutions, libraries found a potent new source of funding in the federal government. The success of the Russians with Sputnik in 1957 had generated an aroused national interest in education, leading to the enactment of the National Defense Education Act of 1958. This provided, among other things, a little money for the purchase of library materials to aid in the teaching of the sciences, mathematics, and foreign languages. More significantly, it was the breakthrough for later acts which brought in a great deal of money indeed. The Academic Facilities Act of 1963 provided for buildings in colleges and universities (including libraries) and Title II of the Higher Education Act (1965) provided specifically for financial assistance to libraries for acquisition of materials, fellowships for library training, research in librarianship, and a National Program for Acquisitions and Cataloging of research materials. Eventually, over $124 million in federal funds were granted for the academic library resources program, resulting in the acquisition of over 13 million library volumes.[38]

Clearly, then, the academic library's whole scale of operations was altered out of all recognition. The money now available to the academic library vastly exceeded any amounts previously known, and this was true even after full allowance was made for the erosion of purchasing power by an unbroken inflation. It was equally true that the supply never seemed to match a demand that had shot up even more abruptly. The classic case in point was Harvard. Paul Buck said that there were more complaints about the inadequacy of the Harvard libraries in the sixties, when the collections exceeded 7 million volumes, than in 1900, when the library had only a million.[39]

A good deal of this dissatisfaction probably represented no more than the usual tendency for expectations of the library to rise as the service improved. For example, librarians had long before noted that a new building was seldom large enough because it tended to attract students who had not previously been users. Similarly, the availability of generous funds for acquisitions seemed always wonderfully to sharpen and extend the faculty's need for materials.

However, much more than psychology was at work in this pressure for expansion. The hard facts of enrollment statistics indicated that academic libraries were now serving a much larger clientele than before. College and university enrollment in the United States went up from 1.5 million in 1940 to 2.7 million in 1950 to 3.2 million in 1960, and reached 5.7 million in 1965.[40] Thus the number of books acquired per student probably had not risen much if at all since the 1940s.

Plotting the library acquisitions against the increase in publications resulted in the same kind of constant ratio. Which is to say that the academic libraries, confronted by an unprecedented expansion in the volume of publishing, were unable to do more than to obtain the same proportion of the published record of civilization. In the United States alone, book production went up from some 12,000 new titles and editions in 1952 to about 30,000 in 1969.[41]

Much more important than the sheer number of publications was the fact that U.S. universities were now becoming interested in the kind of esoteric material which they would have wholly ignored a few years before. Prompted by the war and its political aftermath, aided by special funds from foundations and the federal government, the burgeoning interest in foreign countries crystallized as "area studies programs," which became standard features in the university library scene. Such programs drew the university libraries well out of the narrow orbit of "Western civilization" to which they had previously been confined. The geographical and linguistic scope of their collecting was greatly expanded.[42]

Such expansion brought with it some difficult problems in acquisitions and cataloging. Libraries which had always found it difficult enough to handle materials in the "usual" foreign languages were now faced with some highly unusual ones indeed, from Southeast Asia, the Arab world, the new countries of Africa. And even when the languages themselves offered no extreme difficulty, as with materials from Latin America or the Slavic region, the ineffectiveness of the local book trade or the lack of workable bibliographical apparatus made for constant problems.[43]

The federal government provided some initial relief through its Public Law–480 program, which permitted the Library of Congress to use "blocked currencies" to acquire and catalog publications from such countries as Ceylon, India, Indonesia, Israel, Pakistan, and Yugoslavia. A very much more ambitious plan came into effect in 1965, when the National Program for Acquisitions and Cataloging (NPAC) began on what was intended ultimately to be coverage of the whole world's output. Funded through the Higher Education Act of 1965, NPAC had the purpose of expanding the acquisitions and cataloging program of the Library of Congress to the point where it could provide cataloging copy for any publication which other research libraries might secure. The plan was, in short, to realize the old dream of eliminating duplication of effort in cataloging.

Pending the realization of such hopes and dreams, the university libraries had still to perform most of the technical services tasks themselves. They sought new methods in order to cope with their changed circumstances. One approach was to go outside the profession for needed personnel. Since the library schools could not supply graduates with the necessary linguistic competence, libraries hired foreign language specialists, who thus came to form a kind of third force, alongside the traditional groupings of librarians and support staff.

Another change was even more significant. The selection of materials which had always been a tightly maintained faculty prerogative, was being now taken over by the librarians. In the larger university libraries a corps of "bibliographers" would now divide up responsibility for selection along language or subject lines, consulting with the appropriate faculty members about needs and opportunities but not waiting upon them for decisions.[44]

Interestingly enough, there was very little opposition on the part of the faculty members to this removal of their traditional powers. The sheer volume of acquisitions now meant that few faculty members had time or taste for keeping up with the bibliographical work involved. In any case, affluence, like amor, omnia vincit. Since almost all their specific requests for material were likely to be met forthwith by the library, faculty members had little incentive to struggle over the formalities of control.[45]

The same two factors of volume and money prompted a thoroughgoing change in the techniques of acquisition. Traditionally university libraries had chosen and ordered their materials item by item. In the forties the experience of the Farmington Plan had shown that, for foreign publications, a carefully framed "blanket order" with a reliable dealer could be an effective and economical way of securing material. In the fifties it became common to place standing orders for all publications of the more important university presses since the great majority of these publications were probably going to be ordered individually anyway. By the sixties a great range of "approval plans" was in effect covering most current publications, both foreign and domestic.[46]

The theory behind such plans was that they provided broader coverage, quicker delivery, and substantial savings in staff time as compared to the title-by-title method, especially when the plans could be linked to the computer. The library would draw up a detailed "profile" of its requirements as a guide to the dealer of what and what not to send. Moreover, sales were conditional on the library's "approval" of each item by examination of it after receipt. Practice, however, did not always follow closely upon theory. Mismanagement, by either the dealer or the library, could result in omissions or a plethora of "returns"; a slipshod or harassed staff might be led to approve many inappropriate materials for lack of adequate scrutiny. Some university librarians felt strongly that no form of "block buying" could muster the necessary quality control and, besides, that it was simply wrong for librarians to devolve one of their most basic professional responsibilities upon an outside group. Having just won the power of selection from the faculty, it seemed odd to them to hand such power over to the dealers.[47]

For most librarians, however, such objections were dismissed as theoretical niceties which could no longer be afforded. Perhaps as never before, university librarians sensed themselves under pressure to find methods to make library services faster and cheaper. The pressure was especially acute from the scientists and the administrators. The scientists, whose severalfold increase in numbers epitomized the much-talked-of "information explosion," professed a growing disenchantment concerning university libraries and their services. Libraries, they complained at many conferences, were too slow to acquire and process the current information and they would not package it in convenient form. A number of scientists even boldly claimed that it was now cheaper to do a given piece of research over again than to go through the cumbersome business of searching the library's holdings to see whether the research had already been done.[48] Even among the less disaffected scientists, it seemed that communication with colleagues in "the invisible college" was often a preferred alternative to gathering information through the library.[49]

The scientists were perfectly willing to offer solutions as well as complaints, but the favorite solution they proposed was in effect the most damaging criticism of all. Librarians, they suggested, were simply not taking advantage of the capabilities of the new technology. The computer and, to a lesser degree, microforms and telecommunications, would make possible a "push-button library," where the user had only to dial a few appropriate numbers in order to secure a printout of the information he wanted. The implication, of course, was that librarians were too ignorant or too hidebound to recognize or accept the panacea.

It was a heady prospect which administrators were quick to urge upon their librarians; and along with it probably the implied criticism, too. The fact that considerable sums of money were available from governments and foundations for experiments in automation made the pressures all the more compelling. Not that much pressure was needed. Despite the common assumption, there was never much reason to believe that librarians were inherently reluctant to accept new technologies. As George Piternick had convincingly shown, "the available technologies had . . . always had their influences on cataloging rules, procedures, and products."[50] If anything, indeed, the university librarians were operating on the basis of a reverse psychology. Anxious to avoid the charges of resisting change, they were almost pathetically eager to find projects which could be shown as evidence of progress toward automation.

The result was that there were certainly automation prospects aplenty. Almost every university library of any size had its own systems analyst and what amounted to a whole department of renovation.

Whether all this was progress was, however, a matter of dispute. Harrison Bryan, a visiting librarian from Australia, provided one polite but devastating deflation when he pointed out that in the library automation field there was, in fact, much less than met the eye. Many of the most publicized projects, he explained, had been reported in the wrong tense. They turned out to be merely what was planned or conjectured rather than what was actually done. Even worse were the huge blanks in the reporting. Comparisons of costs were infrequently supplied in any detail and project failures were glossed over or simply not mentioned at all.[51]

Ellsworth Mason went much further. "The computer," he flatly asserted, "is not for library use." In support of this outright condemnation, he listed a whole array of charges. The computer was inordinately expensive to apply to library operations, being primarily designed for quite different uses. Computerized procedures obviated personal service; resulted in frustrating delays and breakdowns; were inflexible and capable of truly monumental errors. Besides, in plumping for automation, the librarians were building up a rival department which would eventually cut drastically into the support available for the library itself.[52]

It is perhaps significant that, while Mason's attacks elicited a number of defenses of the computer, few of them presented their counterclaims with anything like his vigor and sweep. The proponents of library automation were becoming modest and cautious about accomplishments. The push-button library was not just around the corner, and the computer's role was being seen as instrumental rather than revolutionary—making for improvements rather than thoroughgoing change. Visualized more realistically as a device of limited application, the computer could still bring unparalleled power to the performance of the many repetitive clerical operations in the university library. Widely used to speed up and control "routines" in circulation, ordering, production of book-form catalogs, serials records, accounting, and indexing, the computer was itself more and more becoming a routine part of library operations.

Much the same process of reassessment was converting other "prospects" of technological revolution into lesser but solid practicalities. Facsimile transmission, which was going to make interlibrary lending all but instantaneous, proved too expensive for ordinary use,[53] but the teletype came to be standard equipment in the university library and did improve communications considerably.[54] Microforms, which once had been heralded as the replacement for the book, encountered too much consumer resistance to become a day-to-day vehicle for storing and transmitting information. But microforms became important means of publications, adding immensely to the stock of material which a university library might acquire. Whole libraries of historical and literary materials became available in the guise of microfilm, microprint, and microcards, while microfiche became the standard form for the publication of "technical reports."

Probably the major instance of technological change at work was so widely and quickly accepted as to be hardly recognizable for the potent influence it really was. The xerographic copier became an alternative to home lending, brought many books back into print, and all but replaced note-taking by students. The copier also finally brought libraries into direct confrontation with publishers over the issue of copyright infringement.[55]

The pursuit of a significant technological breakthrough continued to excite interest throughout the period as one acronymic development followed another along the trail from prospect to project to (sometimes) well-established practice. MARC (MAchine Readable Cataloging) made the Library of Congress's cataloging data available in machine-readable form to other libraries. COM (Computer-Output-Microfilm) married the computer and the microform. SDI (Selective Dissemination of Information) became the generic designation for the scores of ventures which electronically produced a list of publications to match a given reader's "profile" of interests. MEDLARS (Medical Literature Analysis and Retrieval System) and its "on-line" version, MEDLINE, provided automated searching of the National Library of Medicine's periodicals for a continent-wide clientele.

The significance of MEDLINE actually lay not so much in its highly publicized speed of response to inquiries as in the fact that it represented another long step toward the interdependence of libraries. The new electronics-based services were thus providing new capabilities and incentives to reinforce a principle that had already been amply demonstrated—that libraries could no longer go it alone. Picking up momentum steadily throughout the two decades, the movement toward library cooperation began to show operational successes as well as the usual pieties of rhetoric. Perhaps the two landmarks in the development of working cooperative enterprises were the Center for Research Libraries (CRL) and the Ohio College Library Center (OCLC). The Center for Research Libraries began in 1951 as a foundation-backed grouping of midwestern university libraries for joint storage of materials. The key feature in the plan was that materials held by the Midwest Interlibrary Center (as it was first called) became in effect the property of the center and therefore unwanted duplicates could be disposed of. From storage on behalf of the group, the center moved into acquisitions, securing foreign newspapers and chemistry journals which were useful to the group as a whole but not worth purchase by an individual library. Eventually, the center became a national institution, with more than sixty-five libraries across the continent sharing in its considerable variety of innovative programs.[56]

The Ohio College Library Center (OCLC), as the name suggests, also began as a purely regional enterprise, which eventually expanded beyond its region both in scope and importance. Essentially a processing center, OCLC utilized an on-line linking system to make the cataloging information held in any one of its member libraries available to any other. The success of OCLC elicited not only imitation from other "consortia" or "networks" but also in some cases brought about an extended linking, whereby other groups of libraries contracted for OCLC processing instead of doing their own.[57]

The terms *consortium* and *network* were favorites of the period. While their meaning, beyond the general sense of libraries acting as a group, tended to be somewhat variable and imprecise, their use suggested the new seriousness of the attitude toward cooperation. Co-operation among libraries formerly connoted the willingness to work with others but as courtesy rather than commitment. A consortium implied a binding arrangement whereby for certain purposes the libraries were acting together as a legal entity. A network added the element of electronic linking to the organizational bond. By analogy with a power grid system (hence the name), a network would enable one library to "plug into" the resources of others more or less automatically. The American Library Association's Conference on Interlibrary Communications and Information Networks (1970) grandly visualized the network concept as ultimately leading to "removal of all geographic barriers to knowledge" and making possible "equal access by any individual for any purpose to the sum total of the nation's knowledge resources."[58]

The chief beneficiary of the vaulting plans for networks was the research community, just as it was the research clientele who received the lion's share of university library expenditure for acquisitions, cataloging, and reference services. In a period when research activity of almost any kind commanded unprecedented national prestige and support, such priorities on the part of the university libraries were seldom begrudged or even questioned. Yet library service to research did carry a price. To a large degree it was being provided at the expense of service to the university library's largest clientele, the undergraduate students. Every addition to the library's stock made the library more cumbersome; the mass of esoteric materials secured on behalf of the scholars diminished the undergraduates' chances of finding the publications suitable to their needs.[59]

The resolution of this conflict of interests proved simple enough: the recognition that different interests did exist and would have to be served in different ways. Ergo, for the research group a research library and for the undergraduates an "undergraduate library"—a library with quarters, stock, organization, and staff services selected in according with the special needs of undergraduates and their teachers.

The pioneering undergraduate library was Harvard, where the great size of the collections had long made for corresponding difficulty in their use. The Lamont Library, established at Harvard in 1949, created the essential features of what was to become the standard pattern for undergraduate libraries, a small and manageable collection limited to the "live" books; an unusually (for university libraries) generous provision of audiovisual materials; simplified classification and cataloging; a considerable stress on building design, the goal being to *attract* readers; the materials themselves available on "open access"; a staff organized primarily by function rather than subdivided by subject.[60]

Among the some two dozen undergraduate libraries that have since been built, a few variables developed. The size of the collection has ranged from 45,000 volumes to nearly 200,000, the more recent trend being to provide rather larger collections than was originally visualized. The clientele and purpose varied somewhat as well; the library usually served all undergraduates but sometimes only the students in the first two years. Since graduate students and faculty members often used it as well, it was even possible to see the library as not being primarily for undergraduates at all but rather as the "curricular" or "popular" library for the whole campus.

Whatever the minor differences in organization and service patterns, a survey by Robert Muller showed that undergraduate libraries were substantially successful in their objectives of facilitating and stimulating use. Their accessibility and attractiveness spurred large-scale increases in circulation and prompted faculty members to give more library-based assignments. Muller concluded: "There is no question that the undergraduate library on a large campus represents a service that is needed. It was brought into existence in order to provide appropriate facilities that the traditional research library could not satisfy. It is a notable new development."[61]

With their emphasis on layout, furnishings, and decor, the undergraduate libraries were highly visible manifestations of the fact that, since the end of the Second World War, building design itself had become an important aspect of "professional" librarianship. This is to say that librarians were no longer content, as they had generally been previously, to leave the design of their buildings to the architects and donors. At first through the influence of professional meetings (notably of the ACRL Building Plans institutes, 1952–56) and later through the employment of consultants, librarians learned how to create buildings that would be more usable and less forbidding than before. Where the older style had stressed exterior design and monumentality, the newer library buildings emphasized functionalism, flexibility, and a more human scale. Almost always of modular construction, the libraries no longer segregated books into stack areas but sought to create an atmosphere of "openness" by intermingling readers and their materials. Brighter lighting, a generous use of color, lounge furniture, and carpeting were also standard features that worked toward the goal of trying to give even a large library an inviting quality of ease and informality.[62]

In some of the smaller libraries, notably those of the "community colleges," the new approach to building design sought even larger goals—not just a change of atmosphere but a change of function itself. A new name generally went with the new role. "Learning center," or "media center," or "instructional materials center" were favorite designations to indicate that the facility was to go well beyond the provision of books and magazines. Sometimes this idea meant little more than that audiovisual materials were to receive more prominence in the acquisitions and service program; more often the learning center concept implied combining normal library functions with special facilities such as programmed learning and language laboratories, media production units, and art galleries. At its ultimate, the learning center could offer students individual "wet carrels" fitted out with microphone, sound unit, television, and telephone dial. The carrels thus provided access to the college's whole stock of recordings, films, videotapes, and computerized instructional materials.

The emphasis on audiovisual materials, so characteristic of the community college libraries, probably derived from the fact that these libraries were serving a clientele rather different from that of the traditional four-year liberal arts colleges or even of the "junior colleges." The burgeoning of the community college movement was a major academic phenomenon of the sixties; within that decade the number of such institutions had doubled and they enrolled four times as many students. The "community colleges" increased and grew so rapidly because they had discovered a whole new audience for higher education—"dropouts," older people, the disadvantaged, those seeking technical and vocational training tailored to local community needs. Such students were often "nonacademic" and seldom book-oriented. Correspondingly the community college library reached them not so much with books as with audiovisual materials and a good deal of individual counseling in study skills. The community college librarians thus came to feel that they had a distinctive task and approach, which was soon reflected in the creation of their own standards and associations. Their numbers and dynamism made them an increasingly significant part of the academic library profession.[63]

SINCE 1970: AFTERMATH AND ADAPTATION

In the history of institutions the material circumstances tend to remain fairly stable but the passage of only a few years can produce a substantial alteration in mood and outlook.[64] The fast-changing fifties and sixties appeared to Richard Ducote to have been for academic libraries "the duodecade of dynamic development."[65] In the seventies the rate of change did not diminish but the dynamism and euphoria disappeared.

The principal problem was cost. University appropriations could not keep pace with inflation; a political about-face removed much of the federal government's support for higher education. The library book fund, perhaps the largest single nonsalary item in a university's budget, became the natural target for economies. A number of major libraries suffered outright cuts in their book funds; almost all suffered reductions in their buying power. The result was that the number of volumes added annually by university libraries, long assumed as inevitably due to increase every year, began to hold steady or even decline. The statistics compiled by the Association of Research Libraries showed that in 1973-74, as compared to 1971-72, thirty-six out of fifty-eight libraries added fewer volumes. The total fall-off was 7.8 percent over the two-year period.[66] The "wholesale" collecting style of the sixties was giving way to a new "realism" and "selectivity" in acquisitions.

The financial squeeze was felt most severely on serial orders. As new journals continued to proliferate and subscription prices rose at a much faster rate than monograph prices, serials subscriptions came to take up more than half of university library expenditures for materials.[67] In reaction many libraries canceled subscriptions and began to look seriously for some plan of resource sharing that would lighten their load.

Such resource sharing, when coupled with the new technology for improving the speed and comprehensiveness of bibliographical identification and location, also held good prospects for alleviating the burden of interlibrary lending which weighed heavily upon the larger university libraries. Although in theory all libraries bore equal responsibility for facilitating the interavailability of materials, in practice borrowing libraries tended to concentrate their requests upon the major university libraries, whose collections were big enough to offer a good chance of supplying the needed material. The university libraries thus tended to lend much more than they borrowed. The imbalance was borne as a free service to scholarship at large and cheerfully enough until the rising costs of interlibrary lending became so high they constituted a real drain on resources. When the average cost of an interlibrary loan transaction to the lending library came to $7.50,[68] the traditional "free" system was in jeopardy. Some university libraries, notably the private institutions, initiated fees for services;[69] others, as in New York State, looked to state governments for compensation;[70] a growing number of university librarians were coming to feel that only some national agency for interlibrary lending, perhaps modeled on the British Library Lending Division, could offer a real solution for the problem.[71]

In looking to another agency for relief of their difficulties, academic libraries were giving only one more acknowledgement of a central fact of the seventies: they were having to abandon the old goal of self-sufficiency.[72] There was increasing stress on cooperation, not just in collection development and interlibrary lending but in almost every aspect of library operations. Cooperation was stressed not just among academic libraries but among libraries of all types.[73]

The emphasis on cooperation was by no means wholly voluntary. There was heavy pressure placed on academic libraries, especially by state governments, to seek cooperative measures as a means of saving money. Thus, in California the Audits Division of the state government issued a report on "interinstitutional resource utilization," which came very close to saying, "cooperate—or else."[74]

The intervention of government agencies, at least in the more populous states, was indeed increasingly likely to be seen in many ways. When a state supported a large number of colleges and universities, the interests of economy and equity (so as to avoid difficult subjective judgments regarding relative need and value of programs) dictated a growing trend toward the use of "formulas" in the financing of academic library operations.[75] Some greater degree of standardization and state control was thus certainly inevitable and perhaps even desirable, but it also had the effect of diminishing the library director's autonomy in decision-making while considerably increasing the paperwork.[76]

From every direction, indeed, it seemed that the traditional powers of the library managers were being challenged, altered, and reduced. Arthur McAnally and Robert Downs pointed out the remarkably high rate of job mortality among university library directors in the seventies and attributed the cause to the new stresses and strains placed upon library administrators.[77]

The chief pressure, according to McAnally and Downs, actually came from the libraries' own staffs. Perhaps in reaction to the threat to their position posed by the budget cuts, academic library staffs demonstrated an unprecedented militancy. Among the support staff, trade unions won certification on a growing number of campuses. Among the professional staff, while the union movement made significant gains, the main thrust was toward the achievement of faculty status and a much larger share in the making of policy and administrative decisions.

The goal of faculty status was hardly new, having been pursued with varying success for a generation or more. In the seventies, however, the trend toward faculty status gained immensely in terms of both specificity and vigor. Librarians, it became increasingly clear, were no longer willing to settle for a vague "academic status" but wanted the whole package of perquisites enjoyed by the teaching faculty: title, rank, salary, tenure, peer evaluation, and participation in policy making. What was more, faculty status had become a "cause," with strong emotional overtones. Thus the statement on faculty status, issued by the Association of College and Research Libraries, threatened censure and blacklisting of those universities which refused to grant faculty status.[78]

Even in those libraries where the staffs remained unorganized, the power structure changed considerably. It was no longer hierarchical. Decisions had formerly been made through a "chain of command" culminating in the chief librarian. The new trend was toward some form of "participative management" or "democratic administration." Whether the means used to effect participation were consultative committees, ombudsmen, or a full-fledged "library faculty," they came to the same point: the staff wanted a greater share in the management of the library.[79]

Another new administrative approach lay in scientific management. Computerization had brought libraries not only more and better data on which to base decisions but also the methodologies of systems analysis and operations research. Rigid specification of problems and alternative solutions, stated in quantified terms rather than as assumptions and rule-of-thumb guidelines, could lead to more justifiable policies and action. New management tools such as "performance budgeting" could also help to take the guesswork out of decision-making. It was indicative of changing needs as well as of new interest that the Association of Research Libraries found it worthwhile to set up an Office of University Library Management Studies in 1970. The office not only issued publications indicating general strategies for improving academic library administration but also encouraged and guided individual libraries in undertaking a systematic assessment of their managerial practices. By mid-decade no less than twenty-one large academic and research libraries had participated in this Management Review and Analysis Program (MRAP), the eventual result of which was likely to be considerable change in the structure and methods of administration.[80]

The cool objectivity advocated by the MRAP approach contrasted sharply with the emotional intensity generated by another administrative issue, the place of women and minorities in the library profession. The basic facts were simple enough. As Wendy De Fichy pointed out, "80% of librarians are women but 90% of library administrators are men."[81] Members of certain minority groups (blacks, Chicanos, American Indians, Asians) comprised only 9 percent of academic library staffs, far less than their proportion in the population as a whole.[82]

Such data added up to a picture of marked inequality. Not surprisingly, many members of the affected groups equated inequality with inequity and protested with increasing bitterness against what they claimed was "basic social injustice." Anita Schiller, in a phrase that came to be widely used as a kind of slogan, called women in libraries "the disadvantaged majority."[83] Helen Lowenthal advocated a "healthy anger at situations and individuals which help perpetuate the inequalities in the sex roles."[84] The blacks' sense of resentment was, if anything, even stronger. It was the principal theme in E. J. Josey's 1970 collection of papers by prominent black librarians.[85] Five years later

104 / *Clienteles*

Josey's survey of the situation of minority librarians concluded that there was still "a sorry state of affairs with reference to the employment of blacks and other minorities."[86]

In an earlier era such grievances might have led to little more than grumbling. In the "activist" mood of the seventies, those who felt themselves disadvantaged pushed hard for remedial measures. In individual libraries, notably the University of California (Berkeley), they conducted investigations documenting the degree of inequality in hiring and promotion and produced reports making strong recommendations for change.[87] In library organizations, notably the American Library Association, they won adoption of policy statements advocating equal employment opportunities.[88]

Despite all this ferment among librarians, the major impetus for change actually came from outside the library ranks. With the enactment in 1972 of Public Law 92–261 (the Equal Employment Opportunity Act), libraries were required to prevent and remove all forms of discrimination in their employment practices.[89] As supplemented by guidelines (notably amended Executive Order 11246) and enforced by a zealous agency (the Equal Employment Opportunities Commission), the act became the mainstay of a whole array of federal and state activities which vitally influenced personnel administration in academic libraries.[90]

Under this legislation a university was required to file with the relevant agencies an approvable "plan of affirmative action." As one personnel officer explained, such a plan normally envisaged a two-stage program. At the "corrective" or policing level, the university would undertake to ensure against discrimination. At the "positive" or redressive level, an affirmative action plan would propose steps to be taken in assisting members of the designated groups to overcome the adverse effects caused by past discrimination.[91]

The effect of such affirmative action programs could be far-reaching. A library would now have to engage in aggressive recruiting of personnel from the "protected classes" (as they were called at the University of Washington), including advertising in such hitherto unthought of places as ethnic and underground papers. Selection criteria such as education requirements could no longer be used if they operated to discriminate, regardless of intent. Regulations regarding nepotism, seniority rights, and the ineligibility of women for certain kinds of work might have to be repealed. Special training programs might have to be devised so as to prepare members of the protected groups for higher-ranking jobs.[92]

In their concern for "hard evidence" of the effectiveness of affirmative action programs, the supervising agencies tended to judge them in terms of quantitative results, not intent or effort. A common test at the level of professional employment was to compare the percentage of women and minority members actually employed in the given institution with their percentage in the national "availability pool" of people holding that professional credential.[93] The effect was to impose a kind of quota system on top of the normal procedure for hiring and promotion.

Of course, the full impact of the affirmative action policy was not yet assessable at mid-decade. It seemed likely, however, to be of very considerable influence. At the very least, the affirmative action program meant some loss of autonomy in decision-making and the necessity for constant and expensive communication with the supervising agencies.[94] Much more important, the affirmative action program, which in effect if not in theory required "preference in all employment matters to the [protected] groups," produced a potentially serious conflict of interests. As one university stated with unusual candor for so touchy a subject, "an affirmative action rule selectively certifying, as a correctional policy, minorities and/or women for appointment or promotion, may ignore the merit criterion of the most qualified employee. There is thus . . . a basic ethical conflict."[95]

The "basic ethical conflict" posed by the affirmative action policy constituted one last illustration of the largest problem of American academic libraries in the seventies. That overriding concern was not so much one of improving practices and techniques, challenging and useful as this might be, but rather of determining values, directions, and priorities. In the 1970s, as before in the 1870s and the 1940s, the academic library had to redefine itself. Was it to be essentially a service of supply of material or should it seek to be an active element in the educational process? Was its primary concern the needs of teaching or research? How far did its obligations extend beyond its own campus? What were the appropriate limits of collection size, of local autonomy in planning and operations? Could "professional" considerations be reconciled with concerns for "social responsibility"?

In approaching these and similar wrenching questions, the academic libraries of the seventies could rely on one timeless guideline and one demonstrated competence. They would always be the libraries of their colleges and universities and so could look, indeed had to look, to their parent institutions for their basic character and directions. But the academic library, professionalized in America to a greater degree than anywhere else, had also shown a historic capacity to respond to and even influence developments in higher education. The changing academic library would no doubt continue to be adaptable, responsive, and dynamic.

NOTES

1. James Hulme Canfield, "The College Library," *Outlook* 71:248 (May 1902).
2. U.S. Bureau of Education, *Public Libraries in the United States of America: Their History, Condition, and Management*, Special Report, pt. 1 (Washington, D.C.: Govt. Print. Off., 1876), pp. 762–73.

3. Quoted by Benjamin Kurtz, *Joseph Cummings Rowell, 1853–1938* (Berkeley: Univ. of California Pr., 1940), p. 42.
4. Arthur Bestor, "The Transformation of American Scholarship, 1875–1917," *Library Quarterly* 23:165 (July 1953).
5. Fabian Franklin, *The Life of Daniel Coit Gilman* (New York: Dodd, 1910), p. 227.
6. Justin Winsor, "An Address," in *Public Exercises on the Completion of the Library Building of the University of Michigan, December 12, 1883* (Ann Arbor: Univ. of Michigan, 1884), pp. 30–36.
7. University of Michigan Library, *Annual Report of the Librarian for 1905–1906*, p. 55.
8. Samuel Rothstein, *The Development of Reference Services through Academic Traditions, Public Library Practice, and Special Librarianship*, ACRL Monographs, no. 14 (Chicago: Assn. of College and Research Libraries, 1955), p. 18.
9. Quoted in ibid., p. 25.
10. Ibid., p. 19.
11. Ibid., p. 28.
12. Ibid., p. 29.
13. Keyes D. Metcalf, "Harvard Faces Its Library Problems," in *The Place of a Library in a University* (Cambridge: Harvard Univ. Pr., 1950), p. 38.
14. Robert Vosper, "Expanding Library Horizons: The Significance for Learning," *Pacific Northwest Library Association Quarterly* 37:10–11 (July 1973).
15. J. Periam Danton, *Book Selection and Collections: A Comparison of German and American University Libraries* (New York and London: Columbia Univ. Pr., 1963), pp. 86–87, 90–93.
16. Vosper, "Expanding Library Horizons", p. 12.
17. Albert Predeek, *A History of Libraries in Great Britain and North America*, tr. by Lawrence S. Thompson (Chicago: American Library Assn., 1947), pp. 100–102.
18. U.S. Bureau of Education, p. 60.
19. Ibid. Both statements are quoted by Richard Harwell, "College Libraries," in *Encyclopedia of Library and Information Science* 5:275 (New York: Dekker, 1971).
20. Danton, pp. 69–70.
21. Fremont Rider, *The Scholar and the Future of the Research Library: A Problem and Its Solution* (New York: Hadham, 1944), pp. 3–10.
22. Ibid., p. 12.
23. Ibid., pp. 99–102.
24. Fremont Rider, *Compact Book Storage: Some Suggestions toward a New Methodology for the Shelving of Less-Used Research Materials* (New York: Hadham, 1949).
25. Maurice F. Tauber and Associates, *Technical Services in Libraries . . .* (New York and London: Columbia Univ. Pr., 1953), pp. 25–31.
26. Helen Joanne Harrar, "Cooperative Storage Warehouses," *College and Research Libraries* 25:37–43 (Jan. 1964).
27. Andrew D. Osborn, "The Crisis in Cataloging," *Library Quarterly* 11:393–411 (Oct. 1941).
28. Maurice F. Tauber, "Book Classification in University Libraries," in *The Library in the University: The University of Tennessee Library Lectures, 1949–1966* (Hamden, Conn.: Shoe String, 1967), p. 27.
29. Metcalf, p. 191.
30. Rothstein, pp. 75–77.
31. Ibid., p. 108.
32. Archie L. McNeal, "Divisional Organization in the University Library," in *The Library in the University: The University of Tennessee Library Lectures 1949–1966* (Hamden, Conn.: Shoe String, 1967), p. 211.

33. Ibid., pp. 210–11.
34. Ibid., pp. 212–20.
35. Guy R. Lyle, *The Administration of the College Library*, 2d ed. (New York: Wilson, 1949), pp. 333–34.
36. Harvie Branscomb, *Teaching with Books: A Study of College Libraries* (Chicago: Assn. of American Colleges and American Library Assn., 1940), pp. 12–53.
37. William Dix, "Cause and Effect on University Libraries," *American Libraries* 3:725–26 (July–Aug. 1972).
38. Edmon Low, "Federal Consciousness and Libraries," *American Libraries* 3:722–25 (July–Aug. 1972); *Bowker Annual of Library and Book Trade Information*, 19th ed. (New York: Bowker, 1974), p. 144.
39. Vosper, "Expanding Library Horizons," p. 14.
40. *Libraries at Large: Tradition, Innovation, and National Interest*, Douglas M. Knight and E. Shepley Nourse, eds. (New York: Bowker, 1969), p. 7.
41. Dix, p. 725.
42. Robert D. Stueart, *The Area Specialist Bibliographer: An Inquiry into His Role* (Metuchen, N.J.: Scarecrow, 1972), pp. 17–30.
43. Institute on the Acquisition of Foreign Materials, University of Wisconsin-Milwaukee, 1971, *Acquisition of Foreign Materials for U.S. Libraries*, ed. by Theodore Samore (Metuchen, N.J.: Scarecrow, 1973), sections 2 and 3.
44. Robert Vosper, "Collection Building and Rare Books," in *Research Librarianship: Essays in Honor of Robert B. Downs*, ed. by Jerrold Orne (New York and London: Bowker, 1971), pp. 102–5.
45. Interview with Robert Vosper, in Guy R. Lyle, *The Librarian Speaking: Interviews with University Librarians* (Athens: Univ. of Georgia Pr., 1970), pp. 173–74.
46. G. Edward Evans and Claudia W. Argyres, "Approval Plans and Collection Development in Academic Libraries," *Library Resources and Technical Services* 18:35–50 (Winter 1974).
47. Le Roy C. Merritt, "Are We Selecting or Collecting?" *Library Resources and Technical Services* 12:140–42 (Spring 1968).
48. Cf. Conference Board, *Information Technology: Some Critical Implications for Decision Makers* (New York: Conference Board, 1972), pp. 116–17.
49. Cf. Launor F. Carter, "The Scientific User: The Library and Informational Service Needs of Scientists," in *Libraries at Large*, pp. 143–51.
50. George Piternick, "The Machine and Cataloging," *Advances in Librarianship* 1:1 (1970).
51. Harrison Bryan, "American Automation in Action," *Library Journal* 92:189–96 (Jan. 15, 1967).
52. Ellsworth Mason, "Along the Academic Way," *Library Journal* 96:1675–76 (May 15, 1971).
53. Herman H. Fussler, *Research Libraries and Technology: A Report to the Sloan Foundation* (Chicago and London: Univ. of Chicago Pr., 1973), pp. 47–48.
54. Donald D. Hendricks, *A Report on Library Networks*, University of Illinois Graduate School of Library Science Occasional Papers, no. 108 (Urbana: Univ. of Illinois Pr., 1973), p. 9.
55. "Memo to Members," *American Libraries* 2:1182–85 (Dec. 1971). A report on the Williams and Wilkins case, by William D. North, general counsel for the American Library Association.
56. Gordon Williams, "Center for Research Libraries: Its Origins, Policies, and Programs," in *University and Research Libraries in Japan and the United States*, ed. by Thomas R. Buckman, Yukihisa Suzuki, and Warren M. Tsuneishi (Chicago: American Library Assn., 1972), pp. 264–74.
57. Judith Hopkins, "The Ohio College Library Center," *Library Resources and Technical Services* 17:308–19 (Summer 1973).

58. Joseph Becker, ed., *Conference on Interlibrary Communications and Information Networks . . . Airlie House, 1970, Proceedings* (Chicago: American Library Assn., 1971), p. 1.
59. Irene A. Braden, *The Undergraduate Library*, ACRL Monographs, no. 31 (Chicago: American Library Assn., 1970), pp. 1–4.
60. Robert H. Muller, "The Undergraduate Library Trend at Large Universities," *Advances in Librarianship* 1:113–19 (1970).
61. Ibid., p. 130.
62. Ralph Ellsworth, "Academic Library Buildings in the United States," *Advances in Librarianship* 3:119–36 (1972).
63. Cf. Harriet Genung and James O. Wallace, "The Emergence of the Community College Library," *Advances in Librarianship* 3:29–82 (1972).
64. In addition to the documentary sources cited for this section, it is based on information derived from visits and interviews. I am particularly indebted to the following university librarians for their help in identifying and assessing current developments: Marion Milczewski (University of Washington), Donald Hunt (San Jose State University), David Weber (Stanford University), Earl Borgeson (Stanford University), Janice Lane (Stanford University), John Haak (University of California, San Diego).
65. Richard Ducote, "Spiraling Patterns in College Libraries," *American Libraries* 3:733 (July–Aug. 1972).
66. Cited by Richard de Gennaro, "Austerity, Technology, and Resource Sharing: Research Libraries Face the Future," *Library Journal* 100:917 (May 15, 1975).
67. Ibid., p. 922.
68. Stanford University, Lane Medical Library, "Interlibrary Loan Fees" (Memorandum to borrowing libraries, Sept. 27, 1974).
69. Ibid.
70. Brigitte L. Kenney, "Network Services for Interlibrary Loan," in Becker, ed., pp. 124–25.
71. De Gennaro, pp. 920–23.
72. Ibid., p. 923.
73. Cf. Nina T. Cohen, "The 3R's System and the Academic Library Community in New York State," in E. J. Josey, ed., *New Dimensions for Academic Library Service* (Metuchen, N.J.: Scarecrow, 1975), pp. 239–49.
74. California, Department of Finance, Audits Division, Program Review Branch, *Library Cooperation: A Systems Approach to Interinstitutional Resource Utilization*, Report no. PR-70 (Sacramento: June 1973), pp. 62–63.
75. David R. Watkins, "Standards for University Libraries," *Library Trends* 21:199–200 (Oct. 1972).
76. Interview with Donald Hunt, San Jose State University, May 14, 1975.
77. Arthur McAnally and Robert B. Downs, "The Changing Role of Directors of University Libraries," *College and Research Libraries* 34:103–25 (Mar. 1973).
78. Association of College and Research Libraries, "Standards for Faculty Status for College and University Librarians," *College and Research Libraries News* 33, no. 8:211–12 (Sept. 1972).
79. McAnally and Downs, "The Changing Role of Directors of University Libraries," in Josey, ed., *New Dimensions*, pp. 111, 120–23; Evert Volkersz, "Library Organization in Academia: Changes from Hierarchical to Collegial Relationships," in ibid., pp. 77–85.
80. Duane Webster and Jeffrey Gardner, "Strategies for Improving the Performance of Academic Libraries," *Journal of Academic Librarianship* 1:13–18 (May 1975); Duane Webster, "The Management Review and Analysis Program: An Assisted Self-Study to Secure Constructive Change in the Management of Research Libraries," *College and Research Libraries* 35:114–25 (Mar. 1974).

81. Wendy De Fichy, "Affirmative Action: Equal Opportunity for Women in Library Management," *College and Research Libraries* 34:195 (May 1973).

82. U.S. Department of Labor, Bureau of Labor Statistics, *Library Manpower: A Study of Demand and Supply*, Bulletin 1852 (Washington, D.C.: Govt. Print. Off., 1975), p. 25.

83. Anita R. Schiller, "Women Employed in Libraries: The Disadvantaged Majority," *American Libraries* 1:345–49 (Apr. 1970).

84. Helen Lowenthal, "A Healthy Anger," *Library Journal* 96:2599 (Sept. 1, 1971).

85. E. J. Josey, ed., *The Black Librarian in America* (Metuchen, N.J.: Scarecrow, 1970).

86. E. J. Josey, "Can Library Affirmative Action Succeed?" *Library Journal* 100:31 (Jan. 1, 1975).

87. Cf. Library Affirmative Action Program for Women Committee, *A Report on the Status of Women Employed in the Library of the University of California, Berkeley, with Recommendations for Affirmative Action* (Berkeley: Dec. 1971).

88. American Library Association, Ad Hoc Committee on Equal Opportunity in Libraries, "Draft, ALA Equal Employment Opportunity Policy," *American Libraries* 4:560–61 (Oct. 1973).

89. Bureau of Labor Statistics, p. 26.

90. The legislation affecting the personnel policies of universities could be rather complicated. For example, the University of Washington adduced no less than nine state and federal documents as governing the "legal basis for the University's equal employment opportunity policy and affirmative action program." Cf. University of Washington, *Affirmative Action Program, University of Washington* (Seattle: Sept. 30, 1974), p. 4.

91. Eugene Walton, "Accentuating the Positive in Affirmative Action Plans," *Wilson Library Bulletin* 49:135 (Oct. 1974).

92. "EEOC Guidelines for Preventing Discriminatory Employment Practices: LAD Report," *American Libraries* 3:1207–9 (Dec. 1972).

93. University of Washington, *Affirmative Action Program*, pp. 6–7.

94. At the University of Washington, for example, in all cases where a "nonminority male" was chosen for a faculty appointment, the department had to "document . . . the nature of the recruitment process." Ibid., p. 8.

95. Ibid., p. 41.

6
Service to Special Clienteles

ANGELINA MARTINEZ
California Polytechnic State University

The number of special libraries and information centers that cater to special clienteles in the United States has reached more than 12,000.[1] Growth figures indicate that these libraries have developed rather rapidly during the twentieth century. It is estimated that by the end of the 1920s, the number had reached 1,000. A 1935 directory identified 2,000 libraries, and by the middle of the 1950s the number of special libraries totaled close to 5,000.[2] A directory published in 1963 listed over 8,000,[3] and a 1968 directory included over 10,000 libraries.[4]

Special clienteles are associated with business and industrial companies, government departments or agencies, scientific and research organizations, associations and societies, and institutions such as hospitals and prisons. The libraries serving these constituents are integral functioning units of the organizations to which they belong and exist mainly to provide the information that the organizations need in order to build, prosper, advance, and achieve their ultimate goals.[5]

More than any other type of library, the special library's aims and objectives are designed to meet the needs and interests of the specific clientele that it serves. These clienteles have a common purpose, and their needs for information tend to be specialized. Furthermore, their dependence on information sources is determined by the nature of the work that they do. Some disciplines are more dependent on books than others. For instance, the worker in the humanities and the social sciences is very dependent on the literature of his field, while the worker in the applied sciences relies more heavily on the laboratory. Both need to use the library but their dependence on the library resources varies. Some disciplines place greater emphasis on recent materials and others use both recent and retrospective sources.

The special library, therefore, must tailor its collections and services to meet its clientele's needs. Some typical clientele groups include government officials, lawyers, doctors, engineers, agriculturists, economists, social scientists, bankers, insurance people, and scores of other professional groups.

Musiker, in his book *Special Libraries*, provides a wide variety of definitions of special libraries.[6] Although they constitute the least familiar form of library for the general public, special libraries are easily differentiated from other libraries because of their distinguishing qualities or characteristics. So far this chapter has referred only to their institutional affiliations and their special clienteles. Two other important characteristics include their coverage of definite subject fields or groups of related fields and their emphasis on service or the information function. Special departments of public and academic libraries and national libraries are not within the scope of this chapter, except as they appear in the development of the special library movement.

FROM ALA TO SLA

Although special libraries as we know them today are basically a product of the twentieth century, many special libraries were established before the turn of the century. In fact forty-three librarians from private, society, law, medical, theological, and other special libraries attended the first Conference of the American Library Association in 1876. This first meeting of the association was held in the halls of a special library, the Historical Society of Pennsylvania, in Philadelphia.[7]

Two references to special libraries appeared in the proceedings of the 1876 Conference. In his welcome address, the president of the Pennsylvania Historical Society acknowledged the existence of special collections in limited subject fields, and Charles A. Cutter singled out special libraries as the logical repositories of professional or scientific pamphlets.[8] Needless to say, the founding of the American Library Association had a salutary effect on the development of special libraries, as it signaled the birth of librarianship as a profession.

The year 1876 also saw the appearance of the U.S. Bureau of Education's survey, *Public Libraries in the United States of America,* which devoted several chapters to special libraries. Its lists of "principal libraries" contained 80 federal libraries, 50 law libraries, 30 medical libraries, 52 scientific libraries, 45 prison libraries, 44 theological libraries, and many other libraries attached to state government agencies and historical societies.[9]

A survey of special collections published by the library of Harvard University in 1892 included the libraries of 22 historical societies, 17 federal agencies, 16 state agencies, 14 societies and associations, 16 religious bodies, and 23 other special libraries. In fact, out of 192 entries listed, 108, or 56.2 percent, were independent special libraries.[10]

The early development of special libraries was influenced by several factors including the rise of specialization and professionalism, the emergence of professional and technical associations, the development of special collections in public libraries, and the founding of library associations.

The latter part of the nineteenth century witnessed the rise of specialization and professionalism. Scientific, technical, and professional education became part of the university curriculum and research activities began to emerge as important functions in both government and industry.[11] One of the best illustrations of how this trend affected special libraries can be seen in the field of history. History became a profession and historical research shifted from the historical society to the university. When the historical societies lost their monopoly over historical scholarship, the nature of their library collections changed; they became less affluent and several shifted their orientation to the field of genealogy.[12]

Specialization resulted in the publication of increasing numbers of research monographs and articles. Users demanded more materials and easier access to them. Special collections and libraries were needed to meet these new demands.[13]

Another important development of this period was the emergence of several professional and technical associations and societies. Many of these societies were oriented toward supplying the information needs of their members through annual meetings, the publication of journals and, more recently, the publication of secondary sources, such as indexes and abstracts.

The American Chemical Society, which is also celebrating its centennial in 1976, has the largest information program of any professional association. It began publishing *Chemical Abstracts* in 1907 and publishes several journals. The forerunner of *Engineering Index* was published by the Association of Engineering Societies (1881–1915) from 1884 to 1895.[14]

The American Society of Mechanical Engineers, founded in 1880, and the American Institute of Electrical Engineers, organized in 1884, were two of the four engineering societies known as the Founder Societies, which merged their collections to form the Engineering Societies Library in 1913.[15]

Arguments in favor of special collections in public libraries and independent special libraries began to be heard at the ALA annual meetings. In his presidential address to the ALA Conference in 1882, Justin Winsor urged the "creation of some special department" in the public library.[16] C. Alexander Nelson, on the other hand, in an address to the 1887 ALA Conference, stressed the limitations of the public library and called for the establishment of special libraries to supply the demands of the specialists. He stated that the nuclei of such libraries had already been established in the libraries of the medical, scientific, and historical societies and the legal profession.[17]

Special collections and departments, mainly in technology and business, began to appear in public libraries in the 1890s and early 1900s. The technological library first appeared in the form of a special, scientific collection at the Carnegie Free Library of Allegheny, Pennsylvania, in 1891. Other technological collections were later established in Cincinnati, Brooklyn, Pittsburgh, Providence, St. Louis, Minneapolis, Newark, and other public libraries. The Carnegie Library of Pittsburgh was the first public library to elevate its technology collection to the rank of department in 1903. The Pittsburgh Library is still a nationally important center for technical information.[18]

In 1889 when John Cotton Dana was at the Denver Public Library, he established a shelf collection of business books for businessmen, but failed in his efforts to open a service for the use of the business community. However, with the opening of the Business Branch at the Newark Public Library in 1904, he inaugurated public library service to business. It seems strange that in spite of Dana's pioneering efforts, further developments in public library services to business came rather slowly; no other major business collections were established until 1909.[19] In fact, very few trade association and business society libraries were established before 1909.

There were 114 company libraries at various stages of development in 1909. Of these, 12 or 10.5 percent had been founded before 1874, and 102 or 89.5 percent had been established between 1875 and 1909. Over half or 65.8 percent had been founded after 1900. The first decade of the twentieth century represents the first numerically significant period in the growth of company libraries. Manufacturing companies, including pharmaceutical, chemical, and miscellaneous companies and engineering firms accounted for 74 libraries or 65 percent of the total, and banking, insurance, and accounting firms totaled 40 or 35 percent.[20]

Company libraries evolved gradually and informally through the accumulation of books and other types of publications in offices and laboratories. When these materials were collected and brought together, a library was formed. In some instances libraries developed because of the interest of a company official who would donate his personal book collection. In a few cases technical or business collections were superimposed upon previously established educational or recreational libraries for employees. Several company libraries had their beginnings with the organization of their internally produced records, such as reports, data files, information and research papers. Very seldom was a librarian hired for the purpose of organizing a library.

Company libraries were divided into two distinct categories, the technical library and the business library. The technical library sup-

114 / *Clienteles*

ported the programs of organizations engaged in activities relating to the application of science to industry, such as manufacturing and engineering firms, technical departments in industrial concerns, and public utility companies. Business libraries served the interests of commercial or financial firms, such as banks, advertising, accounting, public relations agencies, and trade associations. Many industrial and technical institutions had both technical and business libraries, either under one roof or in separate departments. The company's line of business determined the name designation of the library, i.e., technical, industrial, bank, business, advertising, and so forth.

Among the leading company libraries started before 1909 were those affiliated with Parke, Davis (1876), Arthur D. Little (1886), Prudential Insurance Company (1895), General Electric (1900), Stone and Webster Engineering Corporation (1900), and National City Bank of New York (1907).[21]

The federal government had a total of 80 library collections in 1876 holding more than 700,000 books and pamphlets.[22] Libraries continued to develop independently from one another, usually as part of an agency of the executive, legislative, or judicial branch of the government. Kruzas's survey shows that 61 government reference and research libraries were established between 1870 and 1909.[23]

The lack of coordination in federal library programs was viewed with alarm by Melvil Dewey, who in 1896 appeared before the U.S. Joint Committee on the Library to suggest the creation of a board to study the "development and consolidation of Federal Library and cultural collections and services." In 1898 John Russell Young, Librarian of Congress, echoed Dewey's suggestion for more cooperation among federal libraries.[24] Dewey and Young were premature in their concept of coordinated federal library programs and many years elapsed before the idea was finally accepted.

The 1876 report lists forty-seven state and territorial libraries with a total of 833,219 volumes. At least fifty-seven libraries were added to state government departments and agencies during the period 1876–1909. They were mostly state historical and archival libraries, law libraries, general state libraries, and departmental libraries.[25]

One of the best examples of specialization in libraries was the development of the legislative reference library. Although the first legislative reference service was established at the New York State Library in 1890, it remained for Charles McCarthy, who started the Wisconsin Legislative Reference Library in 1901, to transform it into a thriving institution where legislators were provided with such services as up-to-date syntheses on current topics, bill drafting and analysis, and other services. Indiana inaugurated its State Legislative Reference Bureau (now Indiana Legislative Council) in 1907, and similar libraries were established in other states. In 1914 the Library of Congress established a legislative reference department patterned after the Wisconsin model.[26]

The 1876 count of law libraries stood at 50, not including the law libraries of the federal government.[27] By the late 1900s, in addition to the federal law libraries, most states had collections of law books for the use of the members of the legislature, state officers, the courts, and the bar. Provision had been made by law for the establishment of county law libraries in most states. Law association libraries and law firm libraries had also been developed. Close to 100 law libraries were established between 1876 and 1909.

Medical collections numbered 120 in 1898. These collections were found in hospitals, medical colleges, and medical societies. In 1898 the Executive Committee of ALA passed a resolution encouraging public libraries to establish medical departments in cooperation with medical societies and physicians. At that point Boston Public Library's new collection of medical books had reached 28,604 volumes (more than the Boston Medical Library had). The public libraries of several other cities soon followed Boston's lead.[28]

Newspaper libraries had their beginnings about the middle of the nineteenth century; at least six major newspapers started their libraries between 1876 and 1909, including the *San Francisco Chronicle* (1879), *Boston Globe* (1887), *New York World* (1889), *Chicago Daily News* (1895), *Kansas City Journal* (1907), and *Christian Science Monitor* (1908).[29]

There were very few collections of books available in prisons and mental institutions during the nineteenth century. Rehabilitation had not replaced punishment as the goal of correctional institutions, and most institutional libraries were collections of donations and discards. For the most part the collections consisted of religious materials.

The idea that librarians belong to a profession and are concerned with the social impact of their vocation was behind the founding of the American Library Association in 1876. Three more professional library associations were established before 1909; all influenced the growth of special libraries and encouraged the promulgation of standards for the development of collections and services. The National Association of State Libraries, which was affiliated with ALA, was founded in 1889 (reorganized in 1898) with the purpose of increasing the usefulness and efficiency of state libraries and other agencies performing library functions at the state level. The Association of Medical Librarians was organized in 1898; its objectives were to foster the development of medical libraries and establish an exchange of duplicate materials for distribution among these libraries. The American Association of Law Libraries was launched during the 1906 ALA meeting; its goals included the preparation of a legal index and the exchange of duplicate materials.[30] The medical duplicate exchange was established in 1899 and, according to its first report, 813 items were distributed to fifteen libraries during the first six months of its operation. The *Index to Legal Periodicals* and the *Law Library Journal* started publication in 1908.

Although the development of special libraries during the period covering the years 1876–1909 was not spectacular, it was steady. Figures compiled by D. N. Handy showed that of all the special libraries that were in existence in 1920, a little less than 4 percent were organized between 1871 and 1880, about 6 percent in the years 1881–1890, about 9 percent 1891–1900, and about 16 percent 1901–1910.[31] It is evident that many special libraries of various kinds were functioning in 1909 but, for the most part, they were small and were under the supervision of nonprofessionals.

FROM 1909 TO WORLD WAR II

The decades at the end of the nineteenth century and the beginning of the twentieth century witnessed impressive advances in science and technology. The growth of the communication and transportation fields greatly expanded the industrial potential of the nation. Industry gave a boost to the economy and influenced the emergence of a predominately urban and industrial society in the nation.

The effects of the nation's industrial growth on special libraries were obvious. Conventional library services did not meet the needs of the specialized clienteles who emerged as new technological and industrial organizations were formed. Special libraries were needed to answer the demands of this new breed of technologists, industrialists, and business people.[32] This was the situation encountered by John Cotton Dana as he and other librarians prepared to usher in a new era in the field of special librarianship.

The second major phase in the development of special libraries began with the birth of the Special Libraries Association in 1909. The organizing meeting of the association was held on July 2, 1909 during the annual ALA Conference at Bretton Woods and was attended by about a dozen librarians. On November 5, 1909 in New York City, the first association meeting was held, attended by representatives of legislative and municipal reference bureaus, state libraries, industrial and business firms, and business and technical departments of public libraries.

Speaking before the librarians at this first regular meeting of the association, Robert H. Whitten defined the special library as "an up-to-date working collection with a 'special' librarian in charge; a collection so complete and well organized that it becomes an efficient tool in the daily work of those for whose use it is designed."[33] The special library was on its way to becoming a utilitarian establishment, or "the working library of the modern man of affairs," as John Cotton Dana called it.[34]

The association embarked on a period of intense activity. Committees of like libraries were appointed, including agricultural libraries, commercial associations, insurance libraries, legislative reference bureaus, public utility libraries, sociological libraries, and technology libraries. Committees on publications and publicity were also established. In 1910 the association introduced its journal, *Special Libraries*, to provide a clearinghouse for news and information of particular interest to its members.

One of the main concerns of the new association was how to retrieve the increasing amount of published information. The search for better bibliographic sources resulted in plans for the publication of three indexes, well-known today as *Applied Science and Technology Index*, *Public Affairs Information Service Bulletin*, and *New York Times Index*.

The organization of librarians into group activities and local chapters suggested means for cooperative efforts and pointed to the need for a national directory of special libraries. The first directory appeared in the April 1910 issue of *Special Libraries* and contained references to nearly 100 special libraries. A directory published in 1925 included 1,000 libraries.

In spite of the depression of the 1930s, the years from 1909 to the beginning of World War II saw the establishment of 1,378 special libraries. Special libraries in the fields of science and technology led in the number of libraries established, followed by those in the fields of medicine, business and finance, history, religion, law, social sciences, art, and publishing.[35] Many of these libraries resulted from merging already acquired resources.

The year 1909 began a new era in special librarianship. Service superseded the custodial function as the primary responsibility of the library, and the librarian became more involved in the information retrieval process. SLA and several librarians of stature, such as John Cotton Dana, advocated the most advanced concepts of service and librarianship, including the idea of library cooperation.

The emphasis on current information began to be reflected in the categories of material available in special libraries. Primary sources of information, such as periodicals and serials, technical reports, documents, patent literature, and research papers from research and scientific institutions started to appear on their shelves. The importance of secondary sources was also realized and libraries began to acquire such tools as indexes, abstracts, and bibliographies.

Because speedy service was so important, special librarians needed to identify all their resources for the purpose of searching for needed bits of information. Since information had become a valuable commodity and many special libraries had to show economic justification to survive, immediate access and easy retrieval systems became goals to achieve. Many librarians used standard classification and cataloging tools, but others engaged in considerable experimentation and modified existing systems or devised original ones geared to their specific needs. Reference services were extended to include the compilation of bibliographies, literature searches, translation work, local abstracting, publication of library bulletins, and other individualized services.

Interlibrary cooperation was encouraged by the existing library associations; union lists were prepared. In 1921 SLA published its first *Union List of Periodicals and Annuals Taken by Eleven Special Libraries in Boston*. Since then many SLA chapters and divisions have sponsored the publication of over sixty-three different union lists.[36] Cooperation resulted not only in an expansion of interlibrary loans but also in other cooperative ventures with other special, public, academic, and governmental libraries.

The resources available to special clienteles continued to expand. Professional and technical societies and associations developed rather rapidly during the 1900s and so did their libraries. Special departments, mainly in business and science-technology, were established in most of the large and medium-sized public libraries of the nation and, with the exception of the 1930s, other special libraries continued to develop at a healthy rate of growth.

From 1911 to 1940, 878 industrial and commercial libraries were founded.[37] Among company libraries a new organizational pattern emerged in the 1920s and 1930s. During this period many companies established a library in conjunction with the opening of a research department. In most cases, however, these "technical" libraries were established for the use of the entire organization and not for the exclusive use of a research department.[38] A few of the leading company libraries established from 1909 to 1940 were affiliated with the Eastman Kodak Company (1912), General Motors (1917), Sears Roebuck (1928), and Caterpillar Tractor Company (1940).

Between 1910 and 1940 new military and civilian agencies were organized by the federal government. Most had libraries which were created through formal authorization within the agencies and operated independently of other federal libraries. The result was costly duplication and a lack of coordination in federal library systems. These problems were the focus of two ALA studies conducted in 1935 and 1937. In 1940 the Committee on Federal Libraries of the District of Columbia Library Association, following ALA's lead, recommended the formation of a Federal Library Council.[39]

The establishment of the presidential library under the control of the National Archives added a new dimension to the already vast resources of the federal government. The Franklin D. Roosevelt Library, the oldest of these libraries, was established by a joint resolution of the Congress in 1939.[40]

The state library as it is known today started to take shape in the 1900s. By 1914, according to some sources, thirty-four states had legislative reference bureaus. Starting in the 1920s some state libraries, such as those in California, Illinois, and New York, developed into major research libraries, while others concentrated on public library development. Many state departmental or agency libraries were established in the 1920s and 1930s.[41] Legislative reference services, which identified themselves with state and law libraries, continued to spread. By the 1930s most state libraries provided general library service to public or state officers, historical and archival service, and legislative reference and law library services.

Very few new law libraries were established before World War I. However, with the increase in the regulatory powers of the federal government during the war and the depression, legal materials proliferated and new governmental and other law libraries were formed. Unfortunately, this was a period of slow growth for law libraries and both budgets and collections were near the starvation point.[42]

Medical departments in public libraries continued to increase until they reached a peak of twenty-eight in 1916. However, a number of factors contributed to their decline, including the initiation of package library services by the American Library Association and the American College of Surgeons in 1924, and the increase in the number of local medical and hospital libraries. Some taxpayers had also questioned the propriety of providing public tax support for collections intended for a specialized clientele. Consequently, the period 1910–30 witnessed a rapid development of medical libraries of all types, including nursing, hospital, dental, pharmaceutical, and veterinary libraries.[43] The first Veterans Administration hospital library was established in 1923.

Newspaper libraries continued to expand in size, importance, and numbers and received recognition as an essential part of the newspaper organization. Many morgues were improved and dignified with the title of newspaper library, and many newspaper libraries were opened to the public.

Libraries in correctional institutions developed slowly. ALA established a Committee on Libraries in Federal Prisons in 1911 and published a *Manual for Institution Libraries* in 1915. The year 1929 marked the beginning of the federal prison library system and the expansion of penal institution libraries. In the 1930s ALA became involved in prison library service and started a series of reports on prison libraries. By this time it had been accepted that the prison library was part of the institution's educational program.[44]

In addition to SLA, four other "special" library associations were established during the period 1909–40. They were the American Merchant Marine Library Association (1921), the Catholic Library Association (1921), the Music Library Association (1931), and the Theatre Library Association (1937).

Another special library-related organization established in 1937 was the American Documentation Institute (ADI), now known as the

American Society for Information Science. Up until 1952 membership in the ADI was restricted to representatives of affiliated societies and institutions rather than individual members, and the organization was mainly involved in the technical aspects of microfilm production.[45]

By the early 1940s special libraries were firmly established as necessary units of business and industrial companies, government departments and agencies, associations and societies, and institutions. Significant increases in the number of special libraries had been brought about by the need to meet the wide range of user requirements in the various subject disciplines.

Like all librarians, special librarians were primarily concerned with collecting, organizing, and utilizing recorded knowledge. However, they frequently referred to *information* rather than *knowledge* to identify the library's stock-in-trade and to stress the function of its services.

As the vast body of library materials continued to expand, it created both storage and organizational problems. Librarians began to search for better means of storage and retrieval. The magnitude of these problems and the intense search for their solution are discussed in the following pages.

FROM WORLD WAR II TO THE PRESENT

Statistical surveys indicate that the greatest period of growth for special libraries began after World War II. The end of the war ushered in a period of unparalleled expansion of special libraries, not only in industry, but also in government, associations and societies, and institutions.

A survey, undertaken in 1961 in connection with the preparation of a directory of special libraries, reported that over 50 percent of the total number of special libraries had been founded after 1940, whereas 30 percent of the total had been founded after 1950. Over 68 percent of the industrial and business libraries were established after 1940, whereas 44 percent were established after 1950. Government libraries showed the same rate of growth: 64 percent were founded after 1940 and 34 percent after 1950. The combined science-technology-medicine group of libraries yielded the following percentages: 64 percent were started after 1940 and 39 percent after 1950.[46]

World War II brought about an unprecedented expansion in the research activities of industrial companies and government agencies. The growth of big business and large-scale industry and the government's preoccupation with national security and welfare gave impetus to basic or applied research programs. Scientific manpower had a tremendous increase, and workers from many disciplines joined forces in developing new approaches to the solution of many technical and social problems.

The rise of interdisciplinary science created new forms of primary and secondary publications. New journals and serials were introduced to promote the confluence of related, but formerly isolated, disciplines, and retrospective bibliographies were compiled to bring together all relevant contributions from the preexisting disciplines to interdisciplinary study areas.[47] New abstracting journals were started and others revised their coverage policies to include materials representing multiple disciplines.

Many new scientific societies and associations were established after World War II and existing ones merged or became affiliated with larger associations. For instance, in 1955 the American Association for the Advancement of Science had 265 affiliated societies, including 42 academies of science and an aggregate membership of more than 2 million. These societies and associations played a very important part in the diffusion of scientific knowledge through the publication of primary and secondary sources, meetings, and their special libraries and information services.[48]

The accelerated growth of the literature, the "publication explosion," was the result of high-geared industrial and governmental research programs and the great urgency of scientists to disseminate research results so that they could be applied to the new technologies being developed. It has been reported that *Chemical Abstracts* took over 31 years to publish its first million abstracts, 18 years to publish its second million, 7 years its third million, and 4 years and 8 months its fourth million.[49] The rapid increase of published and unpublished technical reports, documents, theses, pamphlets, and patents substantially added to the quantifiable universe of scientific and technical literature.

The increase in the volume of publications, together with the desire for faster access to the literature, increased the difficulty of the special librarian's job; vast increases of bibliographic work were necessary in order to provide the same level of service as before. The librarian's problems were also compounded by changes in the composition and needs of the library's clientele. Entirely new groups of users entered the ranks of the various professions, particularly in the fields of technology and medicine. The job-related needs of these users fell into three main categories: the need for creative stimulus, the need for technical information on an ongoing basis to perform a job, and the need for career advancement information.[50] Instead of serving the needs of a homogeneous group of readers with similar educational backgrounds, the library had to provide service to widely varying groups of users. This forced the librarian to stock materials on all levels of sophistication and in many forms and to employ various information transfer techniques.[51]

Proliferation of special libraries followed the "publication explosion." This unfortunately magnified the information problems of the researcher, because it ran counter to the trend in interdisciplinary science toward integration of multidisciplinary fields.[52] Many of these libraries were hampered by lack of funds, facilities, and equipment and were not able to meet the needs of the new breed of researchers.

Many of the literature retrieval problems experienced by libraries and users were also shared by the publishers of scientific literature, including scientific societies. Publishers of journals and abstracting services instituted several innovations in an effort to solve the problem of faster access to the published literature. They included the use of the computer in typesetting, and the development of computer-produced keyword indexes, tables of contents, permuted titles, and citation indexes. The new indexes provided the user with more selective access tools to that segment of the total literature bearing on his needs and interests.[53] Other nonlibrary contributions to the field of communications were the development of microforms, photocopy machines, and the computer.

Libraries contributed to the dissemination of knowledge through document delivery service. Although improved indexing and abstracting tools had speeded up the bibliographical retrieval of individual documents, immediate access to the documents themselves was not always possible. Libraries could not meet the demand for documents from their own collections and had to rely heavily on interlibrary lending. Interlibrary loans were too slow, when the time between request and receipt of a document obtained from another library was measured in weeks and even months.

Librarians realized that local self-sufficiency was not attainable within any institutional complex and that good library service required access to the total literature resources of individual disciplines and their related fields. The concept of cooperative networks gradually replaced the informal system of voluntary library lending.[54] Many of these networks made full use of the new technologies, including microforms, photocopies, TWX, and telefacsimile transmission.

Increasing demands on the scientist's time, growing quantities of literature, and availability of computer technology created the demand for information delivery. This resulted in the development of extra-library information systems or services "characterized by the compilation, creation, synthesis, evaluation, publication, and dissemination of information."[55] It was felt that these functions could not be met by the conventional special library whose role was primarily archival in nature.[56]

Many industrial and business companies developed dual information systems, a library and an information service. In many instances these were combined into a centralized service and the library provided the information center with its primary literature resource. Many corporations supported several libraries: in 1973 the 30 largest supported a total of 262 special libraries and information services for an average of 8 each.[57] Many industrial and business firms sponsored the establishment of information centers in academic libraries and obtained their service on a paying basis. Literature services on a paying basis were also available from the John Crerar Library in Chicago, the Linda Hall Library in Kansas City, the Engineering Societies Library in New York, and others.

The development of federal libraries and extralibrary information systems paralleled the twentieth century proliferation of government agencies. By the early 1970s the federal government had close to 3,000 libraries and several hundred information centers representing a multiplicity of subjects, purposes, and services. The absence of a national policy on information had resulted in much of the duplication of effort and redundancy of the present system. In 1965, as a result of a study of federal libraries undertaken by the Brookings Institution under the direction of Luther Evans, the Federal Library Committee was created, charged with the development and integration of library services at the federal level.[58] The coordination of information center programs had been assigned to the Committee on Scientific and Technical Information (COSATI) but this agency was later abolished and its coordinating function was assumed by the National Science Foundation.

The National Commission on Libraries and Information Science (NCLIS), established in 1970, was assigned to develop a national policy on information services that would eventually lead to the creation of a coordinated national system. Its draft report, *A National Program for Library and Information Services*, appeared in 1974.[59] A new congressional bill was introduced in March 1975 calling for the establishment of a Science and Technology Information and Utilization Corporation to insure the widest possible dissemination of scientific and technical information and to coordinate and manage the distribution of such information.[60] The impact of the NCLIS document and the congressional bill are not yet known.

The states were at varying stages in the development of their state library services. The main state library agency, or state library, emerged in the 1950s as the coordinator of all library resources and services within the state. Beginning in 1956 with the passage of the Library Services Act, it also played an increasing role in the local-federal partnership for library services. Most of the emphasis of state library programs was concentrated on public libraries, while special libraries, including state departmental and agency libraries, were often ignored. For instance, no state library had a consultant for special libraries and, in most states, the special libraries in government departments and agencies remained small and were mostly administered by nonprofessionals. However by the 1960s many state libraries became committed to the network concept and several states, for example, Illinois, Washington, and New York, had operational networks combining the resources of all types of libraries, including special libraries.[61]

Law libraries, with some outstanding exceptions, did not keep pace with the development of other special libraries. The close identification of law librarians with lawyers and legal training had prevented law libraries from adopting innovative and practical library techniques. The flood of new regulations brought about by World War II and the social legislation of the 1960s required the law library to provide nonlegal social information of all types for the use not only by lawyers, but also by other professionals, students, and laymen. Improvements in law libraries had, for the most part, been prompted not by librarians but by publishers, law schools, lawyers, and others. This situation began to be reversed in the 1960s and law librarians began developing new programs and tools for improved library services.[62]

The medical or health science libraries pioneered in equalizing access to information for health sciences personnel through regional library services. The Regional Medical Library Program, originally made possible by the Medical Library Assistance Act of 1965, was based on planned sharing of resources aimed at their maximum utilization. For operational purposes, the network was structured into four levels. Level one included libraries of community hospitals, colleges and junior colleges with health science programs, research organizations, and government health agencies, level two included resource libraries, mostly connected with medical schools; the regional medical libraries were in level three; and the National Library of Medicine in level four. In many instances, libraries in the first and second levels in the same area were associated in consortia of three or more members. Cooperative efforts included widespread use of TWX, distribution of serial holdings and union lists, reference service, consultation, training of personnel, and access to the MEDLARS search service.[63] It is an unfortunate oversight that the draft report, *A National Program for Library and Information Services*, did not acknowledge the existence of the Regional Medical Library Program.

The basic information resource for most newspapers was the clipping morgue which, in many cases, had been elevated to the position of a library. With the aid of microforms and the computer, the *New York Times* developed an information bank with access to the newspaper's clipping morgue retrospective to the 1960s.[64] Other newspapers were in the process of developing and installing information banks of their own.

A new basis for library access to inmates was introduced when the Supreme Court upheld a California decision establishing a prisoner's right to legal materials. Prison law libraries became a much debated issue and obscured many of the problems relating to prison nonlaw libraries which still remained unsolved. Title IV of the Library Services and Construction Act provided funds for correctional library improvements, and several states used these funds to add a library coordinator to their department of corrections, to inaugurate services in institutions without them, and to establish a library consultant position for correctional institutions.[65]

Space limitations permit only a few words about certain other types of special library. Libraries in historical societies and museums are limited. Although it is estimated that there are 4,600 historical societies and 4,000 museums in the United States, only the largest and more richly endowed have libraries. Nor is much information available on the libraries of associations and societies although we know that many of them have library facilities for the use of their members. Church and synagogue libraries probably grow at a faster rate than any other type of special library, and it is estimated that there are 40,000 such libraries in the country.

The American Library Association, the Special Libraries Association, and other library and professional associations and their divisions formulated standards for the development and operation of special libraries. In most cases, however, they were used as "guidelines" and were not implemented. There was frequent misuse of the name library and misunderstanding as to what size collection qualified as a library and who qualified as a librarian. Librarians lacked administrative recognition and, in many cases, there was no clear delineation of the role of the special library in its parent organization.[66]

A slowdown in the growth of special libraries, detected in the late 1960s, continued into the 1970s. This slowdown followed many years of almost unlimited development of library services and signaled a leveling-off period for special libraries. Industrial firms and government agencies began making an intensive evaluation of the function and purpose of the library organization and its contribution to the overall goals of its clientele. Special librarians became aware of the importance of adopting sound management practices to library operations and recognized the fact that alternatives to traditional library services had to be considered.

Special libraries have come a long way since 1876 and today constitute an invaluable national information resource. Their success is due in great measure to the efforts of the two major library associations—the American Library Association and the Special Libraries Association—and their divisions.

NOTES

1. Margaret L. Young and Anthony T. Kruzas, eds., *Directory of Special Libraries and Information Centers*, 3d ed. ((Detroit: Gale, 1974), p. 1241.

2. Jo Ann Aufdenkamp et al., *Special Libraries: A Guide for Management, with Revisions through 1974* (New York: Special Libraries Assn., 1975), p. 3.

3. Anthony T. Kruzas, *Special Libraries and Information Centers: A Statistical Report on Special Library Resources in the United States* (Detroit: Gale, 1965), p. 4.

126 / Clienteles

4. Anthony T. Kruzas, ed., *Directory of Special Libraries and Information Centers*, 2d ed. (Detroit: Gale, 1968), p. 881.
5. Paul Wasserman, "One of a Species: The Special Library, Past, Present, and Future," *Library Journal* 89:798 (Feb. 15, 1964).
6. Reuben Musiker, *Special Libraries: A General Survey with Particular Reference to South Africa* (Metuchen, N.J.: Scarecrow, 1970), pp. 13–33.
7. Edward Holley, "Raking the Historic Coals: The American Library Association Beginnings," in Michael H. Harris, ed., *Reader in American Library History* (Washington, D.C.; NCR Microcard Editions, 1971), pp. 175–85.
8. Ada Winifred Johns, *Special Libraries: Development of the Concept, Their Organization, and Their Services* (Metuchen, N.J.; Scarecrow, 1968), pp. 68–9.
9. U.S. Bureau of Education, *Public Libraries in the United States of America: Their History, Condition, and Management*, Special Report, pt. 1 (Washington, D.C.: Govt. Print. Off., 1876), pp. 169–70, 182, 215–17, 228–29.
10. William Coolidge Lane, *Notes on Special Collections in American Libraries*, Harvard University, Library, Bibliographical Contributions, no. 45 (Cambridge: The University Library, 1892), pp. 1–74.
11. Samuel Rothstein, *The Development of Reference Services through Academic Traditions, Public Library Practice, and Special Librarianship* (Chicago: American Library Assn., 1955), pp. 6–19.
12. Charles F. Hinds, "Historical Society Libraries in the United States," in Allen Kent and Harold Lancour, eds., *Encyclopedia of Library and Information Science* 10:439 (New York: Dekker, 1973).
13. Rothstein, pp. 6–19, passim.
14. Bill M. Woods et al., "Engineering Index (Ei)," in Kent and Lancour, eds., *Encyclopedia* 8:49–50.
15. Ralph H. Phelps, "The Engineering Societies Library," *American Documentation* 9:165–67 (July 1958).
16. Ada Winifred Johns, pp. 70–72, 78–82.
17. C. Alexander Nelson, "Libraries for Specialists," *Special Libraries* 17:97–99 (Mar. 1926).
18. Anthony T. Kruzas, *Business and Industrial Libraries in the United States, 1820–1940* (New York: Special Libraries Assn., 1965), pp. 18–47.
19. Janet Bogardus, "Business Libraries and Collections," in Kent and Lancour, eds., *Encyclopedia* 3:535.
20. Kruzas, *Business and Industrial Libraries*, pp. 48–86, passim.
21. Ibid., pp. 25, 51–60.
22. U.S. Bureau of Education, pp.
23. Kruzas, *Special Libraries and Information Centers*, p. 15.
24. Frank Kurt Cylke, "Federal Libraries," in Kent and Lancour, eds., *Encyclopedia* 8:371–87.
25. Robert J. Havlik, *Survey of Special Libraries Serving State Governments, 1963–64* (Washington, D.C.: U.S. Office of Education, 1967), pp. 115–67.
26. Marion Casey, "Charles McCarthy's 'Idea': A Library to Change Government," *Library Quarterly* 44:29–41 (Jan. 1974).
27. U.S. Bureau of Education, pp. 169–70.
28. Kathleen P. Birchette, "The History of Medical Libraries from 200 B.C. to 1900 A.D.," *Medical Library Association Bulletin* 61:306–7 (July 1973).
29. Charles R. Williams, "The Role of the Newspaper Library" (Master's project, Univ. of Mississippi, 1957), p. 2.
30. Johns, pp. 78–82.
31. D. N. Handy, "Special Libraries Association: Its Origin, Growth, and Possible Future," *American Library Association Bulletin* 20:333–38 (1926).
32. Grieg Aspones, "The State of the Art of Special Librarianship," in Robert J. Havlik et al., *Special Libraries: Problems and Cooperative Potentials* (Washington, D.C.: American Documentation Institute, 1967), pp. 27–39.
33. Herbert O. Brigham, "The Special Libraries Association: Personalities and Projects, 1909–1917," *Special Libraries* 23:204–9 (May–June 1932).

34. D. N. Handy, p. 333–38.
35. Kruzas, *Special Libraries and Information Centers*, p. 15–8.
36. Bill M. Woods, "Regional and National Co-Ordinating and Planning for Library Service to Industry," *Library Trends* 14:295–305 (Jan. 1966).
37. Kruzas, *Business and Industrial Libraries*, p. 80.
38. Ibid., pp. 66–67.
39. Cylke, pp. 371–87.
40. Virginia R. Cole, "Presidential Libraries," *Special Libraries* 59:691–97 (Nov. 1968).
41. Elmer D. Johnson, "Government Libraries in the United States," in his *History of Libraries in the Western World* (Metuchen, N.J.: Scarecrow, 1970), pp. 411–5.
42. Christine A. Brock, "Law Libraries and Librarians: A Revisionist History; or More than You Ever Wanted to Know," *Law Library Journal* 67:325–61 (Aug. 1974).
43. William K. Beatty, "Biomedical Libraries," in Kent and Lancour, eds., *Encyclopedia* 2:554–603.
44. Rhea Joyce Rubin, *U.S. Prison Library Services and Their Theoretical Bases*, University of Illinois, Graduate School of Library Science, Occasional Papers, no. 110 (Champaign: The University, 1973), pp. 3–13.
45. Robert S. Taylor and Harold Borko, "American Society for Information Science," in Kent and Lancour, eds., *Encyclopedia* 1:303–7.
46. Kruzas, *Special Libraries and Information Centers*, p. 10.
47. Scott Adams, "The Scientific Revolution and the Research Library," *Library Resources and Technical Services* 9:133–42 (Spring 1965).
48. Ralph S. Bates, *Scientific Societies in the United States*, 3d ed. (Cambridge, Mass.: MIT Pr., 1965), pp. 193–236.
49. Elizabeth E. Duncan, *Current Awareness and the Chemist* (Metuchen, N.J.: Scarecrow, 1972), p. 39.
50. U.S. National Commission on Libraries and Information Science, *Library and Information Science Needs of the Nation: Proceedings of a Conference on the Needs of Occupational, Ethnic, and Other Groups in the United States* (Washington, D.C.: Govt. Print. Off., 1974), pp. 253–54.
51. Ibid., pp. 256–57.
52. Monroe E. Freeman, "The Science Information Exchange as a Source of Information," *Special Libraries* 59:86–90 (Feb. 1968).
53. Joseph H. Kuney, "American Chemical Society Information Program," in Kent and Lancour, eds., *Encyclopedia* 1:247–64.
54. Vern M. Pings, "Improved Document Delivery Services," *Library Trends* 23:89–107 (July 1974).
55. Alan M. Rees, "Interface of Technical Libraries with Other Information Systems," *Information, Part 2* 1:1–37 (Jan.–Feb. 1972).
56. U.S. President, Science Advisory Committee, *Science, Government, and Information: The Responsibilities of the Technical Community and the Government in the Transfer of Information* (Washington, D.C.: Govt. Print. Off., 1963), p. 29.
57. Young and Kruzas, eds., pp. 1–1241.
58. Luther Evans et al., *Federal Departmental Libraries: A Summary Report of a Survey and a Conference* (Washington, D.C.: Brookings Institution, 1963), p. 115–25.
59. U.S. National Commission on Libraries and Information Science, *A National Program for Library and Information Services*, 2d draft, rev. (Washington, D.C.: Govt. Print. Off., 1974), pp. 1–123.
60. "New Congressional Bill Calls for Merger of National Technical Information Service, Smithsonian Science Information Exchange, and Office of Science Information Service into a Science and Technology Information and Utilization Corporation," *Information News and Sources* 7:195–205 (Sept. 1975).

61. Emerson Greenaway et al., "Libraries Look to the State Agency," *American Libraries* 2:735–42 (July–Aug. 1971).
62. Brock, p. 359.
63. Louise Darling, "Changes in Information Delivery since 1960 in Health Science Libraries," *Library Trends* 23:31–62 (July 1974).
64. John Rothman, "The New York Times Information Bank," *Special Libraries* 63:111–15 (Mar. 1972).
65. Rubin, pp. 6–9.
66. Robert J. Havlik, Bill M. Woods, and Leona M. Vogt, *Special Libraries, Problems and Cooperative Potentials*, prepared for the National Advisory Commission on Libraries (Washington, D.C.: American Documentation Institute, 1967), p. 95.

PART TWO

Personnel

7

A Century of Personnel Concerns in Libraries

DAVID KASER AND RUTH JACKSON
Indiana University, Bloomington

Whose concern is the librarian? Whose responsibility is it to see that his or her cares are met? Who should attend to his or her creature needs, such as salary and benefits, and who should be concerned about his or her psychic needs, such as security and professional fulfillment? The past decade especially has heard these questions argued in great depth in many forums, although hardly to points of resolution. The present paper does not propose to add to debate on the matter but rather to review briefly some of the major developments in the profession over the past century wherein the librarian has been a substantial beneficiary and to attempt to identify the sources of those developments.

The library profession has probably had personnel concerns since the days when the first temple archivist found his responsibilities larger than he could handle by himself and required an assistant, perhaps in the period of Egypt's fabled Old Kingdom. It could probably be substantiated, however, that all but a hundredth part of the library personnel activity throughout history has occurred within the past century. These relatively recent concerns have impacted upon the profession primarily in three ways: (1) by encouraging the establishment of extensive programs, largely formal, for the training of its practitioners; (2) by involving library administrators in structured programs of personnel management; and (3) by giving rise to union activities in libraries. Throughout the last half of the period moreover the federal government has entered the scene in a few special ways, although its role has been kaleidoscopic, halting, and seemingly irresolute.

130 / *Personnel*

This paper will be devoted to reviewing these manifestations of personnel concern in libraries since 1876. For discussion purposes the century is here divided into four unequal but rather "natural" periods as follows: (1) the beginning to World War I, a period of groping and largely primitive experimentation; (2) a "premodern" period from 1915 to 1925, during which a number of incipient programs of personnel import were initiated; (3) a modern period stretching over the next four decades, wherein most personnel programs, although continuing to evolve slowly, were essentially operational; and (4) a "postmodern" period beginning in 1965, during which ferment pervaded the personnel scene in libraries and produced a congeries of unsettling but perhaps promising developments. The following paragraphs will attempt to set these developments into a historical perspective and to point out trends that have occurred, with special effort to determine such factors as may have set them in motion.

THE BEGINNINGS OF PERSONNEL CONCERNS, 1876–1915

It is doubtful that the welfare of the librarian qua librarian ever entered the consciousness of the 103 worthies who came together in Philadelphia in 1876 to form the American Library Association. Certainly there is no record of discussion or minute of action to indicate that there was any concern for the matter whatsoever. The statement of purpose of the fledgling organization—"to promote the library interests of the country . . ."[1]—was totally devoid of interest in the issue.

Discussion at the first Conference of the association ranged over the technical problems of library operation—the handling of pamphlets, the sizes of books, cooperative cataloging, binding, the location of library buildings, mutilation of books, and other practical matters.[2] The nearest that discussion ever came to the subject being examined here was in a paper read by Lloyd P. Smith, entitled "The Qualifications of a Librarian," wherein he vouchsafed that "some knowledge of Latin and Greek is indispensible" to a successful career as a librarian.[3]

Likewise there is little evidence to indicate that the federal government paid any attention at all to the needs of the individual librarian prior to the beginning of the period here under consideration. The monumental 1876 report of the U.S. Bureau of Education, *Public Libraries in the United States of America*, contained a little on almost everything about librarianship in its nearly 1,200 pages, but it is significantly silent about the librarian as librarian. There is discussion of libraries in prisons, in medical schools, in historical societies, in YMCAs, and in art museums; of library buildings, copyright, and professorships of books; of statistics, periodicals, and titles of books, but little of librarians. William F. Poole contributed one paragraph on the qualities he felt were required in a good head librarian,[4] but there is nothing else.

In fact, one of the earliest concerns in the library profession which was to have substantive benefit for the librarian as librarian grew from this discussion of his or her qualifications, and was therefore in the area of library education. Its motivation was not primarily to benefit the individual practitioner but was rather to meet the need for a trained cadre of professionals to populate the rapidly growing number of libraries in the nation. Prior to the establishment of the Columbia College School of Library Economy in 1887, librarians had only three avenues available to them for discovering best methods of library operation, trial-and-error, imitation, and informal apprenticeship. Of these three, the last was perhaps best,[5] although the first was probably the one most frequently followed.

Despite fairly extensive discussion within the profession of the need for library training, the American Library Association balked in 1883 at giving Melvil Dewey the unqualified endorsement he sought for his plan to develop a library school at Columbia. It was only after hard politicking that he was able to get a diluted resolution of support although even that bland statement was adequate for his needs because the Columbia College Board of Trustees did approve his proposal.[6]

The American Library Association was slow to assume an active role in the quality of library education. Although Dewey early invited the ALA to think of the Columbia library school as "its school, and that it is its right, privilege, and duty to help form it,"[7] the ALA chose to ignore the invitation, and it opted against such participation for almost four decades thereafter. It flirted frequently with the idea, however, and sustained committees under various names and of varying degrees of assertiveness to monitor library education almost continuously from 1885 forward. In 1905 its Committee on Library Training submitted the first draft "Standards of Library Training for Library Schools," which were accepted and filed by Council without recorded discussion. Revisions of 1906 moreover were used to evaluate the eleven library schools and the eight summer training programs then in existence, and their deficiencies were noted in the committee's report. The association failed to take the obvious next step, however, and prepare a list of recommended or approved schools. Indeed such rigorous ALA involvement in the quality of library education was not forthcoming until after the First World War.

At the beginning of this period there was also little as yet for librarians to learn from the field of management. In fact, the concept of management as a discrete, identifiable activity, capable of being isolated and studied, had not yet been formulated. The advent of the Industrial Revolution in the 1820s had elicited a few tentative gestures in the direction of general management, but its serious emergence as a separable discipline did not take place until the end of the century. The first professional management association was established in 1914.

Although there were in 1876 a large number of librarians who thought of their responsibilities as being genteel and scholarly, above sullying by comparison with the commercial arena, there were already others who regarded themselves as managers of a sort, obligated to function "with a business point of view." In 1887 Frederick M. Crunden, librarian of the St. Louis Public Library, compared a librarian's duties with those of the manager of a stock company.[8] In the 1890s C. C. Soule, of the Brookline (Mass.) Public Library, observed similarities between the executive obligations of the librarian and those of the business man.[9] In 1897 Frank P. Hill of the Newark Free Public Library opined that the success of a library, as the success of a business firm, depended on effective staff organization with the librarian personally encouraging the self-development of members of the staff.[10] However, such evidences of concern among librarians for their managerial functions were relatively infrequent prior to 1900.

The turn of the century saw a rapidly developing consciousness in the world of private enterprise for what came to be known as *scientific management*. Industrial engineers during the 1880s and 1890s had begun searching for greater output at lower cost by controlling waste and increasing worker or machine efficiency. In 1903 Frederick W. Taylor first presented his basic concepts of stimulating employee performance through piece-rate systems, work which was later built upon by such proponents of scientific management as A. Hamilton Church, Henri Fayol, Henry L. Gantt, and Frank and Lillian Gilbreth.

Both the library literature and the ALA Conference proceedings of the period indicate that there was awareness within the contemporary library community of the systematic approach to management of personnel which developed in industry as a result of the scientific management movement. As early as 1911 Arthur Bostwick, Crunden's successor at the St. Louis Public Library, discussed the public libraries' need to adopt the methods of business efficiency, and he mentioned specifically those being advocated by Frederick Taylor.[11] Bostwick was perhaps as knowledgeable on this matter as any U.S. librarian of his time, having been instrumental during the previous fifteen years in developing fully four personnel grading schemes for public libraries. These schemes were among the first half dozen attempted in the nation and pioneered the way for the subsequent development of position analysis and classification systems in the libraries of the 1920s and 1930s.[12]

In total some thirty documents were published between 1910 and 1920 advocating the application of scientific management principles, including efficiency and business methods, to library operations. Interestingly, however, by far the larger portion of this writing dealt primarily with such limited aspects of scientific management as efficiency in library functions and labor-saving devices and techniques rather than extending generally to the development of job standards for personnel management purposes. Indeed only four of these thirty documents dealt with scientific management as it concerned library personnel, one dealt with motion study, and three concerned time studies in libraries.

In summary, at the outbreak of World War I there was a very limited concern for the personal needs of the individual librarian. Library administrators had expressed a glimmer of interest in improving employee morale and productivity to increase organizational efficiency. The library community had begun to monitor its professional preparation. Although these developments benefited the practicing librarian, they were not initiated for that purpose.

NEW VISTAS, 1915–1925

The general societal unrest of World War I stimulated a number of innovations in the American library industry which were to have marked and lasting impact upon the working conditions and fortunes of the individual librarian. By far the most significant among them were a redoubled concern within the profession for the education of librarians and a widespread interest in the problems of personnel classification in libraries. Also important was the first manifestation of unionization in libraries, an incipent development portending a larger future.

During the war years the attention of much of the profession became focused increasingly upon its manpower problems. The first postwar ALA Conference heard extensive discussion of the shortage of trained librarians and the seeming inability of the several kinds of training programs then in existence to provide an adequate flow of people prepared to assume responsible positions in libraries. No consensus, however, was evident on how to resolve these problems. Perhaps the single most influential stimulus to their resolution was the work done between 1918 and 1922 by C. C. Williamson at the behest of the Carnegie Corporation. His report to the corporation urged the rationalization of library education efforts and their restructuring on a more academic model. Among other things Williamson recommended accredited postgraduate training in university-affiliated schools, the preparation of better instructional materials in librarianship, greater attention to continuing education, and a certification program for librarians.

The Williamson report was published in 1923,[13] and led to the establishment in the following year of ALA's Board of Education for Librarianship, which was charged with improving the quality of library education through standardizing and accrediting training programs and with gaining increased financial support for library education. The direction of U.S. library training in the years immediately following was determined largely by the Williamson report and the Board of Education for Librarianship.

Concurrent with this redoubled interest in library education was a widespread concern during the decade for the classification of personnel in many fields. There was continued pressure by federal employees for wage equalization, and intense recruiting competition among federal departments during World War I prompted Congress to appoint in 1919 a special commission to investigate the compensation rates paid to civilian employees of the municipal government and various executive departments in the District of Columbia. As a result of the commission's work, Congress passed the Classification Act of 1923, the first federal legislation to affect directly the well-being of librarians. The job classification activities of the commission and the final passage and implementation of the act provided the first record of alternative methods of systematizing and standardizing various aspects of library employment.[14]

The job descriptions and standards developed for personnel in the Library of Congress and federal department libraries between 1919 and 1924 led to profession-wide discussion of the virtues of such practices. In 1924 the American Library Association joined with the so-called Bureau of Public Personnel Administration—an agency within the privately owned Institute for Government Research—in an intensive study of the nature of library work and of its appropriate remuneration. The study resulted in the publication in 1927 of a report, entitled *Proposed Classification and Compensation Plans for Library Positions*, a landmark work which elicited improved personnel administrative practices in many libraries, especially large public libraries. This document, known popularly as the Telford report, long served as a model for conducting job studies and for developing job descriptions and specifications in libraries based upon more scientific approaches than had previously been used in the collection of job data. Despite obvious difficulties in the administration of classification plans in libraries, their utilization in most large libraries in subsequent decades probably made for more equitable treatment of personnel than had existed before the 1920s.

Concern for position classification in libraries was also instrumental in the establishment of unions during this period. The New York Public Library Union, established in 1917, was the first to form, and although better salaries and working conditions were its initial goals, its stated purposes included also the attainment of civil service coverage for library employees, equal rights for women, and labor representation on the library administration boards. There is no evidence of the number of librarians represented in this union, although Guyton infers from its published statements claiming that librarianship was not professional work, that few librarians "if any at all" were members of the organization.[15] At any rate, records of the effectiveness of the organization are lacking, although it continued in existence until 1929 before officially disbanding.

Three more library unions were formed during 1917 and 1918. In September 1917 a union was established in the Library of Congress. The Boston Public Library Employees Union, founded in 1918, sought better salaries and working conditions; it claimed to have organized 42 percent of the staff before disbanding in 1923, although again there is no clear record of either the number of librarians among the membership or the accomplishments of the union.[16] The District of Columbia Public Library staff also organized in 1918 with two avowed purposes, to obtain improvement in salaries and to lobby in support of reclassification legislation. At one time this organization embraced fully three-fourths of the entire staff, including a number of librarians; it dissolved in 1924. Again, a defensible appraisal of the effectiveness of the organization is not possible, although the Classification Act was passed in 1923, and there is some evidence that it accomplished several other useful purposes as well.[17] Speaking of the three early library unions, Guyton observes that "each claimed certain improvements in staff conditions as a result of their efforts, but whether the unions actually were successful is difficult to judge."[18] Following 1918 there were no more substantive unionizing efforts in U.S. libraries for fifteen years.

These innovations of the war years and immediate postwar period, coupled with library administrators' increased concern for personnel management theory and practice, largely determined the general working climate for librarians for many years to come.

FOUR DECADES OF EVOLVING PRACTICE

The long period from the mid-1920s to the mid-1960s—although embracing the depression, World War II, and the cold war—was nonetheless one of relative stability for personnel matters in libraries in the United States. Rather "straight-line" evolution of practice took place on all fronts save unionization, where developments were almost entirely limited to the fifteen years between 1934 and 1949.

The interest of the 1910s and 1920s in scientific management virtually disappeared from the consciousness of the library profession until after World War II, when the subject came suddenly to the forefront. In the late 1940s and early 1950s many librarians who had become acquainted during their wartime service with applied scientific management principles returned to positions in libraries now grown large enough to benefit from similar attention. A daily Institute on Public Library Management was held at the first postwar ALA Conference in 1946, with Lillian Gilbreth serving as the keynote speaker,[19] and activity flourished in the years immediately following. In January 1954 Ralph R. Shaw, in an introductory article to an issue of *Library Trends* on "Scientific Management in Libraries," reported that there had been "a trend toward the application of scientific management to libraries—and indeed a rapid one. Such an issue of *Library Trends* would have been quite impossible twenty years ago."[20] Although perhaps a quarter-century late, scientific management at last found itself incorporated into the evolving practice of library administration.

Meanwhile the rest of the management world had gone on to something else. This new matter was a broad-based concern for organization theory, and the library community was much quicker to adopt its benefits than it had those of scientific management. Discussion of organizational theory in the business sector came at exactly the right time for the library community. The library world needed attention to its organizational problems in the 1920s and 1930s, and it was quick to avail itself of the unfolding theories of management thinkers. The first book on library management, John A. Lowe's *Public Library Administration*, was published by the ALA in 1928, and in it the author examined the librarian as administrator. For two decades thereafter writers in both general and library administration concerned themselves with the application of management principles and objectives to organizational activities, leading to the rapid professionalization of managers. Both groups emphasized personnel development and motivation, professional leadership, training, and public service. L. Quincy Mumford, writing in 1942, advocated increasing opportunities for leadership development among librarians by (1) establishing a program wherein promising younger librarians could be identified and given experience in different library departments; (2) giving them responsibility and authority commensurate with their professional growth; (3) affording them opportunity for research and study; and (4) welcoming them into "participation in the larger decisions of the library."[21] In the following year the McDiarmids, in their influential manual on *The Administration of the American Public Library*, pointed out the need for greater attention to the preparation of middle managers and for increased delegation of authority in libraries. Reporting on the results of the Public Library Inquiry in the late 1940s, Robert D. Leigh predicted that as libraries continued to grow they would require greater attention to matters of executive-policy direction and internal administrative management.[22]

Meanwhile another new emphasis was appearing in management literature that would lead to innovations in libraries. This was a new concern for the role of employees in the effectiveness of an organization. This new school of thought on human relations in industry led to elaborate social psychological and sociological interpretations of employee and management behavior.

Librarians were quick to see the potential utility of these new interests.[23] As early as 1934 J. Periam Danton was seeking evidence of staff participation in library administration, although he was able to find little more than its role in book selection and in the preparation of annual reports.[24] Herbert Goldhor also made an early case for democracy in library policymaking,[25] and Archibald MacLeish described efforts during the Second World War to spread policy responsibility more broadly at the Library of Congress.[26] Arthur McAnally wrote a quarter-century ago of the use of a staff council system in administering the departmental libraries at the University of Illinois,[27] and Amy Winslow, then director of the Enoch Pratt Free Library, described staff participation as

> an active and natural sharing in policy formation, decision-making, program planning, personnel administration, budget-making, allocation of funds; a spontaneous working together, a seeking for help on the part of the administrators, and an uninhibited experience of many good minds in the job of running the library.[28]

The concepts thus expressed by Winslow were to be heard very often in the next two decades, but apparently not often enough, because the Public Library Inquiry noted in 1952 that "about 50 percent of the professional assistants [in public libraries] believe that the staff is given too little opportunity for participation in policy determination in their libraries";[29] like comments continued to be heard with increasing frequency in subsequent years.

The years 1925–65 also saw a rapid growth of interest in salary administration in libraries. The ALA had created its first Committee on Salaries in 1922, and two years later it published an intensive report comparing the salaries of librarians with those of teachers.[30] Concern within the association for salaries and benefits continued into the next decade with the appointment in 1937 of a Committee on Salaries, Staff, and Tenure, which later became the Board on Personnel Administration. This group was charged with promoting in all kinds of libraries efficient personnel administration, including such matters as classification and pay plans, staff welfare and tenure, and problems of civil service and merit systems. In 1951 the association published its influential *Position Classification and Salary Administration in Libraries* and in the following year its *Personnel Organization Procedures*.[31] This work is now carried on by the Library Administration Division's Personnel Administration Section.

During the depression years staff unease regarding benefits such as salaries, hours, and fringe programs led to the second of three periods of unionization in libraries in the United States; an average of one new library union came into being per year between 1934 and 1949. The first was an organization of library workers in Butte, Montana, which convened solely for purposes of raising public consciousness in opposition to a plan to close the public library for lack of funds. (It succeeded in keeping the library open and promptly disbanded). There were a number of short-lived and ineffectual union efforts including an attempt in New York between 1934 and 1936 to organize all library employees in the nation, an abortive organization in Grand Rapids in 1937, and a similar failure in Detroit in 1941. Library unions in Cleveland and Detroit were established primarily to benefit support staff; they continued in existence into the 1970s.

Three or four of the library unions established during this second era of U.S. library unionization, however, succeeded in eliciting improvements of a sort for professional staff members. A group of employees at the Chicago Public Library, including a number of librarians, organized in 1937 "to extend and improve library service for the people of Chicago by working with labor, professional, and citizens groups for adequate library income and higher professional standards."[32] This organization successfully supported library appropriations, especially during the 1940s, although it languished somewhat in later periods.[33] Still another union effort took place in the New York Public Library beginning in 1940. Organized by the professional staff, it claimed in 1941 that 83 percent of its membership was from the professional roster. This union's purpose was to improve salaries, and it enjoyed some initial successes. However, in the late 1940s internal dissension disrupted its activities. In 1945 a professional staff union was established in the Minneapolis Public Library. This union enjoyed essentially cordial relations with the library administration over the next three decades; although it never negotiated a contract, it was active in its concern for such matters as wages, the work week, and overtime. Thereafter, there was little union activity in U.S. libraries until the mid-1960s.

Although library education in the half century since 1925 has been primarily one of evolution and consolidation, the first decade of the period witnessed a number of rapid innovations and changes. ALA's new Board of Education for Librarianship, armed with several million dollars granted by the Carnegie Corporation, set out vigorously to implement the sweeping new program for improving professional preparation of librarians delineated by the Williamson report.

In 1926 the board was instrumental in the merging of Dewey's old Albany Library School and the training program of the New York Public Library to form Columbia University's present School of Library Service. It established the nation's first library school for blacks at Hampton Institute in 1925 and was influential in founding the School of Library Science at the University of North Carolina in 1931. For these and other library schools it negotiated grants of $25,000 per year for ten years to enable them to upgrade their programs.

One of the key developments in library education in this period, also due in part to the work of the board, was the establishment of the Graduate Library School at the University of Chicago. The stated purpose of this effort was to bring the professional education of libraries to a new level of quality and profundity commensurate with that of lawyers and doctors. The GLS populated its new faculty with established and productive scholars and teachers from a number of disciplines; it encouraged research and investigation of a higher order of rigor than had prevailed previously; it initiated the first scholarly journal in the field, *Library Quarterly*, in 1930; and it strove to bring exacting standards into teaching through the encouragement of sound textbooks in the field. Understandably the GLS attracted a large number of bright young scholar-librarians to its student ranks and was soon a recognized fountainhead of library administrators and educators who had considerable influence on the development of the profession.

The Board of Education for Librarianship did more. It sought and obtained funds for scholarships in the library schools. It aided in the provision of postgraduate training in librarianship not only at Chicago but also at Columbia University and at the universities of Michigan, Illinois, and California. It sought and gained standardization in admission requirements, curricular programs, and degree recognition. It was a strong board, and its actions largely determined the direction of library education during this important decade.

Some felt that the board was too strong, and its activities evoked considerable adverse comments from the library community. A principal criticism was its rigid adherence to Williamson's concept that only university-based library schools should be accredited and receive grants for program support. The vigor of this criticism, coupled with the completion in 1935 of the Carnegie Corporation's program of massive funding of library education, somewhat diminished the power of the board thereafter. In retrospect, it appears that few of the many important improvements in library education that occurred during this crucial decade would have resulted had it not been for the vision and strength of the Board of Education for Librarianship.

In more recent times the primary work of the board has centered upon the accreditation of library schools. In its initial study of the nation's library schools in 1926 it found fourteen schools that merited accreditation. By 1940 there were thirty, and by the middle of the 1970s the number had risen to more than sixty. The general tendency in library education throughout the half century was concentrated less on the techniques of library practice and more on the theory and principle in order to develop a body of empirical scholarship upon which the profession could improve its social usefulness.

In later decades the Board of Education continued to attempt to fulfill its responsibilities and it continued as well to receive substantial criticism. It was frequently castigated for such things as alleged inflexibility, failure to effect adequate training regimens for special librarians, and inability to stem the proliferation of training programs for school librarians. Despite its problems and the many criticisms lodged against it, the board—and since 1955 its successor, the Committee on Accreditation—has striven to exert quality control over the schools where most practicing librarians have taken their degrees, and librarians have benefited greatly from the effort.[34]

In the period since 1950 the U.S. library industry has received massive federal attention, which also benefited individual librarians. Federal involvement affected the welfare of librarians in the following three ways: (1) thousands of new positions were created; (2) high standards of qualifications and service were required; and (3) a large number of training grants and fellowships were established.

Standards for library personnel were first encouraged by the Public Library Service Demonstration Bill of 1949; although it failed to pass the House of Representatives, it nonetheless attracted attention to the need. The main objective of the bill was to provide funding for demonstration libraries in rural areas, for studying the values and methods of public library service, and for training programs to provide adequate personnel for employment in the demonstration projects. The bill's side effects proved beneficial in three important ways. First, it drew attention to the need for state planning agencies to promote quality library service at the local level. Second, the State and National Planning Committee of ALA's Library Extension Division was placed in a position of putting "plans" into practice for service and personnel standards for rural libraries. And third, the library profession as a whole was forced to think seriously of the functions of the state library agency as a direct service institution and of its possible role in the determination of standards for rural library services.[35]

Seven years later the Library Services Act of 1956 embraced and extended all of the provisions of the earlier unsuccessful bill, including those related to the qualifications of personnel. The 1956 act made funds available, nominally to improve library service in rural areas, but which could be used for salaries to attract and maintain competent personnel and for scholarships for library training. Almost 500 library positions were created during the first two years of the program, and seventeen states conducted in-service training projects, including workshops and conferences; institutes for graduate librarians, library administrators, and library assistants; conferences for trustees; and scholarships for graduate study.[36]

The National Defense Education Act of 1958 was the next major federal legislation to benefit librarians, although that benefit had to wait for fulfillment until the act was amended in 1964 to create Public Law 88–665. In this amendment training institutes were authorized under Title XI to improve the qualifications of library personnel in elementary or secondary schools.[37] The 1964 amendment of Title II established loans through colleges and universities for students in any subject field, including librarianship, of up to $1,000 annually for five years. Title IV moreover authorized fellowships for graduate training of college- and university-level teachers, again including the field of librarianship. The content and design of the institutes mounted under

Public Law 88–665 varied, but most had common features, such as special lectures and consultants, a program of information activities, advisory and counseling services, displays of materials and demonstrations of the use of newer media, and some field trips. For the first time in the history of federal legislation, the NDEA Amendments of 1964 provided specific funds designated for training school library personnel, and extensive use was made of the opportunity by the profession between 1965 and 1967.

RAPID CHANGES SINCE 1965

The year 1965 was a high-water mark for library legislation and saw passage of the Elementary and Secondary Education Act, the Higher Education Act, and the Medical Library Assistance Act, all of which had great significance for individual librarians. Funded in September of that year, the ESEA provided monies to the fifty states to improve library service to meet the instructional needs of children and teachers. Title I of the act was all encompassing and, among other things, made funds available for improving the qualifications of school library personnel. Title II provided direct federal assistance through state plans to enhance services in school libraries.[37]

The Higher Education Act devoted substantial attention to library education in Title II–B. This title authorized the granting of $15 million annually for the next three years to library schools for the training of persons engaged in or about to engage in the practice of librarianship. Funds could be used for regular sessions, short-term programs, or institutes, with stipends and allowances for travel, subsistence, and other expenses. A separate section of the title permitted funds to be used also for the improvement of library training. Although full funding for this act was never forthcoming, it nonetheless provided the largest base of financial support for library training ever attempted, and many librarians profited from it.[39] Among the provisions of the far-ranging Medical Library Assistance Act was a five-year program to train medical librarians at an authorization level of $1 million annually. A number of training grants were administered under this program for purposes of increasing the number of highly skilled individuals in the health information specialties.

Insofar as personnel management in U.S. libraries is concerned, the late 1960s and 1970s was a period of swift change. Staff unease and new theories concerning individuals in work groups combined to generate an array of personnel activities which could hardly have been anticipated a few years earlier. Renewed and more assertive interest in staff participation, redoubled concern for professional growth, rising staff dissatisfaction with salaries and benefits, attention to inequities in minority representation, and a host of other similar concerns required greatly enlarged personnel offices in libraries and much more extensive programs of personnel affairs than had been known formerly. Changes occurred quickly, for the most part resulting in improvements in the professional working environment of librarians, changes which, as in the early 1920s, it may take the library community some years to assimilate fully.

Following 1965 staff impatience with the rate of change in the personnel policies and practices in some libraries precipitated the third and most vigorous period of library unionization in the nation's history. In 1966 a majority of the librarians in the Brooklyn Public Library voted for unionization, and the resulting organization has successfully sought such goals as dues check-off and a grievance procedure. By the end of the 1960s unions claimed to have organized at least half of the professional staffs of the public libraries of New York, Los Angeles City and County, Detroit, San Francisco, Youngstown, and as mentioned earlier, Minneapolis. There were also unions with librarians as members at the City University of New York, the University of Pennsylvania, and the University of California at Berkeley. For the most part these newer unions have sought not only improvement in economic benefits but also a voice in library policy formulation.[40] An undeterminable number of librarians have also joined unions not specifically for libraries.

Five general observations can be made about the most recent period of union activity in libraries.

1. A very small percentage of the library profession has availed itself of this route to greater fulfillment.
2. More library unions have been established in large cities than elsewhere.
3. More unions have been established in large libraries than in small or medium-sized libraries.
4. Most unionization efforts in libraries have occurred along the East Coast, in the Midwest, and in California.
5. Improvement in economic conditions has been the most frequently noted goal of union efforts.

Some unions have been formally recognized, and some have not. Militancy rose during the period. Although there had been no library job actions of record before 1968, a number took place soon thereafter, such as at Syracuse University and the University of Chicago.

SUMMARY

In summary, over the past century there has been a continuing increase in activities and programs which have benefited librarians. The sources of these activities and programs have been quite diverse, including among others the federal government, library administrators, and librarians themselves. It is obviously not possible to quantify the respective contributions of these several sources to the welfare and well-being of librarians or to adjudge the quality of those contributions. A fairly wide range of activities, beginning at an early date, may be attributed to library administrators. In the last sixty years unionization has improved salaries and working conditions for a few librarians. And in the last half century the federal government has benefited librarians through its programs of personnel classification and education for librarianship.

Only the union programs, however, have been established specifically to serve the librarian. All of the others have been established first and foremost to benefit others, with the benefit to librarians resulting as a by-product. The ALA's programs have been intended primarily "to promote the library interests of the country." Programs initiated by administrators appear by inference to have been intended primarily to benefit their individual libraries' constituencies. Federal programs have been intended primarily to serve the commonweal. Although these programs have served the purpose for which they were originally established, librarians have also gained from them.

NOTES

1. "The Constitution of the American Library Association," *American Library Journal* 1:32 (Mar. 31, 1877).
2. "Proceedings [of the First ALA Conference]," *American Library Journal* 1:92–145 (Nov. 30, 1876).
3. Lloyd P. Smith, "The Qualifications of a Librarian," *American Library Journal* 1:71 (Nov. 30, 1876).
4. U.S. Bureau of Education, *Public Libraries in the United States of America* (Washington, D.C.: Govt. Print. Off., 1876), pp. 488–89.
5. Mary Wright Plummer, "Training for Librarianship," *Library Journal* 26:317 (June 1901).
6. This and much of the subsequent story of ALA's role in the early development of library education are related in full in Sarah K. Vann's *Training for Librarianship before 1923* (Chicago: American Library Assn., 1961), passim.
7. "[ALA] Proceedings, 1886," *Library Journal* 11:376 (Aug.–Sept. 1886).
8. Frederick M. Crunden, "Business Methods in Library Management," *Library Journal* 12:335–38 (Sept.–Oct. 1887).
9. C. C. Soule, "The Boston Public Library," *Library Journal* 17:54–55 (Feb. 1892); ibid. 17:88–94 (Mar. 1892); ibid. 17:124–25 (Apr. 1892).
10. Frank P. Hill, "Organization and Management of a Library Staff," *Library Journal* 22:381–83 (Aug. 1897).
11. Arthur Bostwick, "Two Tendencies of American Library Work," *Library Journal* 36:275–78 (June 1911).
12. This information and the analysis of the library administration literature here and in the next paragraph are developed more fully in Ruth Jackson, "Origin and Development of Selected Personnel Management Functions in the Field of American Librarianship, 1876–1969" (Ph.D. dissertation, Indiana University, 1976).
13. C. C. Williamson, *Training for Library Service* (New York: [The Carnegie Corporation] 1923).
14. See George F. Bowerman, "Librarian's Salaries in the District of Columbia," *Library Journal* 45:63–66 (Jan. 15, 1920), and his "Washington Library

Reclassification Substitute," ibid. pp. 687–90 (Sept. 1, 1920); and Miles O. Price, "Victory for Reclassification," ibid. 49:735–36 (Aug. 15, 1924), and his "Reclassification of Librarians in the District of Columbia," *ALA Bulletin* 18:200–202 (Aug. 1924).

15. Theodore L. Guyton, *Unionization: The Viewpoint of Librarians* (Chicago: American Library Assn., 1975), p. 16.

16. C. A. S. Fazakas, "Library Employees' Union," *Library World* 21:179 (1919).

17. G. F. Bowerman, "Unionism and the Library Profession," *Library Journal* 44:364–66 (June 1919).

18. Guyton, p. 16.

19. "On the Other Side," *ALA Bulletin* 40:76–81 (Sept. 15, 1946).

20. Ralph R. Shaw, "Scientific Management in Libraries," *Library Trends* 2:359 (Jan. 1954).

21. L. Quincy Mumford, "Administration," *ALA Bulletin* 36:705–10 (Oct. 10, 1942). This development is discussed fully in Arthur T. Kittle, "Management Theories in Public Library Administration in the United States, 1925–1955" (D.L.S. dissertation, Columbia University, 1961), passim.

22. Robert D. Leigh, *The Public Library in the United States* (New York: Columbia Univ. Pr., 1950), p. 235.

23. Ralph E. McCoy, *Personnel Administration for Libraries: A Bibliographic Essay* (Chicago: American Library Assn., 1953), pp. 75–89.

24. J. Periam Danton, "Our Libraries: The Trend Toward Democracy," *Library Quarterly* 4:16–27 (Jan. 1934).

25. Herbert Goldhor, "Democracy and the Library," *Wilson Library Bulletin* 15:30–31, 33 (Sept. 1940).

26. Archibald MacLeish, "The Librarian Discusses LC Employee Relations," *Library of Congress Staff Information Bulletin* 3:3, 6 (May 24, 1943).

27. Arthur McAnally, "Coordinating the Departmental Library System," *Library Quarterly* 21:113–19 (Apr. 1951).

28. Amy Winslow, "Staff Participation in Management," *Wilson Library Bulletin* 27:624–28 (Apr. 1953).

29. Alice I. Bryan, *The Public Librarian* (New York: Columbia Univ. Pr., 1952), p. 276.

30. Mary Kobetich, "School and Library Statistics," *ALA Bulletin* 18:59–74 (Mar. 1924).

31. American Library Association, Board on Personnel Administration, *Position Classification and Salary Administration in Libraries* (Chicago: American Library Assn., 1951); American Library Association, Board on Personnel Administration, *Personnel Organization and Procedure* (Chicago: American Library Assn., 1952).

32. John Clopine, *History of Library Unions in the United States* (Washington, D.C.: Catholic Univ. of America Pr., 1951), p. 87.

33. In 1971 it claimed to have organized 15 percent of the CPL professional staff. See Guyton, p. 27.

34. For a thorough study of library education during this period, see Charles D. Churchwell, "Education for Librarianship in the United States: Some Factors Which Influenced Its Development between 1919 and 1939" (Ph.D. dissertation, University of Illinois, 1966). See also Louis R. Wilson, "Historical Development of Education for Librarianship in the United States," in Bernard Berelson, ed., *Education for Librarianship* (Chicago: American Library Assn., 1949) pp. 44–59.

35. Loleta D. Fyan, "Some Standards for Library Demonstrations," *ALA Bulletin* 44:111–12 (Apr. 1950), and Marion L. Moshier, "Larger Units of Service: Training Needs," ibid 44:209–10 (June 1950).

36. John G. Lorenz, "Progress and Projects under the Library Services Act," *Wilson Library Bulletin* 33:635–37 (May 1959); Paxton P. Price, "In-Service Training Program," ibid., pp. 678–79.

37. Cora Bomar, "The NDEA Breakthrough: Public Law 88–665," *School Libraries* 14:10–22 (Jan. 1965).
38. New York University, *Planning Guide for ESEA Title II* (Albany, N.Y.: [The University] 1967–68).
39. Germaine Krettek and Eileen D. Cooke, "Federal Legislation," *Bowker Annual 1966* (New York: Bowker, 1966), pp. 142–50.
40. For details of many library union activities, see Melvin S. Goldstein, *Collective Bargaining in the Field of Librarianship* (Brooklyn: Pratt Institute, 1969), pp. 30–103.

8

Women in Librarianship

DEE GARRISON
Rutgers University

> The A-L-Adies sailed one day,
> To voyage up the Saguenay,
> Gay and grim, stout and slim,
> Twenty-five hers to every him.
>
> *Library Journal*, August 1912

In 1896 the influential Mary Ahern, editor of *Public Libraries*, warbled her conviction that "no woman can hope to reach any standing . . . in the library profession . . . who does not bring to it that love which suffereth long and is kind, is not puffed up, does not behave itself unseemly, vaunteth not itself, thinketh no evil . . . ."[1] Eight years later, librarian Frances Hawley held firmly to the tradition of female self-abnegation: "at the very top there is no room for us. . . . ambition must mean more to us than a desire for good pay and perhaps a little honor and authority. . . . it must mean that there will not be a single working day in all our lives when we will not see or hear something that will make for the betterment of our library."[2] The influx of such feminine altruists as these into library work before 1900 assured the successful growth of the early library movement and gave the library profession a stirring heritage of humanitarian service. The feminization of library work, however, had unexpected, long-range results. The prevalence of women in the library worked to stunt the process of professionalization, served to maintain the low status accorded to women in matters of the intellect, and helped to perpetuate the public library's marginal position as a cultural institution.

Since women first flooded into the library world in the last decades of the nineteenth century, forming 75 percent of the profession by 1910, there has been no time when the status of women librarians has been even roughly equal to that of their male colleagues. The woman librarian has consistently earned less than the male librarian, regardless of her amount of general or professional education or of the type of library in which she worked. There is evidence, too, that the salary differentials between men and women widen as the woman gains in experience. Even in federal employment, women librarians are paid less than men. Female library graduates of the 1970s can expect to begin library work at a lower salary than male graduates with identical professional training and experience. Additionally, it is clear that women as a group are systematically excluded from top-level administrative positions in all types of libraries. Women are also apparently the victims of an overall trend, beginning as early as the 1950s, to replace women with men as directors of state libraries and state library agencies and on library school faculties, positions in which women have traditionally held power more commensurate with their numbers. The evidence is overwhelming, then, that in library work, which women have historically dominated in number, sexual discrimination affecting salary and promotion has been consistent, blatant and, until recently, relatively unquestioned.[3]

An understanding of the history of women in librarianship properly rests upon a knowledge of the patterns set in the last decades of the nineteenth century. In common with the founders of other service professions for women, the early women librarians are best understood as proponents of that sexual ideology with strong antifeminist implications which dominated the thought of the great majority of middle-class Americans at the turn of the century. This ideal gave women a separate nurturing temperament which was complementary to that of the male and defined women as biologically superior in their capacity for spirituality and fine emotions. The entry of middle-class women into the professions was channeled so as to extend women's service role into the society at large, rather than to release them toward self-justifying intellectual and economic activity. Librarianship was quickly adjusted to fit the narrowly circumscribed sphere of women's work, for it appeared similar to the work of the home, functioned as cultural activity, was philanthropic in nature, required no great skill or physical strength and brought little contact with the rougher portions of society. The delimitation of women's duties and talents posed no immediate threat to the traditionally male-controlled fields of activity and left men charged with the direction and support of most kinds of intellectual life.

Although recognition of women librarians in the national professional association is high in comparison with other professions, here, too, women have been historically underrepresented in official positions.

Beginning in 1879, when three women presented papers, women have continued to represent an important percentage of participants at the annual conventions, although not in proportion to their domination of attendance or their overall strength in the profession. Significantly, women were early handed major responsibility for the topics which pertained to reading for children or standards for judging immoral literature. Since 1880 women have been regularly elected to the ALA Council, and through the 1890s they tended to compose about one-fifth of the Council members. However, it is important to note that in the nineteenth century it was a few favored women who were repeatedly elected to official posts. For example, between 1880 and 1900, while 54 contests seated women on the Council, only 13 individuals served there. Feminine representation on the Council rose to about 30 percent by 1920 and remained there until World War II, when the share rose dramatically. In 1945 women held about 70 percent of the Council positions. After a decrease in the late 1950s, the percentage of women Council members has hovered around 70.

The first woman vice-president of ALA was elected in 1893, Caroline Hewins, who in 1877 had been the first woman to speak publicly at an ALA convention. In 1911 Theresa West Elmendorf became the first woman president, "following a precedent already set by the National Education Association."[4] Women have held the presidential power in ALA two times per decade between 1911 and 1939 and three times per decade since 1940. Because, as Melvil Dewey pointed out, "the secretary is the mate of all work"[5] and the prime executive officer, no woman has yet served as executive secretary, except for one joint appointment in 1890-91.

A heavy demand for trained librarians in the last decades of the nineteenth century was an important cause of the feminization of librarianship. The rapid growth of libraries coincided with other national developments like the advance of women's education and the increase of women workers; women probably would have moved into any new field into which their entry was not opposed. Because male librarians heartily welcomed women into library service, primarily because of the low cost of hiring competent women, the feminization of the library staff proceeded rapidly. Justin Winsor told British librarians in 1877 that educated young women, able to comprehend Latin, Greek, French, German, Spanish, and Italian, were eagerly accepting library jobs and "for the money they cost . . . they are infinitely better than equivalent salaries will produce of the other sex."[6] The same economic factors were at work at this time in librarianship and teaching, for educated women, with few other job opportunities open to them, flocked into both fields with a depressing effect on wages.

In the post–Civil War years, the feminine movement into service professions and clerical and industrial employment led to the formation of charming theories, developed by both sexes, to explain why the feminine mind and nature were innately suited to the new occupations. Thus it was decided that teaching was much like mothering; women, it was said, were uniquely able to guide children into piety, purity, and knowledge. Women writers were inherently sensitive and blessed with an elevated morality. Women were cleared to work as physicians and nurses because they were intuitively kind and delicate of touch. The woman social worker expressed inborn feminine qualities of sympathy and idealism. Factory and clerical work fit the feminine nature, for women were naturally industrious, sober, and nimble-fingered, as well as better able than men to endure the boredom of detailed or repetitive tasks. Although the gradual expansion of the work of women has eventually served to modify the concept of women's proper sphere, the early phases of the process were on the whole unaccompanied by any feminine calls for radical social change and involved no serious threat to traditional social ideals.

This redefinition of the limits of woman's sphere, always in accord with the characteristics presumed to be innately feminine, also came to include library work as a proper activity for women. Libraries held books; books denoted Culture; the Victorian woman's sphere decidedly included the guardianship and consumption of the national culture. It would be almost impossible to over-emphasize the popular nineteenth-century conviction that women, through their refining and spiritualizing influence, could exalt all human society, tame and soften the materialistically inclined male, and preserve humanistic ideals. Moreover, by the 1870s American literature was consciously designed to please feminine readers. The woman librarian, as a priestess dispensing books like sacraments, could shape the library into "an all-pervading force . . . moulding public opinion, educating to all of the higher possibilities of human thought and action; to become a means for enriching, beautifying, and making fruitful the barren places in human life. . . ."[7] Women in librarianship were merely making more visible the female destiny.

Like the concept of "culture," the provision of education and moral uplift to the masses, a prominent mission of the early library, was also believed to be a suitable female concern. Library literature before 1910 abounds with injunctions to the librarian to guide carefully, though subtly, the reading of her uneducated clients, away from light fiction and toward factual information or the approved and tested classical literature of the past. The popular library brought the librarian "in hourly contact with her constituency of readers, advising, helping, and elevating their lives and exerting a far-reaching influence for good not to be exceeded in any profession open to women. . . ."[8] Because "a library is a source of help and light and sweetness,"[9] the chief requisite of the woman librarian was that she "be earnestly altruistic, of great, big heart and tender sympathies, a woman of character, of steadfast purpose and faith," with "unflinching fidelity" to a low estate.[10] "Library work, on account of its philanthropic aspect, as well as its literary character, appeals more strongly to American women than almost any other vocation,"[11] said Hannah James in 1898.

Nineteenth-century woman's sphere was, above all, the home, for which she was biologically intended and which she was so exactly fitted to adorn and bless. Thus, as women became dominant in library work, it seemed natural that in the ideal library the reader should be treated like a visitor to the home, should be given a cheery greeting, and met with kind and gracious attention. The librarian stood "always ready to serve," to "anticipate wants," to do "the honors of a library as a hostess."[12] The reading room could be made inviting by "a bright carpet on the floor, . . . low tables, and a few rocking-chairs scattered about; a cheerful, open fire on dull days, attractive pictures on the walls, and one can imagine a lady librarian filling the windows with plants."[13]

Of course the comparison of the library to the home was one of several devices used to entice the reluctant patrons into the library but it was also a result of the presence of women librarians whose feminity prevailed in the ordered quietness of parlor-like rooms. So too had the schoolroom been redesigned and likened to the home, in order to make more acceptable the dominance of women teachers. And as women entered the new profession of social work, the same impulse drove them to center their work in the settlement-house domicile—a homey haven of beauty and order amidst the slums. The lady librarians in the United States and Canada were praised because of their ability to "make the library a bright and beautiful home."[14] The position of the public librarian came to require a certain "gracious hospitality" and here "women as a class far surpass men." Nor would women workers resent playing in the library the part they played in the home. "Here it is said her 'broad sympathies, her quick wits, her intuitions and her delight in self-sacrifice' give her an undoubted advantage."[15]

Women workers also excelled, it was generally believed, in the performance of the tedious routine tasks of the library. Again, women were inherently qualified for this work because of their "greater conscientiousness, patience, and accuracy in details."[16] Women had unique, inborn abilities to bear the most monotonous tasks without boredom. They were preferred for "the inner work of the library, the application to routine of . . . qualities, especially those of patience, of enthusiasm and of loyalty—which have served to confine to women that vast mass of detail incidental to the organization of rapidly growing collections. . . ."[17]

Not surprisingly, women librarians placed an early emphasis upon library service for children; before 1900 the children's library had moved into its current position as a major department of the public library. Work with children was "the most important" of all library work, reported Minerva Sanders.[18] Mary Plummer agreed that there was "no more delicate, critical work than that with children, no work that pays so well in immediate as well as in far-off results . . . to modify the adult constituency of the future."[19] Woman alone had that "kind of sympathetic second-sight that shall enable her to read what is often obscure in the mind of the child."[20] The air of romantic tenderness which pervades any discussion of children in the library literature of this period is in sharp contrast to the searching self-criticism which librarians gave to other areas of library work. In the children's section of the library, created and staffed by women, female librarians were free, as in no other area, to express, unchallenged, their self-image. Because their activities blended so thoroughly into the Victorian stereotype of the female, their endeavors remained substantially unexamined by male library leaders.

The particular twist given to the child-saving rhetoric in the early public library movement can be best understood not only as an extension of women's traditional homemaking role into the community but also as an imposition of middle-class morality upon the newly literate masses. In its earliest development, the public library movement was in large part motivated by the desire of a declining social elite to retain some of its power and prestige. As immigration and rural migration swelled the population of the urban slums, the older middle class, characterized by that commitment to hierarchial authority and the romantic idolization of women which is the essence of the genteel culture, felt their ideals to be gravely threatened by the strange new urban and industrial social system. The old New England elite, men and women of education—the class which had once held the respect of a simpler, more deferential society—seemed almost to be aliens in their own familiar land. Business control, political bosses, and mindless materialism were the enemies on the right; wild-eyed radicals and the easily deceived and ignorant masses threatened on the left. Those who stood warily in the middle, the "respectable" educated few, with whom library leaders identified, were caught between what seemed to them the two extremes of U.S. society. Conscious of their real lack of control, they shared the fears of the genteel class and worried about the general breakdown of order and morality. Accordingly, the librarians struggled to uplift the taste, manners, and knowledge of their uncultured patrons. It seemed particularly important, in a time of rising social discontent, that the unquiet laborer understand that in the library persons of culture and learning were eager to assist him in achieving middle-class respectability.

Juvenile literature of a bad sort was seen as a "fingerpoint looking toward change in national character from the conservatism of older days to a restlessness and spirit of adventure, a disregard of the rights of others and the settled relations of life, that are communistic and revolutionary in their tendency."[21] Public libraries, it was hoped, would "tend to refine and elevate the people . . . to make them contented, cheerful and happy . . . to prevent crime by giving a taste for something better than the drinking saloon. Thus they make the whole community more safe and peaceful—they take the place of a police. . . ."[22] Mellen Chamberlain admitted it seemed useless to ask children to be sober moderates or select in choosing their pleasures when all society seemed to be running riot. But "we may hope to change the present aspect of things; and, with this inspiring prospect, that when we have changed the habits of the readers in our public libraries, we shall also have changed the habits of society itself."[23]

Women librarians, like Minerva Sanders at Pawtucket, Rhode Island, who in 1877 was probably the first public librarian to allow children under twelve to use books, responded emotionally to the needs of children, especially to the waifs of the urban poor.

> We may say this [work with children] is the work of charitable institutions and humane societies; not so; this is essentially our work. We call ourselves educators . . . the work of a public library is to teach, to elevate, to enable; there is no limit to its possible influence.[24]

In 1882 Caroline Hewins gave the first formal report to the ALA on the reading of the young. Through the 1880s women slowly evolved the essentials of library work with children—careful censorship of books, separate rooms with small-scale tables and chairs, and a kindly maternal guidance designed to lead the child, unsuspecting, to a predetermined standard of reading.

In the 1890s, as the effects of immigration, social discontent, and economic distress increasingly disturbed the complacency of the native middle class, the crusade directed at children in the library came to encompass much more than just the provision of proper books.[25] In common with many other middle-class women of the time, librarians turned to reform and charitable work with the assurance that their very femininity specially fitted them to the task, for they believed that as women they could make "no compromise with wrong, inquiring only for the truth, always on the right side of questions of liberty, temperance, and equality. . . ."[26] The threat posed by immigration to the "American way of life" was clear. In thirty years, Ada Jones warned in 1892, foreigners and their children would equal one-half of the population, "Christian education . . . to reach the masses, is the power that must secure the future welfare of our beloved land . . . to cultivate their taste for reading; to direct and elevate it, these are the high privileges of the ideal librarian."[27] Library women quickly applied the child-saving methodology popularized by kindergartners and social workers to library work with children.[28] The storytelling technique was widely, almost hysterically, touted in the first decade of the century as an effective method of "Americanizing" the foreigner, improving language, softening voices, teaching punctuality, keeping children off the streets, creating friends for the library, inculcating courtesy, honesty, neatness, industry, obedience, and gentle manners and, rather incidentally, was "the only means by which we can get the children honestly to want the books 'we want them to want.' "[29] Librarians by 1910 worked closely with social workers and charity organizations in the cities, carrying books to playgrounds, reformatories, and branches in settlement houses. From social reformers like Charles W. Birtwell, public librarians borrowed the idea of the home library, a collection of books for about ten children placed in one tenement or neighborhood. The home visitor from the library went about once a week, not merely to exchange books and discuss the reading, but, just as importantly, to exert her divine nurturing upon the children of low parentage and to spread her elevating influence over the home.[30] The early children's librarians were repeatedly reminded that "it is a higher aim to help the boys and girls to be *good* than to be merely wise...." Above all, children would learn from the lady librarian the "higher ideals of manhood and womanhood."[31]

By the turn of the century many public librarians were tiring of their highly unsuccessful attempt to direct the reading habits of their adult patrons. They were disappointed, too, in their inability to attract the working man in the numbers for which they had hoped. Adults, it was generally agreed, were impossibly set in their reading tastes and were, besides, notoriously intolerant of any well-meant efforts to raise their literary standards. Children, on the other hand, could be trained to appreciate the "best" and in the children's room there was little protest from the small clients over library censorship of books. The responsibilities which librarians had claimed as moral guides were channeled by 1900 almost entirely into the care of the minds of underage Americans. Library service for children came to absorb most of the librarian's proclivity to censorship. The children's room was

> the one work of the library where we can see results.... It is almost the only work that gives us real encouragement to go on with the detail, the everlasting round of duty, maintaining the public library and hoping for its influence on humanity. ... We have an axiom that we cannot help an adult very much in his reading; but a child we are certainly forming like clay in the hands of the potter.[32]

What kept the children's librarian laboring "day in and day out with crowds of children trying to see that they put their books back after reading them, that their hands are clean, and that they do not talk," was the knowledge that she must be an agent to counteract the "coarsening effect of promiscuous living in crowded tenements, the narrow range of ideas which life in the city creates and the criminal tendencies...." Yet the librarian, forced to *inhibit* childish activity, could only judge her influence by small outward signs like the improvement in a child's manners or cleanliness. Ethel Underhill, of the Brooklyn

Public Library, related the wonderful way in which parents could be influenced by their children who had come in contact with the gentle librarian. For example, one Rebecca, after reading several books, had begged her mother to buy a tablecloth. Another child had taken home a cookbook, thus giving a distinct raise to the family standard of dining. When "the 'Iliad' and the 'Odyssey' fill the mind of Joe Ginsburg . . . when Esther Lichtenstein . . . reads Dickens and Scott, we know that without their realizing it they are getting ideas of chivalry, courtesy, and courage that are fitting them to be wholesome units of society."[33] Thus, through the child, the elusive adult could be indirectly influenced—a situation which reforming lady librarians, kindergartners, temperance and social workers all recognized at about the same time.

Perhaps the most striking point to be made about women's adaptation to library work is the extent to which they supported the traditional feminine concern for domesticity, altruism, and high-mindedness. Women librarians invoked the Victorian definition of proper female endeavors at the same time as they were widening it.[34] Librarianship, when defined as self-denying and spiritual, offered women the opportunity not to change their status but to affirm it. Women's traditional renunciation of intellectual excellence had a major effect upon the deterioration of the image of librarianship from the ancient scholarly one to the more recent image of an inhibited, little, old lady. When women's advance became justified in terms of the good they could do, rather than of their human right to equality or to intellectual activity, it became conditional in nature.

Even if some women in philanthropic work or in the emerging feminized service professions of the late nineteenth century did not subscribe to the concept of woman's sphere, with all its connotations, they had to appear to do so if they were not to run the fearful risk of being deviants in their society, of being judged abnormal because of a challenge to well-established norms. Even today, the instrumentally active and intellectually aggressive woman is commonly suspected as someone showing signs of neurotic disturbance. Critical male commentators who have studied the dominance of women in the conservative reform efforts of the late nineteenth century have generally failed to acknowledge the supreme courage which would have been required of any deviant group of women who sought emancipation from sexual role playing and thereby suffered the loss of economic security and societal isolation and ridicule.[35] Instead, the great majority of newly restless, educated women spent their energies and talent in extending their roles as housekeepers into the society at large, championing the causes of culture, home, the poor, and children. Their activity had the added advantage of not being seen as competition for jobs which men were believed to have the right to perform. Altruistic work filled the void in their lives created by increased leisure and rising aspirations. It is not surprising that they, like males, served their class interests by attempting to impose their value system upon the immigrants and their children. They defended the sanctity of the family, Protestant nativism, parental discipline, and their nurturant, expressive functions, for these were the ideals which had traditionally given meaning to their lives.

The feminization of librarianship also had a major effect upon the professionalization process. Librarians have been absorbed to a marked degree with the question of professionalization but throughout the debate the influence of women on librarianship has been strangely shunted, buried under a multitude of words concerning recruitment, accreditation, curriculums, and other factors thought to be inhibiting professionalization. Yet the feminization of library work is surely the underlying factor in library education, the image of librarianship, and the professionalization of the field.

Although the service and collectivity orientation of librarianship exhibits most of the qualities expected in the ethical code of a profession, significant elements of a truly professional code of service are missing.[36] Specifically lacking in the librarian's professional service code are a sense of institutional autonomy, a drive to lead rather than to serve other institutions in an ancillary role, and a clear-cut conception of professional rights and responsibilities. The feminization of library work is a direct cause of these deficiencies. Women librarians felt a strong obligation to meet the needs of the public and were self-consciously sensitive to requests and complaints of the client. This passive, inoffensive, nonassertive, and unprofessional "service" provided by the librarian is also a natural acting-out of the docile behavioral roles which females assumed in the culture. Nineteenth-century complaints of high employee turnover and of low commitment to excellence are directly related to the place which women accepted in society. A high commitment to work would have required autonomous values, but the majority of librarians were eager to marry and leave library work.

The prevalence of women librarians also served to strengthen a nonprofessional bureaucratic system of control and low-autonomy base for the library worker. In librarianship, as in teaching and social work, the dominance of women made more likely the development of an authoritative administrative structure with a stress on rules and generally established principles to control the activities of employees. Within feminized occupations the compliance to sex roles led women to assume and expect low levels of autonomy.

By 1900 library work in the United States had become so identified with women that it was generally considered to be a feminine vocation. The great majority of women workers were employed as library assistants. In library literature, between 1900 and 1920, there is constant evidence of the dissatisfaction of head librarians with their staffs. References to assistants are singularly carping in nature; there is frequent mention of the staff's distressing lack of intelligence, accuracy, efficiency, motivation, and amiability. Assistants in turn, in their rare appearances in print, seem to be equally resentful of their low prestige, inadequate salary, and monotonous work. This growing tension in the library field is an important indication of the changing status of women's position in the working world. In the late nineteenth century the limited jobs open to middle-class women, as well as the societal prejudices which caused them to shrink from work in the competitive business world, had served, at first, to bring many competent and educated women into library work. As the new century began, however, and as job opportunities for middle-class women expanded, especially in clerical and sales jobs, it became more and more difficult to attract women with the desired intellectual qualities and professional spirit who would accept the meager pay of a library worker.

The desk assistant in the first decades of the century worked on an average 42 to 50 hours a week for a salary of $25 to $40 a month. She was on duty from one to three evenings a week, often on Sundays. It was "practically absurd," said an anonymous assistant in 1902, for the librarian to lay so much stress "upon the 'spirit of the work' which he feels should be so ardent and zealous as to rise above all considerations of salaries and hours, and to make the assistant feel that sufficient for her work is the joy of doing it."[37] A survey taken in 1917 of the women graduates of eight women's colleges and Cornell revealed that even the traditionally low-paid teacher had moved far ahead of the librarian in salary scale and that those graduates who had entered business or social work were better rewarded than teachers.[38] Slowly, then, the quality of library workers receded as living wages became available to educated, middle-class women in other fields. The head librarian was increasingly forced to recruit women assistants with inadequate preliminary education, many of whom were very young, intellectually unsuited to library work, or entering on a purely temporary basis.

But even the educated woman librarian was a source of concern to some library leaders. Speaking to the graduating class of women at Simmons College in 1912, Herbert Putnam frankly acknowledged the discrimination which they would face in professional life. Women would suffer in the library world, he said, because they lacked "the superior traits of men"—specifically, "manliness," and "a sense of proportion." Fortunately women could develop these traits, Putnam believed. The most debilitating of women's faults, Putnam said, was the tendency to "peevishness," to ascribe sinister personal motives to official actions which affected them unfavorably. Moreover women were hampered in business and the professions because they too often became absorbed in small details and lacked initiative. Still, women's special talents—devotion, loyalty, and a disposition to regard the "personal and domestic virtues as of the utmost concern"—were also needed in the working world. And whereas these latter traits "do not lead to promotion, they at least assure preference in the positions which are subordinate," Putnam noted with wholly unconscious irony.[39]

Not until the changes wrought by World War I did the question of low salaries become a really vital topic of discussion among library leaders. For so long as there were sufficient numbers of young women eager to work for any amount, however small, there was little incentive to rectify the salary situation. Although some librarians, male and female, occasionally commented that women were partly to blame for the low pay, because they "systematically put a low value on . . . [their] own services,"[40] more common was rhetoric designed to raise the performance of assistants by a revival of the idealistic altruism which had once so motivated the service of the library women of the nineteenth century. Once again library workers were assured that they were peculiarly fitted by biology for sacrificial devotion to librarianship, regardless of personal discomforts or material needs. The assistant who could maintain belief in the value of library missionary work was "well on the road toward the real compensation . . . which can never be measured by salary scales. She knows something of that satisfaction which comes of being needed and used. . . ."[41]

Because so much of the assistant's work was strictly routine monotony, a constant effort was necessary to incite enthusiasm for the work. Arthur Bostwick claimed that catalog filing, pasting labels, and addressing post-cards had high professional implications: "A label pasted awry may ruin the library's reputation . . .; a mis-sent card may cause trouble to dozens of one's fellow-assistants. Routine work is dull only when one does not understand its purport."[42] The vice-director of Pratt Institute Library School told her students:

> We won't keep doing monotonous things over and over in a mechanical way because we will find some way to make them interesting and to get benefit or pleasure from them. If mending books be your task you will gain expertness, find out new and better ways of saving the lives of the books and at the same time increase your . . . familiarity with authors and titles, and, by seeing what books are the most worn, you can get an impression of the popularity of certain authors and certain subjects.[43]

In 1916 Putnam again speaking of the special talent of women for detailed, repetitive work, asserted that women librarians are "not merely supplementary to . . . men; they are absolutely complementary . . . the lack in men of the qualities characteristic of women, can never be made good except through the auxiliary co-operation of women themselves."[44] Apparently his chiefly female audience, representative of almost 88 percent of the profession, saw little incongruity in their "auxiliary" relationship to the other 12 percent.

Dissatisfaction with the position of women in the American library did surface briefly in 1919 in a resolution presented at the annual meeting of the ALA by the fledgling Library Employees Union of Greater New York, affiliated with the American Federation of Labor. Defended

158 / Personnel

by Maude Malone, an assistant for nine years who shunned ALA membership, it read, in part:

> WHEREAS, The present low and inadequate salaries paid to librarians . . . are due solely to the fact that all of the rank and file in the work are women, and . . . all the highest salaried positions are given to men by the board of trustees, and . . . the present policy of library boards is to remove women from all positions of responsibility . . . and replace them with men only, and . . . .This discrimination is based on sex . . . therefore BE IT RESOLVED, That we are against this system . . . and are in favor of throwing open all positions in library work . . . to men and women equally, and for equal pay.[45]

The outcome of this abortive attempt to arouse female fury and to unionize library employees was no doubt affected by the startling radicalism of Malone, whose sympathies and origins were too obviously working class and who was openly contemptuous of the "caste" of library leaders who, she said, felt "we are professionals, we will educate the great outside body of the people who are not as good as we are."[46] The resolution was defeated by an audience composed of four-fifths women and by a vote of 121 to 1. Alice Tyler hastened to assure "the men members of the Association . . . that the women understand [that] the men have no thought of crowding women out of the profession."[47]

Nevertheless women librarians were voting with their feet, so to speak, for when World War I began there was a startling general exodus from libraries all over the country as women moved into war work or into positions left vacant by men. The resignations did not stop with the armistice, much to the surprise of many library leaders. Margery Doud, speaking at the ALA Conference of 1920, stated her belief that educated women were leaving the library not simply for better salaries but for more challenging jobs which were not so bound by strict supervision and rigid routine. As a "friendly critic" she warned head librarians not to "wait too long to provide measures of self-expression for your supposedly inarticulate assistants. Conditions of today are forcing self-expression . . . with the lucrative as well as interesting positions open to librarians in other fields, even the meekest assistant has reached an alarming state of independence."[48] Much attention was paid to an article by Clara Herbert which told of her distressing experience in recruiting a training class in 1919. Anticipating a surge of women freed from government war work bureaus, she made ready to select 15 candidates from a group of 500 interested inquirers. Out of the 249 who took away the application, 12 filed, 8 took the examination, and 1 lone woman qualified. Herbert reported that her interview experience had made her feel like "an unscrupulous employer of child labor being grilled by a social service investigator . . . there was a new note of distrust of the value of the work . . . . If the library could pay only $55 a month . . . then [it seemed] the work must be of a simple mechanical character requiring small attainments."[49]

Despite the persistence of the popular myth that the 1920s represented a period of unparalleled economic emancipation for women, in fact the proportion of women who held jobs increased by only 1 percent between 1920 and 1929. Between the wars the proportion of all women who held jobs remained almost constant, barely rising from 23.3 percent in 1920 to 25.7 percent in 1940. In this period the vast majority of American working women continued to toil at menial jobs with inadequate pay; as late as 1930 over 57 percent of all employed women were either blacks or recent immigrants, primarily working as domestic servants or as field and factory workers. Professional women were almost entirely limited to the fields traditionally set aside for women, and the proportion of women engaged in the professions rose a mere .4 percent between 1920 and 1940. Although approximately 90 percent of the women employed worked out of economic necessity to meet the basic needs of themselves or their dependents, the belief that females worked solely to earn pin money continued to be widely held and to encourage the custom of paying women about 50 to 60 percent of what men earned. In brief, increased sexual freedom after World War I did not significantly alter the economic division of sexual roles.[50]

The exodus from librarianship of the genteel lady reformers who had found library work to be a compelling mixture of missionary work and educational reform had a major effect upon the status of library women. At an earlier time when higher education for women was still new, intellectually inclined women had been inspired by a sense of mission and of responsibility to make use of their training. Between 1880 and 1900 about half of the graduates of the best women's colleges did not marry, but pursued independent careers, forming the core of professional women. By the 1920s, however, youthful attitudes had shifted and the role of feminist, reformer, or career woman had little appeal to the burgeoning female college population. Older business and professional women lamented the widespread youthful reluctance to make use of the advances for women so hardly won. The new generation of educated, middle-class women felt little sense of commitment to the cause of women's rights or to personal career goals.

Through the twenties and thirties these wider societal developments had their inevitable effect upon the employment of women in the library. The vicious circle was firmly established: library salaries did not attract men and the salaries remained low because they were paid to women. Library work, for many women, became temporary employment between school and marriage. As a perceptive foreign observer remarked in 1939, that librarianship was "the worst paid profession in the United States" was inextricably related to the situation whereby the *Library Journal* was "probably the only professional journal in the world that runs a regular 'marriage column.'"[51]

The coming of the depression exaggerated the already debased status of the married woman librarian who needed work. With growing competition for fewer jobs, employers increasingly denied married women the right to work. In almost every state, between 1932 and 1940, bills limiting the work of wives were introduced and the National Economy Act pushed many married women out of civil service positions between 1932 and 1937. Societal disapproval of working wives, who theoretically kept jobs from men, had its impact upon librarianship. A 1938 survey revealed that, of fifty-seven libraries polled, 10 per cent did not employ married women, 21 percent required resignation after marriage, and 17 percent as a matter of policy did not place married women in responsible positions.[52] Economic conditions also served to draw a slightly larger percentage of men into library work during the 1930s and by 1938 it was apparent that men were being openly favored over women for the best administrative positions, in recruiting, and in placement by library schools.

The economic tensions created by the depression led to an open discussion of the "women question" in the library literature of the 1930s. A controversy began in 1933 when the *Wilson Library Bulletin* printed a letter from an English librarian in which he stated that he found it regrettable that women dominated the library profession in the United States, for women, lacking the "natural curiosity" of men, were unfamiliar with literature and therefore unable to serve as efficient guides to books. The Englishman hastened to add that he had "no wish to disparage or depreciate the work performed by the large numbers of competent women librarians . . . so far as purely routine jobs are concerned." In short, he argued that until U.S. library users realized that their "feminized Library Service is not good enough—that is, it is now only scratching on the surface of the world of books," then low pay and prestige would continue for the U.S. librarian.[53]

In 1934 the *Wilson Library Bulletin* offered three money prizes for the best response to the question "Should the preponderance of women in the American library profession be considered an evil?" The column under which the contest was run was a popular feature of the journal. Because the majority of prizewinners in the past had been women, it was unusual that the contest regarding the status of women was won by three males, with one woman tying for third place, a situation which led the editor to comment that "perhaps the ladies were embarrassed by being put on the offensive."

First place went to Arnold Borden who evaded any real consideration of the issue by his humorous approach. The worst problem, he said more seriously, was that too many women librarians were lost to marriage and the library thereby suffered a loss of the emotional equilibrium and library esprit de corps which women brought to the profession. Second prize winner, Jesse Shera, was more direct. The dominance of women was an evil, he argued, for it perpetuated the "cradle to college" feminine control of American culture. Shera was one of the first librarians to recognize that the feminization of the American library was a direct cause of librarians' low prestige; he saw that the status of librarianship would be raised if other professional avenues were opened to women and if the public were taught to distinguish between the librarian and the bookhandler. "Reuben," the third prize winner, also agreed that the dominance of "Rachael" in the library was a detriment to the profession as a whole, because the woman librarian was generally submissive, unimaginative, and lacked initiative. Significantly, the female contestant who tied for third place based her defense of women in library work upon their preordained feminine roles—"Women are more naturally sympathetic and patient interpreters of individual tastes." Another reply completely denied the dominant influence of women in American librarianship.

> Women do minor clerical work. . . . Men, however, still hold the senior posts in an impressive and almost impregnable array. . . . As long as the American female librarian continues to concern herself with problems of circulation, cataloging, and the like, and is content to leave the theorizing in the hands of the male, there is no danger of an emasculated library service here.[54]

Provoked by an editorial in the *Library Journal* entitled "The Weaker Sex?," feminine resentment surfaced again briefly in 1938. The editorial pointed out that although 90 percent of librarians were women, there was a marked trend toward the hiring of men for any positions paying over $3,600 and toward the favoring of men by library schools for high placement.[55] Alice Tyler, who had opposed the 1919 attempt to organize on a women's issue, now claimed that the discrimination against women was a recent development and called on library women to "not shrink from being labeled a 'feminist'." The influential Margaret Mann pleaded for women to use their numerical majority in the ALA to seize power there.[56] Other women commented upon "the increasing tendency at ALA headquarters to ignore women or to keep them subservient" or argued that women had too long "been satisfied to be 'the power behind the throne' as assistants to the man in charge." The editorial, another woman said, "at last states in print what has become a bromide among us at meetings."[57] Marietta Daniels called for a "Lady Pankhurst who will champion the cause of women in the library profession."

The heated discussion of 1938 elicited a request by a male librarian that the ladies should "not work up a crusade to put the good positions on a proportional representation basis. To do so would drive out most of the men, and make librarianship even more nearly an all-feminine profession. And that, it seems to me, would keep out more of the best minds than the present system does."[58] Robert Alvarez responded with a careful selection of statistics to show that "women still rule the library world."[59] As W. H. Kaiser quickly pointed out, however, Alvarez forgot to say that although only 8.9 percent of librarians were male, men headed 60 percent of the libraries holding over 100,000 volumes.[60] Still, despite these few protests of the 1930s, the great majority of library women continued to accept their lot with little dissent. Perhaps, as Katherine Stokes suggested, they were "too disillusioned after years of observation to be interested in a situation which they must long since have accepted as inevitable."[61] But it is more likely that their passivity reflected a voluntary servitude, made agreeable by the entire socialization process.

World War II proved to be the catalyst which radically transformed the economic outlook and self-image of working women in the United States. During the war years the female labor force increased 50 percent.[62] More importantly, the manpower shortage caused rigid employment barriers to be broken in many areas of work once closed to women, and public attitudes toward working wives made a dramatic shift. Despite persistent discrimination and unequal wage scales, female employment, aided by a postwar boom, continued to rise after 1945; in the 1950s the female labor force was increasing at a rate four times faster than that of men. Significantly, the greatest postwar gains occurred among married women. In 1900 the young, unmarried, and poor constituted the majority of working women. Fifty years later the female labor force was dominated by the married and middle-aged, with a substantial growth in the numbers of employed, middle-class women. By 1970, 60 percent of all nonfarm wives in families with an annual income of over $10,000 were working and more than half of the mothers of children from ages six to seventeen years of age were employed in full-time jobs. The extraordinary social change which these figures represent set the economic foundations for the revival of feminist ideology in the 1960s—a movement which was to reverberate in the staid conventionalism of the library world.

Women's increased economic activity after World War II was a necessary precondition for the rebirth of feminist consciousness. Maternal employment had its impact upon the distribution of domestic responsibilities, the attitudes of men, and the self-image of female children. Social scientists have pointed out that revolutions tend to begin not among the brutally oppressed but in those groups which have been given a taste of emancipation and are experiencing "rising expectations." Historically women's rights have advanced in times of generalized social reform. First, abolitionism, then progressivism, and in the 1960s the civil rights and New Left movements, all resulted in generating a demand for equal rights for women. But if so many women had not already departed from their traditional roles during the forties and fifties, it seems doubtful that the feminists' call for further change in the 1960s would have met with the response it evoked.

In very recent years a new surge of idealistic fever has shaken and moved the 3-by-5 world of the library system. In a burst of energy maverick librarians are challenging the stultifying content of many library school courses, the image of librarians ("old-made ladies sipping custom's tea"),[63] and stand-pat library bureaucracy, and even the labeling system of the Library of Congress which they insist is sexist, racist, and prissy to boot. As library schooling has become more professionalized and attracted more males, its closer association with the academic community has tended to make the mechanical level of library school instruction less acceptable to library students. Many library science graduates of the 1960s shared with their college peers a strong conviction that the U.S. political and economic system was in basic ways monumentally and monstrously wrong. Although the radicalism, expressed at the 1969 Atlantic City Conference where the ALA made a quavering commitment to social change, has succumbed to the new mood of the seventies, the library system, like all our institutions, has nonetheless felt the effect of that turbulent preceding decade.

In the mid-sixties the first trickle of what would become a flood of articles on women in the library began to appear in the library periodicals. Jesse Shera was again one of the first to suggest that the feminization of librarianship, along with the standardization of library work and the popularization of library collections, might be a cause of the deterioration of the library image.[64] In the same year a speaker at the convention of the National Women's party gave a warning to women librarians that if they did not change their passive attitude, the increased entry of men into librarianship, which had begun in the 1950s, might soon push women entirely out of top and middle management.[65] By 1970 the studies of Anita Schiller and others had collected the statistical evidence that convincingly portrayed women as the "disadvantaged majority" in the profession.[66] The September 1971 issue of the *Library Journal* emerged as a sort of feminist manifesto for women in the library.

Women librarians are now expressing dissatisfaction with the public library's feminized world of propriety and respectability. They urge, for example, that librarians live up to their Bill of Rights, which enjoins librarians to stock material representing all possible viewpoints and to fiercely resist community pressures for censorship of books and ideas. A 1969 article in the *Wilson Library Bulletin* resulted in the placing of thousands of No Silence signs as librarians revolted against the tradition of a shushing woman presiding over decorous and hushed rooms. A Virginia librarian wrote: "Tombs and . . . libraries are silent places indeed. Perhaps we should ask why."[67] In attempts like these to break with inertia, public librarians are in effect considering a course which would place them in opposition to hallowed conservatism within their communities. Such a radical change in the library tradition would require that the librarian defy the traditional concept of feminity and assume a new confidence in her right and duty to protect standards of intellectual freedom by bold exercise of intellectual authority.

The 1970 organization of the ALA Task Force on the Status of Women is symptomatic of the new attitude of women toward their own potential and ability. With the growing consciousness of the effects of sexism on the library profession as a whole has come a formal admission that sexual discrimination "wastes needed professional resources and assaults our sense of human dignity."[68] Because a majority of librarians are now members of that group which feels especially frustrated by traditional ideals, the educated women in America, they desire to fuse personal and professional development within the library system. Not surprisingly, as they denounce passivity in themselves and propriety in the world at large, they extend their criticism to their institution and their profession.

The first generations of library women, in developing the library field as a service profession, had not questioned sex-typed roles for women. There was thus no possibility that the first groups of educated women could conceive of themselves as disciplined intellects, freely operating in all human spheres of competence. In library work, as in the other feminized professions, the only legitimate avenue for the operation of feminine intellect, which in some obscure way was believed to be complementary to that of the male, seemed to be through an extension of domesticity. For women librarians, that expanded maternal role was to mean their early self-definition as the unlearned "tender technician" in the library, moral guardian, cultural guide, gracious hostess. Thus the social roles which women elected to act out did much to shape the development of an important American cultural institution. Until the librarian deals with the implications of feminization, with its varied inhibitory effects upon intellectual excellence and leadership, progress toward professionalization will be limited.

But unlike the older group who resisted radical change, many librarians of today indict traditional ideals and tend to wink at sacred cows. The first meeting of organized feminists within ALA, in 1970, drew a small crowd of 170 women and a few men. Three years later, over 1,000 women and their male allies jammed the convention session on women in librarianship to hear Wilma Scott Heide, president of the National Organization of Women, urge them to action. It had been eighty-one years since a "Woman's Meeting" had been called at an ALA convention. In 1892 the subordination of women in the library profession had also been discussed, and the women there had been counseled to keep patience, to be "divine optimists, who rowing hard against the stream, see distant lights of Eden gleam, and know the dream is not a dream."[69] At the 1973 meeting where Heide spoke, a sympathetic reporter of the event described the library women there as they sat listening, with urgent unblinking attention, their "hands to lips, eyes on a distant horizon."[70]

NOTES

1. Mary E. Ahern, "The Business Side of a Woman's Career as a Librarian," *Library Journal* 24:60 (July 1899).
2. Frances Hawley, "Some Non-technical Qualifications for Library Work," *Library Journal* 29:362 (July 1904).
3. See the excellent bibliography on sexual discrimination by Anita Schiller in her essay, "Women in Librarianship," in Melvin J. Voigt, ed., *Advances in Librarianship* (New York: Academic, 1974). Also see Susan Akerstrom Tarr, *North Carolina Libraries* 31:22–32 (Fall 1973); Raymond L. Carpenter and Kenneth D. Schearer, "Sex and Salary Update," *Library Journal* 99:101–7 (Jan. 15, 1974).
4. Editorial, *Library Journal* 36:321 (July 1911). For statistics of leadership positions held by women in the national, state, and local organizations, see Margaret Ann Corwin, "An Investigation of Female Leadership in Regional, State, and Local Library Associations, 1876–1923," *Library Quarterly* 44:133–44 (Apr. 1974).
5. Dewey to G. P. Putnam, January 18, 1898, Melvil Dewey Papers, Columbia University, New York. This letter refers to a controversy arising in 1897 when Rutherford Hayes, first vice-president of the ALA, claimed his right to succession when Justin Winsor died. Hannah James, who joined the majority of the executive board in a vote for Putnam to replace Winsor, told Dewey that "when Mr. Winsor died my first thought in regard to his succession was one of gratitude that I had not rec'd the most votes for VP and I intended making the occurrence the text for a homily against putting women librarians in such a position." James to Dewey, December 6, 1897, Melvil Dewey Papers, Columbia University, New York.
6. "The English Conference: Official Report of Proceedings," *Library Journal* 2:280 (Jan.–Feb. 1878).
7. Linda A. Eastman, "Aims and Personal Attitude in Library Work," *Library Journal* 22:80 (Oct. 1897).
8. "Library Work vs. the Library Profession," *Library Notes* 1:50 (June 1886).
9. Ahern, p. 61.
10. Lutie Stearns, "The Question of Library Training," *Library Journal* 30:69 (July 1905).
11. Hannah P. James, "Women in American and British Libraries," *Library World* 1:90 (Dec. 1898).
12. Virginia E. Graeff, "The Gentle Librarian: A Transcript from Experience," *Library Journal* 30:922 (Dec. 1905).
13. Lilian Denio, "How to Make the Most of a Small Library," *Library Notes* 3:470 (Mar. 1889); phonetic spelling is transcribed. Andrew Steenberg, "Some Impressions of a Visit to American Libraries," *Library Journal* 28:606–7 (Aug. 1903).
14. Steenberg, p. 607.
15. Mary Salome Cutler Fairchild, "Women in American Libraries," *Library Journal* 29:162 (Dec. 1904).
16. Ibid.
17. Herbert Putnam, "The Women in the Library," *Library Journal* 41:880 (Dec. 1916). Also see: Celia A. Hayward, "Woman as Cataloger," *Public Libraries* 3:121–23 (Apr. 1898); "Female Library Assistants," *Library Journal* 14:128–9 (Apr. 1889); John Dana, "Women in Library Work," *Independent* 71:244 (Aug. 3, 1911).
18. Minerva Sanders, "Report on Reading for the Young," *Library Journal* 15:59 (Dec. 1890).

166 / Personnel

19. Mary Plummer, "The Work for Children in Free Libraries," in Alice I. Hazeltine, *Library Work with Children: Reprints of Papers and Addresses* (New York: Wilson, 1917), p. 81.

20. Annie Carroll Moore, "Special Training for Children's Librarians," *Library Journal* 23:80 (July 1898).

21. "Fit Reading for Boys and Girls," *Springfield Republican*, Apr. 1, 1879, reprinted in *Library Journal* 4:171 (May 1879).

22. "Papers on Fiction and the Reading of School Children," *Library Journal* 4:356 (June–July 1879).

23. Ibid., p. 365.

24. Minerva Sanders, "Possibilities of Public Libraries in Manufacturing Communities," *Library Journal* 12:398 (Sept. 1887).

25. Feminization and the attempt at elitist direction were not the only factors leading to this development. Equally important was the proliferation of nonbook activities in public libraries which resulted when librarians discovered that no great number of the public were going to read commendable books of their own volition. See D.W. Davies, *Public Libraries as Culture and Social Centers: The Origin of the Concept* (Metuchen, N.J.: Scarecrow, 1974) for a discussion of how librarians adopted the activities of the voluntary uplift and cultural societies of the nineteenth century.

26. "Child-Saving Work," *Proceedings of the National Conference of Charities and Corrections, 1884*, p. 116.

27. Ada Jones, "The Library as an Educator," *Library Notes* 3:368–9 (July 1892).

28. Gertrude E. Andrus, "How the Library Is Meeting the Changing Conditions of Child Life," *ALA Bulletin* 188–92 (1913).

29. Harriot Hassler, "Common-Sense and the Story Hour," *Library Journal* 30:8 (July 1905). See also Frances Jenkins Olcott, "Rational Library Work with Children and the Preparation for It," ibid. pp. 71–75; and G. Stanley Hall, "Children's Reading as a Factor in Their Education," ibid. 33:123–28 (Apr. 1908).

30. Mary S. Cutler, "Home Libraries," *Library Journal* 19:13–14 (Sept. 1894).

31. Clara M. Hunt, "Some Means by Which Children May Be Led to Read Better Books," *Library Journal* 24:149 (Apr. 1899).

32. *Proceedings of the ALA, 1906*, p. 246.

33. Ethel P. Underhill, "Crumbs of Comfort to the Children's Librarian," *Library Journal* 35:155, 57 (Apr. 1910).

34. For comments on women's sentimentality in other professions see Jill Conway, "Perspectives on the History of Women's Education in the United States," *History of Education Quarterly* 14:1–13 (Spring 1974); John P. Rousmaniere, "Cultural Hybrid in the Slums: The College Woman and the Settlement House," *American Quarterly* 22:45–66 (Spring 1970); Allen F. Davis, *American Heroine: The Life and Legend of Jane Addams* (New York: Oxford Univ. Pr., 1973). Richard Jensen's study of 879 eminent women listed in *Woman's Who Who in America* revealed that women librarians were the group least sympathetic to the equal rights movement at the turn of the century; only 60 percent of the library women in his sample supported the suffrage amendment. Richard Jensen, "Family, Career, and Reform: Women Leaders of the Progressive Era," in Michael Gordon, ed., *The American Family in Social-Historical Perspective* (New York: St. Martin's, 1973), pp. 267–80.

35. Joseph R. Gusfield, *Symbolic Crusade: Status Politics and the American Temperance Movement* (Urbana: Univ. of Illinois Pr., 1966); David Pivar, *Purity Crusade: Sexual Morality and Social Control, 1868–1900* (Westport, Conn.: Greenwood, 1973); Anthony Platt, *The Child Savers: The Invention of Delinquency* (Chicago: Univ. of Chicago Pr., 1969).

36. For an amplified discussion of the effects of feminization on professionalization, see Dee Garrison, "The Tender Technicians: The Feminization of Public Librarianship, 1876–1905," *Journal of Social History* 6:131–59 (Winter 1972–73).

Also see Elaine Fain's critique of the above article and reply in the *Journal of Library History* 2:99–117 (Apr. 1975). For discussion of the characteristic behavior of women as workers see Richard L. Simpson and Ida Harper Simpson, "Women and Bureaucracy in the Semi-Professions," in Amitai Etzioni, ed., *The Semi-Professions and Their Organization: Teachers, Nurses, Social Workers* (New York: The Free Pr., 1969), pp. 192–265; Cynthia Epstein, *Woman's Place* (Los Angeles: Univ. of California Pr., 1970); and Athena Theodore, ed., *The Professional Woman* (Cambridge, Mass.: Schenkman, 1971).

37. "The Case of the Desk Assistant," *Library Journal* 27:877 (Oct. 1902). Also see "Library Assistants: Shortcomings and Desirable Qualifications," ibid. 29:349–59 (July 1904); "A Few Brickbats from a Layman," *Public Libraries* 18:277–79 (July 1913); "The Desk Assistant: An Imaginary Conversation," *Library Journal* 27:251–54 (May 1902); Margery Doud, "The Inarticulate Library Assistant," ibid. 45:540–43 (June 15, 1920).

38. Mrs. J. T. Jennings, "Statistics of Women in Library Work," *Library Journal* 43:737 (Oct. 1918). Also, Josephine Rathbone, "Salaries of Library School Graduates," ibid. 39:188–90 (Mar. 1914); Charles H. Compton, "Comparison of Qualifications, Training, Demand, and Renumeration of the Library Profession with Social Work," *Public Libraries* 30:115–21 (Mar. 1925).

39. Herbert Putnam, "The Prospect," *Library Journal* 37:651–58 (Dec. 1912). Recognition of the "feminine" traits which hampered professional excellence was by no means limited to male librarians. See Louise Connolly, "Women as Employees," *Public Libraries* 19:196 (May 1914).

40. Arthur Bostwick, "Labor and Rewards in the Library," *Public Libraries* 15:4 (Jan. 1910).

41. Jennie M. Flexner, "The Loan Desk from Both Sides," *Library Journal* 49:412 (May 1, 1924). Also, the series by R. R. Bowker, "Women in the Library Profession," *Library Journal* (1920), and Theresa Hitchler, "The Successful Loan-Desk Assistant," ibid. 32:554–59 (Dec. 1907). For protest see Editorial, *Public Libraries* 15:284–85 (July 1910) and Mabel South-Clifee, "A Protest—'Subordinates' vs. 'Assistants'," *Library Journal* 39:198 (Mar. 1914).

42. Arthur Bostwick, "System in the Library," *Library Journal* 34:477 (Nov. 1909). Also see his "Labor and Rewards in the Library," *Public Libraries* 15:1–5 (Jan. 1910) for a discussion of why women were paid less than men.

43. Josephine Rathbone, "Some Aspects of Our Personal Life," *Public Libraries* 21:54 (Feb. 1916); Ida A. Kidder, "The Creative Impulse in the Library," *Public Libraries* 24:156–57 (May 1919).

44. Herbert Putnam, "The Woman in the Library," *Library Journal* 41:879 (Dec. 1916).

45. *ALA Bulletin* 13:359 (1919).

46. Ibid., p. 380.

47. Ibid., p. 359.

48. Margery Doud, p. 543.

49. Clara M. Herbert, "Recruiting a Training Class," *Library Journal* 44:108 (Feb. 1919). See comments by William Henry, "Living Salaries for Good Service," ibid. pp. 282–84 (May 1919).

50. William H. Chafe, *The American Woman: Her Changing Social, Economic, and Political Role, 1920–1970* (New York: Oxford Univ. Pr., 1972), pp. 48–132.

51. Wilhelm Munthe, *American Librarianship from an European Angle: An Attempt at an Evaluation of Policies and Activities* (Chicago: American Library Assn., 1939), p. 165.

52. "Status of Married Women," *ALA Bulletin*, 32:402 (June 1938); "Married Women Librarians," *Library Journal* 66:650–51 (Aug. 1941).

53. "Problems," *Wilson Library Bulletin* 8:230–31 (Dec. 16, 1933).

54. *Wilson Library Bulletin* 8:403–7 (Mar. 1934).

55. *Library Journal* 63:232 (Mar. 15, 1938).

56. Ibid., p. 296 (Apr. 15, 1938).

168 / *Personnel*

57. Ibid., pp. 342, 343 (May 1, 1938).
58. Ibid., p. 438 (June 1, 1938).
59. Robert Alvarez, "Woman's Place in Librarianship," *Wilson Library Bulletin* 13:175–78 (Nov. 1938).
60. W. H. Kaiser, letter to the editor, *Wilson Library Bulletin* 13:336 (Jan. 1939).
61. Katherine M. Stokes, "Warning: Soft Shoulders," *Wilson Library Bulletin* 13:470–71 (Mar. 1939).
62. Contrary to popular belief, only 5 percent of women war workers joined the labor force for the first time during World War I. The fact that the earlier war lasted only a year and a half also served to lessen the pace of social change in that period.
63. Richard B. Moses, "a library pome," in Celeste West and Elizabeth Katz, eds., *Revolting Librarians* (San Francisco: Booklegger, 1972), p. 3.
64. Jesse Shera, "Without Reserve," *Wilson Library Bulletin* 39:677 (Apr. 1965).
65. Miriam Y. Holden, "Discriminatory Practices in the Recruiting of Women for Leading Positions in the Profession of Librarianship," *Antiquarian Bookman* 36:647–48 (Aug. 23, 1965).
66. Anita Schiller, "The Disadvantaged Majority: Women Employed in Libraries," *American Libraries* 1:345–49 (Apr. 1970).
67. Art Plotnik, "Sweet Library Lips," in West and Katz, eds., *Revolting Librarians*, p. 10.
68. Pat Schuman, "Task Force Meets in Detroit," *Library Journal* 95:2635 (Aug. 1970).
69. *Library Journal* 17:89–94 (July 1892).
70. Hunter S. Thompson, "The Wiltings, Winnings, Losings, Loathings, Fears, and Fortunes of 8,500 American Library Association Conferees Who Went to Las Vegas, Part I," *Wilson Library Bulletin* 48:62 (Sept. 1973). *See also* Anne E. Brugh and Benjamin R. Beede, "American Librarianship," *Signs* 1:943–55 (summer 1976).

PART THREE

Facilities

9

Reference Services and Technology

BUDD L. GAMBEE AND RUTH R. GAMBEE
University of North Carolina, Chapel Hill

THEORIES OF REFERENCE SERVICE

Reference book, reference department, reference libraries are terms which have appeared in library literature for many years, as far back as an 1880 listing in Cannons's *Bibliography of Library Economy* with the title, "Reference Library Arrangement." In addition, a complete, new roster of terms has appeared in recent indexes: *information service, information networks, information retrieval, selective dissemination of information,* and a notably intriguing one, *current awareness services.*

The *ALA Glossary of Library Terms* defines *reference service* as "that phase of library work which is directly concerned with assistance to readers in securing information and in using the resources of the library in study and research." Samuel Rothstein, who has written extensively on reference history, has called reference service the "provision by libraries of personal assistance to individual readers in pursuit of information."[1]

The extent of service to be given by reference librarians has long been a matter of debate. Three theories seem to have been recognized, according to William A. Katz in his *Introduction to Reference Work*, where he has discussed the formulations of James I. Wyer in 1930, and the parallel ones of Rothstein several decades later.[2] The "conservative theory" limits service mostly to the provision of such aids as the card catalog, bibliographies, standard reference books, and a classified collection supplemented by proper labels and directional signs, leaving patrons largely on their own. In the "moderate theory" the reference librarian searches for relatively small amounts of information, generally factual in nature, but expects inquirers to do their own study or research, although guiding them to bibliographical aids. The "liberal theory" proposes that patrons be given as much assistance as they want, an ideal ardently espoused by Wyer.

REFERENCE SERVICES BEFORE 1876

Rothstein has noted some early allusions to assistance given to readers by conscientious librarians, such as George Watterston, Librarian of Congress in the 1820s, and William Alfred Jones at Columbia in the 1850s. In these instances, however, Rothstein was not willing to call occasional courtesies to readers reference service. In his view reference service began only when librarians recognized it as basic to the function of a library, and provided staff, special collections, and separate facilities.

Up to this time, scholars had to buy the books they needed, secure manuscript copies from foreign libraries, or study abroad. Nevertheless, the intellectual climate of the country was rapidly changing in the mid-nineteenth century, fostering scholarship in art, history, science, and literature. Along with the introduction of German methods of university teaching which replaced the lecture-textbook system with programs of individual research, these changes created an atmosphere favorable to the establishment of public book collections. The middle of the century also saw the development of library catalogs and periodical indexes as reference tools. Two librarians were outstanding in this respect: Charles Coffin Jewett, who published catalogs of the Brown University Library in 1843 and of the Boston Public Library in 1858; and William Frederick Poole, whose first periodical index dates from 1848 and his Boston Mercantile Library catalog from 1854.

Certainly the most influential library of the period was the Boston Public Library; its founders recognized from the beginning the distinction, already known in western Europe, between service to the general public demanding popular reading and to the researcher requiring scholarly books. The library's first building reflected the two types of service in its architecture, providing a "lower hall" for popular books and an "upper hall" for what would later be called a reference collection.[3] However, the term *reading room* was often used rather than *reference room* for this feature of library architecture which soon became a standard.

Libraries large enough to amass reference collections and give significant service, however, were primarily concerned with only two functions, the building of the collection and its organization. The reference function was hardly recognized. The head librarian was judged by the size of the collection; the chief assistant was the cataloger.

LAST QUARTER OF THE NINETEENTH CENTURY

One of the best and most frequently quoted descriptions of reference work is that by Samuel Swett Green, originally delivered as a paper at the historic meeting of librarians in Philadelphia in 1876, and later printed in the *American Library Journal*.[4] As librarian of the Worcester Public Library, Green had set about increasing the use of his reference collection by giving extensive personal assistance. He reasoned that most users of public libraries, particularly those in the "humbler walks of life," needed help. "You must make the selection yourself, get the works he needs, and hand them to him."[5] He was also concerned about the validity of the information. "In handing the needed volume to the inquirer . . . caution her that there are many stories and traditions which it will not do to accept as facts without careful examination of the evidence in their corroboration."[6] He recommended that school children be taught to use dictionaries and encyclopedias, but also that they be invited to seek the librarian's assistance. For business people and others whose time was valuable, Green not only secured the needed books "open at the proper pages," but borrowed them from larger libraries, encouraging a type of regional reference service. He also sent out announcements of new material in the library to municipal agencies concerned with specific problems. An early "readers' advisor," he drew up study courses and reading lists.

Green was a "generalist" and defended his position thus: "It would be easy to show that scholars, as well as unlearned persons, receive much aid in pursuing their studies from an accomplished librarian, although he has not the knowledge of a specialist."[7] His general philosophy was that the reference librarian "should be as unwilling to allow an inquirer to leave the library with his question unanswered as a shopkeeper is to have a customer go out of his store without making a purchase."[8] Green's paper constitutes a remarkable description of the work of a reference librarian and brings out many facets that are still being discussed a hundred years later.

On the level of the research and university library, Rothstein has documented the conditions which established reference service as an essential function. Graduate education increased, especially with the founding of Johns Hopkins University in 1876 under Daniel Coit Gilman, a former librarian, who believed the principal purpose of a university was research in laboratories and libraries. Universities began teaching a wider range of subjects, resulting in more varied and larger collections. Their libraries remained open longer hours and gradually permitted greater student access to shelves. However, as scholars preferred to do their own research, or so librarians felt, reference services were generally limited to undergraduate students, and then only meagerly in the course of guiding them to find their own answers.

During this period renewed attention was focused on access to the collections: card catalog versus book catalog; dictionary catalog versus classified catalog, and so on. By 1900 the most commonly accepted solution was close classification, largely by the Dewey system, and the use of the dictionary card catalog employing subject headings. Obviously these were all developments of great interest to librarians engaged in reference service.

Louis Kaplan has stressed the 1880s as the era in which reference service as such began to take definite form in both public and university libraries.[9] The reading rooms of public libraries became the logical depositories for the more popular reference books. It was not long before the provision of reference rooms became a commonplace in the architecture of medium-sized and large public libraries. As libraries became larger, inevitably a certain specialization set in. When the chief librarian could no longer personally answer reference questions, this function had to be delegated, and as a result there evolved the position of reference librarian. In 1884 the resourceful Melvil Dewey at Columbia outlined a "reference" service and appointed two "reference assistants," each with differing subject capabilities, to provide aid for Columbia's students. The Boston Public Library had such positions by 1886, and at the time of the American Library Association meeting in Chicago in 1893, reference assistants were listed on the staff of several libraries, mostly public.

By this time also Kaplan's three requirements for genuine reference service were in operation in leading libraries: staff exclusively or largely devoted to this service; reference collections on open shelves in rooms especially designed for the purpose; and efficient reference guides to a library's resources. Reference work was a recognized part of the library canon. No greater evidence is needed than the fact that in 1891 the index to *Library Journal* changed its old subject heading, *Aids to Readers*, to *Reference Work*, and articles under this new heading appeared with increasing frequency. In 1896 when a group of prominent librarians appeared before the Joint Congressional Committee on the Library of Congress, much of their testimony, especially that of Melvil Dewey, saw the future of the Library of Congress as a national reference library. In 1898 at the ALA meeting in Chautauqua, Charles Davidson outlined an elaborate plan for regional reference service which would make the resources of large libraries available to users of county libraries.

Reference books, published library catalogs, and indexes were becoming more numerous in this quarter century. Poole was occupied with both his index to periodicals and the *ALA Index to General Literature*. Bolton's union list, *A Catalog of Scientific and Technical Periodicals, 1665–1882*, appeared in 1885. The establishment in 1898 of the H. W. Wilson Company in Minneapolis was a major event in reference librarianship. Halsey William Wilson, a Quaker bookseller of charm, business ability, and a "New England conscience," built an enterprise, which he later moved to New York, and eventually described as "the world's largest publisher of indexes and reference works for libraries." Starting with the Cumulative Book Index–United States Catalog series, which soon shared with certain R. R. Bowker Company publications the task of listing the output of the American book trade, Wilson branched out into periodical indexes, beginning with the *Readers' Guide to Periodical Literature* in 1901. Attendance at library conferences and the use of questionnaires assisted Wilson in publishing such world-famous reference tools as the *Book Review Digest*, the Standard Catalog series, and the monumental *Union List of Serials*.

FROM 1900 TO WORLD WAR I

From the turn of the century on, recognizable reference service grew steadily. In public libraries personal assistance to users was considered the keystone of the "modern" library movement. Although Rothstein suggests that the "conservative theory" of reference was still dominant in university libraries, the public universities were freer from the dead hand of tradition. Some of the major ones were leaders in the establishment of reference service: Illinois in 1897, Michigan in 1905, Minnesota in 1906, and California in 1911. By 1915 reference service of varying grades of complexity was being offered by most university libraries.

At this time reference service developed in two somewhat related areas: subject divisions in large libraries and special libraries. At first the subdivision of large libraries tended to be based on nonsubject factors, hence the early formation of foreign language, document, print, map, and periodical rooms. But as both public and university libraries grew, a movement arose for subdividing the large, general reference rooms into subject areas. The demands of business and industry were felt early, and William E. Foster at the Providence (R.I.) Public Library established an Industrial Library in 1900. Cincinnati, Detroit, and Cleveland were early examples of public libraries with special departments covering more or less Dewey's "Useful Arts" class. Next fine arts departments came into favor, followed by reference collections in language and literature, science and technology, geography and travel, social sciences, philosophy and religion. By 1913 the Cleveland Public Library under Carl Vitz was almost completely departmentalized.[10]

As a rule, general reference rooms were reduced to information centers, answering ready-reference questions and referring all others to the proper department. Each subject division included reference and circulating books, pamphlets, and materials in other formats. Typically, circulation routines were taken care of at a central circulation desk, and the staff of the subdivisions were under the general supervision of the main reference department. The number of card and vertical files, and other special reference resources was greatly increased under this kind of organization. With the expertise developed by subject departments, the depth of reference work often approached that of research. Library schools responded by offering separate bibliography courses roughly paralleling the typical library subject departments.

University libraries lagged in subject specialization, but by 1905 it was common to find small departmental libraries scattered about the campus. In some instances, university departmental libraries became famous in their own right, such as the Avery Architectural Library at Columbia.

Although subject departmentalization tended to become the norm for larger public and university libraries, there were criticisms. Some public librarians felt that subject departments became essentially research libraries with the loss of the "common touch." Also patrons whose questions did not fit neatly into a given subject area found themselves shunted from department to department.

Offering still greater depth of service were the special libraries generally formed within large businesses and industries and especially tailored to their needs. A few, however, were supported by private endowments, for example, the John Crerar and the Newberry libraries in Chicago. Still others were under public auspices, such as legislative and municipal reference libraries. In these special libraries reference blended with original research: the librarian was a specialist entrusted with the gathering, selection, combining, condensing, and interpretation of information for highly paid and busy users.

The effectiveness of reference service and of the training of reference librarians was increased during this period by the appearance in 1902 of Alice B. Kroeger's famous text, *Guide to the Study and Use of Reference Books*. The third edition in 1917, published by ALA, was edited by Isadore Gilbert Mudge, entitled *Guide to Reference Books*.

Still, in 1915, despite these many evidences of progress, the phrase, *reference librarian*, was termed by William Warner Bishop, superintendent of the "reading room" of the Library of Congress, the "chief of the startling and novel crop of new phrases in our calling."[11] He defined reference work as "the service rendered by a librarian *in aid* of some sort of study. It is not the study itself."[12]

WORLD WAR I THROUGH WORLD WAR II

During World War I librarians of the United States were deeply committed to the war effort through the ALA War Services Program, which aimed among other things to send a million books to a million men in the armed services, providing essentially recreational reading. During the two years of active U.S. involvement in the war, reference activities, perhaps somewhat curtailed by the shortages of wartime living, progressed much as usual.

A major feature of the period after the war was the tremendous increase in industrial research libraries, needed to assist in the production of materials normally imported from Germany. Furthermore, the old image of the scholarly researcher, working independently, gave way to the research team, with the research librarian forming an integral part. The idea of the research librarian, the expert bibliographer, was much in the air. It was during these years that Herbert Putnam at the Library of Congress installed the "endowed chairs" and the "honorary consultants" which brought to the library the knowledge of specialists. In the 1930s the Carnegie Foundation supported research librarians at the University of Pennsylvania and at Cornell University to test the feasibility of such a commitment in university libraries. The experiment failed to introduce this category of library worker on any great scale.[13]

Responding to reference needs in all libraries was the introduction in January 1930 of a landmark title in the evaluation of reference books, ALA's quarterly, *Subscription Books Bulletin*. It was combined with *Booklist* in 1956, and currently appears twice a month.

A phenomenon of the 1930s which inevitably affected every aspect of U.S. and Canadian life was the depression. Everywhere library funds were cut to the bone. Important reference sets simply could not be purchased. What money was available was channeled into periodicals, because they are extremely difficult to fill in at a later date. Staff positions vacated by death or retirement were often not filled. On the other hand, the use of libraries increased; thousands were out of work, and if nothing else, the public library provided a warm place to sit and read the want ads in those desolate days. Many people used libraries to learn new skills to improve their chances of employment.

Although libraries lost professional staff during the depression, they gained another category of staff because of federal efforts to alleviate unemployment. Through the state-wide projects of the Works Progress Administration, large numbers of clerical workers were given library jobs; and although there was both perplexity and amusement at their presence, on the whole, they contributed a great deal. A major emphasis of WPA library projects was rural library extension, but in urban libraries many workers were assigned tasks in indexing, the compiling of union catalogs, catalog maintenance, microfilming projects, and other activities supportive of reference work.[14]

With the bombing of Pearl Harbor on December 7, 1941, the United States became involved in a massive defense and war effort. An account by R. Russell Munn presents an excellent picture of reference service under wartime conditions at the Cleveland Public Library.[15] He found that the greatest increase in demand came from the fields of technology, business and industry, on questions relating to government contracts, wage and price controls, rationing, munitions, and synthetics. There was intense interest in geography, the military, civilian defense, and vocations connected with radio, electricity, and mechanics. He described in particular the specialized service usually called the War Information Center, consisting of a desk located prominently in the library, with telephone, essential reference books, pamphlets, newspapers, war releases, maps, government documents, and so forth. Desks were manned continuously by expert staff who took an aggressive attitude toward reference work, calling official agencies for latest information, clipping and filing promptly items from newspapers.

This lively, vigorous brand of reference work was to have repercussions long after the war, continuing as information centers which screened calls to the library, answering as many questions as possible, and referring others to the proper department. In his article Munn also described the "advice bureaus" in wartime Britain which gave counseling in solving personal problems. They were set up under social work agencies, but he speculated that something of this sort might be an excellent service for public libraries to offer. In the 1960s and 1970s this extension and intensification of service into the community was to become an important issue.

POSTWAR DEVELOPMENTS, 1945–1975

Dan Lacy, in his discerning study prepared for the 1969 report of the National Advisory Commission on Libraries, suggested that "the two most dynamic forces impelling the social changes that affect the library are probably the changing population patterns and the radically increased social investment in scientific and technical research and development."[16]

By the end of the 1960s the term *population explosion* was in common usage and of common concern. The consequent growth in enrollments across the entire educational spectrum brought a corresponding demand for larger library collections and staffs, and a heavier burden on reference departments. The migration of populations was also a notable trend: from rural to urban areas; from city to suburb; from South to North and West. The civil rights movement, and a new awareness of such minorities as the blacks, the American Indians, Puerto Ricans, and Mexican-Americans, had their impact on libraries and were reflected in vigorous and imaginative programs to personalize and broaden services to masses of people often difficult to reach.

The second force affecting libraries mentioned by Lacy was technology. Stimulated by the vast war machine of World War II, it made a powerful impact on postwar society. Military and defense establishments enlarged their programs as the cold war supplanted the Axis threat, and the space age loomed on the world horizon. Scientific advances resulted in an explosion of knowledge and publications which deluged technical libraries and produced those child prodigies called documentation or information centers. Special technologies were devised for the efficient control of this flood of material, bringing on the electronic digital computer and new photoduplication processes. Abstracting, indexing, and distributing services proliferated. Of necessity these programs called for pioneering legislation and massive federal support. They resulted in another kind of explosion in the library community: commissions, committees, conferences, and surveys studying library operations and needs and calling for increased cooperation on a regional basis as well as plans for a national information system.

Looking back over this era of breathtaking change and innovation, one is tempted to view reference service as operating in a vulnerable and paradoxical situation. On the one hand, documentation centers and specialized libraries were attempting to provide the most comprehensive type of service to their clienteles by means of impersonal and sophisticated machines. On the other hand, to combat the pervasive impersonalization of society that these same machines produced, the readers' advisory and information functions began to shift from public library reference rooms to street-oriented programs, such as the neighborhood information centers. Both of these trends threatened to bypass the traditional reference department, and concern was reflected in speech after speech by prominent librarians and documentalists; in survey after survey probing the workings of the reference and communication process; and in an examination and reorientation of the training of the reference librarian.

Research in Reference

Studies and surveys on reference service have appeared in growing numbers and complexity since World War II, concentrating on the following areas: the reference function and the identity of the library user; measurement of the quantity and quality of service; analysis of the communication process; and the organization of information and its most efficient dissemination. As early as 1926, fifty years after the appearance of *Public Libraries in the United States of America*, ALA brought out its four-volume *Survey of Libraries in the United States*, which included reference service in both public and academic libraries.[17] Since then the research has been extensive, and the candid observer must admit, often inconclusive. To illustrate, in 1922 *Library Literature* listed an article, "Measuring Results in Reference Work," and in 1972 "Measuring the Immeasurable: Reference Standards."[18]

In the mid-1940s there was a spate of user surveys, led off by Dorothy Cole's analysis in 1946 of over one thousand questions from public, special, and academic libraries and by Mabel Conat's survey in 1947 in the Detroit Public Library.[19] At this time, too, appeared the first historical accounts of reference work by Kaplan in 1947 and 1950, and by Rothstein in 1953, and also the landmark surveys of the Public Library Inquiry, particularly Bernard Berelson's *The Library Public*.[20]

Papers of conferences such as those at the University of Illinois in 1959, at Columbia University in 1967, and at Airlie House, Virginia in 1970 have contributed valuable comment.[21] Since 1960 the issues of *RQ*, the official organ of the Reference and Adult Services Division of ALA have furthered research. "Research in Reference," a special section of abstracts, was begun by Charles Bunge in 1968.

In current research the survey is still prominent, but it is now likely to be conducted by a team or institute rather than by a single person. Standards have been considered basic for any assessment of reference service, and many have been issued, principally by ALA in the last fifty years. Much attention has been given lately to research-evaluation methodology, involving the construction and efficacy of interviews, questionnaires, case studies, or test questions.[22]

Special Services and Library Users

What have all the surveys shown, and which people are the "library's public," especially for nontechnical reference service? It may be generally agreed that the majority of users have come to the library for unspecified reading or browsing. Of the smaller percentage who ask for assistance, more than half have been found to be students, with the remainder mainly from business or professional ranks. However, the library's public has also been "out there," and from the beginning of organized reference and reader services, attempts have been made to reach groups such as clubs, factory workers, immigrants, racial minorities, and the disadvantaged. It may be significant that *users* has supplanted *readers* as the accepted current term, most likely because the potential user may not be a reader. In the last quarter century, reference departments have initiated some special services which deserve mention.

As early as 1910 Arthur E. Bostwick stated that "probably the answering of busy men's queries over the telephone is coming to be recognized as a perfectly legitimate part of the reference library's work."[23] It was not until World War II and after, however, that telephone reference came into prominence, and then only in larger libraries. Sarah R. Reed, in her ten-year survey of reference departments in twenty-five libraries, discovered that in New Orleans, for instance, from 1945 to 1955, requests by this means increased 209 percent.[24] The usual reasons given for this phenomenal rise were the movement of people to suburbs, the problems of parking and transportation, and heavier use by business and industry in a technological age. Ten years later in 1964 Katharine G. Harris found that this service had expanded still further. "Cleveland with twenty-five trunk lines and Detroit with eighteen report that about half of all requests for information come by telephone."[25] It should be mentioned that some restrictions were placed on the service:

quiz and contest questions; lengthy information to be read; medical and legal queries; and student assignments.

Also indicative of the complexity of modern life has been the widespread interest in the community or neighborhood information center. It is estimated that more than one thousand of these have been established by both "libraries and private and public concerns east of the Mississippi since 1971."[26] Reference departments have long maintained files on local agencies and services, but this rather static concept of service has given way to an activist one, closely allied to social-work theory and methods, of searching out people and their needs, and locating service in their midst. A highly publicized example of the 1960s was the High John experiment, operated from the Prince George's County Memorial Library in Maryland, and using library students to work with the disadvantaged in an unstructured "library."[27] The community information center is a logical extension of Wyer's liberal theory of reference service.

Traditional reference librarians would hardly conceive of themselves as "floating," and even less of being "communications change agents," in the words of Patrick Penland.[28] The goal of the "floating librarian," in his view, is to foment change, to be a personal advocate for the potential user of a library, to advance the library as a "coordinating structure in the community." This concept is of concern to reference librarians because the merger in 1972 of ALA's Reference Services Division with the Adult Services Division gathered into the newly formed Reference and Adult Services Division such ASD projects as the Materials for American Indians, and the Core Collection for Urban Library Services. Presumably the new division also acquired a group of librarians who share Penland's opposition to what he views as the "large and opaque bibliographic pentagons ... in the urban communities in America."[29]

Cooperation in Reference Service

The commitment of the leaders of the library movement in 1876, that books and information should be shared wherever possible, continued to seem valid and necessary. In 1898 Samuel S. Green discussed this subject in an article, "Inter-Library Loans in Reference Work."[30] This type of cooperation became entrenched in library organization as collections grew, communication by various means improved, and state and regional library systems arose.

Interlibrary loan has sometimes been a function of the circulation department, but more often it has devolved upon the reference librarian, possibly because a search was necessary to verify the bibliographical listing of the title desired. Demand tended to fall primarily on the resources of larger libraries so that by 1952 the Association of College and Reference Libraries worked out a National Interlibrary Loan Code. In 1974 it was found that "by a conservative estimate, the total quantity of interlibrary loan activity in the United States now could well be between six million and seven million requests per year,"[31] with academic and public libraries being equally heavy borrowers, and that from an analysis of several surveys, about 70 percent of requests were being filled within regional and local systems.[32]

Perhaps the greatest advance in cooperation in recent years has come with the establishment of library systems in states and regions. As early as 1898 county-wide libraries were operating in Ohio and Maryland, but the push for state-wide units did not come until the depression years and after. Even in the depths of World War II, library leaders were working in liaison with federal agencies on proposals which resulted in ALA's *Post-War Standards for Public Libraries* (1943), and *A National Plan for Library Service* (1948).[33] The volumes in 1950 of the Public Library Inquiry, and the passage of the Library Services Act in 1956 (PL 84–597), were major spurs to state-wide and multistate development.

It is significant that in *Library Literature* for 1958 through 1960 the heading *Reference work* was supplanted by *Reference services* and had for the first time the subdivision. *Regional centers.* In the 1961–63 compilation the items in this subdivision increased from two to thirteen, as plans for regional service took shape in New York and California. The service, however, was not implemented until the passage of the Library Services and Construction Act of 1964 (PL 89–511), and the amendment of 1966 providing for interlibrary cooperation. By this time many state library commissions were encouraging regional systems. In New York State by 1968, twenty-two public library systems were serving 99 percent of the population, and a state-wide reference and research service had been started.[34] At the beginning of the 1970s thirteen states had enacted interstate library compact legislation and nine other states had such legislation under consideration.

In 1966 Julia Schwartz, chairman of the Cooperative Reference Services Committee of ALA's Reference Services Division, issued an annotated bibliography of what state and regional systems were doing or proposing in the United States and Canada. This listing indicated a degree of coordination and level of services that was impressive.[35] The major elements in these services were the provision of interlibrary loan, photocopy or microform service, long distance information by telephone or teletype, union lists, clearinghouse and referral functions, advisory and consultative services, joint acquisition of reference materials, and literature searches.

A national information system is also not a new idea. Its prehistory includes the proposals by A. Vattemare at the Librarians' Convention in New York in 1853, and by Melvil Dewey in 1896. In 1914 G. W. Lee, librarian of Stone and Webster in Boston, composed a detailed "Outline for a Nation-wide Information System."[36] However, the urgency for such a system was felt only after World War II with the proliferation of research libraries, documentation and information centers numbering more than ten thousand in the United States and Canada by 1966. Because these expensive systems were often competing and overlapping, there were studies beginning in 1958 which recommended the coordination into a national system. The most significant and ambitious of these studies have been the Weinberg report of 1963, *Science, Government, and Information*; the report by the Committee on Scientific and Technical Information (COSATI) of 1965; and in 1969 *Libraries at Large*, by the National Advisory Commission on Libraries.[37] In 1973 the latter was reconstituted as a permanent body called the National Commission on Libraries and Information Science.

In the 1970s the barriers to a functional national information network still seemed formidable: competing information systems and libraries; lack of training and interest in information technology by librarians; lack of national standards in documentation processes; and finally, lack of federal and state funding to implement a system.

Technology in Reference

According to Carlos A. Cuadra, a prominent information scientist, the major challenges that technology has posed for the nation's libraries are the electronic digital computer, microform and audiovisual equipment and techniques, the rapid electrical transmission of materials, and new publication techniques.[38]

Electronic digital computer. Although computerized data processing has leaped into prominence of mind-boggling dimensions only since World War II, it is based on concepts which can be traced back at least as far as France's eighteenth-century textile industry. As to the computer's library and reference applications, its advantages are obvious: "(1) it . . . can store vast amounts of data; (2) it saves hours of human time in sorting . . .; (3) it can rapidly search a whole body of information and come up with specific requested items; (4) it can be used for rapid print-out of materials."[39]

One early form of automatic information retrieval was Key-Word-In-Context (KWIC), begun in the 1950s as a less-expensive and time-consuming method of indexing. More sophisticated experiments and projects swiftly followed. A 1966 survey by the Special Libraries Association, quoted in *Libraries at Large*, revealed that as many as 209 libraries were using data processing equipment, principally in serials management and acquisition. As for reference work or document retrieval, it was used in "131 installations, 76 of which were special libraries in industrial organizations. No public libraries, and only 18 colleges and universities, were undertaking this type of activity."[40] The most famous library retrieval system, Medical Literature Analysis and Retrieval System (MEDLARS), was begun in 1961 at the National

182 / Facilities

Library of Medicine. In 1966 educational institutions cooperated to form Education Resources Information Center (ERIC), a network of clearinghouses to index, abstract, and distribute microfiche material in this field. A significant advance in cooperation and computerization took place in 1967 with the founding of the Ohio College Library Center (OCLC), which offered over 300 member institutions in twenty-eight states as of 1975, a service of on-line union catalog and shared cataloging. The center is organized to provide also systems of serial control, interlibrary loan communications, acquisitions, remote catalog access and circulation control, and retrieval by subject.[41] In 1968 INTREX was started at the Massachusetts Institute of Technology to test applications of the computer for information retrieval by automating its engineering library. In 1972 the *New York Times* Information Bank first offered a limited computer access to its columns for its own staff, since extended to institutional subscribers.

It was a natural outcome of the increased efficiency of the documentation process that it be followed by attempts to control the output for the convenience of the library user. Thus selective dissemination of information (SDI) was born. Reference librarians had been using this process in a nonautomatic way since the beginning of their profession, but it was discovered that machines too could ease the process of identifying specific interests of users and speeding current information to them, generally in the forms of bibliographies and abstracts.

Automation has been successfully applied to such library processes as circulation, acquisition, serials management, and cataloging. However, as Cuadra has noted, "In comparison with other library operations, the reference function shows very little in the way of application of technology for most libraries."[42] Many distinguished library leaders have believed that reference librarians must seriously consider automatic retrieval to some degree. The list includes Jesse Shera, who pioneered in information retrieval education for librarians at Case Western Reserve, Joseph Becker, Frederick G. Kilgour, and many others.

The problem for many reference librarians has been: Can and should this type of mechanization be applied in libraries attempting to serve the mass of citizens in a situation where the reference function and process itself has not been clearly defined, or indeed the library user and his information needs clearly identified? In the last ten years this question has been debated hotly in conferences and in library literature. In 1964 *RQ* carried two articles under the titles. "Goodbye, Reference Librarian!" and "Are Reference Librarians Obsolete?" an unthinkable question up to that moment, but plaintively asked then and since.[43] Among those advising caution has been Dorothy Sinclair, who warned that although "reference librarians . . . must improve their product and enter into alliances with so-called competitors whose techniques and skills can further our goals," the primary function of the reference librarian as a "skilled intermediary" between the "information and user's need" must not be lost.[44] There is also the formidable problem of efficient subject analysis of materials or programming, especially in nonscientific fields where meanings may not be precise, with the consequence of librarians or users being overwhelmed by a flood of citations that may be either inapplicable or redundant.

Microform. Literally a new dimension in reference work was microfilm, introduced in the 1920s as the culmination of a long series of improvements in photography, notably the miniature camera. By the 1930s many scholarly libraries were engaged in microfilm projects using Leica, Eastman's Recordak, or Remington Rand equipment. Microfilming became the topic of round table meetings at ALA Conferences beginning in 1935; and from 1938 to 1942 ALA published five volumes of the *Journal of Documentary Reproduction,* devoted primarily to microfilming techniques in libraries. In the following year Columbia started the first course in microphotography for its library school students. In 1951 the National Microfilm Association was founded; it has produced many publications useful to libraries, particularly guides to equipment.[45]

Microfilm activity was at first seen as a method of saving space and at the same time preserving valuable but fragile materials, such as newspapers. Libraries which had no other microfilm generally subscribed to the *New York Times* microfilm edition, which with its excellent *Index* made a major reference source out of material previously difficult to store and retrieve.

The exact relationship of microfilm to reference work is somewhat difficult to define. Its contributions have been largely in the area of building research collections. Because microfilms are usually referred to, not read at length, and are noncirculating materials, they have been kept most frequently in reference departments. Also the indexes of microfilmed materials are reference books. Among the technologies connected with reference work, microfilm has the longest history, and is the most generally accepted not only in academic but also in public and school libraries.

Since World War II many manufacturers have sought to capitalize on the popularity of microfilm by offering variations, each with its own advantages and disadvantages. The first of these were the opaque microforms, microimages printed or photographed on fine quality card stock, such as Readex Microprint and Microcards. Long runs of serials and whole libraries of books were printed by this means. The opaque microform, however, has been plagued with one handicap: the image when enlarged, coming as it must from reflected light, is not as clear and bright as that from translucent microforms, such as microfilm and microfiche.

Developed in Europe during or soon after World War II, microfiche became very popular in federal research agencies, when it was found ideal for the storage of short scientific reports in minimal space. In standard microfiche, microfilmed material has been reproduced on 4-by-6-inch sheets of translucent film in either negative or positive form, producing images of the same clarity as those obtained from microfilm. As if these microformats were not enough, at least two "high-reduction" microfiche formats have been introduced. Photo-Chromic Micro Images (PCMI), brought out in 1964, provide 4-by-6-inch microfiches, reproducing over 3,000 book-sized pages on one fiche. They are sold in large "libraries" of standard classics in such areas as American history and literature. Somewhat similar in approach is the Microbook program of Library Resources, Inc., a subsidiary of Encyclopaedia Britannica.

In computer-output-microfilming (COM), it has been found possible to record the output of computers much more rapidly on microfiche than by print-outs on paper. This already has extensive use in updating serials catalogs and other computerized records, with the entire serial record of a large university library, for instance, available on five or six microfiche. And more astounding processes of miniaturization are in the offing. The recording process known as holography promises that the "Library of Congress can be recorded holographically on a single slab of recording media."[46]

Audiovisual aids. Another of the technologies affecting libraries cited by Cuadra was audiovisual equipment and techniques. The audiovisual movement is an outgrowth of an educational development at the turn of the century generally known then as "visual instruction." Originally it referred to the use of mounted pictures, lantern slides, and stereoscopic views in teaching, and these visual aids were commonly found in libraries, at least through the period of the First World War. Phonograph records were also accepted by librarians quite early in their history because of the demand by music educators and music lovers. The filmstrip, which largely replaced the cumbersome glass lantern slides, was introduced in the 1920s. In the same decade the 16mm silent motion picture began to be used in classrooms. Indeed, Paul Saettler, in his excellent *History of Instructional Technology*, has pointed out that the period of 1918 to 1924 saw the birth of the audiovisual movement, when the first classes were taught, the first journals published, and the first research done in that field.[47] The perfection of the 16mm sound motion picture in the 1930s provided the first truly audiovisual tool for teaching.

Although audiovisual materials are clearly adaptable to libraries in that they may be acquired, cataloged, classified, and circulated, they were accepted only reluctantly. Public libraries have had success in incorporating them into their collections, but audiovisual materials under school auspices have as often as not been under an administrative agency separate from the school library. Somewhat belatedly, mostly in the 1960s as the result of the availability of abundant federal funds, school libraries were enabled to increase their audiovisual services; and indeed the term, *media center*, has been widely adopted to describe the school library in the hope of replacing the old bookish image with a multimedia one. University libraries have almost without exception scorned these materials, presumably as not being of a scholarly nature, and have witnessed in many instances on their campuses huge film libraries giving nation-wide service under the auspices of education departments or extension services.

Audiovisual materials as such hardly fit the definition of reference materials; that is, materials designed readily to provide brief factual information. Picture files and map collections may fit this definition, but films, filmstrips, recordings, and even slides, are designed to be "read" through. However, guides and indexes to these materials, such as Wilson Company's *Educational Film Guide*, which ran from the mid-1930s to 1962, are clearly reference works. Currently, the reference librarian, with the aid of special volumes of the *National Union Catalog*, the NICEM indexes, and the *Learning Directory*, is able to locate a wider variety of library materials than before.[48]

In the last decade, as a result of research in the areas of behavioral psychology, the comparatively simple tenets of the audiovisualists have been replaced by the complicated theories and sophisticated devices of the educational technologists, culminating particularly in the "teaching machine." Such devices are even more difficult to define as reference materials, and indeed there are many who would deny they are even "library materials." Some libraries serving clienteles in education have insisted that they are not classrooms. However, in some schools and community colleges the library is being transformed into a "learning center," including teaching machines along with traditional materials.

Rapid electrical transmission of materials. Refinements and new discoveries in the communication field have had a great impact on reference service, not changing its essential nature so much as increasing its effectiveness and volume. This has been especially true in carrying out interlibrary loans and long distance reference, which have taken a long leap forward with the advent of Wide Area Telephone Service (WATS), teletype (TWX), and now telefacsimile. In 1967 major TWX installations were operating to link public and academic libraries in Connecticut and Rhode Island, and in a network of sixteen colleges in Texas and Louisiana. At the same time telefacsimile was being tested at the University of California, in New York State, and at the University of Nevada. At the latter a Xerox Magnavox Telecopier was transmitting a ten-page request in less than an hour.[49] Instantaneous communication by way of cathode ray tube terminals or teletype has been fundamental to the success of the Ohio College Library Center.

Publication techniques. The last technology of the four mentioned, new publication techniques, has also been of incalculable benefit to reference work, both in interlibrary loan and in the publication of valuable reference tools. Reprography, the mechanical methods of copying the printed page, has supplanted the age-old reliance on hand-copying. The invention of photography produced copy cameras, the best known of which was the photostat machine, used by the Library of Congress as early as 1912; but its expense kept it from wide use. In 1929 "only very large libraries are provided with a photographic copying service of their own."[50] This remained the case at least through 1945 when devices such as Xerox copiers came into use.

Library users reacted with alacrity to each improvement in copying methods, and reference librarians became concerned lest they appear to condone offenses against copyright law. In 1935 publishers and scholars had worked out an uneasy truce known as the Gentlemen's Agreement, whereby it was understood that single copies for the sole use of a researcher were permissible. But as the copying machines improved, there was increasing concern about the ease with which parts of books and journals could be reproduced. An attempt to revise the law was made in 1955, but a final draft has still not been decided upon.[51]

Photo-offset lithography provided reference librarians with further welcome assistance. Beginning in the late 1930s this process, which eliminated the need for laborious typesetting, made possible the reprinting of many older classic reference sets. Soon there flourished a reprint market, replete with its own bibliographies. As the late Verner W. Clapp noted,

> Without photo-offset lithography the vast majority of current bibliographic publication would not exist: we would have neither the bibliographies and catalogs resulting from mounted cards (like the G. K. Hall catalogs) and from mounted and shingled cards (like the LC publications), nor those created by the sequential camera (like Nuclear Science Abstracts) nor those that result from punched card and computer line print-out (like the various KWIC indexes) nor those that are the product of the photo composing machine (like the new *Index Medicus*).[52]

In addition to the increased store of valuable bibliographic tools produced by computerized publication techniques, the last quarter-century has seen other events of importance to reference collections. The work of Isadore Gilbert Mudge was carried on by Constance M. Winchell, whose eighth edition of *Guide to Reference Books* was issued in 1967. The supplements to it were compiled by Eugene P. Sheehy, who prepared the ninth edition published in 1976. This book in its various editions has been the bible for the training of reference librarians since 1902. Other important guides to reference work have been compiled by Louis Shores, William Katz, Frances N. Cheney, and Bohdan Wynar.[53] Shores and Cheney have also made valuable contributions for many years to reference book selection in their annual lists appearing in library periodicals since 1938.

REFERENCE SERVICES IN ALA

Reference interests in the national organization were represented first in the College and Reference Section, established in 1889. The section always included, however, a fair number of reference librarians from public and special libraries, so that by 1948, of the 756 members in the Association of College and Research Libraries (organized as a division in 1938), only 25 percent were from colleges and universities. The dichotomy of interests spurred the formation in 1952 of the Reference Section of the Public Libraries Division, but many reference librarians belonged to both organizations. Finally, after recurrent demands for separate status, and after the ALA management survey of 1957, the Reference Services Division was created that same year, under the leadership of Louis Shores.[54]

In the next two decades there were further organizational shifts, reflecting the adoption of computer technology in research libraries, and also the effort by public libraries to reach a broader spectrum of the population with a more aggressive concept of service. They resulted in the formation of the Information Science and Automation Division in 1966, and in 1972, the merging of the Adult Services Division with the Reference Services Division to become the Reference and Adult Services Division.

The accomplishments of RASD and its parent sections in ALA have been impressive. Since 1958 one of its committees has helped prepare the annual reference issue of *Library Journal*, and another advises the H. W. Wilson Company on the selection of periodicals for their indexes. In 1955 it began a survey, finally published in 1961 as *Reference Services in American Public Libraries*,[55] and since 1961 the division has issued the quarterly, *RQ*. Its History Section started a series of Occasional Papers in 1962. In 1968 it published a revision of the *Interlibrary Loan Code*. As of 1974 the number of committees totalled twenty-three, plus additional ad hoc and joint committees working in information retrieval, public documents, library education, and technical services. Recent lists of committees reflect the merger with the former Adult Services Division, showing a concern for service to the aging, to American Indians, the Spanish-speaking, and labor. One of its more recently formed committees is that of Information Retrieval, testifying to the impact of automation on reference work.

Obviously the activities of ALA itself have had considerable impact on reference service: in addition to *Subscription Books Bulletin* there have been a succession of surveys, standards, catalogs of best books, and reference guides. In 1964 and 1965 it operated Library, USA at the New York World's Fair in cooperation with the Special Libraries

Association and the American Documentation Institute, where professional librarians demonstrated up-to-the-minute reference service with the aid of microfilm reader-printers and a UNIVAC computer. More recently it has established an Office for Library Service to the Disadvantaged.

A LOOK INTO THE FUTURE

The prospects for reference service are inevitably tied to the future of the library as an institution. The years ahead will undoubtedly see continued interest in the network idea. It is also possible that tomorrow's library user will demand that information from libraries be delivered directly to the home by means of dial access (telephone) and cathode ray tube displays (television).

While the wave of the future may lie with these new concepts and technologies, it is likely to be modified by social conditions difficult to predict. The literature in the communication field tends to be written by enthusiasts seeing a rosy, indeed millenial, outlook for their specialties, ignoring the possibilities of economic depression, war, over- or under-population, and of the depletion of natural resources. In addition, there has been a backlash among librarians concerned about overemphasis on technology, about the fate of the humanities and social sciences in library resources and service. There are those not willing to say farewell to the browsing room and the librarian who reads stories to children and personally helps people select books and answers their questions.

Historically, however, modern culture has seen the realization of its wildest technological dreams, and there is every reason to believe this will continue. Perhaps no one has better expressed the challenge of technological change to libraries than Carlos C. Cuadra: "These functions are going to take place and if the library does not bring them about, some other type of agency will. That agency will then occupy the central role in the information business—the role that was once occupied by the library."[56] It has already been noted how audiovisual services, computerized data banks, or community information centers have developed outside of the library field. In the last analysis, however, it may be that the library with its tremendous momentum from the past will continue in a position of strength, will either absorb these similar-but-separate functions or find ways to cooperate with competing agencies to the ultimate benefit of those seeking information.

NOTES

1. Samuel Rothstein, "The Development of the Concept of Reference Service in American Libraries, 1850–1900," *Library Quarterly* 23:3 (Jan. 1953).

2. William A. Katz, *Introduction to Reference Work*, 2d ed., 2:60 (New York: McGraw-Hill, 1972).
3. Walter M. Whitehill, *Boston Public Library* (Cambridge: Harvard Univ. Pr., 1956), p. 56.
4. Samuel S. Green, "Personal Relations between Librarian and Readers," *American Library Journal* 1:74–81 (Nov. 1876).
5. Ibid., p. 74.
6. Ibid., p. 75.
7. Ibid., p. 78.
8. Ibid., p. 79.
9. Louis Kaplan, *The Growth of Reference Service in the United States from 1876 to 1893*, ACRL Monographs, no. 2 (Chicago: Association of College and Research Libraries, 1952).
10. Carl P. Vitz, "Cleveland Experience with Departmentalized Reference Work," *Bulletin of the American Library Association* 9:169–74 (July 1915).
11. William W. Bishop, "The Theory of Reference Work," *Bulletin of the American Library Association* 9:134 (July 1915).
12. Ibid.
13. Samuel Rothstein, *The Development of Reference Services through Academic Traditions, Public Library Practice, and Special Librarianship*, ACRL Monographs, no. 14 (Chicago: Association of College and Research Libraries, June 1955), pp. 90–93, 94–97.
14. Edward B. Stanford, *Library Extension under the WPA* (Chicago: Univ. of Chicago Pr., 1944), esp. pp. 118–19.
15. R. Russell Munn, "Special Reference Functions in Wartime," in Chicago, University, Graduate Library School, Library Institute, *The Reference Function of the Library* (Chicago: Univ. of Chicago Pr., 1943), pp. 323–40.
16. Dan Lacy, "Social Change and the Library: 1945–1980," in *Libraries at Large*, Douglas M. Knight and E. Shepley Nourse, eds. (New York: Bowker, 1969), p. 3.
17. U.S. Bureau of Education, *Public Libraries in the United States of America: Their History, Condition, and Management* (Washington: Govt. Print. Off., 1876); American Library Association, *A Survey of Libraries in the United States*, 4v. (Chicago: American Library Assn., 1926–27).
18. Winifred L. Davis, "Measuring Results in Reference Work," *Wisconsin Library Bulletin* 18:234–35 (1922); Ruth W. White, "Measuring the Immeasurable: Reference Standards," *RQ* 11:308–10 (Summer 1972).
19. Dorothy E. Cole, "Some Characteristics of Reference Work," *College and Research Libraries* 7:45–51 (Jan. 1946); Mabel L. Conat, "Detroit P.L. Surveys Reference Use," *Library Journal* 72:1569–72 (Nov. 15, 1947).
20. Bernard Berelson, *The Library's Public* (New York: Columbia Univ. Pr., 1949).
21. Illinois, University, Graduate School of Library Science, *The Library as a Community Information Center* (Champaign: Illini Union Bookstore, 1959); Conference on the Present Status and Future Prospects of Reference/Information Service, 1966, Columbia University, *Proceedings* (Chicago: American Library Assn., 1967); Conference on Interlibrary Communications and Information Networks, 1970, Airlie House, Va., *Proceedings* (Chicago: American Library Assn., 1971).
22. Katz, 2:249–57.
23. Arthur E. Bostwick, *The American Public Library* (New York: Appleton, 1910), p. 62.
24. Sarah R. Reed, "1946–56 Public Library Reference Services," *Library Journal* 82:133 (Jan. 15, 1957).
25. Katharine G. Harris, "Reference Service in Public Libraries," *Library Trends* 12:380 (Jan. 1964).

26. Katz, 2:53.
27. Eric E. Moon, "High John: Report on a Unique Experiment in Maryland Designed to Initiate Change in Public Library Service and in Library Education," *Library Journal* 93:147–55 (Jan. 15, 1968).
28. Patrick Penland, "Floating Librarian," in *Encyclopedia of Library and Information Science* 8:501–30 (New York: Dekker, 1972).
29. Ibid., p. 518.
30. Samuel S. Green, "Interlibrary Loans in Reference Work," *Library Journal* 23:567–68 (1898).
31. Rolland E. Stevens, "A Study of Interlibrary Loan," *College and Research Libraries* 35:337 (Sept. 1974).
32. Rolland E. Stevens, *A Feasibility Study of Centralized and Regionalized Interlibrary Loan Centers* (Washington, D.C.: Association of Research Libraries, 1973).
33. American Library Association, Committee on Post-War Planning, *Post-War Standards for Public Libraries* (Chicago: American Library Assn., 1943); Carleton B. Joeckel and Amy Winslow, *A National Plan for Public Library Service* (Chicago: American Library Assn., 1948).
34. Harold S. Hacker, "Implementing Network Plans in New York State: Jurisdictional Considerations in the Design of Library Networks," in Conference on Interlibrary Communications and Information Networks, 1970, Airlie House, Va., *Proceedings*, p. 233.
35. Julia Schwartz, "A Bibliography of Cooperative Reference Service," *RQ* 6:73–81 (Winter 1966).
36. G. W. Lee, "Sponsors for Knowledge. Outline for a Nationwide Information Service," *Library Journal* 39:886–90 (Dec. 1914).
37. U.S. President's Science Advisory Committee, *Science, Government, and Information* (Washington, D.C.: Govt. Print. Off., 1963); U.S. Federal Council for Science and Technology, Committee on Scientific and Technical Information, *Recommendations for National Document-Handling Systems in Science and Technology* (Washington, D.C.: 1965).
38. Carlos A. Cuadra, "Libraries and Technological Forces Affecting Them," *ALA Bulletin* 63:759–68 (June 1969).
39. Katz, 2:217.
40. Knight and Nourse, eds., *Libraries at Large*, p. 302.
41. *Bowker Annual of Library and Book Trade Information, 1975* (New York: Bowker, 1975), pp. 95–99.
42. Cuadra, p. 762.
43. Eli M. Oboler, "Goodbye, Reference Librarians!" *RQ* 4:12–13 (Sept. 1964); R. H. Parker, "Are Reference Librarians Obsolete?" ibid., 3:9–10 (July 1964).
44. Dorothy M. Sinclair, "The Next Ten Years of Reference Service," *ALA Bulletin* 62:59 (Jan. 1968).
45. Budd L. Gambee, "Recent Developments in Audiovisual," *Southeastern Librarian* 22:74–88 (Summer 1972).
46. Anthony Debons, "Holography," in *Encyclopedia of Library and Information Science* 10:458.
47. Paul Saettler, *A History of Instructional Technology* (New York: McGraw-Hill, 1968).
48. Budd L. Gambee, *Non-Book Materials as Library Resources* (Chapel Hill: Univ. of North Carolina, Student Stores, 1970).
49. Karl E. Nyren, "A Reference Roundup," *Library Journal* 92:1582 (Apr. 15, 1967).
50. Charles F. McCombs, *The Reference Department* (Chicago: American Library Assn., 1929), p. 21.
51. Knight and Nourse, eds., *Libraries at Large*, pp. 228–63.

52. Verner W. Clapp, "Three Ages of Reference Work," *Special Libraries* 57:382 (July-Aug. 1966).

53. Louis Shores, *Basic Reference Sources* (Chicago: American Library Assn., 1954); William A. Katz; Frances N. Cheney, *Fundamental Reference Sources* (Chicago: American Library Assn., 1971); Bohdan S. Wynar, *Introduction to Bibliography and Reference Work*, 4th ed. (Rochester: Libraries Unlimited, 1967).

54. Frances N. Cheney, "The Reference Services Division: A Look before and After," *RQ* 4:3-6,16 (Sept. 1964).

55. American Library Association, Reference Services Division, Public Library Reference Survey Committee, *Reference Service in American Public Libraries Serving Populations of 10,000 or More*, University of Illinois Library School Occasional Papers, no. 61 (Urbana: Univ. of Illinois Graduate School of Library Science, 1961).

56. Cuadra, p. 767.

10
Technical Services and Technology: The Bibliographical Imperative

SUZANNE MASSONNEAU
Texas A and M University

The second and third of S. R. Ranganathan's five laws of library science are "Every reader his book" and "Every book its reader."[1] If this statement is updated by substituting the word *information* or *work* for *book* in both laws, it will encompass the mission of the later twentieth-century library. However, the simplicity of the statement should not be mistaken for a truism; it is actually a bibliographical imperative. Its implication is that every library user deserves to make contact with the precise information, neither more nor less, that is needed. If the information is held in the library and the contact is not made, the system and the people who operate it have failed. The impact of this kind of failure may be mild disappointment, but it may also have disastrous consequences when the various uses of information are considered. This is what cataloging—bibliographic and subject organization for retrieval—is all about: pointing the way to information that is ready and waiting to be used.

In the century under review librarians have sought to bring reason, system, and economy to the technical side of their retrieval responsibilities. The latter part of the nineteenth century was a time of gradual realization of the intellectual importance of libraries and the obligation of the custodians to reveal their wealth of resources to the public. Thus systems were born, tried, modified, replaced, and new systems evolved. The aspect of librarianship known as cataloging developed out of this need to organize libraries to serve the user and simultaneously exploit available resources. In this pursuit librarians have made steady progress, although occasionally following a detour, with the net result that some old problems persist but many conditions have improved; librarians have coped with situations undreamed of a century ago.

The group of librarians who came together in 1876 to form the American Library Association was particularly interested in finding ways of cooperating, a single word which might still be used as a rallying cry today.[2] Another enduring concern has been the maximal utilization of resources among libraries, with obvious implications for both cooperation and the techniques of bibliographical organization. A perusal of the early issues of *Library Journal*,[3] *ALA Bulletin*,[4] and *Catalogers' and Classifiers' Yearbook*[5] shows concern for such esoterica as "The Cataloging of Medieval Romances";[6] but most of the space is devoted to such timeless topics as costs, codes, catalog form, catalog use, subject analysis, union catalogs, and administrative matters. Some burning issues of those early days have been solved only to become irrelevant as new trends changed our direction, and technical services became more "technical."

The "desultory reading" referred to by Charles Cutter still exists, but as he observed in 1876, demands on librarians were becoming such that they could no longer depend on memory to find books which are "sometimes wanted very much, although not wanted often."[7] The rapid development of scholarship and technology during the twentieth century created an atmosphere in which the library's resources were strained at every point; at the same time the library faced new demands from the community which sought an "open" institution comparable to the school and the church.

The following sections will cover three major areas of technical services: Catalog Codes and Catalogs, Bibliographic Retrieval, and Subject Organization and Retrieval. The treatment of these topics is not intended to be exhaustive, but rather is an attempt to suggest some of the principal problems, solutions, and trends.

CATALOG CODES AND CATALOGS

Responding to increased demands upon libraries during the nineteenth century, several pioneering librarians produced systematic rules for cataloging books. They recognized that inconsistencies of entry in the printed catalogs of the time were no longer acceptable, and that varous schemes for assigning books on particular subjects to designated shelves did not allow for author or title approach to the collection.

Most notable among the early code-makers was Sir Anthony Panizzi, keeper of the printed books at the British Museum. In his "Rules for the Compilation of the Catalogue," published in 1841, he considers the same problems of choice and form of entry, description, cross-referencing, and filing order that are repeated in codes to the present day.[8]

In the United States Panizzi's ideas were taken up and modified by Charles Coffin Jewett, who needed standardized rules in order to accomplish his plan of collecting bibliographic data and making it available for printing individual library catalogs.[9] This plan to prevent duplication of work failed, but its final realization may be seen today in Cataloging in Publication and in the activities of various networks which now have the technological capacity to further Jewett's dream of cooperation and economy.

The development of catalog codes has fluctuated from a pragmatic approach to an emphasis on "technical correctness to the point of pedantry";[10] often positions on specific issues have changed. One need only trace the treatment of pseudonyms or married women's names through the codes since Panizzi to see each generation reversing the stand of its predecessors. On the other hand, some early positions have been hard to overcome and have probably delayed the introduction of new ideas. A good example is the division of corporate bodies into societies and institutions which persisted in the *Anglo-American Cataloging Rules* (AACR), compromise rules ninety-eight and ninety-nine.[11] This anomaly was finally corrected in 1972,[12] but the Library of Congress practice for established names is at least temporarily perpetuated by the policy of "superimposition," which preserves the previously established forms of names even if they are not consistent with the currently adopted code.[13] Superimposition should not be confused with "successive entry" where a corporate body changes its name, with the result that its various works appear under the name in force at the time of publication.[14]

During the days of Panizzi and Jewett there had been much discussion of the merits of an alphabetical catalog as compared to the classified form. With the publication in 1876 of Charles Cutter's *Rules for a Printed Dictionary Catalog* as part of the Special Report on Public Libraries the dictionary catalog was becoming the dominant form;[15] classified catalogs were becoming extinct in America. Cutter's experience in compiling the catalog of the Boston Athenaeum had acquainted him with the full range of bibliographic problems, enabling him to write the most comprehensive code of the nineteenth century.[16] In his introduction he observed the basic need for "principles" which continues to concern us:

> But for a dictionary catalogue as a whole, and for most of its parts, there is no manual whatever. Nor have any of the above-mentioned works [Panizzi, Jewett, etc.] attempted to set forth the rules in a systematic way or to investigate what might be called the first principles of cataloguing.[17]

In the ensuing decades librarians debated the function of the catalog, advocating everything from an abbreviated finding list to a detailed reference tool. They continued to disagree over Cutter's regard for setting "the convenience of the public . . . before the ease of the cataloger."[18] Nevertheless, there has been recurring agreement with the ideas expressed in Cutter's "Objects."[19] His rules, which went through four editions between 1876 and 1904, increased in coverage and complexity and strongly influenced subsequent codes. The tradition of catalog code development and revision by various committees of ALA also began during that period, and it has continued to the present day.[20] Although this method tends to produce unevenness of style, it offers the advantages of utilizing experts on various aspects of the total cataloging problem and of airing conflicting ideas. Cutter was the only individual to cover the whole range from entry to description, and add subject analysis as well.

The twentieth century began with an event of far-reaching consequences, the issuance of printed catalog cards for sale by the Library of Congress. From that point forward there was a new degree of consistency in our library catalogs, but there was also the question of whether developing codes should rationalize and explain LC practice, or whether they should be designed to produce the most effective retrieval, no matter what precedents were already established.[21] In fact, when the *AACR* was published, our libraries were so tied to LC practice that they had to accept LC's compromises with the principles which had been adopted by the International Conference on Cataloguing Principles.[22] Most libraries even welcomed the LC policy of "superimposition," although it was a denial of a considerable portion of the *AACR* chapters on headings for persons and for corporate bodies; it simply made things easier for the time being.

The 1908 rules, called Anglo-American because of the cooperation between the British and American catalogers, were the offspring of Cutter, plus accommodation to LC.[23] They remained in effect, with a good deal of marginalia built up to interpret LC practice, until the preliminary edition of the ALA rules in 1941. In Great Britain the 1908 rules were followed until the publication of *AACR* in 1967.

The efforts of the 1930s produced the *ALA Catalog Rules: Author and Title Entries* (preliminary ed.),[24] which represented a continuing accretion of rules to cover new problems, with corresponding loss of sight of basic objectives and receding possibility of trying fresh approaches. In a statement facing the title page the publisher noted disagreement between "some catalogers and some administrators" over "too much elaboration" in the rules.[25]

After the publication of the preliminary edition, Andrew Osborn articulated the administrators' ideas and advocated a pragmatic approach to cataloging practice.[26] In 1949 the appearance of the *ALA Cataloging Rules for Author and Title Entries* (2d ed.) brought more criticism.[27] Seymour Lubetzky, who was working at LC, wrote *Cataloging Rules and Principles*, in which he asked, "Is this rule necessary?" and suggested the requisites of a new code.[28] Within the next seven

196 / *Facilities*

years he presented the profession with two draft codes which became the basis of the *AACR*.[29]

Although the tendency in the mid-twentieth century had been toward systematizing practices responsive to new problems and new forms of materials, Lubetzky and the catalogers who achieved agreement at the International Conference on Cataloguing Principles in 1961 found a way to simplify rules, even in the face of a growing diversity of types of materials.[30] As far as possible, they would be guided by the bibliographic conditions of authorship, not by the form of material. They would seek the principle behind each condition, rather than develop a rule for every problem. The bibliographic totality of a work would be analyzed and then shaped into a form which would make systematic retrieval possible and logical. Even audiovisual materials without conventional bibliographic elements could be forced into this pattern, and then integrated into multimedia catalogs. The *AACR* embodies these ideas to a point, but has suffered considerable criticism and is currently undergoing thorough revision. Although published in 1967, its approach did not adequately consider the rigorous demands of computer-based systems, which would not tolerate casual inconsistencies or unnecessary frills.

We are now at a major intersection in the history of cataloging which portends a radical break with the past. Traditional catalogs will certainly not be swept away overnight, but many libraries which must cope with a myriad of increasing demands coupled with shrinking financial support must move toward utilization of new forms of cooperation. In most cases this means computerized operations based on networks. There is a question now whether cataloging codes will be of importance in the future, with on-line bibliographic access available on an ever-widening scale. However, there is also recognition of need for bibliographic standardization of description, as demonstrated by the development of the International Standard Bibliographic Description,[31] and its North American version, chapter 6 of the *AACR*.[32] Interest is also growing in the development of Universal Bibliographic Control (UBC).[33] Even if the computer should diminish the importance of catalog codes treating choice of entry, rules for form of entry and description will have ongoing applications.

No matter what codes are used (and most older catalogs have inconsistencies from Cutter onward) or how correctly they have been translated into catalog entries, the factors of physical form and structure also affect retrieval capability. Over the years the format has changed from book to card to book—handwritten, typed, printed, or computer produced—to various microforms. Fullness of entry has ranged from one line in some of the oldest and newest book catalogs to considerable detail in both book and card catalogs. We now have on-line computer access to author, title, and subject finding data, and the time may have come to find a name other than catalog for this instrument.

Within the various formats the physical arrangement of the basic components of author, title, and subject may be in an integrated alphabetical (dictionary) form or may have the components split into separate alphabetical runs in a variety of horizontal and/or vertical patterns. On the other hand, in the classified catalog the alphabetical approach to subjects is confined to a separate index, which itself may take different forms, with the catalog proper arranged by classification notation.

The classified catalog offers not only flexibility of alphabetical subject approach, but also interesting possibilities of subject browsing in the classified section. Unfortunately, this form of catalog is disappearing from U.S. and Canadian libraries, although the computer would seem to offer ways of reducing costs and expediting its use. Its effectiveness may be observed in the *British National Bibliography*.[34] Perhaps the classified catalog is an example of a great idea which was almost lost, but which could emerge again as new techniques, such as chain indexing, make it once again attractive. The alphabetico-classed catalog, which employed either an alphabetical arrangement of main classes with classed subarrangement, or main classes in classification order with subclasses alphabetized, was popular in the nineteenth century and is now extinct.

Register catalogs, with the complete bibliographic data in accession order, but accessed by frequently updated author, title, and subject indexes in book or computer-access form, offer a partial solution to the excessive costs of maintenance of card catalogs or frequent cumulations of printed catalogs. In this case only the brief form indexes need to be kept up-to-date. This type of arrangement has been proposed as one of the elements of a flexible catalog control system for the Library of Congress; the other elements are batch mode processing and on-line access.[35]

Numerous studies have proclaimed the advantages of one form or structure of catalog over the others. It seems plain from the testimony that comparative effectiveness depends on situations, economic resources, technological capacities, and other variables.

BIBLIOGRAPHIC RETRIEVAL

Bibliographic retrieval as an internal or interlibrary function was born of the realization that once a certain amount of effort has been spent in creating a catalog record it is wasteful to repeat the activity. The history of this endeavor to utilize the work of others ranges from Jewett and his premature plan of using stereotyped plates for creating a general catalog of American libraries to the burgeoning activities of the Ohio College Library Center (OCLC) system and similar networks of today.[36]

The major events in bibliographic retrieval since Jewett may be characterized in several groups.

1. Services—printed catalog card sets available from the Library of Congress (since 1901) and from various commercial sources; also, depository cards and proofsheets available from LC
2. Tools—Library of Congress author catalogs and their supplements (1942-52); the *National Union Catalog* (1953-   ); Library of Congress *Books: Subjects* (1950-75); Library of Congress *Subject Catalog* (1975-   ); and various national bibliographies
3. Internal retrieval systems—printed or microform indexes devised to expedite location of LC data by title, LC card number, series, etc.; LC catalog data available in microforms from which catalog cards may be reproduced
4. Dissemination systems—MARC, the LC MAchine Readable Cataloging creation and control system through which all the extant systems or works noted above are now either created or disseminated; Cataloging in Publication (CIP), derived from MARC, provides basic cataloging data in books issued by most U.S. publishers
5. Networks—computer-based bibliographic systems designed to share data among participating members, making possible the creation of bibliographic records for each. Future plans include centralized control of other library functions which lend themselves to computerized treatment.

As these programs have evolved the burdens on the cataloger have changed from hand-copying or typing cards, through various photocopy and edit procedures, to on-line retrieval at a network terminal. This development of methods of distributing bibliographic information has not only expedited cataloging routines and hastened the books to the shelves, but has also improved the quality of the end product and changed the role of the professional cataloger in the operations.

In the early days head librarians were often employed on the basis of their skills in making catalogs and creating classification systems, as well as for the usual administrative abilities. As various standardized or widely applicable systems were adopted they delegated the cataloging chores to their assistants, and eventually clerks were employed to handle routine work. During recent years community colleges and similar institutions have set up training programs for paraprofessional employees who can perform an increasing range of cataloging tasks. At the same time unquestioning acceptance of LC cataloging has become commonplace, relieving the professional cataloger of the performance of dull routines. Gradually the ranks have thinned, and concern now focuses mainly on adapting to changes within the whole field of librarianship, one's own library, and the catalog department. The challenges which face the professional cataloger today are more akin to those which faced her or his counterpart a hundred years ago than those of the generations who laboriously copied entries from LC publications and, often shunning rules, cataloged by analogy to LC practice. The time has come when one can no longer be satisfied with simply performing the traditional procedures faster and more efficiently. Survival requires thinking in new ways about human communication and the psychological aspects of man-computer interaction (e.g., at a terminal), as well as the changing role of the library and its responsibility to its users.

Most catalogers now welcome technological changes as the best hope of making meaningful contributions to their profession during a period of rapid and radical change. Fear of the computer was common in the 1950s and 1960s, but it waned when librarians learned that automation would have to be a mutual rather than an individual process, that its applications would evolve gradually, and that computer experts would, indeed, listen to their problems and help them to understand system demands. For some there was satisfaction that even manual systems could be improved by applying systems analysis techniques.

SUBJECT ORGANIZATION AND RETRIEVAL

The amount of time devoted to the problems of bibliographic retrieval in the past century is incalculable and ongoing. To this day numerous national and international committees are laboring over entry problems of monographs and serials and the feasibility of standardization. The more complex area of subject retrieval, where the users' needs are often only vaguely known or articulated, is in much less satisfactory condition. Not only is the subject approach more complex in its very nature, but the many techniques which have been used have met with varying degrees of acceptance. The profession, through its committees, has devoted less time to seeking solutions to subject analysis than to bibliographic problems. In the case of traditional subject headings, no attempt to codify rules of structure and application has advanced beyond the thinking stage. The situation is further clouded by the fact that the authors of catalog use surveys do not agree on the importance of the subject approach and generalization cannot be made about all types of users.[37]

In reviewing the development of bibliographic analysis as manifested in catalog codes, it is relatively easy to define the topic and to say that two persons, Charles Cutter and Seymour Lubetzky, emerge as the dominant figures of the century. This is not the case with subject retrieval—the term used here to denote any system used in a library setting for the purpose of placing the library user in contact with the information needed.

It might be argued that Melvil Dewey and S. R. Ranganathan dominated the century in classification, but this must be qualified. At a time when no shelf classification scheme was in general acceptance, Dewey drew upon ideas of his predecessors, Edward Williams Johnson and William Torrey Harris (both of the Baconian persuasion), and created the Dewey Decimal Classification (DDC).[38] This system of shelf arrangement with its own alphabetical "relative index" of subjects and a unique notation, involving subdivision of the ten major classes by tens and "mnemonic features," also allowed for relative (movable) location of the books. Dewey promoted his system indefatigably, and through eighteen full editions and ten abridged editions it has grown to be the most widely used system throughout the world.[39] Its frequent revisions and sectional overhauls in the form of "phoenix schedules" have improved the synthesis of notation and have kept the system up-to-date with the many changes in the world of knowledge. In this process of revision Dewey's "integrity of numbers" has been traded for "subject integrity."[40] This is as it must be, as noted by Godfrey Dewey in the introduction to the seventh abridged edition.[41]

Ever since the fifteenth edition, relocations on behalf of subject integrity have created bothersome problems for librarians, and different solutions have been tried. The introduction to the seventeenth edition, taking a new view toward these problems, begins by playing down the importance of classification and ends with a challenge to the classifier's resourcefulness. It implies a greater burden on the catalog, but fails to consider that tool's ability to "cope."[42] The eighteenth edition no longer scorns the librarian with a "compulsion for consistency" and even mentions bad results from "failure to reclassify older materials."[43] Despite these problems, which are felt most in large libraries using close classification, DDC will no doubt survive as long as it is supported by LC in its revision activities and in the application of Dewey class numbers to the materials it catalogs. As recently as mid-1975 a number of DDC changes were announced jointly by LC and the British National Bibliography, and work has continued on the nineteenth edition, indicating its continuing viability.[44] Many academic librarians have reacted to the problems created by "relocation" by changing to what Robert Fairthorne called the "marking and parking" system, Library of Congress Classification.[45]

The Library of Congress Classification owes its authorship to no single person, although most credit should go to J. C. M. Hanson and Charles Martel, who drew on the outline of Charles Cutter's Expansive Classification and designed the system around the "literary warrant" of the books in the library.[46] Three misconceptions about the classification which are widespread among nonusers of the scheme may help to reveal its character. The first misconception is that it is "new" and "modern," while in fact its beginnings date to the turn of the century, and its enumerative, nonanalytic, and nonsynthetic character make it anything but modern. Another misconception is that it is so detailed that it has a different notation for every conceivable topic. Actually, it is so limited in synthetic devices that even geographic or time boundaries of many topics cannot be denoted. In some areas, such as literature, it is possible to be excessively specific, but this is often complicated by the inordinate amount of space squandered on nineteenth century authors, making it necessary to cram all twentieth-century writers into a very few numbers; Robert Browning alone has more space than all the English writers of the twentieth century. A third misconception is that it is suitable in only the largest libraries—an idea which is neither supported nor rejected by any research studies, although the specificity of numbers cannot be reduced as readily as DDC. Some argument can be made for the use of LC classification in schools and small public libraries, thus acquainting users with it from their earliest library experience.

Despite the system's problems noted above, its lack of a general index (now partially ameliorated by the *Subject Keyword Index to the Library of Congress Classification*),[47] and the poor quality of the indexes to the individual schedules,[48] it has grown rapidly in acceptance in North America in new academic libraries and in older libraries previously classed in DDC or a homegrown scheme. By 1975 the academic library in the United States not yet converted to LC was becoming the exception rather than the rule. This popularity must be based on the ease of its use, resulting economies, and the hospitality of the notation which allows introduction of new topics in their proper hierarchical position wherever needed. David Batty was quoted as describing the movement toward LC as "a great leap forward into the nineteenth century."[49] This may be, but it also gives a semblance of order to books on shelves, which could be quite adequate if we had better subject analysis in our catalogs and made a more serious effort to educate users in the exploitation of various catalogs and retrieval tools.

Ranganathan, the great Indian librarian and philosopher, revolted against the enumerative, rigid, and unlogical character of Dewey's classification system and created the Colon Classification, which is so complex in notation as to be almost useless as a shelf-ordering system. Nevertheless, Ranganathan's theoretical approach to subject analysis has had tremendous influence on his contemporaries and his followers in the development of post-enumerative schemes and in other aspects of subject analysis. The details of his system, which has also gone through several revisions, are difficult to understand. However, the barest grasp of facet analysis, the fundamental categories (PMEST), and simple examples of notational synthesis, reveal why the DDC and LC classifications are now regarded as incapable of dealing with complex subjects and doing what they do in a relatively unmethodical way.

In the field of subject headings, the purely linguistic approach to subject content, Charles Cutter's ideas as expressed in his *Rules for a Dictionary Catalog*,[50] have governed the practice of the Library of Congress, which in turn has had national and sometimes international influence. Although practitioners at LC began to realize the weaknesses and inconsistencies in the system, they were bound by the size of their commitment to it.

In spite of Cutter's "specific entry," which tells us to use specific names for topics which have names, but general class names for topics "which are spoken of only by a phrase or by several phrases not definite enough yet to be used as a heading,"[51] effective subject retrieval has not always resulted. The cataloger who treats a work on a very complex topic or various aspects of the topic may often find no available "specific entries." He then lists the work under general class entries where it is virtually lost to the person who has neither the ability, time, nor patience for an extended search. How many users, taking Cutter's example, would search for a work on the movement of fluids in plants under *Botany* (*Physiology*)? When the cataloger uses several general terms which in combination seem to characterize a topic, this relationship of terms is lost as soon as the headings are dispersed to their alphabetical places in the catalog.

Cutter did not comprehend the full ramifications of subject analysis, nor could he anticipate the importance of vocabulary control or citation order in twentieth-century information retrieval. However, it is unfair to criticize the one who went first for not perceiving and solving all the problems. Verbal subject analysis before his time was accidental (i.e., inverted title indexes) or nonexistent. Today, with subject analysis still in an amorphous state, authors of factual works would be well advised to devise very specific and meaningful titles which are then retrievable directly through title or through various key word indexes. Furthermore, the title approach, which was avoided except as a last resort for many years, has gained new respectability and is particularly evident in serials handling and other internal working files.

Library of Congress Subject Headings (*LCSH*),[52] which is currently in its eighth edition, is the descendant of a list prepared by an ALA committee and published in 1895.[53] From the turn of the century on, various committees of the Division of Cataloging and Classification and staff members of the Library of Congress concerned themselves with the problems of subject headings and the development of lists.[54] It had long been recognized that there was a need for a comprehensive subject headings code, and it was hoped by many that LC's David Haykin would develop it. However, his *Subject Headings*,[55] published in 1951, "sought only to explain and bring some system to what LC practice had done with Cutter's approach to the dictionary catalog."[56] It was the same problem the authors of codes of entry had encountered in divorcing themselves from LC practice.

In her study on subject analysis twenty years after Haykin's work, Jessica Harris found that "The state of the art had not really advanced a great deal since the publication of Cutter's *Rules* in 1876."[57] The Harris study, using a 10 percent sample of the *LCSH* seventh edition headings, found that all but 21 percent of the headings could be restyled clerically for computer arrangement.[58] In another recent work J. P. Immroth studied LC subject headings and the terminology of the indexes to the LC classification. He demonstrated the feasibility of the application of chain indexing procedures to LC subject retrieval and found little consistency between the terms in *LCSH* and the indexes to the classification schedules.[59]

The concern for conversion of the existing list may become academic if the "radical solution" of John Rather's report on catalog control at LC becomes a reality and the opportunity to improve subject analysis is taken.

> When all current cataloging is being converted to MARC, the card catalogs should be closed. The most radical but realistic decision would be to regard the closed catalog only as a reference source. According to this policy, the MARC data base would be complete in itself thus allowing name headings, subject headings, and call numbers to be established solely with regard to related elements on MARC records. The non-MARC catalog entries could then be considered for publication in book or microform.[60]

No matter what course is taken by LC in the future, the need for a comprehensive subject headings code is nonetheless pressing.

Another important name in the development of subject headings is Minnie Earl Sears, who edited the early editions of the *List of Subject Headings for Small Libraries*, a work which is still revised periodically and is widely used in school and public libraries.[61] It was originally based on actual headings used in nine representative small libraries, and in some cases responds more closely to commonly used terminology than *LCSH*. In recent years there has been an attempt to bring it as close as possible to LC practice, while still considering small library needs. Unfortunately, many of the "small" libraries which adopted Sears grew large or joined systems which used *LCSH*, thus creating internal problems within cataloging systems already burdened with changing codes and classification systems. LC is presently issuing supplementary lists of headings particularly designed for children's literature.[62] In 1969 the Executive Committee of the RTSD Cataloging and Classification Section approved the recommendation of the Committee on the Cataloging of Children's Materials to adopt "Library of Congress cataloging of children's materials as the national, uniform standard."[63] Thus far this policy does not seem to have deeply influenced the many users of Sears.

The mid- to later twentieth-century developments in subject analysis have been largely in the area of indexing. In the early 1950s Mortimer Taube developed the Uniterm System which coordinates preassigned terms at the time of search through the coincidence of document numbers.[64] Other more recent systems have sought to achieve the maximum number of subject entry points and rationality of term relationships through rotating and arranging controlled vocabularies and through the application of citation order formulas. This type of system is exemplified in the *British National Bibliography*. Here, PRECIS (PREserved Context Indexing System) produces a chain index which also lends itself to machine manipulation.[65] Such systems are referred to as *post-coordinate* in that "the cataloger deals only in simple concepts, providing a device or devices through which the *user* can combine them to create the compound subjects in which he is interested and so retrieve the relevant documents."[66]

In *precoordinate* systems the coordinating of terms takes place at the indexing stage where the indexer (cataloger) attempts to anticipate user approaches and then assigns standardized terms which are related to each other through cross reference networks.

With minor exceptions the interest and accomplishment in post-traditional classification has come from Great Britain, particularly from the work of the Classification Research Group, which has also concerned itself with the development of a new general classification scheme.[67] David Batty, while teaching in the United States, made this observation about his students:

> It is not that there is any inability to understand *how* complex numbers are put together, or even how facet theory can be used to make a classification scheme: it is rather an inability to understand why they should be.[68]

In a summary of cataloging and classification activities from 1950 to 1970, Paul Dunkin went further than most U.S. librarians, who are simply happy to have the British carry the burden of classification research. He likened the study of classification theory to the study of Greek and Latin.[69] Actually, a close study of a list of 469 doctoral dissertations in library science granted in the United States between 1930 and 1972 reveals only two or three titles which even touch on classification theory.[70] There are several on vocabulary control, subject retrieval effectiveness, and computer indexing. The total number indexed under cataloging and classification, subject headings, and indexing is forty-eight. This is exactly the same number as devoted to the history of books and the book trade in the eighteenth and nineteenth centuries. The periodical literature of the post–World War II period, however, shows considerable concern with indexing, particularly in individual subject disciplines and in special libraries; Dunkin's ideas are also challenged by "Classification: Theory and Practice," a recent issue of the *Drexel Library Quarterly*.[71]

It is interesting, if fruitless, to speculate on where we might be today if Dewey and Cutter had coordinated their ideas on classification and subject headings, if Dewey had allowed the Library of Congress to adopt his scheme with their own modifications,[72] if LC had developed its list of subject headings as an index to its classification schedules, or if someone a hundred or so years ago had said, Let's work out a basic structure for the subject designators in our library catalogs and subject bibliographies and try to get everyone to approve it. Standardization was apparently an idea whose time was yet to come and whose relationship to cooperation was not comprehended in the days of nineteenth-century individualism. The bibliographical imperative was only a glint in Jewett's eye. It took nearly a hundred years for the seed to grow in the minds of such probing thinkers as Ranganathan and Lubetzky, and to mature to the commitment to service expressed in the 1975 report of the National Commission on Libraries and Information Science.[73]

NOTES

1. S. R. Ranganathan, *The Colon Classification*, Rutgers series on Systems for the Intellectual Organization of Information 4:49–61 (New Brunswick, N.J.: Rutgers Univ., Graduate School of Library Service, 1965).
2. *Library Journal* 1:251–53 (Mar. 1877).
3. *Library Journal* (1– 1876–).
4. *ALA Bulletin* 1–63 (1907–69).
5. *Catalogers' and Classifiers' Yearbook* 1–11 (1929–45).
6. Anna Clinger Smith, "The Cataloging of Medieval Romances," *Catalogers' and Classifiers' Yearbook* 6:95–110 (1937).
7. Charles A. Cutter, "Library Catalogues," in U.S. Bureau of Education, *Public Libraries in the United States of America* (Washington, D.C.: Govt. Print. Off., 1876), p. 526.
8. British Museum, Dept. of Printed Books, *The Catalogue of Printed Books in the British Museum* 1:v–ix (London: The Museum, 1841).
9. Jim Ranz, *The Printed Book Catalogue in American Libraries: 1723–1900*, ACRL Monograph series, no. 26 (Chicago: American Library Assn., 1964), p. 67.
10. *Anglo-American Cataloging Rules, North American Text* (Chicago: American Library Assn., 1967), p. 1.
11. Ibid., pp. 141–44.
12. Library of Congress, *Cataloging Service Bulletin* 104:4 (May 1972).
13. Library of Congress, *Cataloging Service Bulletin* 79:1 (Jan. 1967).
14. *Anglo-American*, p. 114.
15. Charles A. Cutter, *Rules for a Printed Dictionary Catalogue* (Washington, D.C.: Govt. Print. Off., 1876); U.S. Bureau of Education, pts. 1–2.
16. Ranz, pp. 73–75.
17. Cutter, *Rules*, 1876 ed., p. 5.
18. Charles A. Cutter, *Rules for a Dictionary Catalog*, 4th ed. (Washington, D.C.: Govt. Print. Off., 1904), p. 6.
19. Ibid., p. 12.
20. *In Retrospect: A History of the Division of Cataloging and Classification of the American Library Association, 1900–1950* (n.p., n.d.), pp. 6–8.
21. Wyllis W. Wright, "A Report of Progress on Catalog Code Revision in the United States," in *Toward a Better Cataloging Code* (Chicago: Univ. of Chicago, Graduate Library School, 1957), p. 82.
22. International Conference on Cataloguing Principles, Paris, 1961, *Report*, ed. by A. H. Chaplin and Dorothy Anderson (London: 1963), pp. 91–96.
23. American Library Association, *Catalog Rules: Author and Title Entries*, American ed. (Chicago: The Association, 1908).

24. American Library Association, Division of Cataloging and Classification, *ALA Catalog Rules: Author and Title Entries*, preliminary American ed. (Chicago: The Association, 1941).
25. Ibid., p. [ii].
26. Andew D. Osborn, *The Crisis in Cataloging* (n.p.: American Library Institute, 1941).
27. American Library Association, Division of Cataloging and Classification, *ALA Cataloging Rules for Author and Title Entries*, ed. by Clara Beetle, 2d ed. (Chicago: The Association, 1949).
28. Seymour Lubetzky, *Cataloging Rules and Principles, a Critique of the ALA Rules for Entry and a Proposed Design for Their Revision* (Washington, D.C.: Library of Congress, 1953).
29. Seymour Lubetzky, *Code of Cataloging Rules: Bibliographic Entry and Description, a Partial and Tentative Draft* . . . (n.p.: 1958); Seymour Lubetzky, *Code of Cataloging: Author and Title Entry: An Unfinished Draft* . . . (Chicago: American Library Assn., 1960).
30. International Conference on Cataloguing Principles, pp. 91–96.
31. International Federation of Library Associations, *ISBD (M), International Standard Bibliographic Description for Monographic Publications* (London: IFLA Committee on Cataloguing, 1974).
32. *Anglo-American Cataloging Rules*, North American Text. Chapter 6, (Chicago: American Library Assn., 1974).
33. *International Cataloguing* 2:2 (Oct.–Dec. 1973).
34. *British National Bibliography* 1– (1950–).
35. John C. Rather, *The Future of Catalog Control in the Library of Congress* (n.p.: 1974)., pp. 2–3.
36. See Joseph A. Borome, *Charles Coffin Jewett*, American Library Pioneers, 7 (Chicago: American Library Assn., 1951), pp. 52–63; and Judith Hopkins, "The Ohio College Library Center," *Library Resources and Technical Services* 17:308–19 (Summer 1973).
37. James Krikelas, "Catalog Use Studies and Their Implications," *Advances in Librarianship* 3:195–220 (1972).
38. Leo LaMontagne, *American Library Classification, with Special Reference to the Library of Congress* (Hamden, Conn.: Shoestring, 1961), pp. 152–62, 173–91.
39. Melvil Dewey, *Dewey Decimal Classification and Relative Index*, 18th ed. (Lake Placid Club, N.Y.: Forest, 1971), p. 15.
40. Melvil Dewey, *Dewey Decimal Classification and Relative Index*, 17th ed. (Lake Placid Club, N.Y.: Forest, 1965), p. 43.
41. Melvil Dewey, *Dewey Decimal Classification and Relative Index*, abr. 7th ed. (Lake Placid Club, N.Y.: Forest, 1953), p. v.
42. Dewey, *Dewey Decimal*, 17th ed., p. 47.
43. Dewey, *Dewey Decimal*, 18th ed., p. 60.
44. *Library Journal* 100:709–10 (Apr. 15, 1975).
45. David Batty, "Christopher Robin and Cutter," *Catalogue and Index* 14:6 (Apr. 1969).
46. LaMontagne, pp. 222–33.
47. *Subject Keyword Index to the Library of Congress Classification Schedules*, 6v. (Washington, D.C.: U.S. Historical Documents Institute, 1974).
48. J. P. Immroth, *Analysis of Vocabulary Control in Library of Congress Classification and Subject Headings*, Research Studies in Library Science, no. 3 (Littleton, Colo.: Libraries Unlimited, 1971), p. 141.
49. Derek Austin, "Two Steps Forward . . ." in Bernard I. Palmer, *Itself an Education*, 2d ed. (London: Library Association 1971), p. 73.
50. Cutter, *Rules*, 4th ed., pp. 66–80.

51. Ibid., p. 67.
52. Library of Congress, Subject Cataloging Division, *Library of Congress Subject Headings* (Washington, D.C.: The Library, 1897–).
53. Paul S. Dunkin, *Cataloging U.S.A.* (Chicago: American Library Assn., 1969), p. 83.
54. *In Retrospect*, pp. 10–12.
55. David J. Haykin, *Subject Headings, a Practical Guide* (Washington, D.C.: Govt. Print. Off., 1951).
56. Dunkin, pp. 65–66.
57. Jessica Lee Harris, *Subject Analysis: Computer Implications of Rigorous Definition* (Metuchen, N.J.: Scarecrow, 1970), p. 217.
58. Ibid., p. 225.
59. Immroth, p. 140.
60. Rather, p. 8.
61. Minnie Earl Sears, *List of Subject Headings for Small Libraries* (New York: Wilson, 1923–).
62. Library of Congress, Subject Cataloging Division, *Subject Headings for Children's Literature: A Statement of Principles and Applications* (Washington, D.C.: The Library, 1969). Supplemented in *LCSH*.
63. Library of Congress, *Cataloging Service Bulletin* 86: sup., 1 (Jan. 1969).
64. C. D. Needham, *Organizing Knowledge in Libraries: An Introduction to Information Retrieval*, 2d rev. ed. (London: Andre Deutsch, 1971), p. 227.
65. A. C. Foskett, *The Subject Approach to Information*, 2d ed., rev. and enl. (Hamden, Conn.: Linnett, 1972), pp. 67–74.
66. Needham, p. 97.
67. Derek Austin, "Prospects for a New General Classification," *Journal of Librarianship* 1:149–69 (July 1969).
68. Batty, p. 6.
69. Paul S. Dunkin, "Cataloging and Classification—the Big IF," *American Libraries* 3:780 (July–Aug. 1972).
70. David H. Eyman, *Doctoral Dissertations in Library Science: Titles Accepted by Accredited Library Schools, 1930–1972* (Ann Arbor, Mich.: University Microfilms, 1973).
71. "Classification: Theory and Practice," *Drexel Library Quarterly* 10:1–120 (Oct. 1974).
72. LaMontagne, p. 232.
73. National Commission on Libraries and Information Science, *Toward a National Program for Library and Information Services: Goals for Action* (Washington, D.C.: Govt. Print. Off., 1975).

11

Technical Services and Technology: Technological Advance

ANN H. SCHABAS
University of Toronto

In October 1876 a historic meeting took place in Philadelphia when librarians gathered to consider the implications of the recently released report of the U.S. Bureau of Education on public libraries in the United States and to consider the formation of a new national association for librarians.[1] On the opening day, October 4, they heard words of greeting, encouragement, and challenge from John William Wallace, president of the Pennsylvania Historical Society:

> I see nothing which in coming years is to stand between the librarian and an issue upon him of books upon books, so vast and so uninterrupted that unless he brings the benefit of something like SCIENCE to his aid, he will be overwhelmed and buried in their very mass.[2]

There is a generally accepted notion that the library profession has, throughout the years, failed to identify and make use of new techniques, but such deprecation is not justified by the record. Looking back over these one hundred years, it would be best to start with a picture of how things were in 1876. Poole's contribution to the Bureau of Education's report deals comprehensively with the operation of libraries and gives the impression that all record keeping for the handling of library materials was done manually.[3] However, there is evidence elsewhere that some libraries were already producing card sets from masters. Cutter mentions casually that the Boston Public Library heliotyped its cards,[4] and a few of the largest libraries had their own printing presses for book catalog production and other printing needs.

Then, as now, the recurring theme of card catalogs versus book catalogs was very much in the minds of the pacesetting members of the profession. Familiar arguments were raised: on one hand book catalogs were more satisfactory for browsing and scanning; they could be printed in multiple copies for distribution and consultation outside the library; on the other, the expense of printing them and the speed with which they went out of date were serious disadvantages.

It was generally assumed in 1876 that a card catalog would be handwritten (manuscript) for use as a backroom working tool, and that a book catalog, *the* catalog, would be sent out for printing and made available to the public.

As card production and duplication techniques improved, card catalogs became more common as public tools. Many methods were tried. The typewriter was being marketed by this time and word was spreading about it. In spite of endorsements from people like Dewey, it was slow to gain widespread acceptance. "I like best of course, the typewriter," commented Dewey on duplicating devices, and "for a large number of copies my experience favors the electric pen."[5] Thomas Edison's electric pen did not fare as well as the typewriter in the years which followed. It consisted of a needle mounted in a pen-like tube, motor-driven to bob up and down rapidly, producing countless small holes when guided by hand over paper. The result served as a stencil for subsequent production of copies of cards or other "printed" material.

In the first library primer by John Cotton Dana, which appeared serially in the first six issues of *Public Libraries* in 1896,[6] there is no mention of the typewriter among the library appliances recommended. An appliance which does appear in the primer is the Rudolph Indexer. The creation of Alexander Rudolph of the San Francisco Public Library, it was the talk of the World's Columbian Exposition. It consisted of frames holding catalog records, linked in a circular, endless chain. A mechanism for displaying a number of these frames at one time had the effect of simulating a page of a book catalog. By turning a crank any part of the file could be so displayed. Additions to the file could be inserted at any link. An editorial in the *Library Journal* extolled its virtues, calling it "a work of great ingenuity" but the writer (unidentified) was quick to add that he was not yet ready to advise all libraries to convert their cards into *machine* catalogs.[7] Despite the initial accolades, this device never gained wide popularity, being cumbersome to update and awkward to use.

Production of book catalogs was grinding to a halt in the last decade of the nineteenth century because of printing expenses and update problems. Card catalogs had become the norm. Librarians were concerned about methods of producing cards and reducing copying effort and copying error. There were a few last ditch efforts, about this time,

210 / *Facilities*

to keep the book catalog alive. Alexander Rudolph tried out the blueprint process.[8] He was the first to devise a way of printing a book catalog directly from cards, bypassing the work of typesetting, proofreading, and correcting. Perhaps because the process involved making the cards translucent by soaking them in a mixture of castor oil and alcohol (!) or because of the negative (white print on blue ground) effect, or, because the need for book catalogs was not sufficiently great, the method failed to gain acceptance.

The linotype method was first used on a trial basis in 1891 by the New London Library, just six years after Ottmar Mergenthaler's linotype composing machine was perfected. E. C. Richardson of Princeton College Library was one of its early enthusiasts.[9] He saw the bar of linotype replacing the catalog card. By cutting down the catalog information for each title to what could fit on one line, i.e., one bar of linotype, the bars from one edition could be saved and interfiled with ones for new acquisitions for a later edition. New book catalogs could be printed as often as required: monthly, weekly, or even daily. The problems here concerned the loss of much catalog information and the handling, storing, and filing of the tiny bars. Princeton and other libraries did use the linotype for producing title-a-line finding lists for a number of years,[10] but the trend to card catalogs was too strong to be diverted. The technique did survive, however, and has continued to be used for cumulating periodical indexes.

After much campaigning, central distribution of printed catalog card sets for new imprints was put into operation in 1893 by Dewey's Library Bureau. This service kept its head above water until 1901 despite difficulties in getting books promptly from publishers. It stepped aside with relief when the Library of Congress agreed to take over the work.

LC's service proved to be a real boon to libraries and contributed to the full acceptance of the card catalog; but libraries still had many books for which no centrally produced printed cards were available. In the first decade of the twentieth century the typewriter was finally acknowledged as a must for internally created cards and for the headings on LC's cards. It was noted that typed letters looked well on the printed cards and did not deteriorate in quality with the fatigue of the cataloger.

Libraries that could afford the equipment and had the volume of work to justify it continued to use small printing presses. Newly developed attachments for mechanical typesetting speeded and cleaned up the process. Smaller libraries were duplicating cards from typed masters using some form of stencil equipment. The smallest libraries were using the ditto technique, and some used a small hand press with movable rubber type.

Around the turn of the century an assortment of labor-saving devices appeared on the scene: desk-top paper cutting machines (essentially like the ones used today), book supports (book ends), carbon paper, nonevaporating ink wells, staplers, pasting machines, to name a few. Telephone counters were recommended for statistics tallying, an improvement over Poole's "peas in compartments' method.[11]

In 1914 the American Library Association organized a grand display of such devices at its Washington Conference, featuring, in addition to printing and copying equipment, such timesavers and worksavers as card sorting boards, adding machines, cash registers (for overdue fines), vacuum cleaners. A library fine *computer* had been devised about this time.[12] It consisted of a board with two parallel scales, one for fines, one for a calendar. The calendar scale was movable and could be set each day to match due dates with the appropriate fines.

A most significant technological development was introduced into library processes in the 1930s, photography. As far back as 1877 Henry Stevens had advocated photo-bibliography with his proposal for a central card-based bibliographical clearinghouse of photo-miniaturized title pages.[13] F. K. W. Drury mentions the coming use of the camera for document copying in 1910.[14] By 1912 a number of libraries had installed equipment for this purpose, primarily for patron use, not as library tools.

It was improvements in camera construction in the late 1920s which finally brought photography and librarianship together. In 1932 the Leica-type Dexigraph camera enabled Yale University to reproduce, in short order, its entire catalog on cards of uniform, standard size from cards of varying sizes.[15]

Microfilming of documents was now possible. The advantages to libraries were numerous. The content of rare and deteriorating items could be preserved. Microfilming could also increase the accessibility of one-of-a-kind and precious items, and offered a dramatic solution to space problems. While microfilm as a storage medium was gaining acceptance, readers and reader-printers were being designed with improving resolution and ease of use.

In the late forties, to look ahead somewhat, the photoclerk camera was developed by Ralph R. Shaw for a number of clerical copying routines in the library: circulation overdue notices, follow-ups on book orders, catalog copy to assist the cataloger, to name a few.[16] Yale followed its successful venture of card catalog replication by introducing a smaller camera for ongoing card duplication.[17] Other libraries did likewise. Some adapted addressing equipment for card production using embossed plates or stencils. Offset printing had come into its own as a library duplication process and was favored by the libraries which could afford it for its flexibility and high-quality reproduction.

Another technological breakthrough for card production was xerography, the electrostatic dry copy process invented in the late thirties and first available in the late forties (one of many examples of the time-lag effect of the Second World War). This process could be used on its own to produce multiple card sets or masters for subsequent offset duplication. It required no specially prepared master, nor did it accentuate offending blemishes in the original as photography did. Simplicity and cleanliness, combined with flexibility of easy correction were its chief assets; with sufficient volume, it proved to be comparable in cost to other methods.

The special catalogers' camera, utilizing the Polaroid camera body, was developed in the sixties. It could capture catalog data from printed bibliographies for subsequent editing, without further error-prone copying and proofreading.

In 1938 Fremont Rider proposed photo-offset lithography as a means of achieving a rebirth of the book catalog.[18] Four years later his proposal became reality with the publication of the *Catalog of Books Represented by Library of Congress Printed Cards*, the first of many card catalog reproductions in book form. Techniques improved. At first the cards were laid out by hand (occasionally going askew as the books themselves will testify) and a photographic master for the offset machine was prepared. Later, automatic sequence mechanisms did the work of layout, and with the added sophistication of shingling the cards to reduce unnecessary white spaces.

The time was ripe for these developments. Libraries were extending concepts of service outside their own walls and needed systematic records of the holdings of other libraries. But these photo-offset book catalogs of the forties were produced from, and supplemental to, the card catalogs from which they were made. They were not seen as replacements, as more recent book catalogs produced from machine-readable copy are.

Rider picked up the microphotography idea in 1944 and proposed the microcard, an opaque microphotograph which could store more than seventy pages on one small card.[19] When combined with headings readable without magnification, microcards could be stored as catalog cards in standard catalog drawers. They have now an established place for small edition publication but have never reached the wide popularity Rider hoped for. User acceptance of microforms continues to be a problem, and the special readers required for microcard opaques have discouraged some libraries from purchasing them. Competition from the more widely accepted transparent microfiche has also been a detriment to microcard use. But the idea of putting the collection into the catalog drawer is compelling.

One of the most interesting library applications of photography is in circulation control, but first some earlier circulation developments should be mentioned. In the late twenties the first mechanical book charger was marketed, the Dickman Book Charger. It was hand-operated. With mechanical pressure, date-due information embossed on a date-due plate and borrower number embossed on a borrower card were transferred to the book card. An electrically operated version, the Gaylord Electric-Automatic Book Charging Machine, appeared five years later. These chargers saved copying time and eliminated copying errors but in no way relieved the filing of circulation records or improved access to the circulation file.

The marriage of photography and circulation was effected in 1940 by Ralph Shaw, when he was librarian at the Gary Public Library.[20] By designing a system around a time-sequential, film-stored file, he opened up a totally new approach to loan procedures. Transaction information was filmed and numbered sequentially. Only numbers missing from the sequence at date-due time needed to be looked up. There was still the manual checking for exceptions to the sequence but this took less time than finding and slipping records to purge a circulation file for every book returned. However, information about the location of a book was lost until date-due time (intolerable for many libraries), and prolonged reading of microfilm for overdues was blamed for staff eye strain. Some libraries tried audio-recording instead of microfilming, but audio-devices never gained wide acceptance in libraries.

The greatest significance of photocharging was the departure from traditional file concepts. The idea of creating a file in which most of the records would never be consulted and would purge themselves by disuse was an early example of innovative file thinking which has characterized recent decades. Library management by exception had begun. This was the beginning of the interplay between copying/storage advances and advances in file concepts. In addition to microphotography, the thirties witnessed the first library uses of two other new media for file storage and handling: edge-notched cards and punched (Hollerith-type) cards. At first edge-notched cards were considered equal to punched cards in sophistication. Edge-notched cards, when added to photocharging, improved circulation by eliminating the manual filing and searching for missing transaction numbers, these numbers being coded as notches on the transaction cards.

Edge-notched cards were first used in circulation work in 1939, but not in conjunction with photocharging. Frederick Kilgour at Harvard University devised a system in which the borrower filled out book and borrower information on a call slip edge-notched for date due.[21] One master file of edge-notched call slips filed by call number replaced the former double entry system, with no loss of access and with decided saving of labor. The file could be needled for overdues without disturbing the call number sequence.

The advantages of edge-notched card systems—quick and accurate sequence sorting on more than one key, mechanical selection of those cards with certain codes, and the master file concept (one file replacing several)—were recognized in acquisitions work too. The University of Illinois maintained a single file of order records, edge-notched to code author, fund, agent, and date ordered.[22] Quick access on any coded field was possible.

But edge-notched systems had drawbacks: the needle sorting procedure was tedious; the file size was limited to a few thousand records. Both filing refinement and the number of access fields were limited by the number of marginal holes, and one at the expense of the other. Complex coding could partially overcome this limitation but introduced greater potential for coding and needling errors.

Punched cards could code much more information for each record, but required more expensive equipment for handling. Punched-card coding could be converted to electrical impulses for machine transmission, machine manipulation, and machine storage; and once the equipment to read these cards was developed to exploit this feature, the applications of punched cards diversified.

As might be expected, the first library application of Hollerith cards was for statistics; this was what they had been invented for. In the early thirties the Boston Public Library used them for reader, reading, and purchase statistics.[23] The first file application of punched cards was set up by Ralph Parker at the University of Texas for circulation.[24] His approach was similar to Kilgour's except that the date-due information was coded by keypunch after the transaction. For overdues the cards were keypunched to record fine information and kept for end-of-term billing. An interesting prototype circulation system was installed at the Montclair (N.J.) Public Library which used a card reader/punch at the circulation desk.[25] This first library data collector, the Punching Judy, punched transaction cards from prepunched book and borrower cards.

Although punched cards introduced a degree of mechanized file manipulation to libraries in the 1930s, there was no widespread mechanization in libraries until a generation later. This was due in part to the war, but also because any degree of automation called for an upheaval of old methods, decisions in unknown territory, and considerable, often prohibitive, conversion effort and costs. Successful ventures into this territory were reported sporadically in the general library periodical literature, with no polarizing in one particular journal or through summaries or reviews until the late fifties. Since then the shoemaker's children have been better shod. With the annual review articles in *Library Resources and Technical Services* from 1958, and the *Annual Review of Information Science and Technology* from 1966, the chronology of library technical developments has been very well documented. Rather than capsulate it here, a general assessment appears appropriate.

Broadly speaking, what did the early punched-card systems offer library technical processes? They offered a file of master records that could be searched on any field to provide, for example, book, subject, borrower, or date-due access to a circulation file; book, subject, fund, agent, order-date access to an acquisitions file; title and reorder-date access to a serials file. They offered a file which could be sorted on any coded field and printed out. And, very importantly, they offered a new fund of statistical data.

But punched-card machines were expensive, noisy, cumbersome, and often frustrating. Machine filing was different from library filing; the crude print-outs were usually in upper case only. The automatic typewriter was the most widely accepted member of this species. Driven by paper tape punched on the typewriter itself, it could type multiple copies, in upper and lower case, of an item such as a catalog card, complete with individualizing features such as secondary card headings.

The next level in the automation ladder was that of batch processing by computer. Files in machine-readable code could have several operations performed on them in one pass through the computer under the control of a machine-stored program of instructions. We have moved from record manipulation to field and character manipulation.

Batch processing of library operations proliferated in the early sixties.[26] What improvements were offered over unit record equipment? Once the programs was written to process a file, human effort was reduced dramatically. No longer did decks of cards have to be fed repeatedly through a number of different machines. More sophisticated sorting was now possible. At least some special library filing rules could be followed, at the expense of more complex programming and longer run times. The files could be stored on magnetic tape for easier handling and storing. Coding could be changed by erasure and recording; and copying of records and files was error-free.

But the catch was with the economics of batch processing. Unit costs were acceptably low only when a great many operations were performed on a single pass of the file. This required deliberate delays. Information contained in the file and represented in the most recent print-out was always somewhat out-of-date. Manual files had to be maintained in parallel to bridge the currency gap. The computer itself could prove cost-effective only when used to capacity. Since few libraries could afford their own computer facility the pattern was to contract out or share a facility, with the associated problems of remote location and competing priorities. Notwithstanding, many libraries set up batch systems for circulation, acquisitions, and book catalog production. Many of these, particularly the successful ones, were reported in library journals and in special publications: the University of Illinois's annual *Clinic on Library Applications of Data Processing* (1963–), the *LARC Reports*, and the *Journal of Library Automation* (1968–).

For acquisitions, print-outs by author, title, agent, fund were possible, as were up-to-date fund status lists, lists of items requiring follow-up notices, and the follow-up notices themselves. One attractive consideration was that using a computer for acquisitions need not involve an initial mammoth effort for file conversion. Provided the old and the new files are maintained in parallel for a time, conversion will evolve, the old file eventually disappearing.

Batch circulation systems provided for the easy handling of overdues and statistics. But circulation staff worked with cumbersome daily print-outs which were always a little out-of-date. Tolerance of these inconveniences was inversely proportional to the level of service. A degree of file conversion is essential for circulation; a brief machine-readable book card must be prepared for each book that circulates.

Punched cards to a small degree, and batch computer systems much more so, brought the book catalog back as an *alternative* to the card catalog. All the old advantages of book catalogs were again recognized and magnified in the light of ever increasing pressures for better service and better access to information about holdings. The problem of keeping book catalogs up-to-date remained, however. The solution—reduction of the cost of producing them to the point where frequent new editions are feasible (perhaps even daily, as Richardson dreamed)—is a reality now in the 1970s with computer-output-microform, at reduction ratios undreamed of by the microfilming ventures of the thirties. In a batch environment a machine-stored catalog is of limited use. It can produce book catalogs, catalog cards, and special bibliographies, but cannot replace all other forms.

Magnetic tape became a new medium for the dissemination of catalog information. MARC tapes have been a machine-readable alternative to hard copy for LC's catalog copy distribution service since the late 1960s. A library can now receive centrally created machine-readable bibliographical records, modify them for local needs if necessary, create cards from them, and augment its own machine-stored catalog.

On-line technology developments in the early 1970s have great potential for technical processes. The machine file can now be *the* file, updated and consulted by way of typewriter or cathode ray tube terminal. The librarian can exchange all the headaches of batch systems—lack of currency, voluminous printouts or reader dependent microfiche, trips to and from the computer—for instant information, at the very high costs associated with on-line file storage and communication links between terminals and computers. An on-line circulation file calls for a data collector at the circulation desk linked to a computer. Transactions can be entered into the file for processing as soon as they occur, and an interactive terminal can be used to interrogate the file to determine the current status of any item.

The gap between librarian and computer filing has narrowed with compromise on both sides. The librarian has accepted some simplification in deference to the machine, and programs have been written to handle some of the librarian's nonalphabetical filing logic.

In the first decades of library automation there has been much tension at the man/machine interface. Input equipment such as keypunches were regarded as necessary evils which had to be tolerated. Likewise, computer print-outs fell far below acceptable library standards of quality. Technology has caught up again. The quiet efficiency, speed, and correctability of cathode ray tube terminals make them now first choice of many librarians for the recording of catalog decisions. Light pens to capture transaction data at the circulation desk look promising. The touchtone telephone may bring access to library files into the home.[27] Computer printers such as the xerographic printer produce copy whose precision, resolution, and variety of typefaces are second to none.

With the spread of mechanization concepts the systems philosophy has grown. Libraries contemplating computer applications have, first, to gain a better understanding of basic objectives. Relationships between library subsystems must be identified. It is dramatically apparent how similar the file operations are in acquisitions, in cataloging, and in circulation, how widely data are shared among the library subsystems. It is clear that the master file concept need not and should not stop at the departmental level.

C. Seymour Thompson wrote in 1914 that "the introduction of scientific management as a fad in library work would be deplorable."[28] It is now assumed that scientific management is the only way to approach library technical processes. As much information as possible about each item entering the library should be trapped early and accurately, and the transfer of this information between operations should be mechanized where possible to avoid duplication of work and copy error. Where multiple access to a file is needed, machine-readable records should be seriously considered.

Rob McGee reflects this idea in his approach to circulation.[29] If the traditional "absence" file is expanded to include a record for each item in the collection (records waiting for loan information) it becomes an "item" file. The item file is then a catalog of sorts, with location information. If records of books on order are added to this file (on loan to the agent) we have a file integrating acquisitions, the catalog, and the circulation file, in fact, a master file for the library as a whole. Put this in an on-line environment and we have given the patron and the librarian a single place to look with up-to-date currency, no limits to accessibility (time, distance, and concurrent use), and no danger of copying error after initial input. And the systems concept is no longer limited to one library. Electronic communication between libraries started in the nineteenth century with the telephone, expanded with teletypewriters, and now includes computer-to-computer and terminal-to-computer links. Several libraries can now share files and file manipulating programs at great savings to each, while increasing the speed and quality of service to patrons. This is occurring in networks such as the Ohio College Library Center and the Ontario Universities Library Cooperative System.[30]

What about standards as they relate to library technology? In 1876 Dewey pressed for standardization of card size. (He was far ahead of his time in his insistence on metrication.) Paper durability has been of concern to librarians over the past one hundred years, both for books and for card stock; great progress has been made in this field recently by the work of the W. J. Barrow Research Laboratory.[31] Some microform standards, both for size and quality, have been set. A number of subcommittees of the American National Standards Institute are actively concerned with matters relating to libraries.[32] The ALA's Library Technology Program was energetic in quality control studies during its existence, and the ongoing *Library Technology Reports* are highly valued.[33]

The computer and international cooperation have put new emphasis on standards. Machine compatibility and interchange of bibliographic records have focused attention on the need to standardize ways of referring to items (International Standard Bibliographic Number) and ways of formatting records (International Standard Bibliographic Description). The mandate for the ALA's new Committee on Technical Standards for Library Automation shows just how complex and important the standards issue is.[34]

What are the realities when it comes to applying the new technology? Librarians are caught between the pressures for more and better service, a larger and more diversified body of knowledge, and a multiplicity of new packagings on the one hand and the economic pressure of having to hold the line and pull in the belt on the other. Technology can relieve the first pressures, but the last pressure, the economic one, holds the veto.

I. A. Warheit has analyzed the situation succinctly.[35] On-line storage capacity is increasing, while unit storage and processing costs are decreasing. For some libraries the point has already been reached where machine-stored files and the handling of them can compete cost-effectively with manual alternatives. The development of minicomputers brings computer technology for inhouse operations within the reach of smaller libraries and provides them with a link to larger central machines with central data banks. Computer-produced microfilm provides an inexpensive way of disseminating copies of machine files with sufficient frequency between editions to ensure reasonable up-to-dateness.

Recent reports on the dilemma of library technology give direction to planners and funders.[36] The consensus is that technology in general and computers in particular will play an increasingly important role in library operations, and libraries must join together more and more in technology-dependent networks, sharing equipment, knowledge, resources, files, programs.

It is always important to keep a perspective on the difference between what can be and what is. In the nineteenth century, despite the printed evidence of typewriter capability, most libraries were still handwriting all cards. Now, in the mid-1970s, many libraries are operating, and operating well, with very little more equipment than the telephone and the typewriter. But this does not mean that the pressures facing librarians are not real. Collectively, librarians cannot overestimate the crisis Warheit and Fussler and others talk about. Just as 1876 was a year for identifying problems, assessing the state-of-the-art, planning on a national scale, so the mid-1970s are years for decisive planning to use technology where appropriate to control the ever increasing records of civilization in the national and international arenas.

Reminiscent of the words of Wallace almost one hundred years before, Henriette Avram puts her advice for the future on a more practical note:

> Getting from here to there will require talent, hard work, imagination, risk-taking, patience, cooperation, and common sense. We must attack the problems that are feasible of solution leaving aside the more glamorous possibilities that are beyond the present state of the art or that require system capabilities that have not yet been developed.[37]

NOTES

1. U.S. Bureau of Education, *Public Libraries in the United States of America: Their History, Condition, and Management* (Washington, D.C.: Govt. Print. Off., 1876).
2. *Library Journal* 1:92 (Nov. 1876).
3. William F. Poole, "The Organization and Management of Public Libraries," in U.S. Bureau of Education, pp. 476–504.
4. Charles A. Cutter, "Library Catalogues," in U.S. Bureau of Education, p. 543.
5. Melvil Dewey, "Duplicating Processes," *Library Journal* 4:165 (May 1879).
6. John C. Dana, "ALA Library Primer," *Public Libraries* 1:5–10 (May 1896); ibid. pp. 39–45 (June 1896); ibid. pp. 79–82 (July 1896); ibid. pp. 115–30 (Aug. 1896); ibid. pp. 167–72 (Sept. 1896); ibid. pp. 211–15 (Oct. 1896).
7. Editorial, *Library Journal* 18:69 (Mar. 1893).
8. Alexander J. Rudolph, "The Blue-Print Process for Printing Catalogs," *Library Journal* 24:102–5 (Mar. 1899).
9. E. C. Richardson, "The Linotype Method," *Library Journal* 17:377–78 (Sept. 1892).
10. E. C. Richardson, "Cumulative Printed Catalog for Large Libraries," *Library Journal* 41:28–31 (Jan. 1916).
11. Poole, pp. 503–4.
12. "A New Mechanical Device," *Public Libraries* 19:260 (June 1914).
13. Henry Stevens, "Photo-Bibliography; or, a Central Bibliographical Clearing-House," *Library Journal* 2:162–73 (Nov.–Dec. 1877).
14. F. K. W. Drury, "Labor Savers in Library Service," *Library Journal* 35:542 (Dec. 1910).
15. Anna M. Monrad, "The Use of the Dexigraph in Making an Official Catalog," *Library Journal* 57:218–22 (Mar. 1, 1932).
16. Ralph R. Shaw, *The Use of Photography for Clerical Routines* (Washington, D.C.: American Council of Learned Societies, 1953).
17. Frederick C. Hick, "Reproduction of Catalogue Cards by Photographic Methods," *Law Library Journal* 27:122–31 (Apr. 1934).
18. Fremont Rider, "The Possibility of Discarding the Card Catalog," *Library Quarterly* 8:329–45 (July 1938).
19. Fremont Rider, *The Scholar and the Future of the Research Library* (New York: Hadham, 1944).

20. Ralph R. Shaw, "Reducing the Cost of the Lending Process," *ALA Bulletin* 35:504–10, 512 (Oct. 1941).
21. Frederick G. Kilgour, "A New Punched Card for Circulation Records," *Library Journal* 64:131–33 (Feb. 15, 1939).
22. George B. Brown, "Use of Punched Cards in Acquisition Work," *College and Research Libraries* 10:219–20, 257 (July 1949).
23. Ethel M. Fair, "Inventions and Books: What of the Future?" *Library Journal* 61:48 (Jan. 15, 1936).
24. Ralph H. Parker, "The Punched Card Method in Circulation Work," *Library Journal* 61:903–5 (Dec. 1, 1936).
25. Margery Quigley, "Library Facts from International Business Machines Cards," *Library Journal* 66:1065–67 (Dec. 15, 1941).
26. Frederick G. Kilgour, "History of Library Computerization," *Journal of Library Automation* 3:218–29 (Sept. 1970).
27. Joseph Becker, "Trends in Library Technology," *Special Libraries* 62:430–31 (Oct. 1971).
28. C. Seymour Thomson, "The Exhibit of Labor-saving Devices," *Library Journal* 39:520 (July 1914).
29. Rob McGee, "Two Types of Designs for On-line Circulation Systems," *Journal of Library Automation* 5:184–202 (Sept. 1972).
30. Frederick G. Kilgour, et al., "The Shared Cataloging System of the Ohio College Library Center," *Journal of Library Automation* 5:157–83 (Sept. 1972); Ralph E. Stierwalt, "Cooperative Library System for Ontario Universities," *Ontario Library Review* 58:83–89 (June 1974).
31. W. J. Barrow, *Manuscripts and Documents, Their Deterioration and Restoration*, 2d ed. (Charlottesville: Univ. Pr. of Virginia, 1972).
32. Jerrold Orne, "Standards in Library Technology," *Library Trends* 21:286–97 (Oct. 1972).
33. Verner W. Clapp, "LTP: The Rattle in an Infant's Fist," *American Libraries* 3:795–802 (July–Aug. 1972).
34. "Standards for Library Automation and ISAD's Committee on Technical Standards for Library Automation (TESLA)," *Journal of Library Automation* 7:126–38 (June 1974).
35. I. A. Warheit, "The Automation of Libraries, Some Economic Considerations," *Special Libraries* 63:1–7 (Jan. 1972).
36. System Development Corporation, *Technology and Libraries*, Technical Memorandum 3732 (Santa Monica: 1967); Herman H. Fussler, *Research Libraries and Technology: A Report to the Sloan Foundation* (Chicago: Univ. of Chicago Pr., 1973).
37. Henriette D. Avram, "Library Automation: A Balanced View," *Library Resources and Technical Services* 16:18 (Winter 1972).

12
Library Buildings

A. ROBERT ROGERS
Kent State University

CONTROVERSY AND CONSOLIDATION, 1876–1893

In 1876 libraries in the United States were making use of such nineteenth-century advances in building technology as iron, central heating, and gas lights. American architects were influenced by famous European models like the Bibliothèque Ste. Geneviève (1843), the Bibliothèque Nationale (1854), and the British Museum (1857). Several notable colleges (Harvard, Yale, Williams, Amherst, Wesleyan, Mt. Holyoke, Brown, and Princeton) had separate library buildings and public libraries were increasing both in numbers and in size.

In many cases the buildings designed to cope with the rapid growth which occurred after the Civil War were less than ideal because the planners by using a combination of balconies and alcoves tried to accommodate all users and entire collections in one room. The result was frequently a hall fifty to sixty feet in height with a roof skylight and/or high windows. Lighting in the lower alcoves was sometimes poor despite augmentation of natural daylight with gaslights, while heat in the upper galleries caused serious damage to bookbindings. Examples of this type included the Cincinnati Public Library (1874) and the Peabody Institute in Baltimore (1878). Because of these deficiencies, libraries of the book-hall style were passing from the scene in 1876 to be replaced by libraries on the bookstack plan described by Justin Winsor in the 1876 *Report* or the book-room type (forerunner of the subject division arrangement) advocated by W. F. Poole.

Winsor's chapter on library buildings in 1876 included plans for a public library which could house a million volumes with closed stacks and a central delivery desk. The main book room was to have seven stories, glass floors, and a glass roof. Each level was to be eight feet in the clear with shelving around the walls and crosswise in the room. Aisles were to be 2 feet 10 inches wide. Spiral staircases would connect the floors. Bookcases would be eight feet high and divided into three-foot sections with nine shelves per section. Shelves and uprights were to be of wood. A mechanical conveyor system would bring books to the delivery desk.

The 1870s also witnessed the beginning of the long struggle to plan and erect a separate building for the Library of Congress. Ainsworth Spofford first mentioned the need in 1871. In his annual report for 1872 he specified that there should be a large central reading room similar to the British Museum, and that the building should expand outward from that point, including bookstacks for 2 million volumes. It was to be fireproof with an iron interior and a stone exterior. These and other details were contained in directions given to architects who entered the competition of 1873, won by Smithmeyer and Pelz. The late 1870s saw numerous disappointing delays at the hands of congressional committees. Spofford tried to accelerate matters by arranging for ALA to meet in Washington in 1881. Smithmeyer presented a paper describing plans for the national library and W. F. Poole presented a paper sharply critical of what he regarded as the conventional approach to library buildings.

The clash of Smithmeyer and Poole at the ALA Conference of 1881 served to bring into focus an alternative approach. Poole opened his paper by attacking the Peabody Institute, Baltimore for its conventional main hall and alcoves six stories high. He criticized waste of space, cost of heating, destruction of bookbindings in upper galleries from overheating, staff time wasted in retrieving books from galleries, danger of total destruction in event of fire, excessive noise in the central hall, difficulty in expanding, and great cost per volume shelved. His proposed floor plan showed subject reading rooms around the sides of a quadrangle. Each book storage room was to be separated from all others by firewalls extending through the roof. The central building was to have stairs and an elevator. Poole was soon given an opportunity to put his theories into practice. In 1885 the sum of $2 million became available for construction of the Newberry Library. Poole was appointed librarian in 1887. He advocated subject departments in separate rooms, as he had done since 1876; his 1881 plans served as the basis for the Newberry building, which was opened in 1893.

The most controversial building, apart from the Library of Congress, was the Boston Public Library. The architect, Charles Follen McKim, designed a large, square building around an interior court. At the street level were hallways, processing departments, and popular rooms. On the second floor was a long, high-ceilinged reading room and on the third floor were various special collections. The books were stored on six levels in the southwest corner, using book cases on solid floors rather than bookstacks. Major artists of the day participated with murals and sculpture. Civic enthusiasm was dampened when ALA met in Boston in 1890 and Poole launched his most scathing attack since his criticism of plans for the Library of Congress. Among his objections were: a main reading room too large for quiet study; stacks too far from the reading rooms; closed shelving, a bad idea; inadequate work rooms for the staff; refusal of the trustees to consult with knowledgeable librarians; and high cost. The building was estimated at $1.175 million but the total cost eventually exceeded $2.8 million.

The number of public library buildings completed rose rapidly in the period from 1876 through 1893. In the category of large buildings (costing $100,000 or more) the figure was twenty-three, compared with five in the preceding quarter century. These new libraries were heavily concentrated in New England and the middle Atlantic states. The construction cost index declined slightly between 1870 and 1880 and remained stable for the rest of the period. Three-quarters of the funding was private before 1893.

Meanwhile, the founding of Johns Hopkins University in 1876 symbolized the change that was occurring from a lecture-textbook method of instruction to a research-oriented and library-dependent style. As a result, library usage increased and buildings which had seemed adequate were in need of expansion or replacement. The extension to Gore Hall at Harvard University in 1877, for example, consisted of six levels of iron bookstacks, 7 feet 6 inches high, with floors grated for light and ventilation. Planned in collaboration with Henry Van Brunt, architect, it made the first use of iron bookstacks in America, and Justin Winsor contended that 300,000 books were within one or two minutes of the delivery desk.

By 1890 the new University of Pennsylvania Library was regarded as the best and most advanced building of its kind. The stacks were in a separate wing with a fireproof wall to cut them off from the main building and were roofed entirely in glass, presenting the appearance of a large greenhouse. The stacks were only three stories high with floors of translucent glass. It was said that lettering on the spines of all books could be read without artificial light. Provision was made for expansion to the south one bay at a time. Criticisms of the building centered on inadequate provision for readers and staff.

The World's Columbian Exposition of 1893 in Chicago furnished ALA with an opportunity to survey progress since 1876 and to issue the papers of its conference as a manual of recommended contemporary practice. There was much progress to report. ALA's Committee on Library Architecture had been meeting for several years and an impressive array of papers had been presented at annual conferences.

Librarians, often excluded from the planning process in 1876, were making their voices heard and architects were beginning to listen. Papers by W. I. Fletcher on the relations of architects and librarians had been published in *American Architect and Building News* and *Library Journal*. Even more important, C. C. Soule's "Points of Agreement among Librarians as to Library Architecture," which had been adopted by ALA in 1891, was being widely used by librarians and architects. Electric lighting had been introduced into libraries in the 1880s and found superior to gas, although natural daylight was still the first choice of many. The old book-hall style buildings were no longer being erected, although professional opinion was still divided between the stack style advocated by Justin Winsor and the plan of books and readers in separate subject rooms supported by W. F. Poole. Separate reading rooms for women were still being provided in some buildings. Reading rooms for children began to appear in public libraries in the 1880s, along with reference and newspaper rooms. Public libraries tended to be larger and more highly developed than academic, although the latter were more likely to grant open access to their shelves. Except for the Library of Congress, planning attention was focused exclusively on public and academic library buildings with no consideration of quarters and equipment for school or special libraries.

EXPANSION AND INTERRUPTION, 1894–1918

The World's Columbian Exposition of 1893 influenced construction of libraries from 1894 through 1918. The classical styles of France and Italy predominated. Light-colored marble and Indiana limestone replaced dark exteriors of brick, granite, and sandstone. In a period of accelerated library construction, the Library of Congress (1897), the New York Public Library (1911), and the Widener Library of Harvard University (1915) were most noteworthy.

General acceptance of bookstacks as the most efficient means of housing large collections occurred during this period. The design patented by Bernard R. Green and manufactured for the Library of Congress by the Snead Iron Works was widely accepted as standard for large libraries, although other firms competed avidly, especially for small library orders. Snead recommended cast-iron uprights and open-bar shelves of polished strip steel which hooked into teeth in the uprights. The firm also made bracket-type shelves with uprights of thin steel but did not recommend them.

Opened November 1, 1897, the Library of Congress was substantially as planned by Spofford twenty-five years earlier. The Italian Renaissance building with its golden dome was designed to accommodate sightseers as well as library users. In size and complexity it was unparalleled. The outside dimensions were 470 by 340 feet and the floor space exceeded 3.75 acres. There were nine stack levels, each seven feet high, carefully coordinated with the floor heights. A system of automatic book conveyors connected the central desk in the octagonal reading room to all parts of the stacks. Trolleys on parallel rails went by underground tunnel to the Capitol and provided speedy delivery of books to congressional staffs. Scarcely a decade later, Congress approved $320,000 to enlarge the book capacity and in January 1910 the new stacks in the southeast courtyard were completed and occupied.

Although the New York Public Library was not completed and occupied until 1911, its planning began shortly after John Shaw Billings was appointed director in 1896. He arranged for preliminary plans to be published in *Library Journal* and discussed at the ALA Conference in 1897. Designed by Carrère and Hastings, it cost $8 million and was the most expensive public library building erected until after the Second World War. Housing both reference and circulation facilities, the building consisted of four stories with two light courts. Offices and a variety of specialized reading rooms were located around the perimeter. The main reading room was at the rear of the building on the third floor, atop several tiers of stacks. The building was planned so that expansion could take place at the rear. When opened, it had space for 3 million volumes and 1,700 readers.

The pace of public library construction rose sharply in the 1890s and peaked in 1900, with a slightly declining plateau between 1900 and 1910 and a marked decline between 1910 and 1918. Although there was still a very heavy concentration in New England and the middle Atlantic states, more libraries were opening in the Midwest and Far West. The number of large libraries ($100,000 or more) completed during these years was fifty-nine, compared with twenty-three in the earlier period. The cost of construction remained stable until 1915; it doubled between 1915 and 1920. About two-thirds of the new buildings were constructed with tax money, as against one-fourth in the preceding period. Of those constructed with private funds, about half were the result of Carnegie donations.

Prior to 1908 there was little Carnegie supervision of building plans. In that year James Bertram, Andrew Carnegie's private secretary, aware of poorly planned and inefficient buildings in some communities, began to require that plans be submitted for approval before grants could be made. After conferring with leading librarians and library architects (notably W. H. Brett and Edward L. Tilton), he prepared a leaflet entitled "Notes on Library Buldings" [sic], which was first issued in 1911. Economical and flexible use of interior space was stressed and four sample floor plans were included. Wasted space and monumentality in libraries (e.g., the building in St. Louis cost $1.5 million but had no more usable space than that in Springfield, Massasetts, which cost $350,000) led Carnegie to shift his emphasis to support for the construction of branches. No new applications for library buildings were accepted after November 7, 1917, although applications in process were completed and a few grants made after the war.

The years from 1894 to 1918 saw rapid growth of college and university libraries. By 1910 three main types had evolved: a linear arrangement with reading and book rooms side by side in a rectangular building; a centralized plan with a square or octagonal reading room in the middle; and an angular arrangement with one or two wings. A variant of the last pattern was the T form, in which a bookstack extended to the rear from the middle of the building. The delivery desk was usually in the main reading room, ordinarily on the first floor. A sloping site was often selected to allow windows in the lower floors of the multi-tier stacks. In 1911 the University of Texas placed the reading room on the second floor to permit the entrance to be in the center of the main wing and to isolate the reading room from noise. Whereas Texas followed a T pattern, the University of California (1912) added lateral and rear wings around the stack. Both were widely imitated.

Harvard's Widener Library (1915) was a hollow rectangle with a central court divided by a section housing the Widener collection. The rooms on the first floor included: a large hall (with stairs to the second floor); a book room with a collection of standard titles; the rare book room; administration; and technical services. The main reading room was located on the north side of the second floor. The other three sides of the building were taken up mainly with nine tiers of bookstacks, although there were special collections and seminar rooms on the third floor. Numerous individual stalls or carrels were provided in the stacks along with seventy-four individual study rooms nearby. The capacity of the stacks was 2 million volumes.

State library buildings were discussed for the first time at the ALA Conference of 1905. Melvil Dewey spoke against putting a state library in the capitol. A separate building, like a large warehouse but fireproof and with good heating, lighting, and ventilation would be best. In a large city, Dewey thought, the reading room should be on the top floor, above the dust and noise and easily reached by elevator, with bookstacks underneath. Plans announced in 1908 called for the New York State Library and Library School to be located on the second and third floors of a new education building. The main reading room, on the second floor, was lighted on three sides by eleven large, arched windows. The stacks (seven levels) were directly below without windows, thus totally dependent on artificial light and ventilation, and serviced by four elevators. The capacity was 2 million volumes. Before the state library could move to its new quarters in 1912, fire desroyed a large portion of its collection.

ALA's Committee on Library Architecture was active throughout this period. In her 1894 report Theresa H. West noted the need for more discussion of the best method of selecting an architect. In 1902 the ALA Publishing Board announced plans for a supplement to Soule's *Library Rooms and Buildings* and invited submission of plans, exteriors, and other information on good buildings. The ALA Conference of 1906 included talks by architects as well as librarians. In 1907 C. R. Dudley reported that ALA had collected floor plans of over 100 library buildings, but that classification and evaluation would make the collection more useful. C. S. Andrews presented a paper on the economics of library architecture in 1916, by which time ALA had a committee on this specific aspect of the topic.

Relations between librarians and architects improved. In 1898 William Foster noted that library boards were increasingly consulting with librarians and that architectural publications were devoting more attention to libraries. Indeed, the entire November 1897 issue of *Architectural Review* bore that character and "Modern Library Buildings," by Charles C. Soule was the feature article in its January 1902 issue, which included nearly fifty pages of library building plans. Sidney K. Greenslade's paper on "Libraries in the United States," presented at a meeting of the Royal Institute of British Architects in 1902, was later published in their *Journal* and reprinted in *American Architect*. At the 1906 ALA Conference, A. D. F. Hamlin described the role of a consulting architect as that of an intermediary and adviser on all matters of doubt and controversy.

Professional thinking underwent substantial change. William R. Eastman's 1906 collection of plans contained a warning against unnecessary partitions, urging use of bookcases, desks, or hand rails instead. By 1911 Willis K. Stetson was also arguing forcefully that most libraries had too many rooms, thus increasing personnel costs and user inconvenience, and that all major adult services should be on the main floor. Similar ideas were expressed by the New York architect, Edward L. Tilton, whose concept of the "open plan" was a key feature of the Springfield (Mass.) City Library (1912).

In 1915 Chalmers Hadley surveyed the library architectural scene, noting the influence of the Columbian exposition of 1893 and changes in the 1905–15 period away from the classical building with its leaky dome toward better adaptations to meet local climatic conditions. He mentioned the trend to put main public libraries in civic centers and warned of problems when expansion became necessary. He spoke with distaste of recent efforts to design libraries like stores (display windows, entrances at sidewalk level) and thought people should be willing to climb a few steps in order to use libraries. He regarded stacks in the center of library buildings (now feasible because of artificial light) as more efficient in terms of accessibility. Other recent improvements which he noted were: better provision for the staff; much less space devoted to entrance halls, stairs, and corridors; and an open plan for interiors with use of bookcases and furniture to divide areas. Even in

228 / Facilities

his omission of quarters and equipment for school and special libraries, Hadley's address to ALA was an accurate summary of the state of the art of library planning and construction prior to the First World War.

DEPRESSION, WAR, AND TECHNOLOGICAL IMPROVEMENTS, 1919–1945

Despite the economic dislocations caused by inflation during and after the First World War and the Great Depression of the 1930s, the period from 1919 to 1945 was a time of substantial, sometimes even spectacular, advance.

The number of large public library buildings ($200,000 or more) rose slowly during the 1920s and dropped sharply during the 1930s. The total, twenty-eight, was smaller than for the preceding period. Private funding declined in importance, representing only 14 percent of the total. The construction cost index peaked in 1920, dropped substantially during the 1920s, and sharply in the early 1930s. By the end of the 1930s it had risen to the level of the late 1920s. Buildings were more widely distributed across the country. The Wilmington Institute Free Library (1923) and the Enoch Pratt Free Library (1933) were pacesetters in the open plan with stacks beneath the main floor. There were nine public libraries which cost over $1 million each: Crerar, Chicago (1921); Detroit (1921); Cleveland (1925); Los Angeles (1926); Philadelphia (1927); Baltimore (1933); Rochester (1936); Brooklyn (1940); and Toledo (1940).

The Wilmington Institute was a development of the open plan which Tilton had used earlier in Springfield. The main floor was but a few steps above street level. Only glass partitions and bookcases were used as dividers between the delivery hall and adult reading room. A mezzanine housed offices, a lecture hall, and an exhibit area. The building was recognized as outstanding, and its design influenced the planning of other buildings, most notably the Enoch Pratt.

Opened in 1933 the Enoch Pratt Free Public Library in Baltimore represented the combined efforts of Joseph L. Wheeler, Edward L. Tilton, and Alfred M. Githens. The main floor was at sidewalk level with numerous display windows in front. There was a large central hall with the public catalog and circulation desk. Seven subject reading rooms, a general reference room, and a popular circulating room were located around the periphery, each with a large collection on open shelves and with rapid access to the three-tier bookstacks in the basement. The basement also contained workrooms and a children's room with its own entrance. The second floor (around the upper part of the main hall) housed offices and special reading rooms, a lecture hall, and a classroom. The building was air-conditioned and could house 1,400 readers and 1.6 million books.

During this period public libraries made substantial progress in site selection, the planning process, and building design. Although the role of consultant did not fully develop until after the Second World War, more librarians were actively involved in planning their own buildings and several wrote books on public library planning. Chalmers Hadley's *Library Buildings: Notes and Plans* was devoted to buildings costing less than $50,000;[1] Arthur E. Bostwick's *The American Public Library* devoted a lengthy chapter to library buildings;[2] further updating was provided by H. S. Hirshberg's *Elements of the Library Plan*.[3] But the definitive treatise in scope, thoroughness, and practicality was *The American Public Library Building*, by Joseph L. Wheeler and Alfred M. Githens.[4] Most large public libraries were planned on a subject division basis. Cleveland and Los Angeles put stacks in the center and subject departments around the periphery on several floors. Baltimore, Brooklyn, Rochester, and Toledo put subject departments on the main floor at street level with bookstacks underneath. Design improvements noticeable in public libraries of this period included more compact, rectangular shapes; less space devoted to hallways, lobbies, and stairs; more space for reading rooms and other public services; greater flexibility of interior arrangement; and larger and more efficient quarters for staff.

College and university library buildings became larger and more complex. External architectural styles were often dictated by campus master plans. In most buildings the second floor was the main service level with such functions as reserve reading rooms on the first. Multitier bookstacks encompassed more levels (up to twenty in a few instances) than was customary in public libraries. A tendency developed to put stacks in the center, surrounded by reading rooms and offices (e.g., South Hall, Columbia University) which was to pose expansion problems later. The stack tower became a feature on such campuses as Fisk, Rochester, Yale, and Texas. Newspaper stacks became common in large libraries after 1919, as did map and rare book rooms. A major development was the increase in seating capacity. Whereas the University of California had planned for only 10 percent of the student body in 1912, the University of Michigan planned for 20 percent in 1919, and the University of North Carolina for 33.33 percent in 1929.

Among the major buildings of the period were Michigan, Yale, the New England Deposit Library, and Joint University Libraries. Opened in 1919 the general library of the University of Michigan incorporated the fireproof bookstacks of the old building. It faced north, was four stories high, and had light courts on both sides of the old stack (five levels) and a book conveyor at the point where the two new stacks (eight levels) and the old were joined. Among the novel features were reinforced concrete construction, which permitted better light and fireproofing, and bookstacks designed for research as well as storage. The second-floor reading room had eleven large windows on the north side and three at each end as well as indirect overhead lighting and table lights concealed in wooden frames, with reflectors and diffusing glass. The building cost $615,000 and could seat 1,000 readers. Stack capacity was 1 million volumes with provision for expansion to 2 million.

The Sterling Memorial Library at Yale featured a stack tower with sixteen floors and seventy-five miles of shelves (2 million volume capacity). The building shell as a whole resembled a great cathedral of Gothic design made of gray granite with limestone trim. Constructed within the shell by Snead and Company, the stacks included 330 carrels, 20 studies and seminar rooms, 2 public and 3 staff elevators, 2 dumbwaiters, an electric book conveyor, pneumatic tubes, and 4,500 lights. The main floor of the building was at ground level with public catalog, delivery desk, and several reading rooms including the undergraduate library with 20,000 volumes on open shelves. The central bibliography room was designed to serve readers as well as the order and cataloging staffs.

Overcrowding in the Widener Library led Keyes Metcalf to propose the New England Deposit Library for little-used books owned by various libraries in the Boston area. Located on inexpensive land, the reinforced concrete building was shaped like a T, with six levels (8 feet 4 inches high) in the stack area, which held 1 million volumes. The service section across the front consisted of a basement and first floor. Cooperative and economical sharing of resources and facilities was exemplified in the Joint University Libraries (Nashville). The library was H-shaped with eight tiers of flexible stacks (capacity 500,000 volumes). Planned to offer various possibilities for alteration and expansion, the building also included advanced technological features: air conditioning, treatment of ceilings with celotex acoustical tile, use of rubber tile on reading and reference room floors, and fluorescent lighting.

Information to assist college and university librarians in planning new buildings or the renovation and expansion of old ones became more plentiful. James T. Gerould's *The College Library Building*, funded by a Carnegie grant, was a landmark work which served until after the Second World War.[5] Less analytical, *College and University Library Buildings*, by Edna R. Hanley, was very useful for its photographs and floor plans.[6] From its very first issues in 1939 *College and Research Libraries* carried articles on library planning and individual new buildings. Substantial chapters on these subjects were included by Guy R. Lyle in *Administration of the College Library* and Louis R. Wilson and Maurice F. Tauber in *The University Library*.[7]

The annex to the Library of Congress (1939) was essentially a solid stack core, surrounded by offices and reading rooms.

By the early 1930s state libraries were being placed in office buildings rather than capitols. Descriptions of buildings completed or under construction in New Jersey, Ohio, Pennsylvania, Indiana, California, and Nebraska were contained in L. J. Bailey's reports to the National Association of State Librarians. In 1939 a paper on the Virginia State

Library was presented at the Association's annual conference. Opened that same year was the Oregon State Library, constructed with $825,000 of WPA money.

An article in *Special Libraries* in 1920 noted the lack of published information on planning and equipping special libraries and the need for a collection of floor plans and pictures. Practically nothing was published on these subjects in the next two decades.

The planning and equipping of school libraries began to receive attention in the early 1920s. Hadley's *Library Buildings* included the Omaha Technical High School Library. By 1930 Tilton noted a rapid increase in provision for school libraries. He stressed that the library should be centrally located and readily accessible from study halls. Provision for adequate daylight could be made by means of high windows equal to 20 percent of the floor area. Skylights were not recommended. Artificial light should come from ceiling fixtures suspended twelve feet above the floor and spaced at intervals to insure even distribution and nine to ten footcandles of intensity at table height. The reading room should seat at least 10 percent of the student body. Shelving in reading room and stacks together should hold 100 volumes per reader. There should be one or more small conference rooms with glazed partitions up to the ceiling, a classroom for instruction in library use, a small workroom, and a stack room near the charging desk, which should be so located that one person could control the library. A teachers' room would be desirable. At least twenty square feet per reader should be allowed (twenty-five would be better).

Recommendation in the three editions of Lucille Fargo's *The Library and the School* did not always come up to the level of those by Tilton.[8] Nor did the recommendations of educational administrators in the numerous articles which appeared in the late 1930s and early 1940s in *American School and University, American School Board Journal,* and *Nation's Schools.*

Noteworthy during the years 1919-45 were technical advances in lighting. Windows were used for both light and ventilation when the period opened. By 1929 Bostwick was stressing artificial light. Writing in 1930 Angus S. Macdonald noted a rise in intensity level considered necessary and made the following recommendations: entrance hall, six to ten footcandles; information or delivery desk, ten to fifteen footcandles; areas of intensive work or fine print, twenty footcandles. Gerould discussed both windows and artificial light, noting that sunlight caused deterioration of paper and binding and calling attention to the rare book stack of the Huntington Library which was both artificially lighted and air-conditioned. J. W. Barker discussed effect on the eyes at the Conference of Eastern College Librarians in 1933 and the same theme was explored in 1934 by O. G. Henderson and H. G. Rowell. The problem of glare was treated at length by F. F. Lee in 1937. The theme of eye comfort was revived in 1938 by M. A. Tinker.

232 / Facilities

A paper on lighting systems was presented by R. C. Engelken at the 1941 ALA Conference. That same year J. O. Kraehenbuhl described requirements for an adequate lighting system and recommended fluorescent lights for library tables. By this time several major libraries including Joint University Libraries were using fluorescent lights with average illumination of twenty-five to thirty footcandles.

Substantial advances were made in heating, cooling, and ventilating library buildings. In 1924 Hadley noted that hot-air systems were being avoided and expressed a preference for steam heat. By 1929 Bostwick preferred an indirect system in which fresh air would be drawn from the outside, warmed, and then circulated. Gerould in 1932 noted that central heating plants on college campuses were relieving libraries of the need to have furnaces and boilers with the result that danger from fire was considerably lessened. When the Enoch Pratt library opened in 1933, it was equipped with an air-conditioning system which controlled temperature and humidity and filtered the air to remove dust, bacteria, odors, and acids. The air-conditioning system in South Hall, Columbia University filtered, cleaned, cooled or warmed, and humidified or dehumidified. In 1937 the Temperature Research Foundation of the Kelvinator Corporation reported that air conditioning would aid substantially in the preservation of books and manuscripts. In 1941 it was reported that Harvard University would install air conditioning in the new Houghton Library to protect its rare books.

Changes in floors and flooring were smaller and more gradual. In 1924 Hadley preferred cork carpet or battleship linoleum to wood. In 1929 Bostwick mentioned that linoleum might be laid directly over cement. He also reported that terrazzo and marble blocks or tiles were used in some of the more expensive buildings, but that they tended to be noisier. Gerould in 1932 mentioned that use of wood was declining. He observed that battleship linoleum was often used but that flooring tile of ground cork, asphalt, or rubber was more satisfactory. Gerould also noted the acoustical properties of cork and rubber tile. In 1939 ALA published a book on flooring by C. D. Plaister.

Wall shelving of wood was common in small libraries and in the reading rooms of large ones. For large libraries, this was the age par excellence of the multitier stacks. The preeminence of the Snead standard stack continued, especially in the towers of academic libraries. In addition, considerable attention was now given to the percentage of books in different size categories and the most economical and efficient shelf sizes. Two trends were in evidence: greater standardization in shelf lengths (three feet became universal in new installations) and depths; and abandonment of glass in multitier stack floors in favor of marble and, later, of reinforced concrete. Standard definitions of terms (e.g., range, tier, deck) emerged and continued to be used in the next period.

ALA's Library Architecture and Planning Committee held programs at annual conferences and sponsored *Small Public Library Buildings*, by J. A. Lowe.[9] The Library Buildings Round Table provided an additional forum. The Cooperative Committee on Planning of New University and College Libraries, chaired by J. P. Boyd of Princeton, had representation from eleven educational institutions which were planning to spend over $25 million on new library buildings after the Second World War.

New theories arose on how libraries should be planned and constructed. In papers which appeared in 1933 and 1934 Angus Snead Macdonald proposed virtual elimination of fixed interior walls, ceilings throughout the building approximately eight feet high, walls made up of insulated interlocking panels which could be taken down and reassembled elsewhere, uprights (even in reading areas) placed nine feet apart to facilitate interchangeability, buildings composed of these units or modules, interspersing of readers and books, making departments and subject areas for readers out of portions of the bookstack, complete temperature and humidity control, and excellent artificial lighting. In 1945 Ralph Ellsworth, then chairman of the Committee on College and University Library Buildings of ACRL, presented a paper which gave evidence that Macdonald's ideas had been seriously considered and many would shortly be implemented at Iowa, MIT, and Princeton.

THE MODULAR REVOLUTION AND THE GOLDEN AGE, 1946–1976

The period from 1946 to the present has been one of unprecedented activity, fed at first by the pent-up demand created during the Second World War. This was later sustained by population and industrial growth, enrollment increases, and in the late 1960s by an infusion of federal funds. The trends already noted in a few leading libraries (air conditioning, fluorescent lighting, modular planning) became widespread.

Academic libraries met the challenge of growth with new main buildings, decentralization of facilities, cooperative storage arrangements, or some combination of these alternatives.

Princeton, Iowa, and MIT led the way with plans for new buildings to be constructed on modular principles. A summary of Ellsworth's description of proposals for Iowa is instructive in terms of its attention to flexibility and placement of fixed elements as well as its attention to the means of conducting heat, light, and ventilation. All ceilings were to be 8 feet 6 inches high. All floors would be supported by columns spaced 19 feet 6 inches apart in one direction and 13 feet 6 inches in the other. Columns would be 18 inches thick, leaving a clear space of 12 feet by 18 feet. Partitions (with or without doors) or shelves could be hung between any pair of columns. Lighting and ventilation through ceilings and columns were to be such that all spaces could be used interchangeably for reading, book storage, faculty offices, seminars, conference rooms, microforms, listening rooms. There would be no separate stacks as such, but reading areas adjacent to book areas. The fixed elements (stairs, elevators, mechanical equipment, plumbing) would be concentrated in a core in the front and center part of the building. Floor and wall construction would be dry and would consist of thin steel boxes resting on beams supported by the columns. It was hoped that prefabricated lights, and ventilating ducts, would effect substantial economies.

Subsequent experience with modular building design indicated that use of hollow columns for ventilation ducts posed fire and other problems. Ventilation ducts and electrical wiring were then placed between floors, necessitating substantial increase in thickness. Electrical outlets on walls and columns often proved insufficient, especially in technical processing areas. Floor outlets introduced lack of flexibility and posed cleaning problems. An innovative solution arising out of the Study of Educational Facilities (Toronto) was the use of portable energy columns which could be plugged into outlets from an electrical grid in the ceiling and relocated at other outlets on the grid whenever the need for changes might arise.

Other new main libraries were also constructed along modular lines. Wayne State adopted a subject division arrangement. Washington University, St. Louis used an architectural competition to produce the design for its new main library, which was subsequently judged one of the most successful of the postwar modular buildings. The new central libraries at Cornell and Notre Dame were similar in design, with a broad base to handle heavy traffic reader areas and technical services and a tower for stacks and research facilities. The Regenstein Library of the University of Chicago was the largest in floor area (577,045 gross square feet) and the new library at Northwestern University (both designed by Walter Netsch of Skidmore, Owings, and Merrill) was one of the most controversial because of its three round towers, lengthy corridors, and radial bookstacks.

Harvard set the pattern for decentralization with the opening of the Lamont Library for undergraduates in 1949. Michigan followed with its Undergraduate Library (the first on a state university campus) in 1958. Michigan also opened a storage library of 400,000 volumes on its North Campus and later added a new wing to its general library. Cornell converted its old main library to undergraduate use. Yale's first expansion was the Beinecke Library, when translucent wall panels were used instead of windows and rare books and manuscripts were housed in a glass-enclosed interior display stack; it was followed in less than a decade by the Wilbur Cross "intensive use library," which was constructed underground to house about 225,000 books and journals used most heavily by faculty and students. Another successful underground building was the Undergraduate Library of the University of Illinois.

Inspired by the success of the New England Deposit Library, a group of universities in the Midwest established the Midwest Inter-Library Center in 1951, with a building in Chicago which was essentially a large book warehouse, with some facilities for visiting scholars.

Jerrold Orne, who began his series of annual reports on academic library buildings in 1967, referred to the period from 1967 to 1971 as the Renaissance or Golden Age of academic library building because of the tremendous upsurge of activity stimulated in part by burgeoning enrollments and in part by federal grants under the Higher Education Facilities Act of 1963.

Developments in the public library field included large programs of branch expansion, some new central libraries, and a number of renovations and additions. In 1946 A. M. Githens and Ralph Munn prepared a plan for the public libraries of New York City. An extensive building program for the Los Angeles County Library was announced in 1950 and that same year ALA issued a book with new designs for branches. By 1960 Chicago had developed a standard plan for its branches, and standards for branches prepared by the Los Angeles Public Library had reached a third edition. Miami, Cincinnati, Denver, Seattle, Minneapolis, Dayton, Nashville, and Washington, D.C. erected modern functional main buildings. Newark decentralized some of its functions with the erection of a service building. New York took some of the pressure off the main building by erecting the Donnell Library Center and renovating a commercial structure to create the Mid-Manhattan Library with collections and facilities geared to the needs of college students. Philadelphia's building was renovated. Cleveland doubled its size by purchasing an adjacent newspaper building and constructing an underground tunnel. Detroit doubled its capacity by expanding to the rear of the old building with two new wings and a street-level entrance facing Wayne State University. Boston opened a substantial new wing in modern style but designed to harmonize with the 1894 building. Pressures from citizens' groups to preserve a historic site forced Chicago to retain its 1897 building but plans were made to transfer certain specialized functions to a separate new one.

There was a marked increase in public library building activity following passage of the Library Services and Construction Act of 1964. When federal funds for construction were cut off in the early 1970s, state and local funding took up much of the slack. In 1968 H. R. Galvin began a series of annual statistical reports on public library construction in the December 1 issue of *Library Journal.*

The Library of Congress completed refurbishing and air conditioning its entire original building in 1965. Approval of a third expansion was given that same year and ground was broken in 1971 for the James Madison Memorial Building with completion projected for 1977.

Several state libraries gained separate buildings, new quarters, or additions, mainly after 1960. One of the earliest was award-winning Louisiana, followed closely by Washington, which designed its modern structure to harmonize with the neoclassical state capitol. Texas shared its new quarters with the state archives, as did Idaho. Connecticut built an addition. North and South Carolina gained new quarters. New Jersey erected a large new building specifically designed for library purposes.

School libraries received early postwar attention from librarians, educators, and architects. A revised chapter appeared in the fourth edition of Lucille Fargo's *The Library and the School* (1947). *Dear Mr. Architect*, an ALA publication devoted to planning school libraries, appeared in 1946 and in a revised edition in 1952. Concern with elementary as well as secondary school libraries was evident by this time, although the extent of elementary provision increased most rapidly after passage of the Elementary and Secondary Education Act in 1965. Provision for audiovisual services began in the 1940s. By the 1970s, standards for media centers routinely included viewing, listening, production, and storage facilities.

After 1950 special librarians began to write and publish articles and books on library quarters and equipment. By the middle of the 1950s articles on specific libraries were appearing with regularity. A monograph was published in 1955. From 1958 through 1962 *Special Libraries* carried a series of more than thirty articles about different libraries on the general theme, "planning the new library." The New York chapter, especially active, was responsible for books which appeared in 1963 and 1972.

Library buildings became increasingly accessible, comfortable, and attractive. During the 1960s and 1970s great emphasis was placed on planning new buildings so that they would be accessible to and usable by the physically handicapped. Entrances at sidewalk level, elevators, and special restroom facilities were incorporated in most plans. Air conditioning, still something of a luxury reserved for a few leading libraries at the beginning of the period, was being included routinely in over 90 percent of new public library buildings by the early 1970s. Despite this progress, problems with the mechanical functioning (heating, ventilation, air conditioning) of new buildings were frequent and sometimes severe. Other flaws cited by W. H. Jesse included misuse of glass and provision of mezzanines which undercut the economies of modular planning. Fluorescent lighting became widespread and the number of footcandles of illumination increased. Standards by the Illuminating Engineering Society were revised in 1950, 1959, and 1972. At least one noted authority, Keyes Metcalf, questioned whether recommended illumination levels of 70 to 100 footcandles might not be far too high and whether 30 to 35 footcandles for most purposes, with lower levels in halls, might be more appropriate.

Meanwhile, a continuous stream of articles in the 1940s and 1950s called for more color in libraries and for increased use of art work. By the 1960s and 1970s these pleas were having substantial effect and new libraries were increasingly attractive. Floors received intensive study as the result of a grant to the Library Technology Program from the Council on Library Resources. Vinyl tile and carpeting proved popular choices. Indeed, 88 percent of all new public library buildings erected in 1974 contained some carpeting in public areas. School and academic libraries were also making extensive use of carpet.

The planning process was further defined and clarified. The roles of librarians, architects, and consultants received much attention and ALA increased its already substantial involvement. E. J. Reece wrote a practical article on preparation of library building programs. Working drawings and specifications received attention from L. Kaplan. ACRL and ARL sponsored a research project which resulted in the publication of a landmark work, *Planning Academic and Research Library Buildings*, by Keyes D. Metcalf.[10] Robert McClarren and Donald Thompson prepared a planning checklist and Ellsworth Mason wrote on questions which a librarian might raise with architects and engineers in order to insure lighting and ventilation systems adequate to the library's needs. The modular approach to planning and construction, which had captured the academic library field immediately after World War II, eventually spread to other types of libraries. One variant of this approach known as "systems building" (extensive use of prefabricated components to reduce cutting and fitting on the construction site) was first applied on a large scale in the "instant libraries" of West Virginia. Edward Tilton's concept of the "open plan" evolved into "office landscaping" (flexible use of furniture and movable partitions to create individualized work areas which could readily be modified as work flows changed).

Early in the postwar period, Donald Bean called attention to the role of a consultant in the selection of library equipment. By 1960 the heading *Consultant services* had appeared in *Library Literature*. Ellsworth and Ulveling wrote of the roles of consultants and training institutes were held during the 1960s. The ALA committees noted in the preceding period continued to be active. A particularly significant activity was the sponsorship of preconference institutes on library buildings. Librarians and architects presented plans for proposed new buildings and heard the criticisms of experts as well as others in the audiences. The papers and the discussion highlights were later published. Despite substantial clarification of roles in the planning process, the gap between theory and practice was sometimes wide. W. H. Jesse cited failure to involve all the participants at a sufficiently early stage as the most common source of difficulty, but lack of expertise and personality clashes also resulted in some buildings that were less satisfactory than they might have been.

The period from 1946 to the present has been one of unprecedented activity. New buildings have appeared in record numbers, more compact and economical of space and staff than in earlier periods. Modular planning has been almost universally accepted and the first real test is about to come as large numbers of buildings erected in the 1940s and 1950s must be expanded. Buildings have become more accessible (especially to the physically handicapped), more colorful, better lighted, and more comfortable. In addition to its practical qualities (acoustics, ease of cleaning), carpeting adds a touch of luxury. ALA continues to play a vital role in the dissemination of new information on library buildings. One can look forward with confidence to ALA's contribution in its second century.

NOTES

1. Chalmers Hadley, *Library Buildings: Notes and Plans* (Chicago: American Library Assn., 1924).
2. Arthur E. Bostwick, *The American Public Library*, 4th ed. (Chicago: American Library Assn., 1929).
3. H. S. Hirshberg, *Elements of the Library Plan* (Chicago: American Library Assn., 1930).
4. Joseph L. Wheeler and Alfred M. Githens, *The American Public Library Building* (New York: Scribner, 1941; reprint Chicago: American Library Assn., 1941, 1950).
5. James T. Gerould, *The College Library Building* (Chicago: American Library Assn., 1932).
6. Edna R. Hanley, *College and University Library Buildings* (Chicago: American Library Assn., 1939).
7. Guy R. Lyle, *Administration of the College Library* (New York: Wilson, 1945); Louis R. Wilson and Maurice F. Tauber, *The University Library* (Chicago: Univ. of Chicago Pr., 1945).
8. Lucille Fargo, *The Library and the School* (Chicago: American Library Assn., 1930); 2d ed. rev., 1933; 3d ed., 1939.
9. J. A. Lowe, *Small Public Library Buildings* (Chicago: American Library Assn., 1939).
10. Keyes D. Metcalf, *Planning Academic and Research Library Buildings* (New York: McGraw-Hill, 1965).

SELECTIVE BIBLIOGRAPHY

Items cited fully in the Notes are not reported here. Articles in *Library Journal* (numerous in almost every volume) are not listed, but may be found by consulting the years indicated in the text.

American Association of School Librarians and Association for Educational Communication and Technology. *Media Programs: District and School.* Chicago: American Library Assn., 1975.

American Library Association. Library Architecture and Planning Committee. *Buildings for Small Public Libraries, Remodeled and Adapted, Including Branches.* Chicago: American Library Assn., 1950.

Bailey, L. J. "New Housing for State Libraries." Summaries in *ALA Bulletin* 25:648-49 (Sept. 1931); and 26:684 (Aug. 1932).

Bean, Donald E. "Role of the Equipment Specialist in Building Plans." *Public Libraries* 2:38-40 (May 1948).

Bean, Donald E., and Ellsworth, Ralph. *Modular Planning for College and University Libraries.* Priv. Print., 1948.

Berkeley, B. *Floors: Selection and Maintenance.* Chicago: American Library Assn., 1968.

Bobinski, George S. *Carnegie Libraries: Their History and Impact on American Public Library Development.* Chicago: American Library Assn., 1969.

Boll, John Jorg. "Library Architecture 1800-1875: A Comparison of Theory and Buildings, with Emphasis on New England College Libraries." Ph.D. dissertation, University of Illinois at Urbana-Champaign, 1961.

"Brooklyn's New Library Building." *Wilson Library Bulletin* 15:640-41 (Apr. 1941).

Brough, Kenneth J. *Scholar's Workshop: Evolving Conceptions of Library Service.* Urbana: Univ. of Illinois Pr., 1953.

Bryan, J. E. "Building Planning and the Use of Color in the Library." *Wilson Library Bulletin* 28:570-73 (Mar. 1954).

Church, W. W. "New Virginia State Library Building." *National Association of State Librarians Proceedings and Papers* 42:16-21 (1939).

Cole, John Y. "The Main Building of the Library of Congress: A Chronology, 1871-1965." *Quarterly Journal of the Library of Congress* 29:267-70 (Oct. 1972).

———. "Smithmeyer and Pelz: Embattled Architects of the Library of Congress." *Quarterly Journal of the Library of Congress* 29:282-307 (Oct. 1972).

Coman, W. M. "Planning and Equipping the School Library." *American School Board Journal* 108:22-24 (Jan. 1944).

Douglas, M. T. P. "Design and Equipment of Consolidated School Libraries." *American School and University* 297-303 (1939).

———. "Plans and Equipment for School Libraries." *Library Trends* 1:324-32 (Jan. 1953).

Dudley, C. R. "Report of the Committee on Architecture." *ALA Bulletin* 1:119-23 (July 1907).

Eastman, William R. "Library Building Plans." *New York State Library Bulletin* 107:87-137 (1906).

———. "Report of the Committee on Library Architecture." *ALA Bulletin* 3:215-16 (Sept. 1909).

Ellsworth, Ralph E. "Buildings and Architecture." *College and Research Libraries* 6:279-81 (June 1945).

———. "Consultants for College and University Library Building Planning." *College and Research Libraries* 21:263-68 (July 1960).

———. *Planning Manual for Academic Library Buildings.* Metuchen, N.J.: Scarecrow, 1973.

Engelken, R. C. "Lighting Systems." *ALA Bulletin* 35:117-19 (Sept. 1941).

"Firestone Addition of 1971: Symbol of Continuity and Change: Dedication." *Princeton University Library Chronicle* 33:89–103 (Winter 1972).
Franckowiak, Bernard. "Considerations in Planning School Media Centers." *Wisconsin Library Bulletin* 66:2–9 (Jan. 1970).
Hadley, Chalmers. "Some Recent Features in Library Architecture." *ALA Bulletin* 10:18–21 (1916).
Hand, W. J. and others. "Special Library of the Future." *Special Libraries* 42:13–18+ (Jan. 1951).
"Harmony without Imitation: Modern Library Building Faces Washington State's Neoclassical Capitol in a Manner Befitting Both." *Architectural Forum* 113:104–7 (July 1960).
Herner, S. "Physical Planning of Special Libraries." *Special Libraries* 42:5–12 (Jan. 1951).
Hilker, Helen-Anne. "Monument to Civilization: Diary of a Building." *Quarterly Journal of the Library of Congress* 29:234–66 (Oct. 1972).
Hilligan, M. P., ed. *Libraries for Research and Industry: Planning and Equipment* . . . New York: Special Libraries Assn., 1955.
Hirshberg, H. S. "Four Library Buildings." *ALA Bulletin* 27:732–37 (Dec. 15, 1933).
Hoefler, E. J. "Color Dynamics as Applied to Libraries." *Wilson Library Bulletin* 22:532–33 (Mar. 1948).
Jesse, William H. "Some Common Faults in Planning Library Buildings." *Southeastern Librarian* 14:28–34 (Spring 1964).
Kaplan, L. "Librarian's Function with Regard to Working Drawings and Specifications." *ALA Bulletin* 48:369–71+ (July–Aug. 1954).
Kaser, David E. "Institute for College Library Building Consultants." *College and Research Libraries* 25:424–25 (Sept. 1964).
Kraehenbuhl, J. O. "Lighting the Library." *College and Research Libraries* 2:306–17 (June 1941).
Kuhlman, A. F. "Program of the Joint University Libraries." *College and Research Libraries* 3:108–16 (Mar. 1942).
Lewis, Chester M., ed. *Special Libraries: How to Plan and Equip Them* . . . New York: Special Libraries Assn., 1963.
Library Journal 1–99 (1876–1974).
Los Angeles. Public Library. *Building Standards for New Branches*. 3d ed. Los Angeles: 1960.
Lowe, J. A. "How the Rochester Public Library Resembles and Differs from the Enoch Pratt Free Library, Baltimore." *ALA Bulletin* 31:792–94 (Oct. 15, 1937).
Macdonald, Angus Snead. "A Library of the Future." In *Overbibliotekar Wilhelm Munthe*. . . . Oslo: Grondahl, 1933.
―――. "Some Engineering Developments Affecting Large Libraries." *ALA Bulletin* 28:628–32 (Sept. 1934).
Mason, D. D. "Mies van der Rohe's Design for the New D.C. Public Library." *D.C. Libraries* 37:23–25 (Spring 1966).
Maurer, H. V. "Planning Library Facilities for an Elementary School." *School Executive* 66:63–66 (Sept. 1946).
―――. "Planning Library Facilities for a Secondary School." *School Executive* 66:66–69 (Sept. 1946).
Metcalf, Keyes D. "Lamont Library Building: Function." *Harvard Library Bulletin* 3:12–30 (Winter 1949).

———. *Library Lighting.* Washington, D.C.: Association of Research Libraries, 1970.
Miller, H. M. "New State Library and Archives Building." *Idaho Librarian* 23:47–49 (Apr. 1971).
Minster, M. "Librarian Chats with Architect." *American School Board Journal* 98:63–64 (Jan. 1939).
Mount, Ellis, ed. *Planning the Special Library* . . . New York: Special Libraries Assn., 1972.
"New Quarters for N.C. State Library." *North Carolina Libraries* 26:149 (Fall 1968).
New York. Planning Commission. *Program for the Public Libraries of New York City.* Prepared by Alfred M. Githens and Ralph Munn. New York: 1946.
"Northwestern's New Library." *American Libraries* 1:443–45 (May 1970).
"Notes on Industrial Library Planning." *Special Libraries* 11:20a–25a (May 1920).
Oehlerts, Donald. "The Development of American Public Architecture from 1850 to 1940." Ph.D. dissertation, Indiana University, 1974.
Plaister, C. D. *Floors and Floor Coverings.* Chicago: American Library Assn., 1939.
"Planning for Audio-Visual Service." *School Library Association of California Bulletin* 18:22–24 (Mar. 1947).
Purdy, G. F. "Wayne State University Library Buildings." *College and Research Libraries* 14:143–46 (Apr. 1953).
Reece, E. J. "Library Building Programs: How to Draft Them." *College and Research Libraries* 13:198–211 (July 1952).
Reynolds, Helen M. "University Library Buildings in the United States 1890–1939." *College and Research Libraries* 14:149–57 (Apr. 1953).
Roberts, M. A. "New Annex of the Library of Congress." *ALA Bulletin* 31:795–98 (Oct. 15, 1937).
Rufsvold, Margaret I. *Audio-Visual School Library Services: A Handbook for Librarians.* Chicago: American Library Assn., 1949.
Sargent, D. K. "Library Planning." *Nation's Schools* 24:41–42 (Oct. 1939).
Schunk, R. J. *Pointers for Public Library Building Planners.* Chicago: American Library Assn., 1945.
"Seminar for Experienced Building Consultants, 1968, Rutgers University." *Library Building Consultant: Role and Responsibility.* Ed. by Ernest R. Deprospo. New Brunswick, N.J.: Rutgers Univ. Pr., 1969.
Snead and Company Iron Works. *Library Planning, Bookstacks, and Shelving.* Jersey City, N.J.: Snead, 1915.
"South Carolina State Library Gets Collection under One Roof." *American Libraries* 1:511 (June 1970).
Ulveling, Ralph A. "Problems of Library Construction." *Library Quarterly* 33:91–101 (Jan. 1962).
U.S. Office of Education. *Report of Commissioner, 1892–93.* Washington, D.C.: Govt. Print. Off., 1894.
Van Hoesen, Henry B., and Kilpatrick, Norman L. "Heights of Books in Relation to Heights of Stack Tiers." *Library Quarterly* 4:352–57 (Apr. 1933).
Wagman, Frederick H. "Undergraduate Library at the University of Michigan." *College and Research Libraries* 20:179–88 (May 1959).

White, Lucien W. "University of Illinois Award Winning Undergraduate Library." *Illinois Libraries* 50:1042–46 (Dec. 1968).

Willard, Ashton R. "College Libraries in the United States." *New England Magazine* 17:422–40 (Dec. 1897).

Winsor, Justin. "Library Buildings." In U.S. Bureau of Education. *Public Libraries in the United States of America.* . . . Washington, D.C.: Govt. Print. Off., 1876.

PART FOUR

Environment

13

The National Libraries of the United States and Canada

JOHN Y. COLE
Library of Congress

The Library of Congress developed into the de facto national library of the United States of America during a relatively short period of time, roughly speaking, between 1861 and 1901. Furthermore, its two sister libraries, today known as the National Agricultural Library and the National Library of Medicine, were established during the same fruitful decades. The development of a Canadian national library proceeded at a slower pace, culminating with the establishment of the National Library of Canada in 1953. Although events in the United States greatly influenced the establishment of the National Library of Canada, there is a considerable difference between the two national library patterns. This essay is a brief historical comparison of their respective courses.

DEVELOPMENT IN THE UNITED STATES

In 1876 when the American Library Association was founded, the Library of Congress was the largest library in the United States. Its book collection totaled over 400,000 volumes and it was growing at a rapid rate. Such expansion created serious problems, however. Located in cramped rooms in the west front of the U.S. Capitol, the Library virtually was out of shelf space and its staff of fifteen was too small to cope adequately with the collections or with service to Congress. The Library had one tremendous asset, however, a shrewd and aggressive Librarian who was determined to make the Library of Congress a library of truly national significance. His name was Ainsworth Rand Spofford. After his appointment as Librarian by President Abraham Lincoln on December 31, 1864, Spofford made considerable progress toward the accomplishment of his goal.[1]

Spofford was responsible for reviving the idea of an American national library, an idea that had flourished sporadically throughout the nineteenth century. New England intellectuals such as Rufus Choate and George Perkins Marsh, for example, were strong promoters of the notion of the Smithsonian Institution as the national library of the United States. Charles Coffin Jewett, the Smithsonian librarian from 1847 to 1854, had the support of Choate and Marsh in his effort to shape the Smithsonian into both a national library and a national bibliographic center. Unfortunately for Jewett his superior, Smithsonian Secretary Joseph Henry, was not nearly as enthusiastic about the development of a national library at the Smithsonian. Henry, the foremost U.S. scientist of his day, favored a library designed solely to support what he viewed as the true purpose of the institution, the increase of knowledge through scientific research and the subsequent diffusion of this knowledge through publication. Henry dismissed Jewett in mid-1854, bringing to a halt any notions that the Smithsonian might someday be the national library.[2]

With Spofford's appointment as Librarian, the Library of Congress began its transformation from a small legislative library into a national institution. Between 1865 and 1897, Spofford provided his successors at the Library of Congress with the comprehensive national collections and the spacious new building necessary for the development of a modern national library.[3]

Ainsworth Spofford saw no conflict between the functions of a legislative and a national library. He was convinced that there was no book on any subject that might not at some time "prove useful to the legislature of a great nation in their manifold and responsible duties." A comprehensive collection was therefore as important to Congress as it was to scholars and the general public. Once this collection was developed for the use of the national legislature, it should be made available to the rest of the American people, for the strength of the Republic depended on "the popular intelligence."[4] Spofford viewed the national library as a unique, independent institution; it was to be a single, comprehensive collection of national literature used freely both by members of Congress and by the U.S. people. This great national collection was to be patterned after the famous national libraries of Europe, particularly the British Museum.

Between 1865 and 1870, taking advantage of a favorable post–Civil War political and intellectual climate, as well as his personal friendships with several prominent politicians, Spofford gained congressional approval for the rapid expansion of the Library. Two of the most significant events were the purchase of the personal library of Peter Force and the approval of the copyright law of 1870. Peter Force, an archivist and historian who resided in Washington, D.C., had accumulated probably the most important collection of manuscripts, books, and newspapers relating to the United States in existence at the time; in 1867 Spofford convinced Congress to appropriate $100,000 to purchase the collection for the Library of Congress. Three years later, he orchestrated passage of the copyright law of 1870, which centralized all U.S. copyright registration and deposit activities at the Library of Congress, thereby bringing to the Library without cost two copies of each copyrighted book, pamphlet, map, print, photograph, and piece of music. In five years Spofford had made great strides in gathering his "national collection" and the Library of Congress had become the largest library in the United States.

Moreover, this sudden, permanent expansion made a separate Library of Congress building a necessity. The Librarian first asked Congress for such a structure in 1871. The next year he presented a detailed plan for the building, but it was not until 1886 that its construction was authorized. In the meantime, the Library ran out of shelf space and until the new building was finally completed in 1897, Spofford was faced with severe problems. But the new Library of Congress building, located across the east plaza from the Capitol, is truly the capstone of Spofford's effort, for its monumental nature enhanced the Library's national character and permanently ensured its national role.[5]

The origins of the working relationships between the Library of Congress and its two sister national libraries, the National Library of Medicine and the National Agricultural Library, can also be traced to the era of Spofford's administration. The National Library of Medicine was founded in 1836 as the library of the Office of the Surgeon General, but its growth into a national institution occurred during the administration of Dr. John Shaw Billings, from 1865 to 1895. In 1872 Billings asked Spofford if one of the two copyright deposits "of each American printed treatise relating to Medicine, Surgery, and Hygiene" could be sent to his library. Already becoming overwhelmed with copyright deposits, Spofford agreed to the request and the transfer of medical books from the Library of Congress to the surgeon general's library began almost by return mail. For a brief period during the 1880s, Spofford had second thoughts about the trend toward independent growth among U.S. governmental libraries, including that of the Office of the Surgeon General. Accordingly, he advocated a plan which would consolidate the medical library and other federal departmental libraries within the Library of Congress, once the new building was completed. However the lengthy delays he encountered in obtaining authorization for the new structure soon forced him to abandon such plans. The library of the surgeon general continued its independent growth into the twentieth century and in 1922 was named the Army Medical Library. It was designated as the Armed Forces Medical

Library in 1952, and in 1956, when it became part of the Public Health Service of the U.S. Department of Health, Education, and Welfare, it was officially named the National Library of Medicine.[6]

The National Agricultural Library was established in 1862 as the library of the U.S. Department of Agriculture. In 1893 its librarian, William P. Cutter, asked Spofford to send him copyright deposits in agricultural subjects; but the Librarian of Congress, by then immersed in growing piles of books, maps, prints, and newspapers, was unable to comply. However, Herbert Putnam, Librarian of Congress from 1899 to 1939, did start such an arrangement in 1900. The library of the Department of Agriculture was designated a National Agricultural Library in 1962.[7]

Ainsworth Spofford developed the Library of Congress into a national institution quite independently of the U.S. library movement or the American Library Association. Between 1876 and 1896 the leaders of ALA showed great personal respect for Spofford, but they also came to expect from the Library of Congress an aggressive leadership in national library matters that Spofford simply was unable to provide. As the new Library of Congress building neared completion, the ALA, led by Melvil Dewey and Richard R. Bowker, became anxious to exert its influence on the reorganization that obviously would take place once the new structure was occupied. When the Joint Congressional Committee on the Library of Congress scheduled hearings in late 1896 on the "condition" of the Library prior to its move into the building, the ALA sent seven witnesses to testify. Those hearings, held from November 16 until December 7, 1896, are of great interest as a discussion of the proper role of the U.S. national library. In addition to Spofford, the principal witnesses were two of the ALA delegates, Melvil Dewey, then director of the New York State Library, and Herbert Putnam, librarian of the Boston Public Library. Both men carefully avoided direct criticism of Spofford, but their views of the proper functions of a national library plainly differed from those of the aging Librarian of Congress.[8]

The testimony of Herbert Putnam is of special interest, for less than three years later he was to become Librarian of Congress and implement many of the ideas that he expressed during the hearings. Putnam wholeheartedly endorsed Dewey's description of the desirable role of a national library as "a center to which the libraries of the whole country can turn for inspiration, guidance, and practical help." Centralized cataloging, interlibrary loan, a national bibliographic center, and the equivalent of what today is the national union catalog were among the needed functions described by Dewey and Putnam. The Boston librarian also stressed the need for stronger national leadership in other library services, and tactfully expressed his opinion that the services of the Library of Congress should be expanded far beyond those offered under Spofford's administration. Herbert Putnam, unlike

Ainsworth Spofford, shared a view expressed by U.S. librarians as early as 1850, when Charles Coffin Jewett presented his plan for centralized cataloging through the Smithsonian Institution: that the national library should offer comprehensive services to other libraries of the nation and that a logical starting point would be the centralized distribution of cataloging information.

The hearings of 1896 marked a sharp turning point in the relations between the American Library Association and the Library of Congress. For the first time the association, albeit cautiously, offered its advice to Congress about the organization and functioning of the Library of Congress. Moreover, Congress listened with great interest. The Joint Committee on the Library, however, never actually issued a report about the reorganization of the Library. Instead, provisions for its reorganization were included in the legislative appropriation bill, which was approved by the president on February 19, 1897, before the committee's hearings were even available.[9]

The reorganization, which expanded all aspects of the Library's operations and gave the Librarian of Congress the unique powers which that office still holds, went into effect on July 1, 1897. On that date President William McKinley also appointed a new Librarian of Congress, a personal friend, the veteran journalist and diplomat John Russell Young. Spofford stepped down, but by prearrangement. Young's first act was to appoint the former Librarian to the post of chief assistant librarian. Young's career at the Library of Congress was productive but brief; after a short illness, he died on January 17, 1899. His successor, as a result of a concerted campaign by the American Library Association, was Herbert Putnam, who took office as the new Librarian of Congress on April 5, 1899.

The appointment and the administration of Herbert Putnam firmly linked the policies of the Library of Congress with the broader interests of librarianship in the United States. Putnam was vitally interested in the issues that concerned the rest of the profession, particularly cataloging and classification, and he quickly brought his extensive experience to bear upon the Library's collections and services. By 1901 he had introduced new cooperative cataloging, classification, and loan services that established the Library of Congress as the leader among U.S. libraries. His lengthy annual report for 1901 describes the Library's collections, facilities, organization, and the operations of each administrative unit. It is a guide to the best library practice of the day and sets high standards for every aspect of library operations. In all, Putnam's administration reflects the coming of age of ALA influence on the Library of Congress. Putnam himself twice served as ALA president: in 1898, when he completed the term of the deceased Justin Winsor, and again in the year 1904. More importantly, however, during at least the first two decades of his career as Librarian of Congress, the views of Herbert Putnam about the role of the Library of Congress as the national library were synonomous with the views of the American Library Association.

From the ALA standpoint, there nevertheless was one major issue that was never resolved during Putnam's administration. In fact, it became more complicated. This was the question of the official designation of the Library of Congress as the U.S. national library, and it included the question of the location of the national library in the legislative branch of the government. In 1896 and early 1897, Dewey, Bowker, and others in the American Library Association had hoped that the reorganization of the Library of Congress would result at least in its formal designation as the national library of the United States, and perhaps even in its transfer to the executive branch of the government.[10] This was one area, however, in which the ALA carried no influence. Congress refused to consider seriously either a change of name or giving up its jurisdiction over the Library, even though it did provide funds adequate for the latter's expansion into a truly national library. As a result, while during the Putnam administration the Library of Congress developed into a national library in the general manner advocated by the leaders of the American Library Association, that national library remained under the direct control of the U.S. Congress. The reference and research needs of the latter, accordingly, had priority over the demands from the Library's other "national" constituencies, including the American Library Association, other federal libraries, scholars, and the general public.

Herbert Putnam served as Librarian of Congress until 1939. During his forty-year term of office, the size of the Library's book collection increased from 900,000 to over 6 million volumes, the staff from 230 to 960, and a new Annex building was constructed. He continued the expansion of both the legislative and the national functions of the Library. The Legislative Reference Service was founded in 1915 to serve Congress more directly, and in the last two decades of his administration the Librarian also made a concentrated effort to develop the Library into a research center for scholars from the United States and abroad. This expansion of functions, in turn, helped create the major problem of Putnam's administration. A strong, even dictatorial personality, Herbert Putnam kept tight personal control over the institution in his charge. As Putnam grew older the result, unfortunately, was a certain degree of administrative stagnation, especially in the 1930s when the depression made additional funds for expansion and for new activities virtually unavailable. The administrative redistribution of the new functions and responsibilities acquired during the Putnam years was left to his successor.

In 1939 President Franklin D. Roosevelt nominated the poet and writer Archibald MacLeish to be Librarian of Congress. The American Library Association protested the nomination to no avail; the U.S. Senate easily confirmed MacLeish's appointment. The new Librarian, with aid from outside and staff committees, devoted a great deal of effort to a thorough administrative reorganization of the Library. He also provided, in his "Canons of Selection" and "Canons of Service," a concise definition of the Library's objectives. MacLeish fully accepted the dual nature of the Library as it had developed during previous administrations: the Library of Congress served both Congress and the nation, but the Congress had priority. He nevertheless defined the Library in his own terms: it was a "people's university which provides to the people, through their representatives in Congress, and their officers of government, as well as directly, the written record of their civilization."[11]

MacLeish's successor as Librarian, political scientist Luther H. Evans, served from 1945 until 1953, when he resigned to become director general of UNESCO. Shortly after he took office, Evans attempted to expand the Library's national functions rapidly and decisively: his budget request for fiscal year 1947 called for nearly a 100 percent increase in the Library's appropriation. The House committee on appropriations refused to approve the Librarian's full request, even though a modest increase was approved. Moreover, in its report, the committee posed a question of fundamental importance with regard to the Library's national role:

> If it is the desire to build and maintain the largest library in the world which, according to testimony, the Library of Congress is at present, that is one matter, and if it should be the policy to maintain a library primarily for the service of Congress, it is quite another matter from the standpoint of fiscal needs.[12]

Because of such Congressional doubts, and budgetary concerns, Evans never was able to expand the Library of Congress in the style or at the pace he felt appropriate.

L. Quincy Mumford, Librarian of Congress from 1954 through 1974, was more successful than Evans in obtaining increased congressional appropriations. All aspects of the Library's activities expanded during Mumford's administration. For example, the size of the book collection increased from 10 to over 16 million volumes, the Library's map, music, graphic arts, and manuscript collections approximately doubled in size, the number of permanent staff positions increased from 1,564 to 4,250, and the Library's appropriation soared from $9 million in fiscal year 1954 to over $96 million in fiscal year 1974. Development of plans for a third major library building, the establishment of overseas acquisitions and cataloging programs, and the expansion of the Legislative Reference Service (renamed the Congressional Research Service in 1971), were three of the most significant achievements of his administration.

L. Quincy Mumford, like Ainsworth Spofford and Herbert Putnam, was an expansionist Librarian of Congress. Mumford also faced some of the same problems as did his distinguished predecessors, especially lack of space. Spofford obtained authorization for the Main building in 1886, Putnam for the Annex in 1930, and Mumford for the James Madison Memorial Building in 1965. While waiting for construction to be completed, these three librarians endured crowded conditions that curtailed services and brought criticism from the Library's various categories of users. In each instance, rapid growth and the lack of space also contributed to the need for future administrative reorganization.

An important national development during the Mumford administration was the formal coordination, for the first time, of Library of Congress activities with those of other federal libraries and specifically with the other two national libraries.

The Library of Congress, with the cooperation of the U.S. Bureau of the Budget, took the initiative in the establishment of the Federal Library Committee on March 11, 1965. The purpose of the new committee was "to improve coordination and planning among research libraries of the Federal Government, so that common problems may be identified, solutions sought, and services to the Government and the Nation improved."[13] The committee has its headquarters at the Library of Congress.

An important step toward the development of a national library "system" in the United States was the creation, on May 25, 1967, of the U.S. National Libraries Task Force on Automation and Other Cooperative Services. Its general purpose, as announced by the three national library directors, was to encourage closer cooperation among the national libraries in the development of national library objectives and services. To undertake the studies necessary for the establishment of compatible procedures and alternative designs for a national library information system, working groups were assigned to pursue specific problems, for example, bibliographic codes, machine-readable formats, and aspects of a national serials data program. Although the National Library of Medicine and the National Agricultural Library are considerably smaller than the Library of Congress, each has gathered the most extensive worldwide collection within its specialty. Moreover, the limited size and specialized scope of each has enabled these two institutions to inaugurate unique and especially useful services for their respective clienteles. The computer-based Medical Literature Analysis and Retrieval System (MEDLARS) established by the National Library of Medicine in 1964 is worthy of special mention.

In 1966 President Lyndon B. Johnson established a U.S. National Advisory Commission on Libraries to recommend methods for achieving a coordinated, nationwide library and information services policy. One of the commission's principal recommendations was the "recognition and strengthening of the role of the Library of Congress as the National Library of the United States." In 1970 when the U.S. National Commission on Libraries and Information Science was created, as a result of another advisory commission recommendation. the Librarian of Congress was named to the commission. Librarian Mumford frequently stated his opposition to the oft-repeated idea that the Library of Congress be transferred to the executive branch of government, as well as his opinion that the formal designation of the Library of Congress as the U.S. national library was "unnecessary." Mumford continued to emphasize a point that he had explained at great length in his 1962 annual report, that the Library of Congress already performed "more national library functions than any other library in the world."[14]

In its final report published in May 1975 and entitled *Toward a National Program for Library and Information Services: Goals for Action*, the U.S. National Commission on Libraries and Information Science stated its belief that the Library of Congress "should be designated as the National Library." The commission's emphasis, however, was on the responsibilities it felt the Library should accept in the proposed national program, for example, expansion of its lending function, its National Program for Acquisitions and Cataloging (NPAC), machine-readable cataloging program (MARC) and its automation programs, and the development of an expanded general reference program to support a national system for bibliographic service.[15] The degree to which the Library of Congress can implement these recommendations in the face of increased research demands from the U.S. Congress and the Library's continuing space crisis is perhaps the major challenge facing the new Librarian of Congress.

A LIBRARY FOR CANADA

Cultural development in the United States has been characterized by its fragmentary, hurried, and even accidental nature, and the evolution of the idea of a national library has been no exception. The actual institution, meanwhile, was vital not only at home but to the Canadian library community. In 1946 at the organizational meeting of the Canadian Library Association (CLA), it was generally agreed that "the Library of Congress has played during the last fifty years the part that a Canadian National Library ought to have been playing in Canada."[16]

The National Library of Canada is an infant among national libraries. Although a Canadian national library was advocated as early as 1883 by Sir John A. MacDonald, the first prime minister, no such institution existed before 1953, nor did it occupy its own building until 1967. However frustrating to the supporters of a national library, this long delay was not necessarily harmful: when the time came for its establishment, the basic role of the Canadian national library had been debated and in large measure agreed upon. In particular its promoters wanted to avoid, as far as possible, the dilemmas posed by the fragmentary pattern of national library development in the United States. By the early years of the twentieth century, they were promoting the idea of a centralized national library in the executive branch of government, separate from the older and established Library of Parliament. In the middle of the twentieth century they achieved their goal by carefully molding a new national institution out of other Canadian institutions that previously had performed national library functions.

There are many similarities between the early histories of the Canadian Library of Parliament and the U.S. Library of Congress. One parallel could not be more direct: during the War of 1812, the U.S. forces burned the Parliamentary Building in York (Toronto), including the library. A year later on August 24, 1814, the British invaded Washington and destroyed the Capitol and its small legislative library. Half a century later, after the new Dominion of Canada had been proclaimed on July 1, 1867, the Library of Parliament was legally constituted under a Joint Library Committee.

Shortly thereafter, however, the joint committee recommended the creation of a separate national archives, an event that did not take place in the United States until 1934 when President Franklin D. Roosevelt approved the establishment of the U.S. counterpart. The Public Archives of Canada was established in 1872, and four years later another event occurred that did not have its parallel in the United States until many years later, the Library of Parliament moved into its own separate building.

In the late nineteenth century there was considerable support for the idea that Canada should follow the U.S. example and expand its Library of Parliament into a national library. The argument had a certain practical appeal to its advocates, men such as the parliamentary librarian, Alpheus Todd. In an 1882 request to the Treasury for additional funds, Todd used arguments similar to those used by the Librarian of Congress, Ainsworth Spofford, and ended by imploring the Treasury to contribute "to the enlargement and improvement of our National Library."[17]

Prime Minister Sir John A. MacDonald agreed on the need for a national library. On April 16, 1883 in the House of Commons, he asked the Library Committee to take up the question, since "we really ought to have a National Library containing every book worthy of being kept on the shelves of a library." However, at the time Sir John did not think that the Library of Congress was a particularly good example for the Parliamentary Library to follow.

> Our Library is neither one thing nor the other just now. It is not a British Museum, or a Canadian Museum, or a National Library. It falls, as it were, between two stools. . . . I may say the same thing, however, with regard to the great library at Washington. It is assumed from the number of volumes that it has the character of a National Library, and yet it is commonly and technically, merely a Parliamentary Library.[18]

After librarian Todd died in 1884, however, MacDonald filled the post with two librarians, one called the general librarian and the other the parliamentary librarian. In other words, despite his doubts, the prime minister *did* attempt to pattern the Parliamentary Library after the Library of Congress where Librarian Spofford was, in effect, serving as both the general and the parliamentary librarian. The prime minister explained that a general librarian was needed because "here, as in Washington, we have no British Museum, no general library considered as a national one, but under the name of a Parliamentary Library, we have increased the number of books so as to make it a national one." As F. Dolores Donnelly points out in her excellent study, *The National Library of Canada* (1973), MacDonald's compromise of trying "to cast the Library of Parliament into the mold of the Library of Congress by creating the illusion that the former was fulfilling the role of national library as well as the legislative function—with two heads instead of one—may have postponed the real issue for sixty years."[19]

It is obvious, however, that at least until the early decades of the twentieth century, the lack of a national "cultural consciousness" impeded Canadian national library development. Regional library associations were founded, but attempts to establish a national library association failed, in part because of the strength of the regional movement and in part because of the convenience of the American Library Association. Canadian librarians attended the annual ALA meetings in Montreal in 1900 and 1934, in Ottawa in 1912, and in Toronto in 1927, as well as nearby annual meetings in the United States. Canadians tended to rely on the leading library association in the United States as they relied on the Library of Congress for bibliographic, interlibrary loan, and union catalog services.

The most prominent regional association, and the center of Canadian library activity, was the Ontario Library Association, founded in 1901. In 1910 its president, Lawrence J. Burpee, librarian of the Ottawa Public Library, delivered a speech at the association's annual meeting on the subject of a Canadian national library. His statement, entitled "A Plea for a National Library," soon revived the Canadian national library movement. It also helped crystallize differences between the Canadian and U.S. approaches to a national library.

Burpee pointed out that the Parliamentary Library was not by any means serving as a satisfactory national library and suggested a complete separation of the two functions, along with a separate national library building. He admired the Library of Congress, but felt that "only the genius of the present Librarian" made it a workable institution. He especially approved of Librarian of Congress Herbert Putnam's willingness to cooperate with other libraries and to share the resources of the Library of Congress as widely as possible, in contrast to the more conservative administrations of the British Museum and the

Bibliothèque Nationale. Finally, Burpee made one practical suggestion that proved to be prophetic: "Let the government remove from the Library of Parliament to the national library all books and other materials that would properly find a place in such an institution, but which serve no very useful purpose in a purely legislative library."[20] Interestingly enough, one librarian who endorsed the concept of separating legislative collections from the more general collections was none other than Librarian of Congress Putnam, who also was the organizer of the Library's separate Legislative Reference Service.[21]

The Library of Congress became the de facto national library of the United States without assistance from the American Library Association, even though the ALA has had an important influence on the Library's development since, roughly speaking, the beginning of Putnam's administration. In Canada, by contrast, the organization of the Canadian Library Association proved indispensable for the establishment of the National Library of Canada. Between the time of the personal crusade of Lawrence Burpee and the founding of the CLA in 1946, the Canadian government was preoccupied with two World Wars and an economic depression, and the government itself changed hands several times. Recommendations favoring a national library and a "national library policy," such as those included in the Ridington report, *Libraries in Canada: A Study of Library Conditions and Needs* (1933), went unheeded. Canadian scholars, as well as librarians, became increasingly concerned. By 1946, for example, the Canadian Political Science Association authorized its head "to act with the Royal Society of Canada or any other learned society or public body in urging upon the government of Canada the establishment of a National Library."[22]

The Canadian Library Association was finally organized in June 1946. Its establishment was a major victory for national library advocates: the CLA was recognized as a bilingual and bicultural organization with an English/French title, the Canadian Library Association/ Association Canadienne des Bibliothèques. Under the determined and skilled leadership of individuals such as Elizabeth H. Morton and Freda F. Waldon, the new organization wasted no time in coordinating a renewed effort to convince the Canadian federal government of the pressing need for a national library. Within two months a comprehensive document outlining the arguments was prepared under the sponsorship of the CLA, the Royal Society, the Canadian Political Science Association, the Canadian Historical Association, and the Social Science Research Council of Canada. The statement, or joint brief, introduced a new notion into the national library argument: it urged that a bibliographic center be established as a first step toward a national library. In other words, essential functions should be undertaken immediately; details regarding the formal creation of the library and provision for its separate building could be worked out later.

At last there was a positive government response, even though Prime Minister MacKenzie King added a new facet: he wanted to combine the administration of the Public Archives with that of the proposed national library. This was acceptable to the CLA and to Dr. W. Kaye Lamb, librarian of the University of British Columbia and seemingly the unanimous choice to become the first national librarian. On September 11, 1948 Prime Minister King announced the appointment of Lamb as dominion archivist "with the special assignment of preparing the way for the establishment of a National Library in Ottawa."[23]

On May 1, 1950 in accordance with the recommendations of the joint brief, the Canadian Bibliographic Centre was created. It was administered by the dominion archivist and had as its primary purposes the publication of a current national bibliography and the compilation and servicing of a national union catalog. Since 1923 the Toronto Public Library had compiled and published the annual *Canadian Catalogue of Books*; this function was assumed by the Bibliographic Centre, which replaced it in January 1951 with a new bilingual national bibliography entitled *Canadiana*. The union catalog activity was deemed essential since it was obvious that the new Canadian national library would probably never be able to accumulate a truly comprehensive national collection. The location of research materials around the nation therefore became the key to national library planning. As it did in many other areas, the Library of Congress provided the Canadians with equipment and technical assistance to aid the development of the union catalog.

In 1951 the Royal Commission on National Development in the Arts, Letters, and Sciences (known as the Massey Commission) urged that a Canadian national library be formally established "without delay." The government agreed and a national library bill was finally approved on June 18, 1952. On January 1, 1953, accordingly, the National Library of Canada was established, absorbed the functions of the National Bibliographic Centre, and began to automatically acquire certain categories of Canadian publications under the terms of a new deposit law. Subject to the direction of the government ministry, moreover, the national librarian was authorized to purchase, lend, and exchange materials and direct the work of the library "in such a manner that the facilities of the Library may be made available to the Government and to the people of Canada to the greatest possible extent."[24]

The next task for national library supporters was to obtain a new building for the National Library, which was housed with the Public Archives and in temporary facilities. Only with additional space could its functions be expanded properly. Once again, the Canadian Library Association took the lead, organizing a national campaign for a library building. As usual there were delays, and funds were not appropriated until 1963; the new National Library and Public Archives Building on

256 / Environment

Wellington Street in Ottawa was officially opened on June 20, 1967. Perhaps the most immediate benefit of the new building was that it provided the space needed for the National Library to implement the various agreements that it had already worked out with other Canadian libraries and research institutions.

The Library of Parliament had, of course, been accumulating Canadiana for over a century. It also had been receiving copyright deposits and participating in international exchanges on behalf of the Canadian government. A new agreement was initiated whereby the National Library assumed responsibility for most, though not all, international exchange activity. Certain useful but essentially nonparliamentary reference services were transferred to the National Library, along with sizable portions of the Library of Parliament collections. These included approximately 720,000 bound volumes of newspapers and about 250,000 other volumes of seldom used materials, primarily Canadiana but also including foreign public documents and many duplicates. Bound newspaper volumes were also transferred from the Public Archives to the National Library, but the archives retained its rich collections of manuscripts, maps, and graphic arts.[25]

The major advantage of including the National Library and the Public Archives in one building was that it combined the unparalleled Canadiana resources of both institutions in one location and also permitted the sharing of certain facilities. From the beginning, however, national library supporters had urged an autonomous institution, one that would not be subordinate to any other agency. Upon the retirement of Dr. Lamb on June 1, 1968, the administrative structures of the National Library and the Public Archives were formally separated.

In 1967 the idea of a unified Canadian national library was challenged by a statute of the Province of Quebec. The new law transformed the Bibliothèque St. Sulpice in Montreal (founded 1844) into a national library for French Canada, to be known as the Bibliothèque Nationale du Québec. Moreover, the declared functions of the new national library, which include the acquisition and preservation "of every document published in Quebec or relative to Quebec, and even every document published in French in Canada," augur duplication of effort and possible conflicts of interest with the National Library of Canada. Since its establishment, the latter institution has accepted equal responsibility for the French and the English library interests of Canada. The situation was complicated further in 1968 when the CLA ceased to be the official bilingual library organization of Canada. By mutual agreement between the two organizations, the CLA was recognized as the English-speaking association and the L'Association Canadienne des Bibliothécaires de Langue Française (ACBLF) as the French-speaking association. In late 1968 the two associations presented a joint brief to the national librarian, Guy Sylvestre, on "The Role of the National Library." One of its recommendations was that the National Library of Canada "develop close liaison with the National Science Library, the Bibliothèque Nationale du Québec, and other research and documentation centers in Canada."[26]

One response to this challenge was the approval of a strong new National Library Act on June 29, 1969. The new law confirmed the original national mission of the library and provided for the expansion of its functions; it defined the role of the National Science Library, but did not mention the Bibliothèque Nationale du Québec. Its most significant feature was the allocation to the national librarian of the responsibility for coordinating all aspects of Canadian government library services. There was one exception to this provision, full autonomy for the Parliamentary Library. On the other hand, the 1969 act made the National Library the legal deposit library, completing the removal of copyright deposit responsibilities from the Parliamentary Library.

The 1969 National Library Act also clarified the complicated relationship between the National Library and the National Science Library. The latter had started as the library of the National Research Council of Canada, created in 1924 and still the library's parent body. The science library's national responsibilities expanded until, in 1966, it obtained statutory recognition as the National Science Library, responsible for national services in the fields of the natural sciences, engineering, and technology. The 1969 act formally placed the many national functions performed by the science library under the general direction of the national librarian, even though the National Science Library operates with a considerable degree of autonomy. Of particular significance is the development of a national scientific and technical information system, a responsibility given to the National Research Council in December 1969.[27]

In conclusion it is obvious that librarianship in the United States, and particularly the Library of Congress, has had a significant impact on the development of the National Library of Canada, both through example and through specific activities. This "dependency" is part of the historical pattern of U.S. influence on Canadian cultural development, a situation that has encouraged the rekindling of Canadian nationalism in recent decades. At the organizational meeting of the Canadian Library Association in June 1946, the keynote address was given by Luther H. Evans, Librarian of Congress from 1945 to 1953. In his speech, entitled "The National Library in the Life of the Nation," Evans compared library development in the United States and Canada, reminding his listeners that they had been "able to read the diary of our failures and successes while we have had to work out major solutions somewhat in advance of you." However, he welcomed the advent of a Canadian national library and commented that "we are happy if our experience may furnish you with an opportunity to avoid a number of pitfalls."[28]

258 / Environment

Yet, in a more fundamental sense, the National Library of Canada, thanks to the growth of Canadian nationalism, is really a variation of the overall pattern of U.S. influence on Canadian institutions. Compared to the Library of Congress, the National Library of Canada is relatively small; nevertheless, it now stands at the center of a clearly defined national library system in the executive branch of the Canadian government. The different approaches to national library development in each country are directly linked to the political and cultural differences between the United States and Canada. As Verner W. Clapp, Acting Librarian of Congress, declared before the Canadian Library Association on August 27, 1953:

> The minimum requirements for a national library are that it should be a national institution and that it should attempt to form a comprehensive collection of the national publications; beyond that, each national library will create its own personality.[29]

NOTES

1. A full account of Spofford's collection-building efforts is in John Y. Cole, "Of Copyright, Men, and a National Library," *Quarterly Journal of the Library of Congress* 28:114–36 (Apr. 1971).

2. The Henry-Jewett dispute is described in Wilcomb E. Washburn, "Joseph Henry's Conception of the Purpose of the Smithsonian Institution," in *A Cabinet of Curiosities: Five Episodes in the Evolution of American Museums* (Charlottesville: Univ. of Virginia Pr., 1967), pp. 119–29.

3. The views of Spofford and his successors on the legislative and national roles of the Library of Congress are outlined in John Y. Cole, "For Congress and the Nation: The Dual Nature of the Library of Congress," *Quarterly Journal of the Library of Congress* 32:118–38 (Apr. 1975).

4. A concise statement of Spofford's views on a national library is his "The Function of a National Library," in *Handbook of the New Library of Congress*, comp. by Herbert Small (Boston: Curtis and Cameron, 1899), pp. 123–28.

5. The story of Spofford's efforts to obtain a separate building is told in John Y. Cole, "A National Monument for a National Library: Ainsworth Rand Spofford and the New Library of Congress, 1871–1897," *Records of the Columbia Historical Society of Washington, D.C., 1971–1972* (Washington, D.C.: The Society, 1973), pp. 468–507.

6. Billings to Spofford, February 12, 1872, Library of Congress Archives, Library of Congress, Washington, D.C. Also see Dorothy M. Schullian and Frank B. Rogers, "The National Library of Medicine," *Library Quarterly* 28:1–17, 95–121 (Jan.–Apr. 1958).

7. See Foster E. Mohrhardt, "The Library of the United States Department of Agriculture," *Library Quarterly* 27:61–82 (Apr. 1957).

8. U.S. Congress, Joint Committee on the Library, *Condition of the Library of Congress*, 54th Cong., 2d sess., March 3, 1897, S. Rept. no. 1573. Dewey's testimony is on pp. 139–68, 172–79; Putnam's is on pp. 179–203; 216–28.

9. Ibid., pp. I–II. For a discussion of the hearings and the reorganization, see John Y. Cole, "LC and ALA, 1876–1901," *Library Journal* 98:2965–70 (Oct. 15, 1973).

10. See Richard R. Bowker, "The American National Library," *Library Journal* 21:356–57 (Aug. 1896); Edith E. Clarke, "A Congressional Library or a National Library?" ibid. 22:7–9 (Jan. 1897); and Cole, "LC and ALA," pp. 2969–70.

11. U.S. Library of Congress, *Annual Report of the Librarian of Congress for 1940* (Washington, D.C.: Govt. Print. Off., 1941), p. 24.

12. U.S. House of Representatives, 79th Cong., 2d sess., May 14, 1946, Rept. no. 2040, p. 6.

13. Marlene Morrisey, "Historical Development and Organization of the Federal Library Committee," *Drexel Library Quarterly* 6:215 (July–Oct. 1970).

14. U.S. Library of Congress, *Annual Report of the Librarian of Congress for 1962* (Washington, D.C.: Govt. Print. Off., 1963), p. 95. Also see "The Library of Congress as the National Library: Potentialities for Service," *Libraries at Large*, ed. by Douglas M. Knight and E. Shepley Nourse (New York: Bowker, 1969), pp. 435–65.

15. U.S. National Commission on Libraries and Information Science, *Toward a National Program for Library and Information Services: Goals for Action* (Washington, D.C.: Govt. Print. Off., 1975), pp. 66–70.

16. This statement was made by William Stewart Wallace, librarian of the University of Toronto. See Canadian Library Association, *Proceedings of the Organizational Conference at Hamilton, Ontario, June 14–16, 1946* (Ottawa, 1946), p. 21.

17. Todd to Sir John A. MacDonald, November 8, 1882, MacDonald Papers, Public Archives of Canada, Ottawa. Quoted in F. Dolores Donnelly, *The National Library of Canada: A Historical Analysis of the Forces Which Contributed to Its Establishment and to the Identification of Its Roles and Responsibilities* (Ottawa: Canadian Library Assn., 1973), p. 20.

18. Canada, House of Commons, *Debates*, April 16, 1883, pp. 630–31.

19. See note no. 17. I am indebted to Donnelly for her analysis, which provided useful background information for the portion of this paper dealing with the National Library of Canada. Another interesting account is William Kaye Lamb's "Canada, National Library," *Encyclopedia of Library and Information Science* 4:165–69 (New York: Dekker, 1970).

20. Lawrence J. Burpee, "Canada's National Library," *Library Journal* 37:23 (Mar. 1912).

21. Lawrence J. Burpee, "A Plea for a Canadian National Library," *Library Journal* 59:499–502. This article is reprinted from *University Magazine* (Montreal) 10:152–63 (Feb. 1911).

22. Quoted in Donnelly, p. 56.

23. Ibid., pp. 72–74.

24. Canada, Statutes of Canada, *An Act Respecting the Establishment of a National Library*, I Elizabeth II, 1952, chap. 31.

25. Erik J. Spicer, "Canada, Library of Parliament, Ottawa," *Encyclopedia of Library and Information Science* 4:157–65.

26. See discussion in Donnelly, pp. 185–87, 211–13.

27. Canada, Statutes of Canada, *An Act Respecting the National Library*, 17–18 Elizabeth II, 1969, chap. 47. For a full discussion of the 1969 act and its importance for the future of the National Library of Canada see Guy Sylvestre, "The Developing National Library Network of Canada," *Library Resources and Technical Services* 16:48–60 (Winter 1972).

28. Luther H. Evans, *The National Library in the Life of the Nation*, an address delivered before the Organizational Conference of the Canadian Library Association, Hamilton, Ontario, June 15, 1946, (Washington, D.C.: 1946), pp. 1–2.

29. Verner W. Clapp, *The National Library*, an address delivered at the 8th Conference of the Canadian Library Association, Ottawa, August 27, 1953 (Ottawa: Canadian Library Assn., 1953), p. 10.

14
The Principal Library Associations

PETER CONMY
Oakland Public Library, California
and
CAROLINE M. COUGHLIN
Simmons College

The purpose of this article is to reflect upon the implications of past activities of various library associations in order to be prepared to explore issues which will confront library associations in the next hundred years. We must assume that to some degree problems repeat themselves, if we believe that a study of history has value. With this perspective the history of library associations becomes a ripe and reasonable subject for a systematic analysis in a simplified framework.

Although some recognition of the specifics of the historical development of various library associations will be a part of this essay, full documentation of the past one hundred years of association growth is not the authors' aim. Nor is this article a compendium of information concerning the current organizational arrangements of various library associations.

Certainly patterns recur in the development of the major library associations. The question is, Can we describe them in a way which permits us to learn enough for the future from the examples of the past? Jerome Davis's work on social movements will serve as a framework for this discussion of library associations.[1]

> Every social movement tends to traverse a cycle of change. First of all, there arises a tangible need, and some individual or group begins to voice this need more or less publicly. Second, propaganda and agitation result. Third, there follows a growing

consciousness of this need in a small or large group. Fourth, they organize. Fifth, concerted action and strong leadership develop and new converts are won. Sixth, if the movement is successful it becomes institutionalized—becomes the pattern of the majority and group control sets in. Any one who does not conform to the new pattern code is disciplined. Seventh, eventually bureacracy, inflexibility, and reaction become dominant. When this occurs some one usually feels a new need and either the institution changes to meet that need or in time it is superseded.[2]

It must be noted that other scholars in the field of social movements, such as Cantril, Rush, or Denisoff would view Davis's approach as historical, rather than psychological or sociological. They would not necessarily agree with his definition of a social movement, that is, the "reaction on the part of individuals and groups to unsatisfactory conditions in their social life. The movement develops in an effort to bring about harmony."[3] Although there are valid arguments for not viewing fully developed, stable, status quo-oriented associations as the equivalent of social movements, it is also valid to consider the origins and developments of associations within the framework of a historical, social movement focus. It is the thesis of this paper that the individuals and groups involved in the development of library associations viewed their actions as movements for the social good of all citizens including themselves. The unsatisfactory conditions in their social life were the absence of library service for all the people and the low esteem society held for librarians acting as instruments of social development, if not social change.

Like any complex subject, categories can overlap, types can appear similar, and solutions for one aspect of a situation may also apply to another. Social movements theory is not the only way of viewing library associations. It is necessary to supplement this type of theory with organization theory, to give one outstanding example. This paper expands in one direction with no prejudice against other approaches or future integrated approaches. What follows is a brief, descriptive categorization of Davis's cycle, as modified and applied to library associations, a conceptualization of the types of library associations to which Davis's theory can be applied, and a discussion of specific examples of the phases in the life of library associations. This modification collapses Davis's first 4 cycles into phase 1 and his fifth cycle into phase 2. The sixth Davis cycle is expanded into phases 3 and 4. His seventh cycle is this study's phase 5.

Like most educational and social efforts in society, library associations were begun by dedicated volunteers who wished to spread the word about libraries, to make them available to the less fortunate, and, in some cases, to learn the skills necessary for running one. In 1853 a conference of librarians was held in New York. It was the first of its kind and closed with a resolution to seek a permanent, professional organization. A committee of five was to be appointed to draw up a constitution and arrange for a second conference to be held in Washington, D.C.[4] Nothing came of this action for a number of reasons, one of which was the chaos which beset the country in the years preceding, during, and after the Civil War. The next move toward the establishment of an association came twenty-three years later. Initiated by Melvil Dewey and supported by a committee of twenty-four, the call for the 1876 conference attracted 103 delegates. The call to meet combines practicality with an understated but obvious example of what Jerome Davis would identify as the missionary stage.

> The undersigned, connected with library interest of this country believing that efficiency and economy in library work would be promoted by a conference of librarians, which should afford opportunity for mutual consultation and practical cooperation, issue this preliminary call, inviting librarians and all interested in library and bibliographical work, to meet at Philadelphia, on the 15th of August next, or otherwise as may be found more generally acceptable.[5]

This missionary stage is preliminary to an association's development. The length of this stage is not fixed. It depends upon the zeal of the workers and the impact of their message upon the audience. The preliminary missionary period is followed by stage one, in which there is concern for initial stability of the movement. Typical stage one activities, according to Davis, center on the development of bylaws and membership drives. The founders needed to expand their membership. Not all of the 103 delegates present at the 1876 Conference signed up to be members of the new American Library Association. According to Holley, 41 had done so by the end of the year. By 1877 the membership was 110, and a year later had reached 197. Although the association was immediately recognized as representative of the profession and soon influenced librarianship materially, membership increased slowly. At the opening of the new century, twenty-four years later, it was only 874.

Once the tasks of stage one are accomplished, stage two of association life may begin. Evangelical messages and organizing tactics are now supplemented by demonstration projects designed both to involve the membership and achieve greater visibility.

The third stage of association life occurs when a decision is made to go beyond exhortations or demonstrations to assure the future viability of the chosen activity. Regulatory processes are incorporated into the mission of the organization, and attempts are made to stabilize and evaluate efforts in order to produce a consistent product that meets a recognized need.

Finally, the fourth phase begins when those people involved in the development of the association, either the original missionaries or their converts, become concerned about their own welfare. They recognize that their job satisfaction is a necessary part of the work of creating a stable, effective organization capable of producing a product or service over the long run.

Of course all four levels operate to advance the needs or purpose of the association, and there may be more than one purpose. The American Library Association is a classic example of a multipurpose, educational association. It recently reaffirmed it after much debate, when the membership accepted the Activities Committee on New Directions for ALA (ACONDA) statement that the purpose of the association was to promote libraries and librarianship.[6]

A final phase must also be acknowledged. The seventh Davis cycle asserts that eventually bureaucracy, inflexibility, and reaction become dominant in social movements. Since this study's phase 5 is the Davis parallel, questions must be raised about the dangers library associations face. Is stagnation normal and/or necessary?

Examples of each level in library association life over the past one hundred years are numerous. The following section will expand upon the stages described by presenting a description of four possible models for the organization of associations. Although the strategies may differ, each experienced the above stages of growth.

UMBRELLA MODEL

In the initial stage of organizing, an association, in order to regularize its drive for the betterment of the profession, can and has utilized different strategies. ALA, the first library association, chose an umbrella approach, opening its membership rolls to anyone interested in the development of librarianship in its broadest sense. On the final day of the 1876 Conference the following resolution was adopted:

> For the purpose of promoting the library interests of the country, and of increasing reciprocity of intelligence and good will among librarians and all interested in library economy and bibliographical studies the undersigned form themselves into a body to be known as "The American Library Association."[7]

After the initial national membership drive, attempts were made to attract members by developing separate state and/or regional associations. These attempts were tangential to the main drive for ALA membership, but were perceived as having a positive impact on ALA.

The great American library leaders in the last decade of the nineteenth century believed strongly that a state professional organization should receive and disseminate information from ALA to local librarians on the one hand, and promote better public support for libraries on the other. When the American Library Association met in 1890 at a White Mountains resort, concern was expressed over the absence of professional organizations on the state level. During 1889–90 Frederick Morgan Crunden, librarian of the St. Louis Public Library, had served as ALA president, and he strongly urged the organizing of a library association in each state.[8] ALA enthusiastically endorsed his sentiments and the appeal was carried on by his successor in office, Melvil Dewey.[9] In back of the sentiment for state library associations was the new awareness that many librarians were unable to travel around the country to attend the conferences and meetings of ALA and its committees. It was realized, also, that throughout the United States, there were many differences, geographical, political, economic, and social.[10] This was especially true in the South, which, as late as 1890, was suffering the economic exhaustion resulting from the Civil War. Education associations also provided a model as they were organized on both the state and local level; public librarianship at this period was closely allied with the public schools. In fact in several cases the librarian's home was the "librarians' section" within state educational associations; in some states this section became the nucleus for a state library association.

In response to the American Library Association's advocacy of the formation of state library associations, eighteen states and the District of Columbia formed associations during the decade 1890–99. The states were California, Colorado, Connecticut, Georgia, Illinois, Indiana, Iowa, Maine, Massachusetts, Michigan, Minnesota, Nebraska, New Hampshire, New Jersey, New York, Ohio, Vermont, and Wisconsin.[11] Between 1900 and 1909 associations were formed in fourteen more states, eight of which were in the South, namely, Alabama, 1904; Florida, 1901; Kentucky, 1907; Mississippi, 1909; North Carolina, 1904; Oklahoma, 1907; Tennessee, 1902; and Virginia, 1905. The librarians of Louisiana formed their association in 1910 followed by Arkansas in 1911, Texas in 1912, West Virginia in 1914, and South Carolina in 1915. In 1920 librarians in Alabama, Florida, Georgia, Kentucky, Mississippi, North Carolina, South Carolina, Tennessee, and Virginia formed the Southeastern Library Association on the theory that as a regional unit their combined efforts would win greater support and advancement for librarianship. Two years later Arkansas and Texas joined with the professionals of several other states to form the Southwestern Library Association.

Progress has been made since ALA first sent out the call for state library associations. Associations have been established in every state, the District of Columbia, Puerto Rico, the Virgin Islands, and Guam.

The following summarizes the growth of state associations in the last nine decades.

Decades	Number Formed
1890–99	19
1900–9	15
1910–19	8
1920–29	4
1930–39	1
1940–49	2
1950–59	0
1960–69	3
1970–	1

Most of the state library associations were formed between 1890 and 1909, during ALA's first stage of association development. The distinct roles played by men and women librarians during this formative period have been explored recently by Garrison, Corwin, and Wells. Their historical research provides additional insights into the various strategies which may be deployed by leading members during the organizational stage of association life.[12]

Another strategy to attract members in this umbrella-type organization was to promote divisions within the association along the lines of type of library and type of activity. In 1889 the Association of College and Research Libraries became the first type of library division; it was followed in 1890 by the American Library Trustee Association, a type-of-activity division.[13]

Both of these strategies to attract members have continued to the present. The particulars of the life of the separate interest groups and the state associations are often involved, and each example could be viewed in the framework of Davis's social movement theory.

The third major strategy to attract members selected by the new national organization was to publish materials about librarianship and the activities of librarians. This was a means of achieving cohesiveness among a scattered membership and a method of education. Thus in this first period, professional publishing began with the appearance in 1886 of the official *Bulletin*, now known as *American Libraries*. In 1905 the *Booklist*, an important aid in book selection, was inaugurated on a monthly basis. In Corrine Gilb's study, *Hidden Hierarchies: The Professionals and the Government*, the influence of a publishing program is recognized.

> Through their magazines and journals, scientific and technical conferences and meetings, continuing education programs and the informal social interchange at association meetings, the collective "mind" of the profession is molded, skills and techniques are developed and transmitted, the limits of the intellectual scope of the profession's knowledge are established, and the avenues in which knowledge might advance are marked out.[14]

National, international, and local associations such as the Library Association of the United Kingdom followed the ALA example of an umbrella organization.

SPECIALIST MODEL

All of the options offered by ALA were not sufficient to meet the needs of medical librarians. In 1892, 65 librarians of medical institutions formed the Medical Library Association, an organization which now numbers over 2,500 members. As early as 1902 the Medical Library Association published the *Bulletin of the Medical Library Association*. In addition this association has developed standards for medical library service, provides in-service training to its members, and offers certification to those who meet the standards.

In 1909 another group of special librarians broke away from ALA to form the Special Libraries Association. The Medical Library Association offered enough examples of success to indicate that other organizational arrangements were viable. It can be argued that the special library proponents had the benefits of studying the broad geographical and subject approach while they were members of ALA. Thus, their design was meant to overcome difficulties they had experienced in communicating with each other while part of the ALA model. Consequently, the founders carefully provided for local chapters and particular rather than general subject divisions.

Other subject associations, such as the American Society for Information Science and the Theatre Library and Music Library associations, pattern themselves on the specialist model begun by the Medical Library Association.

FEDERATION MODEL

A third organizational option developed much later. The Canadian Library Association was founded in 1946 and based its membership on the provincial associations. Thus it formed a federation which provided librarians with an affiliation with the national group, but maintained the subject interest areas on the local level. A recent report from the executive director underscores the role of the provincial associations as interactive components forming the body of CLA.

> As anticipated in the Association's new structure, the participation of provincial library association representatives, at the executive level in our Council deliberations, has made it easier for matters of provincial concern to gain the support of other provinces and to receive national attention. The effectiveness and speed with which action has been taken in the area of library service to the handicapped is exemplary. The response of the National Library of Canada to this particular concern has been well noted and is much appreciated.

On the other hand provincial participation has also made it easier to communicate national needs or concerns to other parts of the country. The readiness of the Ontario, Manitoba, and Saskatchewan Library Associations in agreeing to fund and carry out several of the small data opinion collection projects recommended in the Status of Women's report is illustrative. The offer of the Manitoba Library Association to assist in the local arrangements for the annual conference in Winnepeg and to provide office space for the Local Arrangements Committee Chairperson, is another example of provincial participation.[15]

This federation model of organization was a natural consequence of the history of Canada. When the American Library Association was formed in 1876 during the United States's centennial year, the Dominion of Canada was only nine years old. Although theoretically it is possible for nationwide organizations to exist without the presence of a strong national government, it is unlikely because there seems to be a correlation of inspiration between a national association and a national government.

There were some early attempts to form a national association in Canada. In 1900 there was an attempt in Ontario, but it resulted in the formation of the Ontario Library Association instead.[16] Parallel developments occurred in the other provinces. It was not until 1940 when Margaret Gill, president of the Library Association of Ottawa, sounded a call for a national association that the response was favorable and the time was ripe.[17] In June 1946 the Canadian Library Association was organized. Thus, the missionary stage of development in Canada had a longer duration.

The International Federation of Library Associations has some parallels with the Canadian Library Association experience.

CALIFORNIA SPLIT MODEL

Although it is really too early to judge, a fourth organizational model seems to be emerging in the structure of the reorganized California Library Association. The distinction of this model is the separation of the educational concerns of the members from their professional concerns. The ambiguity and overlap implicit in this division is indicative of the difficulties facing this new hybrid. At present two organizations, one centering on librarians' professional concerns and one dealing with the problems of libraries, coexist within the parent association.

SELECTIONS FROM THE PAST

The history of library associations offers examples of each stage or phase of the social movement pattern. Five phases will be discussed. Although the examples chosen may not be the most significant occur-

268 / Environment

rences faced by the associations, they reveal patterns that offer insights for today's participants in multipurpose library associations.

Phase 1

Phase 1 corresponds to the early four cycles in Jerome Davis's theory of social movement: a "tangible need" arises; propaganda and agitation result; there is a growing consciousness of this need on the part of a small or large group; and they organize.[18]

ALA actions during phase 1 range from the preliminary 1853 conference to the establishment of a paid, executive secretariat in 1909.[19] The missionary fervor permeating the organization during this period is indicated by one of the first association-related statements on record. "We meet," said Charles C. Jewitt, in his address as president of the 1853 convention, "to provide for the diffusion of a knowledge of good books, and for enlarging the means of public access to them. Our wishes are for the public, not for ourselves."[20] In this case the need was to explain libraries to the public and librarianship to the untrained people employed in libraries.

The organizational birth pangs of SLA and its structural imitators, as well as other national and international associations, are similar with one important exception. Each of these groups had an existing model, ALA, to react to and to modify in order to better meet their own needs.

It should be stressed that multipurpose institutions such as ALA have a high birth rate of separate interest groups within the accommodating family circle. This is a result of the essentially open-ended umbrella associations. In the more restricted subject organizations, although some accommodation to new interests occurs (as in the development of the aerospace divisions of SLA), the tendency is to form a new and distinct subject organization, for example, the American Documentation Institute, now the American Society for Information Science.

Phase 2

Phase 2 in the development of an association is marked by actions designed to demonstrate the worth of an idea and the capability of an association to help bring the idea to fruition. For ALA, phase 2 was marked by an illustrious program. It coordinated World War I library work, and by the end of the war the committee responsible could claim credit for developing the largest library system ever operated.[21]

In 1920 Carl Milam, fresh from his work with the ALA-sponsored war library program, accepted the position of executive secretary of ALA. He remained with the association for twenty-eight years and must be considered its prime mover during the development of phase 2 and 3 activities. His influence was so great that one is tempted to dwell solely on his activities.[22] However, tantalizing examples of his influence during each phase must suffice. When he left ALA in 1948, a special series of programs was presented at the 1948 Annual Conference. Ralph Munn in honoring Milam the administrator mentioned that it was no accident that the most active boards during the past twenty-eight years of Milam's service were the ones Milam himself had an interest in—library extension, adult education, education for librarianship, and international relations.[23]

Munn's analysis is confirmed by Milam's own accounting of the significant developments achieved by ALA during the latter's term as executive secretary. Milam's list begins with the phrase "expansion of activities" and includes other informal references to major programs of the association such as "beginnings of an international organization, two million in endowment from the Carnegie Corporation, beginnings of state and national plans, increased relations with the national government, completion of a national plan, and new headquarters."[24]

Detailed records of official committee or board activity trace the history of these major programs over a period of years. For example, the World War I library program was the model for ALA's Enlarged Program, an unsuccessful domestic version. Although the Enlarged Program was not developed in toto, segments of it did succeed. One facet of the Enlarged Program can be seen in the work of the Library Extension Board, begun in 1925. Its aim was to provide library service to the unserved; although the board cannot claim direct credit for each result, the percentage of Americans not receiving library service dropped from 40 to 8 percent by Milam's retirement in 1948.[25] The tasks of the Library Extension Board were primarily phase 2 demonstration activities. However, the Board itself provided its members with the supplemental bonus of tangible involvement (concerted action) with the association; committee members were more than anonymous faces in a growing crowd.

Eventually the work of the Library Extension Board was diverted into a variety of division channels. However, the search for foundation monies to support demonstration activities and the desire of membership to be involved in such activities has continued for the past fifty years. Milam acknowledges as one of his achievements the endowment received from the Carnegie Corporation for demonstration projects.[26] This was not the only money received from the Carnegie Corporation,[27] nor was the Carnegie Corporation the only source of foundation support for phase 2-type demonstration projects.

The Adult Education Board was helped by the millions of dollars in grants made available from the Carnegie Corporation during the period 1924 to 1941 and from the Fund for Adult Education between 1951 and 1961. According to Monroe, "the grants drew attention to the field, irrespective of the merits of the program itself, and created an important emphasis in the ALA program. ALA's role in stimulating public libraries to carry out the adult education services conceived and developed at national headquarters was both eagerly abetted as leadership and strenuously resisted as pressure."[28] Monroe chronicles the activities of the Adult Education Board during the 1920s and 1930s as well as the arguments of prominent librarians skeptical of both the adult education movement philosophy and the ability of the Carnegie Corporation to dictate its terms.[29]

In the 1950s when the adult education idea resurfaced as the American Heritage Project, it was an attempt to combat the McCarthyism of the time. Funded by a Ford Foundation offshoot, the Fund for Adult Education, the project had two stated objectives: It "not only makes a contribution to a better understanding of our American Heritage; it also provides libraries with an unusual opportunity to demonstrate the effectiveness of the public library as an essential community agency."[30] When the book discussion project was completed, the subsequent projects from this fund were focused on the single goal of promoting adult education as a service for public libraries to consider.[31]

The history of international activities generated by ALA is both illustrious and sporadic. From the time of Milam to the present day, the primary policy appears to be a phase 2 one of reliance on foundation support for the completion of library demonstration projects desired by various internationally minded groups. Another type of international activity in which ALA has played a continuing and decisive role is in the development of other library associations. During Milam's tenure the International Federation of Library Associations was founded;[32] the Canadian Library Association was influenced by David Clift's advice.[33]

To date many of the parts of ALA such as divisions or offices are involved in library demonstration activities. The purpose of the recent J. Morris Jones Goals Award to the Intellectual Freedom Committee was to develop a leadership workshop model to demonstrate how state associations could mount continuing education efforts in the area of intellectual freedom. The SRRT Task Force on Ethnic Materials likewise makes the point with the publishing of *Alternatives in Print*; and Reference and Subscriptions Books Committee, when they publish reviews in *Booklist*. The list could continue indefinitely. One recent activity, the production of booklists for mass distribution during the U.S. Bicentennial, indicates that the second stage of development is still occurring in ALA.

Other associations, particularly subject-oriented associations, have a different orientation in their demonstration stage. Their audience is not the general public but the specific groups who need distinctive library services, such as business people, executives, doctors, or museum personnel.

Phase 3

Phase 3 in the life of an association is marked by the development of regulatory processes (standards) to stablize the demonstrations and to guide others to similar successes. "Perhaps the greatest spur to the improvement of library service was the passage of the Library Services

Act in 1956. . . . ALA had opened its National Relations Office in Washington in 1946 so that ten years of planning and acquiring legislative know-how had preceded this success. . . . It is hardly coincidental that standards for services for all types of libraries were formulated and approved during the period."[34]

Some ALA members had favored federal aid to libraries as early as 1919.[35] In the 1930s philosophical differences concerning its desirability accounted for the tabling of a plan by Carleton Joeckel for federal library legislation.[36] It was then necessary for the proponents of federal legislation to use another strategy to establish the concept of federal responsibility for libraries. The tactic chosen was to accept a slot within the education hierarchy of the executive branch of the New Deal government in order to achieve some visibility for libraries and to wait for a more favorable mood of the membership. World War II intervened, and it was not until 1944 that ALA was able to raise funds to support a separate Washington office. When the office was established, and later, when library legislation was passed and funded, the outlines of the original ideas proposed by Joeckel were still visible.[37]

"The importance of *Public Library Service: A Guide to Evaluation with Minimum Standards* appearing as it did at the same time as passage of the Library Services Act can hardly be overestimated. Its recommendations formed the basis for nearly all the state plans required by the Act, and they in turn served as a means of testing the validity of the Standards."[38] These standards were the work of an ALA committee, assisted by twenty-eight professional committees within and outside ALA and the model of the standards developed earlier by the California Library Association.[39] Thus phase 2 activities (concerted action, strong leadership, demonstration projects) emerged naturally into phase 3 activities and a cycle of activity which stressed planning, funding, guidelines, demonstrations, and evaluation captured many diverse elements of ALA.

Ambivalent attitudes are frequently expressed in establishing measures to evaluate services. Some wish to regulate with no accurate base to build from, others wish to build the base first. Sections, divisions, and individuals within ALA have repeatedly grappled with the issue of regularization. In some cases, particularly in the subject-oriented associations, a degree of firmness has been achieved. The Medical Library Association certifies librarians on three levels and is now considering a continuing education component as an addition to their certification system. The major attitude in this stage is to promote the values of order, stability, and a measured growth in the drive towards excellence. The major technique used is the carrot approach, or the stimulation of acceptance through special funding provisions.

Librarians with iconoclastic or isolationist attitudes or higher standards than the norm often focus on stage 3 activities in their attempts to prevent any development of controls or domination by others.

Phases 2 and 3 frequently overlap. The overlapping aspects become clear when the combined demonstration/regulatory activities of associations are examined. After the ALA membership rebuffed Milam's attempt to develop an Enlarged Program, ALA turned its attention to recruitment, certification, a headquarters employment bureau, and development of county libraries.[40] Both the certification program and the development of public libraries exemplify combined demonstration/regulatory activities.

Certification (regulatory) implies the development of an educational program (demonstration). Similarly, the development of county libraries (demonstration), assuming an existent tax base and legal structure to support the new institutions, implies a concept of what functions they should perform (regulatory). The development of both certification and county libraries depended upon the original ideas, money to fund demonstration projects to explicate the ideas, and standards by which to judge the quality of the endeavor.

Certification and county library development were a strong part of ALA's life in the 1930s and 1940s; in fact the growth pattern of these phase 2- and 3-type activities demonstrate a strong link between the administration of Carl Milam, which began in 1920 and ended in 1948, and the almost as lengthy span of David Clift's term as executive director, which began in 1952 and ended in 1971. (During the interim period John Mackenzie Cory was the executive secretary.)

Three other outstanding examples of the overlap between phase 2 and phase 3 activities are the history of library education in the twentieth century, the growth of standards for all types of libraries, and the drive for federal legislation for libraries.

Although Munthe believed Louis Round Wilson's essay on the history of library education was biased toward the Chicago wonders of that day, it provides a succinct overview and analysis of the early developments. Wilson cites five major steps in the development of library education; at each step the impact of ALA was felt. The first step was to select a school model rather than an apprenticeship to educate librarians. Dewey's efforts to establish the School of Library Economy with the approval of ALA signals the start of the drive for the creation of library schools.[42]

The second step listed by Wilson is the establishment of the Association of American Library Schools (AALS) in 1915. Wilson and other scholars, notably Donald Davis, Jr., in his dissertation, have judged the impact of this association as negligible. Their criticisms center around the inability of the association to control its own membership or its destiny. To be specific, the power to accredit schools belonged to ALA, the practitioner group, as exercised through the Board of Education for Librarianship and its successor, the Committee on Accreditation, not with the educator group, AALS. The growth of this accrediting power was an outcome of an embryonic version of the 1923 Williamson report, a paper read by Williamson at the 1919 ALA Conference, entitled, "Some Present Day Aspects of Library Training."[43] In 1920 ALA appointed a National Board of Certification for Librarians to adopt standards. These next steps were not as faltering as they might have been if taken unassisted. The financial and intellectual resources of the Carnegie Corporation were behind both, and their Ten Year Plan of Library Service provided the funds and impetus for accomplishments ranging from the preparation of minimum standards for different types of schools to the publication of textbooks, the provision of fellowships, and, in 1933, the development of qualitative rather than quantitative standards.[44]

Although ALA has continued its accrediting activities to this day, revising the Standards for Accreditation in 1951 and again in 1972, it has not allocated funds nor recommended the establishment or the endowment for schools as the earlier board did when it provided for the establishment of a library school for Negroes at Hampton Institute and a million dollar endowment for the Graduate Library School at Chicago.[45] That funding power has been dispersed and the power remaining within the association is that of quality control and the articulation of policy such as the recent Library Education and Manpower Statement, passed by Council in 1971.

The bold actions of the Board of Education for Librarianship in the 1920s were followed by the imaginative work of its creation, the Graduate Library School at Chicago in the 1930s. Their example of an interdisciplinary teaching and research faculty grew slowly, and it was not until the 1950s and 1960s that any appreciable number of schools followed their example with respect to post-master's degree students. Since then, the quantum jump in the number of researchers in the field seems to be attributable to the availability of federal fellowships in the early and middle sixties.[46] At this point it is again reasonable to assign some credit for the results to ALA, the association which has pushed for federal funds since the 1930s.

Examples of combined phase 2 and 3 activities from other associations include an occasional series in *Special Libraries*, the official journal of the Special Libraries Association. Articles under the following kind of heading, "This is an X Type Library," are written to achieve two purposes: to give a verbal demonstration of services to the vast potential audience of organizations in need of that kind of library (stage 2) and to indicate the minimum level of support necessary to maintain a library of x type (stage 3). Another example is the recent award citations of a new organization, Art Librarians Society of North America (ARLIS/NA). Publishers of quality art books are honored by ARLIS in order to demonstrate the fact that there is a group concerned about quality and to establish, through the award evaluation process, some guidelines or criteria for art book publishing. The Association of Research Libraries' (ARL) massive support for the Booz, Allen, and

Hamilton study of Columbia University is another illustration of stage 2 tactics in action.

Phase 4

In phase 4 association members are concerned with their own welfare in addition to the growth of service to clients. Membership interest in educational opportunities, salaries, benefits, and status are indicators of an association reaching this stage. There seems to be no library association (including library trade unions) which devotes all of its efforts to this stage of development. Rather, it appears that each association has a certain segment of membership concerned with these issues and active in promoting them, while a parallel group in an association focuses on phase 5 activity.

The struggle by black librarians to achieve equality with their white counterparts is illustrative of one kind of phase 4 activity. In order to present a compressed, but evolutionary account of the role of black librarians in the American Library Association, a series of incidents will be recounted.

In 1926 the Board of Education for Librarianship encouraged the founding of a library school for Negroes at Hampton Institute;[47] in 1940–41 it assisted in the development of Atlanta University's library school.[48] In both instances, the demonstrated need for a training school for southern Negroes resulted in interracial cooperative action, moral and financial encouragement, integration of planning meetings and conferences, and, finally, assumption of responsibility by the black community. Today, the greatest number of black librarians are graduates of Atlanta University, which is not to say that the overall number is either overwhelming or sufficient.[49]

In 1936 a letter describing conditions under which Negro librarians could attend meetings was sent out to over 200 Negro librarians. The author of the letter was Wallace Van Jackson, librarian of Virginia Union University, a local black college. To quote in part, "those meetings which are a part of breakfast, luncheons, or dinners are not open to Negroes . . . . Provisions will be made to seat Negroes in the front right hand section (at other meetings)."[50]

The letter was published in *Library Journal* before the annual meeting, and comments were invited. The majority of the letters printed voiced the opinion that ALA should not be meeting in a segregated city. Although the Conference did take place in Richmond, the report of the Conference includes the information that a committee of the Executive Board had been appointed to consider the matter of future conferences and places where they will be held. Council in December of 1936 accepted the report of the committee, including a "declaration of adherence to the principle of complete professional equality and the recommendation that, in order to secure this equality for all its members, the selection of all future meeting places be conditioned upon acceptance and enforcement of the following stipulations: that in all rooms and halls assigned to the Association for use in connection with its conferences, or otherwise under its control, all members shall be admitted upon terms of equality."[51] ALA did not meet in the South again for twenty years, after the Supreme Court ruling in the *Brown vs. Board of Education* case.

The next challenge faced by black librarians interested in full participation in ALA was the decision to remedy the "situation in the South with respect to chapter memberships."[52] In 1944 the North Carolina Negro Library Association was recognized as a legitimate chapter and its representative, Mollie Lee Huston, was seated in Council.[53] In 1948 Ralph Shaw, chairman of the Fourth Activities Committee, recommended a reorganization based on regionalism and offered the idea of special national membership for those southern black librarians unable to join their segregated state chapters.[54] By 1952 the procedural strategy of changing bylaws to restrict each state to one chapter, one which could only be recognized if it accepted all races as members, in accordance with section 3 of the constitution of ALA, was accomplished with very little fanfare reported in print.[55] The result was that certain southern state library associations, notably, Georgia, Mississippi, and Alabama, did not apply for chapter status under the new rules. Other southern library associations, Louisiana in particular,[56] waited until the 1962 policy, "Individuals, Membership, and Chapter Status," clearly pinpointed the actions by which a chapter could be judged as having denied membership rights to a minority group and then withdrew as a chapter.[57] Although the 1962 policy and procedures included the threat of Council censure to state associations found to be lying about their eligibility rules, action was never taken against any southern state which remained a chapter.

The passage of the Civil Rights Act in 1964 had a parallel in activities within ALA. Within a day or two of passage of the U.S. law, the Council of ALA passed a motion presented by E. J. Josey.[58] This motion, which barred ALA officers from attending library meetings in the states not able to meet chapter status served, with the Civil Rights Act, as a catalyst; by 1966 all of the southern states with library associations had regained their chapter status.[59] Black librarians living in the south were at last recognized as equal with respect to their rights as ALA members.

For many blacks, the question of success within the association remains. In E. J. Josey's book, *The Black Librarian in America*, two essays, by Robert Wedgeworth and A. P. Marshall, discuss the problems still to be faced in 1971.[60] Although by 1975 tangible power gains have been made by minorities seeking representation within the affairs of the association, more needs to be done by the association as a whole to ensure that the minority viewpoints truly influence policy and programs.

ALA was not the only association of interest to black librarians; however, it did serve as a professional home for these black librarians unable to participate in local associations. The Special Libraries Association seems to have experienced less difficulty in achieving an integrated status for its southern chapters.[61] Earlier the North Carolina Negro Library Association was founded in 1934, and in other southern states black librarians belonged to sections of state Negro educational associations.[62] In this chronicle of a search for professional equality it must be stressed that at no time did black librarians from the south refuse to be integrated; their meetings were always open to participation by other racial groups. It was the local white library associations which were separate and unequal.

In addition to actions taken to ensure the participation of blacks in the affairs of the American Library Association, there are various other types of activities which can be viewed as having phase 4 characteristics. Without going into precise details, it does appear that the record of ALA in the 1930s presents a pattern of strong interest in personnel matters which is quite similar to the interest manifested in this subject by ALA in the 1970s. Many of the programs developed by the Office for Library Personnel Resources have their antecedent or counterpart in the work of the Board for Personnel Administration in the 1930s. The earlier version of such activities as a placement service was cut in 1948 due to budgetary problems and a shortage of librarians to fill the requests for trained employees. The former threat is always with ALA, the latter seems to be the exact opposite of today's problem. For today, one must look further back at the employment picture of the early 1930s. At the height of the depression there were many more librarians than the nation could afford to employ, while the shortage in the late 1940s was a product of a boom economy. ALA actions with respect to the encouragement (1950s) or discouragement (1930s) of the establishment of library education programs can be seen to be as a necessary pattern of reaction to the larger economy of the nation rather than simply a matter of keeping its own treasury solvent.[63]

Phase 5

Phase 5 corresponds to Davis's final cycles of a social movement; if it "is successful it becomes institutionalized . . .; bureaucracy, inflexibility, and reaction . . . dominate."[64] Notwithstanding the work of various reform activities committees, most recently ACONDA and ANACONDA in ALA, it is reasonable to assume that some of the above elements have become part of an association reaching its one hundredth year of operation. However, it is also possible, and would make for an interesting discussion, that the continuing history of partial successes and the incorporation of new movements are the result of living in one or more stages at once. It may be that multistage living has at least prevented the development of a self-satisfied closed bureaucracy.

Other library associations show evidence of phase 5 activities. The Association of Research Libraries and Beta Phi Mu offer more possibilities for reaching phase 5, because their policy of selective memberships tends to breed institutionalization. SLA's rejection of a merger with ASIS can also be viewed as inflexibility, a phase 5 problem. The inability of the Medical Library Association and the newest division of ALA, Health and Rehabilitative Library Services Division, which includes hospital librarians, to work closely together is another example of phase 5 problems.

INTERNAL TENSIONS

In the shadow of this sketchy approach to an understanding of an associations behavior and history lurks the dilemma of the past one hundred years: the reappearance of familiar old problems at various stages of association development. Often these problems are not peculiar to any one age of association life but are indicative of the difficulties of multipurpose associations which are simultaneously experiencing life in five different ages. The popular book, *I'm OK, You're OK*, by Thomas Harris, discusses the alternating child, parent, and adult personalities in most of us and illustrates the erratic nature of behavior which results from the presence of all three roles in one person.[65] In a sense the first four phases of organization development parallel the child, parent, adult stages, and consequently the same type of confusion about choice of role behavior results. Knowledge about the problems in light of the peculiar organizational environment of associations may help us avoid phase 5 in the future. In the past we seem to have recognized the problem but have attempted solutions separate from or unconscious of the particular environment.

This is not meant as a censure of the past decades of work by librarians involved in strengthening their association. Instead it is a recognition that voluntary, educational associations and their cousins, professional associations, have a very short life in the history of organizations. The Catholic church, the military, and manufacturing enterprises are the more familiar models for organizational theorists. Consequently, the literature on organization effectiveness and efficiency has a cultural historical bias towards these more hierarchical and closed forms. While modern authors such as Etzioni may criticize modern organizations severely,[66] the criticism often evolves from the classic definition of an organization which in turn is based on the early models mentioned above.

An association is an organized form of activity; but it is not the exact equivalent of an organization, nor should it be judged as such. Different evaluative mechanisms are needed to judge the effectiveness and efficiency of voluntary membership or professional associations. We cannot measure ourselves against an outdated, inappropriate model. Thus the starting point for the next one hundred years is to recognize the difference and capitalize on the openness of voluntary membership organizations and the nonhierarchical strengths of professional associations in attempting to devise solutions which recognize the problems of our own models and permit the cycle of social movement to occur within the social order of librarianship and information science.

NOTES

1. M. E. Anders explores the development of public libraries in the Southeast, using Jerome Davis's work as a framework. See Mary Edna Anders, "The Development of Public Library Service in the Southeastern States, 1895–1950 (D.L.S. diss., Columbia Univ., 1958). Her articles on the history of the Southeastern Library Association are also appropriate. Mary Edna Anders, "The Southeastern Library Association, 1920–1950," *Southeastern Librarian* 6, no. 1:15–39 (Spring 1956), and ibid., no. 2:161–91 (Summer 1956).

2. Jerome Davis, *Contemporary Social Movements* (New York: Century, 1930), p. 8.

3. Ibid.

4. The first professional conference of librarians in the United States, or the world for that matter, took place in New York City, September 15–17, 1853. The leading authority on this subject, who also reproduced the minutes of the convention, is George B. Utley, *The Librarians Conference of 1853, a Chapter in American Library History* (Chicago: American Library Assn., 1951). A good article on this subject is Gardner M. Jones, "The Librarians' Conference of 1853," *Library Journal* 27:254–56 (1902).

5. This is reproduced in Edward G. Holley, *Raking the Historic Coals, the ALA Scrapbook of 1876* (Pittsburgh: Beta Phi Mu, 1967), p. 54. The last paragraph, which had to do with a possibility of visiting the Centennial Exposition in Philadelphia, has been omitted here. The document was signed by Justin Winsor (Boston Public Library), J. L. Whitney (Boston Public Library), Fred B. Perkins (Boston Public Library), C. A. Cutter (Boston Athenaeum), John Langlor Sibley (Harvard University Library), John Fiske (Harvard University Library), Ezra Abbot (Harvard University), S. F. Haven (American Antiquarium Society, Worcester), J. Carson Brevoort (Astor Library), F. Saunders (Astor Library), W. S. Butler (New York Society Library), W. T. Peoples (New York Mercantile Library), Jacob Schwartz (Apprentices' Library, New York), S. B. Noyes (Brooklyn Mercantile Library), H. A. Holmes (New York State Library), Lloyd P. Smith (Philadelphia Library Company), Reuben A. Guild (Brown University Library), J. D. Hedge (Providence Athenaeum), Addison Van Name (Yale College Library), Franklin B. Dexter (Yale College Library), A. S. Packard (Bowdoin College Library), Melvil Dewey (Amherst College Library), James G. Barnwell (Philadelphia Mercantile Library), John Eaton (Bureau of Education, Washington), William F. Poole (Chicago Public Library), Charles Evans (In-

dianapolis Public Library), Thomas Vicker (Cincinnati Public Library), and John N. Dyer (St. Louis Mercantile Library).

6. The issues are clearly stated, "ACONDA Revised Recommendations on Democratization and Reorganization," *American Libraries* 2, no. 1: 81–92 (Jan. 1971), and "Recommendations from ANACONDA," ibid., pp. 93–97. See *Constitution and By-Laws of American Library Association* as amended in Dallas, June 1971. The amended constitution was printed in *American Libraries* 2, no. 10: 1093–1102 (Nov. 1971).

7. The organic resolution is reproduced in George B. Utley, *Fifty Years of the American Library Association* (Chicago: American Library Assn., 1926), p. 12. The names of the 103 registrants may be found in *American Library Journal* 1, no. 1: 143–45 (Jan. 1907).

8. Frederick Morgan Crunden had a long experience both in education and librarianship. He had been a grammar school principal in St. Louis, 1869–72, and a professor in Washington University, 1872–76. In January 1877 he was appointed secretary and librarian of the Public School Library, which he converted into the St. Louis Public Library, serving as its librarian until 1900.

9. Dewey while at Columbia University had been active in forming the New York Library Club, a professional group from in and around New York. He had been active also in forming the Association of State Librarians in 1890.

10. The effect of the frontier on civilization and the reactions of the pioneers to it are discussed both philosophically and factually in Ray Allen Billington, *The Frontier and American Culture* (Sacramento: California Library Assn., 1965).

11. The New Hampshire Library Association was formed August 21, 1889.

12. Three articles which reflect this viewpoint are Dee Garrison, "The Tender Technicians," *Journal of Social History* 6:131–59 (Winter 1972–73); Margaret Ann Corwin, "An Investigation of Female Leadership in Regional, State, and Local Library Associations, 1876–1923," *Library Quarterly* 44, no. 2:133–44 (Apr. 1974); and Sharon B. Wells, "The Feminization of the American Library Profession, 1876–1923" (A.M. thesis, Univ. of Chicago, 1967).

13. Utley, *Fifty Years*, passim.

14. Corrine Gilb, *Hidden Hierarchies: The Professions and the Government* (New York: Harper, 1966), p. 79.

15. Canadian Library Association, *Annual Reports* 1973–74, pp. 5–6.

16. The minutes of this historic meeting may be found in Ontario Library Association, *The Ontario Library Association: An Historical Sketch, 1900–1925* (Toronto: Univ. of Toronto Pr., 1926), p. 117.

17. Margaret Gill, "CLC to CLA," in Bruce Peel, ed., *Librarianship in Canada 1946 to 1967* (Victoria, British Columbia: Canadian Library Assn., 1968), pp. 11–12.

18. Davis, p. 8.

19. Utley, *Fifty Years*, p. 15.

20. Ibid., p. 9.

21. Ibid., p. 18.

22. Peggy Sullivan, "Carl H. Milam and the American Library Association" (Ph.D. Dissertation, Univ. of Chicago, 1972).

23. Ralph Munn, "Carl Milam: The Administrator," *ALA Bulletin* 42:3–6 (Sept. 15, 1948).

24. "From Corner Office," *ALA Bulletin* 42:203 (May 1948).

25. Munn, p. 3.

26. "From Corner Office," p. 203.

27. Louis Round Wilson, "Historical Developments of Education for Librarianship in the United States," R. B. Berelson, ed., *Education for Librarianship* (Chicago: American Library Assn., 1949), pp. 44–59.

28. Margaret E. Monroe, *Library Adult Education, The Biography of an Idea* (New York: Scarecrow, 1963), p. 4.

29. "In 1920 the Enlarged Program became a center of a whirlwind that threatened for a year to tear the American Library Association apart." Monroe, pp. 26 and 71–72.
30. Eleanor Ferguson, "Inevitable Change for Public Libraries," *American Libraries* 3:747 (July–Aug. 1972).
31. Ibid.
32. H. M. Lydenberg, "Carl Milam—The Internationalist," *ALA Bulletin* 42:7 (Sept. 15, 1948).
33. Elizabeth Morton, "American Conferences: CLA and ALA," *American Libraries* 3:815–24 (July–Aug. 1972).
34. Grace Stevenson, "ALA: The Fight for Library Service," *American Libraries* 3:711–16 (July–Aug. 1972).
35. Carleton B. Joeckel, "Report of the American Library Association Committee on Federal Relations," *ALA Bulletin* 30:470 (May 1936), as reported in James Stewart Healey, *John E. Fogarty: Political Leadership for Library Development* (Metuchen, N.J.: Scarecrow, 1974), p. 9.
36. Healey, p. 11.
37. Ibid., p. 13.
38. Ferguson, p. 747.
39. Ibid.
40. *ALA Bulletin* 15:18 (Jan. 1921) as cited in Monroe, p. 72.
41. W. Munthe, *American Librarianship from a European Angle* (Chicago: American Library Assn., 1939).
42. Wilson, p. 44.
43. Ibid., p. 45.
44. Ibid., p. 46.
45. Ibid.
46. William Summers, "The Emergence of Library Education," *American Libraries* 3:791–94 (July–Aug. 1972).
47. Wilson, p. 47.
48. Atlanta University, *Library Conference* (Atlanta: Atlanta Univ. Pr., 1941).
49. V. L. Jones, "A Dean's Career," in E. J. Josey, *The Black Librarian in America* (Metuchen, N.J.: Scarecrow, 1970), p. 40.
50. Wallace Van Jackson, Letter, *Library Journal* 61:387 (May 15, 1936).
51. *ALA Bulletin* 31:37 (Jan. 1937).
52. Ralph Shaw, "Fourth Activities Committee Report," *ALA Bulletin* 42:123–28 (Mar. 1948).
53. "ALA Handbook," in *ALA Bulletin* 38:H–77 (Dec. 15, 1944).
54. Shaw, pp. 123–28.
55. "Conference Report," *Library Journal* 79:1345 (Aug. 1954).
56. "Midwinter Report," *ALA Bulletin* 57:232–33 (Mar. 1963).
57. "Statement on Individual Membership, Charter Status, and Institutional Membership," *ALA Bulletin* 56:637 (July–Aug. 1962).
58. "Conference Report," *Library Journal* 89:2921 (Aug. 1964).
59. "ALA Organization and Information, 1966–67," in *ALA Bulletin* 60:1003–4 (Nov. 1966).
60. Robert Wedgeworth, "ALA and the Black Librarian," in Josey, pp. 69–76; A. P. Marshall, "Search for Identity," in ibid., pp. 173–83.
61. Jones, p. 39.
62. Ibid.
63. Theodore Guyton, *Unionization and Libraries* (Chicago: American Library Assn., 1974), chap. 3.
64. Davis, p. 8.
65. Thomas Harris, *I'm OK, You're OK* (New York: Harper, 1969).
66. Amatil Etzioni, *Modern Organizations* (New York: Prentice-Hall, 1964).

15

The Library World and the Book Trade

GRANT T. SKELLEY
University of Washington

In 1876 U.S. and Canadian librarians and members of the book trade, two groups of strongly motivated, hard-working people, began to formalize a relationship that has ever since been expressed in sweet and sour ways. At times rich in language and rhetoric, manifesting both cooperativeness and antagonism, the record consistently reveals a fundamental ambivalence that neither group has entirely resolved.[1]

It is the purpose of this essay to describe how librarians, publishers, and booksellers have interacted during the period between the founding of the American Library Association and the centennial of that event. The range of interaction has been so broad and varied that a brief essay can attempt only to survey some of the more prominent areas in which that interaction has taken place. Thus, no effort has been made to show systematically the involvement and influence of either ALA or any other library organization, or of the book trade organizations. (A full history of library/book-trade relations in North America needs to be written. When it is, it will have to be based extensively upon the activities of all such groups.)

The focus here will be on (1) general relationships (including the promotion of books and reading, and the library market), (2) discounts, (3) copyright, (4) library acquisition methods, and (5) the influence of librarians on publishing.

This essay was prepared with the assistance of Meta Johnson, research assistant at the University of Washington School of Librarianship.

282 / *Environment*

GENERAL RELATIONSHIPS

First to emerge was one of the basic, perhaps the most potent, underlying factor: the contention that libraries are in competition with publishers and booksellers. (When books can be borrowed, who will buy them?) Both sides have made numerous assertions through the years, but hard facts have always been scarce. As early as 1877 *Library Journal* editorialized as follows:

> This [question] expresses a frequent objection of publishers, shared in by some literary people, but on which most librarians will be quite ready to join issue. The most that can be admitted is that lending libraries may have some tendency to change the direction of book-buying, since by supplying ephemeral books they enable those who have money to spend for this purpose to purchase books that are more lasting. . . . [Libraries] ultimately increase book-buying by increasing reading, and the publisher who publishes the best books has the most reason to be grateful to them.[2]

If that seems like a tenuous argument, the publishers and booksellers were unable to come up with anything less impressionistic. In 1913, for example, George P. Brett, president of the U.S. branch of the Macmillan Company, declared that while libraries "are worthy of all encouragement," they are nonetheless "detrimental to the interests of publishers in that there can be no doubt that the purchase of books by individuals is curtailed by the increasing library facilities."[3]

Meanwhile, Edward W. Mumford of Penn Publishing Company was moved to generalize his feelings in a way that left no doubt where he (and very likely many of his colleagues in the trade before and since) stood:

> The librarian, freed, as he believes, from all taint of commercialism, looks with ill-concealed contempt at the bookstore window filled with shrieking "best-sellers" . . . and wonders what sort of man can peddle that harmful stuff and sleep well o'nights. And the bookseller . . . is just as vehement on his side in condemnation of the impractical librarian, who may have his head in the clouds, but who the bookseller firmly believes has seldom more than one foot on the ground.[4]

Having thus given the librarian, deservedly or undeservedly, the status of an only sometime and incompletely terrestrial being, Mumford goes on to describe with blunt clarity what functionally has always been the crux of relationships between libraries and the book trade in many sectors of their contacts. "This attitude of mutual disrespect is naturally fostered by the differences born of bargaining between two parties, one of whom has little to spend and the other very little to make."[5]

Hardly surprising is the confession four years later, in Edward Stevens's address as president of the New York Library Association:

"I soon discovered that it was considered professional to regard the interests of publishers and librarians as inherently antagonistic."[6]

More encouraging forces were at work too. It was said in 1916 that "the libraries of the country are agencies for book publicity,"[7] and one can cite Melvil Dewey's "a book ownd is better than a book loand"[8] (in his famous, ill-fated, simplified spelling) and the later comment, "those who borrow most tend to buy most."[9] By 1921 *Publishers Weekly* opined that "all those who have to do with the distribution of books [including librarians] now understand each other and their respective difficulties as never before."[10] A decade later the Cheney report stressed the importance of the influence of libraries on the book market represented by library readers, asserting that "the work of the libraries in the promotion of reading is too obvious to require discussion." Cheney went on to conclude that "the antagonism of booksellers and publishers who felt that libraries are bad for the trade has largely disappeared—although, at times, it seems to recur."[11] And so it does, in spite of reportedly improved communication and substantial gains in cooperation during the 1960s.[12]

Publishers, on their part, have not been inactive in promoting libraries in later years of the period. The most conspicuous examples of this are their sponsorship of the National Book Committee (withdrawn in 1974), their participation in National Library Week, and the considerable, if indirect, contribution they make by exhibiting at librarians' conferences. It has also been suggested, at least implicitly, that publishing promotes libraries without actually trying to do so. One publisher's representative offered (1963) the imaginative hypothesis that "the advent of paperback publishing and its subsequent exploitation" had drawn so many readers to public libraries that they "could have an influence on public libraries as important as that of Andrew Carnegie."[13]

In spite of library participation in general book promotion programs such as Children's Book Week, the National Book Committee, International Book Year, the Committee on Reading Development, and the Freedom to Read Foundation, it is apparent that the general economic downturn of the early and mid-seventies, the rising cost of published materials, and the then obviously growing tensions over copyright matters (the latter could be both elicited and summed up at the time merely by a mention of the Williams and Wilkins case) were sufficient to give one pause about the future amicability of library/book-trade relationships.

There was some indication that in the 1970s Canadians were also experiencing some of the disjunctive forces that seemed to be at work in the United States. In 1973, for instance, a survey was conducted for the Canadian Booksellers Association in order to report on the problems of getting books to Canadians. One of the conclusions drawn as a result was that booksellers and librarians, who represent the quality-control element in the book world, do not seem inclined to cooperate, and that their time should be spent on cooperative book promotion and not on "meaningless and petty squabbles."[14]

Differences between librarians and the book trade seem to achieve more visibility than what the two groups have in common. There is, however, one basic similarity, other than involvement with books and the promotion of reading, that is mentioned in the literature throughout the period, probably more often by librarians than by publishers and booksellers: the social and cultural value of their role as public servants. At times this presumed likeness between the two groups was expressed in rather high-flown phrases, like "the spirit of devotion to a noble cause" and "the joy of service,"[15] though such would seem to be the pardonable results of genuine enthusiasm, in this case on the part of a librarian. Regardless of language, however, the impression is strongly made that practitioners in both fields felt they were doing something that was ipso facto worthwhile.

How libraries affect the sale of books and how the sale of books to the public affects libraries are related to the matter of libraries themselves as a market. In other words, how important are libraries as customers to publishers and booksellers? What percentage of the total published output goes to libraries in any given year? Nobody really knows, although there have been numerous guesses, estimates, and opinions. The principal reason for this lack of information is the nature of book distribution in North America, which has so far made clear, reliable, and comparable industry-wide statistics almost impossible to produce.

For the earlier part of the period nobody seems to have given the matter much thought; John Tebbel, in the first two volumes of his *History of Book Publishing in the United States,* covering 1630–1919, does not mention it.[16] *Publishers Weekly* reported that, of 34.5 million trade books sold during 1913 in the United States, 35 million (a little over 10 percent) were bought by libraries.[17] Three years later one commentator said he had "the impression that, while the library business is undoubtedly important, still, the books purchased by libraries are a very small part of the entire book sales of the country."[18] In the 1920s *Publishers Weekly* approached the matter from a different angle. "The total book consumption of the country has been estimated at about $1 per capita including textbooks, so that the total library expenditure is perhaps 5 percent of the entire amount."[19]

As late as 1949 public libraries' purchases of trade books were considered to be an insignificant part of the publishers' market,[20] but it was said that during the 1950s and 1960s "publishers generally 'discovered' the library market, and came to realize its importance and potential."[21] Publisher Henry Z. Walck, Sr., "guesstimated" that in 1970 sales of nontextbook books to "institutions" in the United States amounted to 20.9 percent of the total sales.[22] A 1973 *Publishers Weekly* article, in which the author tentatively enumerates what libraries "appear to have acquired" in terms of consumer dollars spent, puts the 1972 domestic library market at $328 million, or 11 percent, of total expenditures for books that year, excluding $40 million in school library expenditures. Including the latter, the total becomes $368 million, or what works out to 12.3 percent. The 1974 *Bowker Annual* includes what is said to be a reprint of this article, and in so doing contributes to the mystification that generally surrounds quantified descriptions of libraries as consumers. In the *Annual* the estimate for school libraries has unexplainedly gone up by a factor of three, from $40 million to $120 million, which would bring the total of library purchases to about 19.5 percent of the market.[23] All in all, the investigator will believe the figures he or she chooses to believe. Common sense indicates, however, that the library market is one that many publishers cannot afford to ignore completely, and one that some publishers could not exist without.

Informed opinion in the early seventies seemed to be that children's book sales were heavily dependent upon libraries, but that most adult book sales were not, with the possible exception of many professional, technical, and university press books.[24]

However important libraries may or may not be in the eyes of the trade, and even though libraries and their committees have been involved in negotiating with the trade about everything from the width of margins to relations with publishers, the most durable causes of discord and confrontation have been the economic issues of discounts and copyright.

DISCOUNTS

The question of book discounts has always brought forth emotional reactions. The whole story was aptly summed up in 1940 in a remark that might be considered by some to be in substance just as valid over thirty years later: "Verily, library discounts have had their ups and downs. Ups, against vehement protestations of 'the trade.' Downs, with critical and cynical opposition of librarians."[25]

In 1876, perhaps stimulated by the Tweed Ring, *Library Journal* mentioned "the booksellers' ring" in commenting on an apparent victory over the then prevailing 20 percent limitation on discounts, achieved at the first national conference of librarians.[26] But the "victory" was short lived. The position of the librarians was, and has continued to be, based on three contentions: libraries are (1) public service, educational institutions, (2) practically wholesale buyers, and (3) in many cases tax-supported. Because of these characteristics, the argument goes, libraries are entitled to a more favorable price break than the ordinary customer. In 1902 *Library Journal* declared that the profession was willing to help work out a reform that would be more equitable, and added that, although "the publishers, on the whole, have appreciated the tone of the library profession," the booksellers had not.[27] Typical of the latter's point of view is a statement by Charles E. Butler of Brentano's, who also chaired the Board of Trade of the American Booksellers Association (the Board of Trade made recommendations on prices and discounts).

> Our greatest complaint as to economic grafting and unfair trading is against . . . the public libraries of the United States. For their own selfish purposes and gain, ignoring absolutely the right of others to exist, they have waged war bitterly and remorselessly against the booksellers of the United States, with the purpose and determination to break down the last line of defense which the bookseller has built up about himself that he might survive, that of fair trading and standardization of price.[28]

That is rather strong stuff. But with retailers and jobbers both competing for discounts from publishers, and librarians shopping around for the best deal, implicitly inviting price-cutting in the process, the worries of the booksellers, operating in a notoriously low-margin business, take on considerable legitimacy. Even with the increased use of jobbers for library purchasing, and direct ordering from publishers, the squeeze went on, and with it the differing points of view have become, if not reconciled, at least stabilized. In fact, one might even say "standardized," for it is not unlikely that in the 1970s the same situation prevails that was said to have prevailed at the 1920 Federal Trade Commission hearings on price maintenance. "In the end, everybody was able to show beyond question that everybody else was taking a narrow and selfish view of the problem and that therefore his arguments were not grounded on broad truth and should be disregarded."[29] The Cheney report, in 1931, said flatly "there is no justification for increasing discounts to libraries."[30] (In Canada, the trade feared the effect of Canadian library purchasing from U.S. and English wholesalers, from whom librarians said they could generally receive better discounts and better service.)[31]

COPYRIGHT

The U.S. Congress has shown fitful interest in copyright since at least 1789. In this essay the main concern will be with how librarians reacted and/or participated in the earlier years of our period, and with the controversies that became increasingly divisive during this last decade or so. Major legislation revising the first (1790) U.S. copyright law was enacted in 1831, 1870, 1891, and 1909. In addition, there were the necessary amendments for ratification, in 1955, of the Universal Copyright Convention. As of September 1975 it was basically the law of 1909 under which we operated.

The various historical accounts of international and domestic copyright in the United States do not indicate that the role of librarians was very significant in affecting copyright law. But the record shows that the American Library Association, other library organizations, and librarians individually have been making themselves heard, if not always heeded, from the 1880s on. The record also shows that they were not always in agreement. During the period we are concerned with here, the story of librarians' involvement begins with matters pertaining to the law enacted in 1891.[32] This law is significant in that it was the first to grant protection to foreign authors and because it restricted importation of foreign editions of works copyrighted in this country. The latter, as will be seen, was a major cause of disagreement between librarians and the trade. The act also introduced the controversial "manufacturing clause," requiring that books be manufactured in the United States if they were to be copyrighted there.

In 1886, as the 1891 law was taking shape in characteristically glacial fashion, Ainsworth Spofford, Librarian of Congress, presented what has been called "the most lengthy and most important observations" on international copyright at the hearing on the Hawley and Chace bills before the Senate Committee on Patents on March 11.[33] Since Spofford did not explicitly endorse either of the bills, but mainly the principle of international copyright—that is, the protection of works by foreign authors published in this country—one cannot be sure that his remarks had any definite bearing on the fact that it was substantially the Chace Bill that emerged as the new copyright law in 1891. (Spofford's testimony may have been "important," but it seems probable that he was upstaged somewhat by Mark Twain and James Russell Lowell, who were among the witnesses.)

In a detailed listing of bills, reports, laws, petitions, resolutions, memorials, hearings, Thorvald Solberg's *Copyright in Congress, 1789–1904* mentions the American Library Association only once, for its petition laid before the Senate February 7, 1891. The petition, "praying the passage of an international copyright law," was tabled.[34] Besides the ALA petition, there were only three identifiable as having been submitted by librarians, all in the House, and all on May 19, 1890, nine months or so before ALA offered an official reaction. The three were submitted by "Librarian of Indiana University," "Librarians and libraries of New York," and "Librarians of University of Virginia."[35] Just what effect the petitions had on the eventual legislation of 1891 is apparently not ascertainable.

Nor is it known whether librarians were behind the petitions presented in the names of college and university faculties, or "citizens" of some city or state. The fact that the Senate received seventy-seven petitions, and the House seventy-four, in favor of the Chace-Platt-Breckenridge Bill (passed on March 3, 1891 as the Platt-Simmonds Act) has been attributed to the Conference Committee of the American Authors' Copyright League and the American Publishers' Copyright League. The committee members were said to have employed "every conceivable effort in their final campaign to insure [its] passage," including the promotion of petitions.[36]

The next significant legislative activity came in the three or four years before the enactment of the 1909 law, and librarians were more active than they had been before. In 1906 ALA was even described as "a very powerful and very diligent and active association . . . which has been very much interested" in copyright matters.[37] It should be pointed out, however, that this statement may have been political window-dressing since it was made by Stephen H. Olin, counsel for the American Publishers' Copyright League during attempts at negotiating a compromise that would satisfy both publishers and librarians.

There are indications that ALA, even though it had a copyright committee, was not highly effective, the most important testimony coming from its own ranks. In 1906 William P. Cutter of the Forbes Library, Northampton, Massachusetts, proposed the formation of a Library Copyright League because, as was later pointed out at a congressional hearing, the ALA committee's views did not adequately represent the libraries of the country. Membership in the league grew, and its executive committee subsequently congratulated the league on the passage of a copyright act which was in every "essential feature" what the league had striven for.[38]

Probably the outstanding obstacle to accord was, until "fair use" became a major issue about a half-century later, the matter of importation (of foreign issues of works that were copyrighted in the United States). One student of American copyright law observed in 1961 "the librarian has tended to wear blinders which focused his attention upon [that] problem to the exclusion of others."[39] Whether or not that overstates the case, the problem had motivated the Library Copyright League, the American Authors' Copyright League, and the American Publishers' Copyright League, causing a serious rift between librarians and the trade.

The 1891 copyright legislation permitted libraries to import foreign editions of copyrighted works (which were often preferred by librarians because they were less expensive and of better physical quality) "for use and not for sale . . . not more than two copies of such book[s] at any one time."[40] The 1909 law contained the same clause, but limited the number of copies per invoice to one. The permission was not retained without a struggle, however, with both librarians and publishers lobbying heavily, and it polarized the two groups.

Perhaps representative of the feeling involved was an exchange between officers of the Library Copyright League and George Haven Putnam in 1909 in the *Dial*. In these letters the librarians, Bernard C. Steiner of Enoch Pratt Free Library, league president, and William P. Cutter, secretary, spoke of Putnam's "glaring misstatements" and made somewhat inflammatory remarks about publishers establishing price controls, which, they said, would put the U.S. buyer "just where the publishers of books have been trying to put him, entirely at their mercy."[41] Putnam was no less rancorous in objecting to the librarians' denial that the importation privilege led to unfair competition from foreign publishers, which was the contention of the trade. He accused the librarians of being "disingenuous," ending up by saying, "I can but think that the Library Copyright League might more accurately be entitled The League of (certain) Librarians for the Undermining of Copyright."[42]

What may have been the crowning reprimand for the alleged single-mindedness of those who supported importation came from a perhaps unexpected source. In 1926 R. R. Bowker, an outstanding publisher-friend of North American libraries and librarians, scolded them for having been

> misguided into considering the importation section as an iniquitous conspiracy of publishers because you have emphasized only an inconvenience for libraries while ignoring the right of the author. The manor of your attack has aroused hostility between classes otherwise friendly in the common cause of the wider distribution of books.[43]

Bowker's criticism may have been deserved in the twenties, but had he been around in the sixties and seventies he probably would have had to admit that librarians had widened their area of concern. In 1964 ALA adopted eight principles on the general revision of copyright law:

> 1. The principle of "fair use" be reaffirmed.
> 2. The requirement of printing of notice and date of copyright be endorsed as absolutely essential to libraries and library users.
> 3. Proposals to make the duration of copyright for a fixed term, both for published and unpublished works, be endorsed.
> 4. The principle that libraries be exempted from import restrictions and penalties be reaffirmed.
> 5. The principle that government material should not be subject to copyright be reaffirmed.
> 6. Proposals to have copyright subsist in the federal government after its expiration in the hands of the copyright owner be opposed.
> 7. The requirement of American manufacture as a qualification for securing copyright of works by American authors be opposed.
> 8. The "not for profit" principle as now embodied in the copyright law be endorsed.[44]

Since 1964 ALA's Washington Office and the ALA Committee on Copyright Issues have labored to achieve these ends. By 1975 accord or satisfactory compromises had been reached on all but "fair use," duration of copyright, and "not for profit."

290 / Environment

As ALA approached its centennial year, the main event was what came to be popularly known as the Williams and Wilkins case, the circumstances of which it will be possible only to summarize here. In, 1968 Williams and Wilkins, medical publishers, sued the National Library of Medicine and the National Institutes of Health for violation of copyright in their photocopying activities. A commissioner to the Court of Claims recommended for the publishers in 1972. On appeal, the full Court of Claims decided for NLM in 1973. Later that year the U.S. Supreme Court agreed to rule on the case, and in February 1975 rendered a four-to-four decision, Justice Blackmun not participating. The reaction of librarians to the Williams and Wilkins suit was reflected in the fact that ALA publicly supported NLM, and filed an *amicus curaie* brief with the Court of Claims.[45]

The Supreme Court tie-vote, of course, left standing the judgment of the lower court. But it set no precedent and had no effect on the law of the land, so the hope for clarification of "fair use" rested solely with congressional action on copyright revision. In early 1975 there was some optimism that legislation would be passed by the end of that year.[46]

Finally, it should be noted that in the sphere of copyright, as elsewhere, librarians have been oriented to the needs of the public and to the free flow of information and culture. Early in the period they were the only active group without some vested economic interest such as that of authors, publishers, printers, and binders. Although there is the possibility that they felt their livelihood was threatened, and thus were being defensive, there appears to be no evidence to support this. At times their protestations have sounded a trifle righteous. However, it seems evident that many of the debates over copyright were genuine advocacy situations on the part of the librarians, and, as Verner Clapp pointed out, "the publishing industry has the whole copyright bar working for it, but the public has no legal talent to represent it."[47] The American Library Association, at least in recent years, has worked hard to change not only the law, but also the state of affairs referred to by Clapp. Early in 1975 the association's opposition took on an added dimension with the formation of the Coalition for Fair Copyright Protection, which represented eleven associations of publishers, media producers, bookstores, and authors.[48]

LIBRARY ACQUISITION METHODS

Since 1876 little of fundamental significance has changed in the basic consumer/supplier relationship of libraries and the book trade. Libraries a hundred years later wanted to acquire materials as quickly, conveniently, and economically as possible, just as they always had, and the trade was still in the business of supplying these materials, generally competitively, in such a manner that they could earn a profit. A classic "free economy" formula remained, even though the number of participants and the volume of trade had increased. (The unprecedented number of mergers during the 1950s and 1960s, which often resulted in the absorption of publishers into conglomerates, has caused some alarm in the library profession. That alarm may be justified on certain grounds, but there is little indication at this writing that from an acquisitions standpoint these changes have significantly altered the basic consumer/supplier relationship.)

The mechanics of this relationship—the day-by-day nuts and bolts operations of ordering, shipping, corresponding, invoicing, paying, collecting, returning, claiming, and so forth—have likewise changed very little. Very little, that is, except for the fact that the widespread applications of computer and automation technology have both speeded up and slowed down the transaction of business. Otherwise, the same old complaints about each other are heard from both librarians and members of the trade. Chief among the perennials are publishers' and booksellers' complaints that they must cope with a wide variety of billing requirements, bureaucratically slow payments, garbled bibliographic information, and what they often consider to be unreasonable demands for service. Librarians are moved to comment feelingly about slowness in filling orders, duplication, books without invoices, invoices without books, wrong titles, wrong editions, too many or too few copies, and what they often consider to be an unreasonably low level of service. All participants have lately protested against the frustrations of "communicating" with computers.[49]

In spite of the essential sameness of buying and selling library materials through the years, there have been some innovative plans and operations that deserve attention in this survey. Those selected for brief description are: (1) approval plans, (2) lease-purchase plans, (3) the "Greenaway Plan," (4) the Farmington Plan, (5) PL-480, (6) the Cooperative Acquisitions Project (LC), (7) the U.S. Book Exchange, and (8) the Library Book Club.

Approval Plans

The fairly recent development and spread of approval plans has caused controversy, mostly among librarians, but with opinions voiced by members of the trade as well. Most aspects of the controversy have been published, and the principal arguments can be conveniently summarized.[50] On the pro side, an approval plan (1) offers broad coverage, (2) gives better service, (3) assures faster receipt of books, (4) enables librarians and others to select with book in hand, (5) involves less paper work, (6) frees staff time for selecting on the antiquarian and out-of-print markets, (7) provides better coverage in some areas than the library could achieve independently, and (8) results in lower clerical costs. On the con side, an approval plan (1) constitutes an abdication of selection responsibilities, (2) amounts to book collecting or gathering (both pejorative terms in this context) rather than book selecting, (3) ignores the factor of use of the materials purchased, (4) causes at times higher unit cost of books, and (5) results in higher clerical costs.

What was probably one of the most ambitious and wide-ranging approval plan packages was that of Richard Abel and Company. The essence of its method of providing bibliographic control of new books, both foreign and domestic, of interest to academic or other research libraries has been described in the following way:

> The Approval Program is a fully automated method for the distribution of new books. Four major mechanisms make up this program: (a) the acquisition mechanism, (b) the new title profiling mechanism, (c) the SDI (selective dissemination of information) mechanism, and (d) the update (or feedback) mechanism.[51]

Lease-Purchase Plans

Lease-purchase plans may vary in the details of their operation but are basically the same, in that this manner of acquisition allows a library to add current books to its collection on a temporary basis while retaining the option of purchasing them outright if they so desire. The model used for this description is the program offered by the McNaughton Book Service, more familiarly known as the McNaughton Plan, which began in about 1940 as a rental service.[52]

The library first determines the size of what is called a "basic collection" of leased books it wishes to maintain. This ranges from 100 to 5,000 or more books (not titles), and the size of the base determines both the number of books to be added (with an equal number to be returned each month—usually 10 percent in the McNaughton Plan) and the cost of the program. The library selects from monthly lists, popular fiction, nonfiction, or young adult, supplied by the company, and may, by special arrangement, make other requests. The books are contracted to be supplied very close to their publication dates, and to come cataloged and in plastic jackets, "ready for shelving and immediate circulation." Should the library wish to purchase any of the books, it may do so at a 75 percent discount.

The principal advantages claimed for lease-purchase plans are (1) promptness (as one librarian administering the plan for her library system told the author, "it's great PR—gets books to the patron much faster" than ordinary channels), (2) economies in in-library processing costs, and (3) one solution to the space problems caused by shelving permanently accessioned books of transient interest.

Most of the lease-purchase subscribers appear to be large public library systems, although school and other types of libraries have been noted.

The Greenaway Plan

Toward the end of the 1950s Emerson Greenaway, director of the Free Library of Philadelphia, conceived a method of blanket (not "approval") ordering that has since borne his name. In the Greenaway Plan a library contracts with a given publisher to be sent, and to purchase, one copy of each of that publisher's new titles. The advantages of this plan to a library are purported to be that librarians can examine the book itself before "selecting" it for addition to the collection, and that sometimes copies come before the official publication date. In order to be attractive to publishers, because of the additional operational costs to them, they would have to limit their participation in the plan to libraries with a good potential for multiple-copy orders.

The Farmington Plan

Stimulated, among other things, by Hitler's suppression of books, was the Farmington Plan,[53] born in 1942 and named after the Connecticut city in which the planning meetings were held. A cooperative effort to enrich American library resources in foreign materials, the plan was put into operation in 1948 under the auspices of the Association of Research Libraries (ARL), which secured an initial grant from the Carnegie Corporation.

Eventually to involve some sixty research libraries, the plan worked on a basis of participating libraries accepting assignments for collecting in specific subject areas or from specific geographical areas. Some parts of the plan called for acquiring current material only, and some for current and retrospective. Some used blanket order arrangements, others not. All libraries agreed to make their material readily available on interlibrary loan.

The foreign countries covered at first were limited to some of those in Western Europe (excluding Great Britain), but subsequently programs were added for Australia and New Zealand, as well as for countries in East and South Asia, Latin America, Africa, Eastern Europe, and the Near East.

The Farmington Plan was formally terminated by ARL as of December 31, 1972. However, a number of libraries continued their Western European responsibilities, and activities in other parts of the plan went on in varying degrees. Philip McNiff, chairman of ARL's Foreign Acquisitions Committee, gave three reasons for ending the program: "(1) The increasing use of blanket order programs by member libraries (which presumably duplicated the Farmington program); (2) the

Library of Congress' national program of acquisitions and cataloging; and (3) the reduction in many libraries' acquisition budgets in recent years."[54]

Although it has been controversial and described in ways ranging from "a milestone in American intellectual history" (Robert Vosper) to "a large, costly, and rather clumsy sledge-hammer to crack so small a nut" (J. P. H. Pafford),[55] final assessment of the Farmington Plan as an attempt at nationally coordinated, cooperative acquisitions is yet to be made.

PL-480

The terms of Public Law 480, 83rd Congress (the Agricultural Trade and Development Act of 1954), as amended, authorized the use of foreign currencies owned by the United States for the acquisition and analysis of publications from certain countries that issued those currencies.[56] In 1961 Congress appropriated funds for a pilot project involving India, Pakistan, and the United Arab Republic. Countries added later were Indonesia, Ceylon, Nepal, Poland, Israel, and Yugoslavia (the latter two programs being discontinued in the early 1970s). The operation is directed by the Library of Congress, which also provides cataloging.

PL-480, as this program came to be called, began in 1962 with the Library of Congress, 21 college and university libraries, and the New York Public Library participating. As the period this essay covers drew to a close, something on the order of 17 million pieces of current material had been received by more than 40 full participants, plus English-language publications that went to some 300 other libraries as well.

Materials were received on a blanket order basis at first, but later became more selected; juveniles, for instance, were for the most part eliminated. Libraries have no commitment to add all they receive, but must agree to keep discards out of the trade (although depositing with the U.S. Book Exchange is permitted), and must agree to interlibrary lending.

Cooperative Acquisitions Project (LC)

A program of short duration, but highly acclaimed, was the late 1940s Cooperative Acquisitions Project of the Library of Congress, concerned with getting World War II European publications into American libraries.[57] Priorities were assigned by subject among the initial 113 participating libraries. Distribution of materials began in May 1946 and ended in September 1948, by which time the number of libraries taking part had been reduced to 56. The publications acquired were predominantly German, but also included French, Italian, Dutch,

Belgian, and Swiss. About 25 percent of the ultimate total of nearly 2 million items were confiscated; the rest were purchased by the Library of Congress Mission for acquisition of these materials at a total expense of around $627,000. Surplus items were given to the U.S. Book Exchange.

Robert B. Downs, in evaluating this cooperative project, wrote that "We have available in the United States an unsurpassed collection of European wartime publications, far richer than would have been possible if we had been forced to depend upon the efforts of individual institutions."[58]

The U.S. Book Exchange

The venerable library acquisition method known as "exchange" (which may have started in antiquity) is not discussed per se in this essay because of the fact that exchange arrangements entered into by libraries, whatever the degree of formality, have usually involved material that is not readily available for sale through regular book trade channels. The U.S. Book Exchange, however, partakes of both trade and nontrade characteristics.

The U.S. Book Exchange, Inc., is an outgrowth of the American Book Center for War Devastated Libraries, Inc. (ABC), which was formed in 1944 under the sponsorship of the Council of National Library Associations.[59] The ABC worked with the Division of Cultural Cooperation of the U.S. Department of State, with its organizational costs covered by funds from the Rockefeller Foundation. By 1947 it had received for distribution more than one million volumes, contributed by libraries, publishers, and individuals.

The USBE was incorporated in 1948, its stated purpose being to promote the distribution and interchange of books, periodicals, and other scholarly materials among libraries and other educational and scientific institutions of the United States, and between them and libraries and institutions of other countries. It is a private, nongovernmental, nonprofit, self-supporting corporation. As an outgrowth of the ABC, in its earlier years it continued to serve foreign libraries, subsidized by the U.S. Agency for International Development (AID). When AID funds were withdrawn in 1963, USBE was forced to serve only those libraries abroad that could pay the fees, which reduced the number considerably. Thus, although its international operations were curtailed, it has continued to serve as a national bureau for both domestic and international exchange (with a fee).

Headquartered in Washington, D.C., USBE in the early 1970s claimed 1,500 regular, fee-paying, library members, and in its role of worldwide clearinghouse had around 4 million periodical issues (more than 30,000 titles) and 100,000 books. From this collection, built and rebuilt primarily by deposits of duplicates from member libraries, the exchange moved about 650,000 pieces per year among its members.

Participating libraries pay a membership fee and per-item service charges for most transactions.

In early 1975 the Board of Directors voted to change the name (but had not yet decided upon one) to one that would not give the impression that it was a government agency, and would more accurately describe its function. Also announced was a request for funds from the Council on Library Resources and the National Science Foundation to finance a two-year interlibrary loan pilot project.

The Library Book Club

An account of a somewhat utopian proposal closes this brief survey of library acquisition methods during the period.[60] In 1938 a columnist for the *Wilson Bulletin for Librarians*, taking note of an in-house company report showing that U.S. libraries each year spent "the staggering minimum total" of nearly $21 million on books, proposed that librarians organize a consumers' buying unit, or cooperative. This co-op was to be called a Library Book Club, and the originator of the idea argued that it would convert the libraries' collective buying wealth into economic power and substantial savings. By such tactics as ordering large editions ("with library bindings") for distribution to club members, and supplying catalog cards, the club would have books in libraries "by the day of publication." As well as affecting economies, it was claimed, the club would make "an important cultural contribution" by coordinating book selection.

The reaction of librarians to this scheme was generally (naively?) favorable, that of publishers at best cautious and skeptical. At any rate, the proposal's brief flowering in the twilight of the thirties seems to have been its last.

THE INFLUENCE OF LIBRARIANS ON PUBLISHING

One aspect of library relationships with the book trade that has manifested itself on and off from the earliest days of the period is the matter of librarians' influence on what is published (or the lack thereof), other than solely through being a market. It is reported that in the 1950s one publisher (unnamed) was heard to say, "To hell with librarians. Our customers are booksellers, and we do what *they* want."[61] At least part of the message is that publishing is, for most of the people engaged in it, a business, and must therefore make money. Quite often librarians have seemed to overlook this fact, and thus have been prone to grumble about the nonfulfillment of their wishes for higher quality fiction, better made books, in-print longevity, and so forth.

There are two areas in which librarians have had perhaps the most noticeable, interactive influence on publishing. The first of these is children's books, the second reprints. In the children's field, which is largely dependent upon libraries as pointed out above, an effective agency has been the Joint Committee of the ALA Children's Services Division and the Children's Book Council, which acts as a sounding board for publishing ideas.

Although ALA's and librarians' interaction with the reprint industry goes back at least to the 1920s, they did not become a significant force until the mid-1960s.[62] The rapid growth of libraries during the 1950s and 1960s created a ready-made market. Beginning in the late 1950s, partly through the efforts of the Reprint Expediting Service of the Resources and Technical Services Division of ALA, publishers began to respond encouragingly to librarians' suggestions about reprinting, and some ten years later started to openly solicit the library market. The ALA Reprinting Committee has continued to work at improving library/publisher relations.

Underscoring the economic nature of the situation is a remark made by Daniel Melcher in 1972. "One thing comes clear as you review the publishing for libraries of the past two decades: Libraries can have just about anything they want whether or not anyone else wants it, *if they are ready to pay for it* [emphasis added]."[63] This is probably true, considering the human and technical resources of publishers, but it represents a different kind of influence than librarians have generally had in mind (or pocket). They can look with more satisfaction at the influence they have exerted, collectively and individually, on such publishing ventures as indexes, bibliographies, and reference works, as well as at the large number of these works upon which they themselves have done the creative work. Collectively, their contribution has been substantial, and deserves more attention than it can be given here.

CONCLUSION

The first one hundred years of the American Library Association has been a period marked in North America by growth and achievement in librarianship and in the book trade. But it has also been a trying time, as members of the two groups sought in their respective ways to cope with a coexistence that they knew was necessary and inevitable since both had evident virtues and unique roles, but about which both felt ambivalence, and saw on occasion to be inimicable to their particular interests. All through the period, it is clear, efforts have been made on both sides, either by individuals or organizations, to arrive at a mutually satisfactory working relationship. The success of these efforts can safely be described as varying.

In the ninety-ninth year of this first century of formalized coexistence, there were strong indications that a complex mingling of factors was contributing to an increasingly unstable situation. It seems appropriate to quote one expression of this idea.

298 / *Environment*

The battle lines are being drawn for a great debate over the emotionally and politically charged issue of how library and information services are to be funded in the coming decades. Most librarians will be on the side of "conservatism" and "democracy," favoring the continuation of traditional modes of tax-supported public library service with information freely available to all as a matter of right. Information industry people, publishers, government officials, engineers, and even, perhaps, authors will be on the side of "progress" and "profits," advocating a new concept of for-profit or pay libraries, user charges, and information as a salable commodity.[64]

One of the uses of history is as a means of understanding how we arrived at where we are or were. Librarians and members of the book trade have arrived at ambivalence and discord most often when money was involved. What the future holds for relations between the two groups is fair game for speculation. It is obvious, however, that money will be a dominant factor.

NOTES

1. The term *book trade* has been restricted for purposes of this essay to mean book publishers and in-print booksellers. Only a small amount of the documentation is from Canadian sources. Search turned up little in the literature (compared with the output about conditions in the United States) that could be satisfactorily encompassed in a presentation the length of this one. Some problems in Canada are unique. Even so, one might assume that Canadian librarians, publishers, and booksellers probably also have or have had many of the same interests and problems as their colleagues to the south. If the problems seem to be given a large share of attention in this essay, it is because they have been given a proportionate amount of attention in a hundred years of writings about this topic.

2. Editorial, *Library Journal* 1:321 (May 31, 1877).

3. George F. Bowerman, "Co-operation between the Library and the Bookstore," *Library Journal* 38:325 (June 1913).

4. Edward W. Mumford, "The Librarian and the Bookseller," *Library Journal* 38:136 (Mar. 1913).

5. Ibid.

6. Edward F. Stevens, "An Honorable and Lasting Peace," *Library Journal* 42:852 (Nov. 1917).

7. Matthew S. Dudgeon, "Librarian and Bookseller: Comparison and Cooperation," *Publishers Weekly* 89:1743–44 (May 27, 1916).

8. Melvil Dewey, "Libraries as Book Stores," *Library Journal* 45:493 (June 1, 1920).

9. Susan Severtson and George Banks, "Toward the Library-Bookstore," *Library Journal* 96:163 (Jan. 15, 1971).

10. "The N.A.B.P. Meeting," *Publishers Weekly* 99:188 (Jan. 22, 1921).

11. O. H. Cheney, *Economic Survey of the Book Industry, 1930–1931: Final Report* (New York: National Association of Book Publishers, 1931), p. 45. This work was reprinted by Bowker, with minor supplemental additions, in 1949 and 1960.

12. See, for instance, Helen Welch Tuttle, "Library–Book Trade Relations," *Library Trends* 18:398 (Jan. 1970); Theodore Waller, "The Indispensable Partnership," *Library Journal* 98:1543–49 (May 15, 1973); Fred DeArmond, "Books—To Buy or Borrow?" *Library Journal* 84:2890 (Oct. 1, 1959).
13. Lawrence F. Reeves, "The Other Side of the Coin," in Carl H. Melinat, ed., *Librarianship and Publishing* (Syracuse, N.Y.: Syracuse University, School of Library Science, 1963), p. 24.
14. Jim Lotz, ". . . Some of My Best Friends Are Librarians . . . ," *Canadian Library Journal* 31:48–52 (Aug. 1974).
15. Paul M. Paine, "The Book-Trade and the Library," *Publishers Weekly* 95:1453 (May 24, 1919).
16. John Tebbel, *A History of Book Publishing in the United States*, 2 vols. (New York: Bowker, 1972–75). Tebbel does say that as of about 1900 "libraries had probably increased the sale of books" (2:60).
17. Fredric G. Melcher, "The Retailer's Place in Book Distribution," *Publishers Weekly* 92:1091 (Sept. 29, 1917). Melcher refers to "1913 Government figures" for the number of library purchases.
18. W. H. Brett, "The Library and the Book Trade," *ALA Bulletin* 10:402 (Mar. 1916).
19. "Book Expenditures of Libraries," *Publishers Weekly* 103:997 (Mar. 24, 1923). Cheney, p. 311 gives a 1929 total of $13,886,280 in library purchases, but does not indicate what percentage this is of the total of all sales for that year.
20. William Miller, *The Book Industry* (New York: Columbia Univ. Pr., 1949), p. 125.
21. Daniel Melcher, "Two Decisive Decades: Discovering the Library Marketplace," *American Libraries* 3:811 (July–Aug. 1972).
22. Ibid., p. 812 (table by Henry Z. Walck, Sr.).
23. John P. Dessauer, "Where the Book Buyers' Money Goes," *Publishers Weekly* 204:42–43 (July 30, 1973); the same (with noted exception) in *Bowker Annual of Library and Book Trade Information*, 19th ed. (New York: Bowker, 1974), pp. 189–93.
24. See, for instance, the D. Melcher article cited in note 21, and the Walck table cited in note 22. On the other hand, the results of a joint Association of American Publishers/American Library Association survey of 61 publishers in 1974 led to this comment: "Librarians probably represent the largest single market for most nontext book publishers." Sandra K. Paul and Carol A. Nemeyer, "Book Marketing and Selection: Selected Findings from the Current AAP/ALA Study," *Publishers Weekly* 207:43 (June 16, 1975).
25. Oscar C. Orman, *Library Discount Control: A Survey to January 1940* (Chicago: American Library Assn., 1941), p. 10.
26. Editorial, *Library Journal* 1:91 (Nov. 30, 1876).
27. Editorial, *Library Journal* 27:244 (May 1902).
28. Charles E. Butler, "The Direct Selling Problem," *Publishers Weekly* 91:1684 (May 26, 1917).
29. William B. Colver, "The Present State of Price Maintenance," *Publishers Weekly* 97:1667 (May 22, 1920).
30. Cheney, p. 319; also see p. 312. Cheney says that with regard to wholesalers, discounts from publishers are "a payment for definite services" (p. 231).
31. See "Library-Publisher Relations," *Canadian Library Association Bulletin* 9:30–34 (Sept. 1952), and Trude Pomahac, "The Institute on Publishing in Canada, University of Alberta, Edmonton, 27–30 June 1971," *Canadian Library Journal* 28:262–65 (July–Aug. 1971).
32. Public Law 565, 51st Cong., 26 Stat. 1106–10.
33. Aubert C. Clark, *The Movement for International Copyright in Nineteenth Century America* (Washington, D.C.: Catholic Univ. of America Pr., 1960), p.

142. See also U.S., Congress, Senate, 49th Cong., 1st sess., S. Rept. no. 1188, (Washington, D.C.: Govt. Print. Off., 1886), pp. 120–30.

34. Thorvald Solberg, *Copyright in Congress, 1789–1904*, Copyright Office Bulletin no. 8 (Washington, D.C.: Govt. Print. Off., 1905), p. 300.

35. Ibid., p. 285.

36. Clark, pp. 157, 158.

37. Thorvald Solberg, "Hearing on the U.S. Copyright Bill," *Library Journal* 31:321 (July 1906).

38. See "Library Copyright League," *Library Journal* 31:172 (Apr. 1906); ibid. 32:14 (Jan. 1907); "Second Public Hearing on the Copyright Bill," ibid., pp. 16, 18 (Jan. 1907); "Library Copyright League," ibid., 34:409 (Sept. 1909).

39. Joseph W. Rogers, "Libraries and Copyright Law Revision: Progress and Prospects," *ALA Bulletin* 55:58 (Jan. 1961).

40. U.S., *Statutes at Large*, p. 1108.

41. Bernard C. Steiner and William P. Cutter, "From the Library Copyright League," *Dial* 46:321 (May 16, 1909). For what prompted this letter see George Haven Putnam, "Copyright and the Importation Privileges," ibid., pp. 252–53 (Apr. 16, 1909). The *Dial* had come out editorially in favor of the importation privilege and even advocated its extension to booksellers; see "The Copyright Advance," ibid., pp. 217–19 (Apr. 1, 1909).

42. George Haven Putnam, "The Importation of Copyrighted Books," *Dial* 46:395 (June 16, 1909).

43. "The Copyright Controversy: Letter from R. R Bowker to Dr. M. Llewellyn Raney," *Library Journal* 51:767 (Sept. 15, 1926).

44. Charles F. Gosnell, "The Copyright Grab Bag: Observations on the New Copyright Legislation," *ALA Bulletin* 60:55 (Jan. 1966).

45. See "ALA Backs Copying Stand on Medical Library," *Library Journal* 96:1312 (Apr. 15, 1971); "ALA Supports NLM," *American Libraries* 2:608 (June 1971); U.S. Court of Claims, *The Williams and Wilkins Company v. The United States, No. 73–68, Decided Nov. 27, 1973* (slip decision), (Washington, D.C.: Govt. Print. Off., n.d.). For a summary of arguments supporting the libraries' position, see American Library Association, *Libraries and Copyright: A Summary of the Arguments for Library Photocopying* (Washington, D.C.: American Library Assn., 1974). It was first published in June, revised and reprinted in October.

46. "[Representative Robert W.] Kastenmeier and Copyright Legislation," *American Libraries* 6:137–38 (Mar. 1975).

47. "Publishers vs. Librarians on Copyright Issue," *Publishers Weekly* 192:29 (Aug. 14, 1967).

48. "New Coalition Aims for Copyright Protection," *Publishers Weekly* 207:15 (Mar. 24, 1975).

49. This is a consensus, arrived at by the author, based upon a conscientious survey of about a hundred years of the literature, and his own twenty years or so of both making and hearing these complaints.

50. For a review of the literature see Kathleen McCullough, "Approval Plans: Vendor Responsibility and Library Research: A Literature Survey and Discussion," *College and Research Libraries* 33:368–81 (Sept. 1972). To her inclusions might be added Margaret Dobbyn, "Approval Plan Purchasing in Perspective," ibid., pp. 480–84 (Nov. 1972); Gayle Edward Evans and C. W. Argyres, "Approval Plans and Collection Development in Academic Libraries," *Library Resources and Technical Services* 18:35–50 (Winter 1974).

51. Donald P. Chvatal and Gary L. Olson, "A Computer-based Acquisition System for Libraries," American Society for Information Science *Proceedings*, 8:217 (Westport, Conn.: Greenwood, 1971). Richard Abel and Co. encountered financial difficulties and went into receivership in early 1975. Shortly after, some of its operations were assumed by a newly created descendant of Blackwell, the

old and respected British booksellers. The new firm, Blackwell's–North America, planned to emphasize supplying North American books to North American and overseas libraries. See "Blackwell Takes Over Abel Assets; Sets Up New Firm," *Publishers Weekly* 207:223 (Jan. 27, 1975).

52. Information is synthesized here from five sources: (1) "The McNaughton [Adult] Plan," a brochure, and (2) "The McNaughton Young Adult Plan," another brochure, both undated, and both supplied to the author by Elaine N. Keller, product marketing director, Bro-Dart, Inc. (of which the McNaughton Book Service is a subsidiary) on February 26, 1975; (3) Keller's letter to the author, February 26, 1975; (4) what little information there is in the literature, and (5) the author's conversations with librarians familiar with lease-purchase plans.

53. Information in this section is based upon the following (in chronological order): *Foreign Acquisition Newsletter* (formerly *Farmington Plan Letter* and *Farmington Plan Newsletter*) (Washington, D.C.: Association of Research Libraries, 1949–); Edwin E. Williams, *Farmington Plan Handbook*, (Cambridge, Mass.: Association of Research Libraries, 1953); Association of Research Libraries, *Farmington Plan Survey: Final Report*, directed by Robert Vosper and Robert Talmadge (Chicago: Association of Research Libraries, 1959); Edwin E. Williams, *Farmington Plan Handbook Revised to 1961 and Abridged* (Cambridge, Mass.: Association of Research Libraries, 1961); Robert G. Vosper, *Farmington Plan Survey: A Summary of the Separate Studies of 1957–1961* (Urbana: Univ. of Illinois Graduate School of Library Science, 1965); James E. Skipper, "National Planning for Resource Development," *Library Trends* 15:321–34 (Oct. 1966); Hendrik Edelman, "Death of the Farmington Plan," *Library Journal* 98:1251–53 (Apr. 15, 1973).

54. "Research Acquisitions Programs Fold," *American Libraries* 4:78 (Feb. 1973).

55. Quoted in "Farmington Plan Ends after 30-Year Run," *Library Journal* 98:374 (Feb. 1, 1973). The original quoting of these two opinions is ascribed to Edwin E. Williams in the *Harvard Librarian*, issue unspecified.

56. The information presented here is based primarily upon "PL 480 Program Already a Success," *Wilson Library Bulletin* 37:22 (Sept. 1962); "PL 480 Celebrates 10th Anniversary," Library of Congress *Information Bulletin* 31:[19] (Jan. 20, 1972); William L. Williamson, ed., *The Impact of the Public Law 480 Program on Overseas Acquisitions by American Libraries* (Madison: Univ. of Wisconsin Library School, 1968).

57. See "Cooperative Acquisitions Project," Library of Congress *Information Bulletin* [no vol. no.] 9 (Aug. 19–25, 1947); ibid., p. 7 (Nov. 11–18, 1947); ibid., p. 4 (Apr. 20–26, 1948); R. B. Downs, 'Report on the . . . Cooperative Acquisitions Project," ibid., 7–10 (Jan. 25–31, 1949).

58. Downs, p. 10.

59. Information in this section was derived mainly from the following (in chronological order): "American Book Center," *Special Libraries* 36:213–14 (July–Aug. 1945); Kenneth R. Shaffer, 'The American Book Center Makes Its Plans," *Library Journal* 70:671–72 (Aug. 1945); Laurence J. Kipp, "The American Book Center Reports Progress," *Library Journal* 72:14–16 (Jan. 1, 1947); "United States Book Exchange to Continue under Grant," *Library Journal* 74:184–85 (Feb. 1, 1949); Henry T. Drennan, "Cooperative Book Selection and Book Ordering," in Herbert Goldhor, ed., *Selection and Acquisition Procedures in Medium-sized and Large Libraries* (Champaign, Ill.: Illini Bookstore, 1963), p. 63; "Brief History of USBE," *Library Resources and Technical Services* 14:607–9 (Fall 1970); U.S. Book Exchange, *Operating Instructions* (Washington, D.C.: U.S. Book Exchange, Apr. 2, 1973); "United States Book Exchange, Inc.," in *Bowker Annual of Library and Book Trade Information*, 19th ed., (New York: Bowker, 1974), pp. 511–12; USBE *Newsletter* 27 (April 1975).

60. Information is drawn primarily from S. J. K. [Stanley J. Kunitz?], "A Li-

brary Book Club," *Wilson Bulletin for Librarians* 12:392–93 (Feb. 1938); S. J. K., "Comments on the Library Book Club Proposal," ibid., pp. 458–59 (Mar. 1938); Lila Stonemetz, "Hurrah for the Book Club!," ibid., p. 530 (Apr. 1938); "A Library Book Club," *Publishers Weekly* 133:1265–66 (Mar. 19, 1938).

61. "Library Promotion: An Adclub Seminar," *Publishers Weekly* 187:29 (Mar. 8, 1965).

62. However one defines *reprint*. Carol A. Nemeyer, in her comprehensive work on the subject, *Scholarly Reprint Publishing in the United States* (New York: Bowker, 1972), cites fourteen definitions of *reprint, facsimile,* and *type facsimile* (pp. 159–61). Most of the information given here about reprints derives from this source.

63. Melcher, "Two Decisive Decades," p. 812.

64. Richard DeGennaro, "Pay Libraries and User Charges," *Library Journal* 100:363 (Feb. 15, 1975). The author concludes somewhat plaintively with the refrain heard repeatedly from 1876 on, "We are allies, not adversaries; our interests are complementary, not competing" (p. 367).

16
The Image of Librarianship in the Media

NEAL L. EDGAR
Kent State University

Librarians, until very recently, have often remained neutral and passive on public issues. Although some statements from librarians did appear in the media, they tended to be scholarly or bland. Little could be said of the librarian as a cultural force. Although this is changing, the change is slow. For a change to be faster and meaningful, the profession must realize what its image is currently and relate that image to the condition surrounding professional practice.

This chapter addresses the images of librarianship in the nonlibrary media and relates them to problems raised by the journals of library science. And both contribute to an evaluation of the profession. The literature of librarianship is little known outside the library profession. How the nonlibrarian perceives the profession is shaped to some degree by statements made about it in the nonlibrary literature. Few of these statements come from librarians, a circumstance that tends to develop misunderstanding. Library literature is important as a facet of the profession, as is the attitude toward the profession held by those outside it, and both are blended in such a fashion that speaking of one require an examination of the other. Both measures should be involved in the profession's self-examination as the second century of the American Library Association begins. But this study can only emphasize the second.

304 / *Environment*

SOME GENERAL CONSIDERATIONS

The major measure of librarianship in this brief study is the "image" of the library in nonlibrary media, one measure of the library in this case being the librarian. First, it should be recognized that the image of the librarian, like many other images, is a stereotype, and as such does violence to reality. Second, space allows for only a small sampling of what nonlibrarians consider the image of librarians to be; but perhaps, they will not be too biased.

The sources used to establish the image will be newspapers, magazines, advertisements, and broadcast media; and a few other means of communication. Before analyzing these media, the stage should be set by considering half a dozen other sources for parts of the image. Although some of them are not "media" per se, they do form a part of the picture and a platform from which to examine the media themselves.

Perhaps a first question is, "Are librarians professionals?" Some recognized measures for a profession do exist in the literature of sociology: a system of licensing, some widely accepted groups of standards and systematic theory, a strong and enforced code of ethics, some form of self-regulation with effective sanctions attached, colleague performance evaluations, professional education, organizations which oversee some of the hallmarks of the profession, and a literature. To the observer and the practitioner alike librarianship clearly lacks many of these, perhaps most. And this vacuum tends to be a part of the popular image.

A second observation is that the U.S. librarian seems to have slipped below the level of esteem his or her European counterpart enjoys, and which he or she enjoyed one hundred years or more ago. One reason for this might relate to education for the profession. Although some other professions require an education lasting from two to four years or more, librarians usually qualify for a master's degree in a year and a summer or some such combination. Much of the preparation is theoretical, not practical; and many graduates cannot perform adequately in a job situation without undergoing considerable on-the-job training. These characteristics of the training seem to some to be mediocre preparation. Justified or not, the public impression of the new library school graduate is that of a person not well-prepared to run a library, let alone produce its literature.

Still another view is provided by a survey of popular images of librarians held by students.[1] Over half the impressions were negative, one-third were positive, and the rest were neutral. The negative terms included: eccentric, frustrated, inhibited, and intolerant. And this was a survey of students, a group with fairly high library contact.

A dozen books, published mostly in the 1970s, on mass media and higher education hardly mention libraries. One 312-page, 1974 book on public higher education in California includes one sentence which names five university research activities in forty-three words. Only one of these activities is the library.[2] Perhaps twelve books do not comprise a good statistical sample, but at least the choice was random. The lack of concern for the library in these books constitutes a strong, disturbing statement. Not recognizing the library as an essential aspect of higher education says a great deal about these authors' attitudes toward the library.

Another revelation about the library in education appears when the academic budget is examined. What should be the center of the academic financial circle receives little more than a token portion. And this seems true for academic libraries at all levels, as well as for public and special libraries. Clearly, this is another area worth separate attention.

The American Association of University Professors (AAUP) has only recently admitted librarians to membership. The controversy on rank and status of librarians as faculty is another indication that at least some educators do not consider librarians eligible to be members of this group. Within many academic institutions, the responsibility of serving as departmental representative to the library is reserved for the newer, the older, or at times the least effective department member, the one who needs a job and still hangs on because of tenure. What a comment on the library that is! Frequently, the department which complains about the library sabotages its own relationships with an ill-considered assignment.

Because only a very few of the media considered in this examination date back to 1876, this chapter is divided into types of media, not time periods. Any one of the media touched on here could be the basis of an extensive study on attitudes toward libraries and librarians.

NEWSPAPERS

The earliest sustained column devoted to library news was written by Asa Wynkoop for the *New York Evening Post*.[3] Called "The Librarian," its statistics and general library news did not seem popular, but did set a trend. In the early twentieth century newspaper reporting about libraries was usually supplied by librarians. One outstanding example, possibly inspired by Asa Wynkoop, is "The Librarian," by Edmund Lester Pearson, who wrote 734 columns published on Wednesdays in the *Boston Evening Transcript* from March 28, 1906 until May 26, 1920. His articles ranged from statistics extracted from library reports to the activities of the satirical Exra Beesly Free Public Library of Baxter. Although Pearson was a librarian, he published in the nonlibrary newspaper press. He was a strongly conservative thinker who criticized many of the procedures of libraries. His column angered many librarians and probably created an image standing somewhat to one side of the real picture.

306 / Environment

Pearson had detractors, but he also had imitators. Among them were columnist Malcolm W. Bayley who appeared in the *Louisville Times* in 1913 and the anonymous author of "The Librarian's Corner" in the *New York Sun* in 1918. The *Christian Science Monitor* had two such series: "Libraries and Librarians" in 1918 and "The Library Alcove," by Sam Walter Foss, which was published from October 6, 1909 up to March 1, 1911.

The library columns in newspapers by men such as Pearson and Foss were a type and in a style which no longer exists. Pearson's column continued until 1936, written by others, but it lacked Pearson's spark. After its death in 1936, this type of general coverage of library news was sharply reduced. Since that time, serious library coverage in the newspaper press has been limited, in Norman Stevens's words, to "censorship controversies, new buildings, or large bequests."

One syndicated columnist of the 1970s who is a friend of the library is Sydney J. Harris. His column, "Strictly Personal," has frequently spoken up for libraries and librarians. And he has done this with perception, intelligence, and an understanding of the roles of both the library and the librarian in our culture and society. But his column seems to be one of the very few exceptions. That is not to say that other columns are negative; they simply have not been discussing libraries and their functions.

The same does not always hold true for all writers of articles which mention librarians. The librarian appears in phrases such as: "in his baggy uniform . . . he looked more . . . like a librarian," or "looks like Maureen O'Hara in Librarian's glasses." Letters to authors of such phrases generally are unanswered. Perhaps the authors are not serious, or perhaps they are simply using a common image.

The Brooklyn Public Library devotes time and energy to public relations through its director of public relations, Irene E. Moran.[4] She relates that Brooklyn's twenty or so weekly papers print practically everything sent in by the main library as well as by the branches. Few communities can claim such high performance. And, naturally, there are catches. The big New York dailies treat foreign countries with more respect than they do their neighbors across the East River. However, there is an exception to that: if stories arise which focus on vandalism or a reduction of hours, a reporter may appear. One of the library's contacts is "an old-time police reporter who is constantly after the crime-type stories, like discipline problems, robberies, vandalism, etc." Television coverage in one period, according to Moran, was limited to a film clip on the book protection system. In November 1974 Irene Moran believed that, "Our 'image' is obviously still that of a silence-shrouded repository of knowledge—at least among the media people."

Newspaper stories constantly refer to the "library worker," and the number of stories with inaccuracies and misinformation is legion. The stories show a basic ignorance of the field of librarianship. The impression is strong that the writers simply have not asked, and perhaps asking a question of a librarian as their stories developed simply did not occur to the authors.

MAGAZINES

Partly as a substitute for the lack of a professional literature in the late nineteenth century, articles about libraries frequently appeared in literary magazines. Charles A. Cutter wrote editorial notes for the *Nation*. Also, periodicals made other attempts to keep readers informed.

In retrospect the coverage in magazines was uneven. One 1864 article on U.S. libraries described the American Antiquarian Society, the Boston Athenaeum, the Redwood Library in Newport, and a half-dozen other major collections but failed to mention the Library of Congress.[5] Perhaps the idea of a national library had not yet been realized.

As was true for the newspapers, magazines covered the library meetings of 1853 and 1876 quite well. The Columbian Exposition was news in 1893, and the library meetings held there were covered. Norton's *Literary Gazette*, the *Nation*, and the *Dial* also treated all of these meetings as information of importance to society at large. The *New Republic*, a literary journal with a wide audience, established in 1914, contained a scattering of news and information about librarians from its beginning. If the articles were critical, they were not carping, and they were often helpful. One such editorial position of the *New Republic* was that state governments should subsidize libraries and fund statewide library systems. But such items were not numerous. An informal survey of the *Readers' Guide* in recent years indicates that the vast majority of references to librarianship are to the professional literature, with most of the rest being found in only a few titles.

Some formal studies have been done. For example, in 1952 Eunice Wilson examined several hundred articles which discussed library service in broad terms in 167 nonlibrary periodicals. The image of librarianship was not specifically treated or analyzed.[6] Perhaps this examination needs to be undertaken again.

Various viewpoints on libraries and librarianship can also be found. A recent dialogue on academics and athletics begins with, "I think every dollar you put into an intercollegiate athletic program that could have gone into books for the library ... has to be looked at very hard."[7] *Playboy*, despite the denial of its editorial librarian, has had at least one librarian as a Playmate.[8] And in an otherwise sensible 1973 article on children's books, an anonymous author refers to "nervous librarians" reacting to the newer Sendak illustrations by doctoring them a bit, and personifies one of the librarians as Mrs. Grundy.[9]

Also, there is the banal (vintage 1946):

308 / Environment

> Apparently, men don't go for brainy wives. Take a look at women physicians, scientists, and lawyers. Their marriage odds are near the bottom of the roster, only slightly above school teachers, who, low in prospects, are out-old-maided by only women librarians, who get fewer proposals than women in any other profession. If you want to get yourself married, don't be scientific or technical. And above all, stay out of the library.[10]

It can therefore be stated that reaction to librarianship is mixed. Although articles on, and mentions of, librarians and libraries appear in magazines, they are not frequent; of the two, libraries seem to have a somewhat more favorable image than librarians. But there is no great interest in the library nor is there respect for its importance. Again, in the words of Norman Stevens, scholarly journals in other disciplines limit library news to "matters of common concern such as copyright and the proliferation of journals."

When any library decides to add a journal title to its collection, it frequently pays an institutional charge, often many times higher than an individual's rate, probably to counter for lost subscriptions. Another recent development is a renewed postal service enforcement of its definition of a periodical in relationship to second-class mailing privileges. Both of these money-raising ideas have understandable rationales, but both also seem based, in part, on an image of the library. This image probably includes the concept of the library as a passive institution which will not fight back.

LITERATURE

The most obvious place to look for the image of the librarian is in literature. Some of this research has already been done. One brief list by Agnes Greer appeared in 1935: the eleven titles indicate that librarians appeared simply because they happened to be needed as characters in the plot.[11] In addition, libraries themselves have issued cognate lists. They vary from a short group of titles on a library-related topic to somewhat more serious bibliographies.

In a substantial analysis, Lucille Long found the picture of librarians in some literature not based on fact, and in fact not true.[12] In general, the librarians she identifies appear as images of authority, as enforcers, and at times, as comic relief. Often, the librarian is not presented in a vital, interesting way. Generally, she (!) is an old maid, lacking style, taste, charm, and the will to compete, but having high morals, virtue, gentility, a scholarly mind, little training, and less salary. Importantly, the librarian protects books from people.

At least three other master's theses have listed literary works which feature librarians in one way or another.[13] Taken together, they analyze some 200 titles: novels, short stories, poetry, plays, and some essays. These theses take a stab at statistical analysis with some focus on the characteristics, physical and psychological, that each librarian displays. The results are predictable: librarians are people. Although they may lead quieter lives than football players, they are not, as a group, negative. Rather, they are merely characters used to enhance a plot, seldom being cast in a negative role as the butt of a joke or for derogatory purposes.

An article published in 1974 by Julian Moynahan mentioned eighteen novels which feature librarians in some role.[14] Moynahan's intent was to explore the image without a serious attempt at evaluation. But evaluation would not display the librarian as a figure exercising power, even where librarians are described with sophistication.

Quotations, too, can be found to praise librarianship, but there is more praise for the library than the librarian. A few at random are: "librarianship is one of the few callings in the world for which it is still possible to feel unqualified admiration and respect";[15] "What we are most pleased with in our western civilization is found largely on shelves and is held together by buckram binding";[16] "I never would have comprehended the total frustration of college without the four-story undergraduate library, a sterile, glass-enclosed cage fronted by a gravel-pit lawn";[17] and "Public libraries should be efficient. They are places to which you go to get useful but uninteresting information."[18]

A 1975 contribution by Katherine M. Heylman analyzes twenty-two juvenile books published from 1932 to 1973, which include portraits of twenty-five librarians. The examination reveals that

> the librarian in children's books is female (24 to 1), young (11 to 6), either married or likely to become so (10 to 5), attractive (13 to 3), has a positive attitude toward patrons (22 to 3), and presents a generally positive image (19 to 2). All neutrals, "indeterminates," and "so-so's" are omitted.[19]

The image in these children's books is more flattering than that found in the adult books and perhaps better than the average stereotype of some other groups. One of the books, incidentally, *Rufus M*, contains what may possibly be the most amusing scene set in a library anywhere in literature.

A poem by Leonard Randolph speaks eloquently of one man's attitude toward a librarian and what he learned from her: "She was a shy woman, a stereotype of the librarian the ALA would ultimately deny. . . . She was always there when I needed her to make me feel at home among books. . . . She had a reverence for the printed word. And she loved the feel of a beautiful book."[20]

TELEVISION

In 1963 an episode in "The Defenders" series had a librarian defending censorship. In 1973 "The Other Woman" was aired on ABC. In *TV*

Guide the program was described in a fairly normal way on one page, but on another the lead, a librarian, was described as an ugly duckling.[21]

Television has used librarians in both commercials and dramas. The networks carry many programs, and a great number of occupations would naturally be portrayed in the long hours of this sort of broadcasting. Many different trades and professions are shown in many lights and from many viewpoints. Some librarians feel that their particular profession has been shown in a consistent manner over the years, one that is, to say the least, gray. All four networks were asked to respond to this feeling. Two did not answer the inquiry. One sent a printed, dear-viewer type of card which said simply, "We are unable to fulfill your request." The one network which did respond declared that it had "no set policy guiding creative or executive personnel," and even more astonishingly asserted that "a comedy or drama character is never a statement of position and certainly not meant to be a stereotype."[22]

ADVERTISEMENTS

Advertisements frequently use actors to portray the trusting souls in the world who must wash clothes, buy cars, dye their hair, or whatever else the advertisers are trying to get the listeners or readers to do. The actors usually portray types of people, who, by their uncritical acceptance of the ads' statements, often appear gullible and stupid. The ads stereotype both people and occupations. Among the occupations represented are librarians. Some examples even achieved special attention and a bit of newspaper coverage. Nabisco's Chipsters were eaten by a persimmon-mouthed librarian; American Motors's Javelin was supposed to scare librarians; Ex-Lax was alleged to be recommended by a librarian; *Intellectual Digest* pictured a "librarian" with a stamp firmly clenched in her teeth; McDonald's has a hair-in-a-bun type stamping a book with a vicious swipe of her date-due stamp; and the gentleman should have offered a Tiparillo to the librarian!

Most of the advertisements featuring or mentioning librarians do so with some negative implications. It might not always be possible or realistic to show the all-American type who is good, clean, and upholds all the tenets of the scouting oath. A few can have faults. But all of any type should not be poorly represented. When other groups are shown in a bad light, some letters or other reaction often results. Usually, a retraction follows. This did happen with some of the unfavorable ads published in the early 1970s, but not always. In most cases, the manufacturers ignored the objections of librarians and ALA. That, in itself, is a statement on image.

One firm which sells coats-of-arms designed to be ego-building and "decorative" moved into a house formerly used by a library and began sending out letters signed by an employee. After doing some market research, the firm discovered that many customers had visions of a "little, gray-haired lady in a library" who did all the research herself and who licked the stamps. The firm decided to maintain the image as one which would foster sales.

A potentially poor image of the library results from the advertising produced for books from the Disney empire. A 1976 mailed-to-the-home advertisement from "Disney's Wonderful World of Reading" should have given second thoughts to the commercial firms who are mentioned in the ad. Of course librarians, and some others, know that Disney did not really create Pinocchio, Cinderella, and Bambi, but most people exposed to Disney advertising garner the impression that these and other characters are Disney originals.

The stories produced by Disney bear little resemblance to the originals, and perhaps the omission of the real authors' names is a service to their memories and reputations. The advertisement says, "Let the Disney magic of Disney characters help your child to *love reading on his own!*" As the characters exist in Disney they are Disney's, but the impression can be otherwise on those who receive the ad.

One part of the advertisement reads:

> Leading educators tell us there comes a time during these early years when parents can help their children's reading most simply by their general attitude towards books and reading, and by recommending suitable books and making them available. It isn't always necessary to sit and read to your child in order to stimulate reading! DISNEY'S WONDERFUL WORLD OF READING is just the kind of program these educators are referring to. . . .

The advertisement contains many other loaded statements, for example, "Clearly, it would take many long hours of tiresome shopping through bookstores in order to find even a few books that might—or might not—suit your child's reading needs." Why "tiresome"? And where is the library in all of this? Not mentioned. Not even a hint. Perhaps it's poetic justice that the "Special Bonus Gift" is a FREE Mickey Mouse Book Rack! The term "junk mail" may be offensive and inaccurate in some cases, but here, from the librarian's viewpoint, the nail is hit squarely on the head.

CARTOONS

The library and librarian are frequently the victim of cartoonists. Hardly ever is the humor anything other than teasing and spoofing. And sometimes the humor points to services offered by librarians, thus acting as a public relations tool. No one should resent being made fun of, especially in a witty way, and if librarians are in fact made the point of cartoons, they should obtain copies, frame them, and hang them up where everyone can enjoy them. Librarians should rejoice in the knowledge that these cartoonists feel that librarians can take a little jab now and then.

A few examples may be amusing. Conversation: "I understand you come from a small town. How small was it?" "The public library was a big-little book." Wife to a husband in four-way traction: "Here's a card from the public library. . . . your book 'Roof Repairs Made Easy' is two weeks overdue." Two generous-sized ladies in a library, one to the other, "It's a book you're really going to love! It's called 'Fat Is Beautiful'." Three youngsters standing in the school hall looking at a door with a new sign which reads, Media Center, "Just when I learn to spell 'library' they change its name." And then there is the non-cartoon comment by Sydney Harris, "A Learning Resources Center is a library that finagled federal funds." Dennis the Menace has a number of confrontations with the library, usually resulting in his being tossed out. Perhaps one of the favorites of librarians is the series of *Peanuts*, drawn by Charles M. Shultz, recounting Charlie Brown's search for a library card. And then the whole Peanuts gang became involved when the school library banned Miss Helen Sweetstory's *Six Bunny-Wunnies Freak Out*.

CENSORSHIP

Still another reflection on the library is the whole area of censorship. How many groups have served as self-appointed, if not self-annointed, judges and have descended in one way or another on the library? Nearly always the matter of the librarian's judgment is involved, or at least the librarian's authority to build a collection is questioned. In the early 1960s, for example, federal agents tried to find out what Lee Harvey Oswald had read. It is to the everlasting credit of the librarians concerned that they refused to reveal the information. It happened again in the early 1970s when Treasury Department employees tried to discover who was reading what about Che Guevara. But librarians do not always fare so well or easily. From the time the first American newspaper, *Publick Occurrences*, was closed after one issue in 1690, up to yesterday, somewhere, someone is trying to expunge or expurgate something because that someone thinks he or she knows better than the librarian.

When the Supreme Court was pontificating on pornography, one of the tests created was the judgment of whether or not a work is "serious." But librarians are not to be the judges; librarians are not to be the arbiters. They probably were not excluded consciously. The court probably just did not consider the librarian as a possibility. But how does the censor define pornography when the Supreme Court cannot? What is a foul or filthy word? What is the pure position which will satisfy everyone as the philosophical basis from which to judge the radical or the cynical? How does the censor answer rational curiosity set afire by the artificial prohibition of some words or texts? The questions are endless. The librarian starts off on the defensive and unfortunately often loses. That the librarian is seldom used as an ally is a comment on what all sides think of the keeper of the books that others want destroyed.

The press in the 1970s frequently has carried stories of repressive actions against books and libraries. Some incidents involve whole communities and even some school systems in acrimonious debate with both sides seeking some form of control and neither side "winning." In these cases the librarian is often in the middle and, in an attempt at neutrality, can leave the impression of passivity.

ADDITIONAL CONSIDERATIONS

A few miscellaneous sources may add to the mosaic of the librarian's image.

Who hasn't heard of Marian the librarian? It's not too bad an image at that. One of the better movies is *Storm Center* in which Bette Davis plays a librarian who, while prim, hotly defends the freedom to circulate ideas and strongly describes the damage done to society when this freedom is abridged. And that isn't a bad image either. A winner of five awards is a charming, library-made film called *Fiction Friction* which is a view from the librarian's side of the desk. Another film, 30 years old, is *Adventure*. Although the librarian is prim, bespectacled, and single, she manages to tame the hero and bring him to bay.

In a 1953 study of the personality of librarians, Alice McKinley arrived at the conclusion that librarians are relatively homogeneous and that they manifest receptive traits more than aggressive traits.[23] Although the study was of library school students, it is safe to assume carry-over to the profession. It is interesting to note that McKinley uses the word "vocation"; likewise, it is interesting to note that no outstanding cluster of characteristics was discovered, especially not the negative ones.

A few words from our national library seem important. At the end of L. Quincy Mumford's tenure as Librarian of Congress, he should have an opportunity to distill his twenty years of service at the focal point of U.S. librarianship. He has summarized his relationship with Congress, saying:

> I have found the attitude of Congress sympathetic to the needs of librarians in general and of the Library of Congress in particular.... Members came to Washington aware of the service librarians render the public ... and see how the work of the Library of Congress affects ... libraries all over the country.[24]

He adds this, however, "As Librarian of Congress I have found that the attitudes of non-librarians toward the Library of Congress are as various as the number of non-librarians at large."

In the 1970s the National Commission on Libraries and Information Science worked to identify problem areas in the profession and to seek solutions where needed. In 1974 one project of the commission, completed by the Graduate Library School at Catholic University, reported on continuing education in library and information science.[25] The word *continuing* is important because the study does not deal with the basic graduate preparation. The commission issued its final report in 1975 along with its national program and goals for action.[26] Nothing was said in this report about the characteristics expected of the librarians who are to achieve the goals, the process of information development and communication—what might be called the literature of librarianship—or the structure of a librarian's basic education needed to implement the commission's program. Perhaps the report should have dealt with these specifics in order that it could have addressed some of the basic problems surrounding the library profession and its popular image.

CONCLUSION

Under present conditions a favorable image of the librarian may be impossible. Although professions have parameters, from a reading of the professional literature it would seem that librarianship has no limits in its attempts to satisfy the demands of those who have need of the profession's services. Not having limits does not mean that the occupation is not a profession; rather it means the occupation is a profession whose limits have not yet been defined, codified, or perhaps even perceived. It is also interesting that libraries are among the very few sources which commonly provide both sides of an issue, and books and magazines are still the major source of self-improvement. Yet they are not used in the United States and Canada as much as other media. The interesting paradox is that although the strength of the U.S. system is decentralization of control and support, it is the great weakness of libraries. Libraries lack the funds which seem to be available to support the other media which are more highly centralized and controlled.

Basic changes in the society which the library serves seem to indicate that the library must change. The urban centers are changing their make-up and structures. Street crime in and around the library and the lack of library parking or convenient public transportation also change the patterns of library use.

Still another icon of the librarian is status quo—not only the librarian's, but also the library's. The drive to serve all equally, sympathetically, and without bias adds to the protective coloration of the library. That is one of the ironies of equality: it is supposed to be equal for all, and can easily become nothing special to anyone. The attempt to achieve absolute equality for all, at least in terms of library service, then becomes a barrier to library service and creates yet another problem for the librarian. This type of arrangement may lead to a middle-of-the-road balance, a sort of bibliographical mugwumpery, in which, although most can find something, that something will be mainly bland. A further consequence is having little with which to disagree, and disagreement, or at least informed questioning, is the beginning of discovery.

Over and over again the professional literature has discussed the problems mentioned in the first volumes of *Library Journal*. That these problems still face librarians after a century of national organization suggests that librarians have not clearly identified them, or cannot articulate their perceptions, or perhaps have problems which are insoluble. The latter seems unacceptable, and if so, signals the need for solid, meaningful research on major problems in librarianship. One thing is clear: many solutions, if they exist, have not been published in the periodicals.

An examination of the professional literature of librarianship reveals the expected image: that of a qualified profession too little understood outside the ranks. Another dilemma of the profession's literature is a reflection of its attempt to be of service to all. If the journals remain neutral, they seem passive; if they take sides, they seem biased. If the journals do not express editorial opinions, they appear to have none; if they advocate one book, they may seem to dislike others. Impartiality ought not to be synonymous with objectivity and fairness. Every viewpoint does not warrant representation. Naturally enough, the middle-of-the-road approach may be taken as the lack of an opinion.

One reason is that, despite an available market, librarians tend not to write in the nonlibrary periodicals, except for the scholar-librarian publishing in his subject area or the dissenting librarian who tends to criticize the profession in a negative manner. An example of the latter is a 1974 article by Bonnie Collier in *Change* which attempts to describe and evaluate current library periodicals.[27] She asserts, among other things, that, "The journals librarians read serve to sketch a fair portrait of the profession," and that "librarians in academic libraries have been crusading . . . for years . . . that their professional concerns fundamentally correspond to the faculty's. If library literature is indicative, the proposition does not stand." Other articles which gore the profession can be found in places like the *AAUP Bulletin*. Constructive criticism quite clearly has its place; but when articles by librarians published in the nonlibrary press are negative, the majority of what nonlibrarians see contributes to a negative image.

Perhaps librarians' schedules are such that little time is available for the work needed to prepare for publication. However, the Public Relations Board discovered that being published in *American Libraries* was not mentioned as an important goal by those interviewed.[28] Robert Stueart reports a study done of the articles in the *PNLA Quarterly* which indicated that 27 percent of the articles in the journal were by nonlibrarians and that most of the rest were by academic librarians.[29]

Although this is only one library journal, one conclusion is that most professional writing is done by only one part of the profession, and most of it is limited to professional journals. Because library journals are almost unknown outside the profession, those outside the profession have little opportunity to learn what the profession is doing, except for the carping articles which do appear in the nonlibrary press.

The general attitude toward libraries and librarians which seems a characteristic of most media is probably not a conscious attempt to denigrate the library's role in society; rather it is circumstantial evidence of the lack of a strong, well-formulated attitude. Most writers are not aware of the role librarians play, even if they are heavy consumers of library services. Perhaps the positive image of the librarian in children's literature results from the author's own positive library experiences.

Librarians need to organize for a strong, professional, public relations program to sell libraries as any other service is currently sold in the market place. The protective coloration of neutrality will no longer do. Sue Fontaine received a Council on Library Resources grant to examine the public relations in selected libraries.[30] Her survey concerns approaches to media and publicity, media relationships, and effective public relations and publicity techniques for mass media. Work to foster in the media a new concept of librarians, especially in hitherto unrecognized roles librarians are playing, has indeed begun in public and school libraries. At the very beginning of her survey Fontaine found good media images in several cities which had hired professional media people rather than librarians to handle public relations. In these cases the director was personally active in becoming visible in the community. At the outset it became apparent that a good, positive image relates to a well-run public relations campaign. When librarians are not public relations oriented or skilled, they should use the talents of those who are trained in advertising and marketing. Why librarians do not use this tool in a wider sense remains a mystery. Manufactured products and commercial services "sell" by advertising campaigns, and many are well done; some are even informative. Except for occasional television and radio spots and a few booklists, information about any library is found infrequently in the mass media. Why? Perhaps because of the nature of librarians.

In 1950 Norman Cousins wrote a compelling plea for the public support of libraries, saying, in part, "One thing seems certain: public library service in the United States cannot carry on much longer without major reinforcements."[31] Although the 1960s did bring some federal assistance, it was not long-lasting or stable and was treated as a political pawn.

On the other hand, one Ohio newspaper, in a 1976 opinion poll, asked if the government should offer more aid to financially troubled public libraries. The answers were 70 percent in favor saying things like "the public library is one of the greatest facilities we have" and "A good library is one of the most important social influences in a community."[32]

Over a century ago, Samuel Benjamin, himself a librarian, held that "most libraries are either pleasing to the eye and unsuited to the purpose for which they were erected, or conveniently planned and contrary to the rules of good taste."[33] Some observers of the library architecture scene would hold that not much has changed in a century of library building. Benjamin also felt, "There is only one way entirely to obviate the difficulty: the architect should be at once a librarian and architect. . . ." How many library buildings in a century have been built on the basis of harmonious cooperation between librarian and architect? Rather too few. And here also is a view of the librarian and his abilities as a planner.

One other building controversy involves the Madison Building of the Library of Congress. The whole series of squabbles says volumes about congressional attitudes toward libraries in general, and the not-overwhelming defense of the Library by librarians may also say something about the profession itself. What will the resolution of this be as the profession starts its second century?

Change is needed in other ways as well. Local support has as many variations as there are libraries. Poor appointments to library boards also cannot help, and often obviously hinder, library operation and growth. Professional education might change its emphasis or at least make some new things available. For all of these and more, the only real answer is money; and the only probable source is federal funding. But first must come a course of action from within the profession to change some of the aspects of the profession.

One example of hope for the future is ALA's Office for Library Personnel Resources.[34] This office is producing some attractive, eye-catching, and innovative materials geared toward attracting young, fresh, talented people to the profession.

In the vast literature written by visitors to the United States, one picture frequently presented has local citizens asking how the visitor "likes" the United States. A psychologist might say this action reveals a national insecurity; so also with librarians in their own literature. Dozens of articles have appeared asking if librarians are mice, nice, people, polite, and other things. In 1974 Margaret Bingham Stillwell, one of the more respected scholar-librarians, published her fascinating memoir, *Librarians Are Human*. What else? Should anyone for an instant think otherwise? Yet that title expresses what must be a widely held sense of professional inferiority. If the profession itself has this self-image, others will perforce follow along, agree, and transform it into a definition before long. Librarians are not in a strong position to argue against an image they themselves helped construct.

The Public Relations Board's communications audit has suggested many areas for improvement. A major effort should be made through "an information bank, the development of adequate press lists, and by media." Several examples are given for the development of a better image by using nonlibrary periodicals to publish

> more long-range features. *McCalls* is into oral history; *House Beautiful* wants to cover things the citizen can do to help libraries locally; *Women's Day* is covering continuing education in libraries; and, as you might expect, *Cosmopolitan* is fighting for lib on the library scene, too.[35]

These seem to be signs of a change in attitude on the part of many magazines outside the library sphere.

All in all, the totality of the image in all the media at the centennial mark seems more bad than good. And the fault lies with the librarian. The literature of librarianship needs revamping, and maybe the image of the librarian needs a little vamping. A change is occurring, but it needs concerted and organized encouragement.

Oscar Handlin remarked that "the library will strengthen its demand for support by clarifying its own function and by retooling for the job new conditions have created."[36] That was certainly true in 1964. Twelve years afterward, the demand for support has not become strong, and the profession badly needs a clarification of its function. The later seventies and beyond will make available a vast new array of tools for the profession. It is up to the librarians to make fuller and better use of library and nonlibrary media alike in changing the image of the library and in developing ways for all libraries to fulfill their roles in U.S. and Canadian society.

One image problem libraries and librarians have yet to deal with, but must in the decades after 1976, will develop from a combination of forces including a new copyright act, organizations such as the Authors League of America, and the copying syndrome. Surely librarians will have to deal with copying, and librarians have an opportunity to act decisively in leading the way toward a reasonable solution to the problem.

A century ago the public library survey remarked, "The influence of the librarian as an educator is rarely estimated by outside observers, and probably seldom fully realized even by himself."[37] Not much has changed for librarians or libraries in a century of change in other areas. If librarians and libraries are to change before 2076, librarians should take to heart the words of Porky, a friend of Pogo, who once remarked, "We have met the enemy, and he is us."

NOTES

1. William H. Form, "Popular Images of Librarians," *Library Journal* 71:851–55 (June 15, 1946).
2. Neil J. Smelzer and Gabriel Almond, eds., *Public Higher Education in California* (Berkeley: Univ. of California Pr., 1974).

3. Norman D. Stevens, "Newspaper Columns on Libraries," typescript. This and other references to the late nineteenth- and early twentieth-century newspapers are based on the Stevens article, correspondence with him, and thoughts his ideas have suggested.
4. Irene E. Moran, director of public relations, Brooklyn Public Library, New York. Letter to the author, November 21, 1974.
5. Samuel Greene Wheeler Benjamin, "Libraries," *Harper's New Monthly Magazine* 29:482–88 (Sept. 1864).
6. Eunice C. Wilson, "Study of Articles on Librarianship in Non-Library Periodicals from 1947 through 1951" (Master's diss., Atlanta University, 1953).
7. "Academics vs. Athletics," *College and University Business* 55:15 (Sept. 1973).
8. *Playboy*. Citations and names are available, but added publicity here seems pointless.
9. "A Happy Year to Be Grimm," *Time* 102:102 (Dec. 10, 1973).
10. Judith Chase Churchill, "Your Chances of Getting Married," *Good Housekeeping* 123:314 (Oct. 1946).
11. Agnes Greer, "The Librarian in Fiction," *Wilson Library Bulletin* 9:317–18 (Feb. 1935).
12. Lucille Eileen Long. "The Stereotyped Librarian as Portrayed in Modern American Belles-Lettres" (Master's diss., Kent State University, 1957).
13. Ruby Othella Denman, "Librarianship as Revealed in Seven Recent Teen-Age Career Books" (Master's diss., Texas State College for Women, 1954); Mary Kirkpatrick, "American and Foreign Fictional Librarians: A Comparison" (Master's diss., Western Reserve University, 1958); Margaret Ann Nation, "The Librarian in the Short Story: An Analysis and Appraisal" (Master's diss., Florida State University, 1954).
14. Julian Moynahan, "Libraries and Librarians: Novels and Novelists," *American Libraries* 5:550–53 (Nov. 1974).
15. Joyce Maxtone-Grahame, *Pocketful of Pebbles* (New York: Harcourt, Brace, 1946), p. 397.
16. Jacques Barzun, *Teaching in America* (Boston: Little, 1945), p. 61.
17. Roger Rapoport and Laurence J. Kirshbaum, *Is the Library Burning?* (New York: Random, 1969), p. 10.
18. Joyce Kilmer, "The Inefficient Library," in Robert Cortes Holliday, *Joyce Kilmer* 2:54 (New York: Doran, 1918).
19. Katherine M. Heylman, "Librarians in Juvenile Literature," *School Library Journal* 21:25–28 (May 1975).
20. Leonard Randolph, *Scar Tissue* (Washington, D.C.: Some of Us Pr., 1973), pp. 50–52.
21. *TV Guide* (Cleveland ed.) 21:A58, 61 (Dec. 1, 1973).
22. "Audience Services" of one of the networks whose name is omitted here to protect the guilty to the author, November 18, 1974.
23. Alice Roberts McKinley, "Personality and the Choice of Librarianship as a Vocation" (Master's diss., Western Reserve University, 1953).
24. L. Quincy Mumford, then Librarian of Congress, to the author, December 31, 1974.
25. *Continuing Library and Information Science Education*, Final report to the National Commission on Libraries and Information Science, May 1974 (Washington, D.C.: Govt. Print. Off., 1975).
26. U.S. National Commission on Libraries and Information Science, *Toward a National Program for Library and Information Services: Goals for Action* (Washington, D.C.: Govt. Print. Off., 1975).
27. Bonnie Collier, "The Library Journals: Putting Things in Order," *Change* 6:59–61 (May 1974).

28. Roger D. Isaacs, Presentation to the American Library Association, January 24, 1975, summarizing a communications audit conducted for ALA by the Public Relations Board, Inc. Unpublished and untitled document in typescript furnished by Peggy Barber, director, ALA Public Information Office, 1975.

29. Robert D. Stueart, 'Writing the Journal Article," typescript of a conference presentation supplied to the author, 1975.

30. Sue Fontaine, information officer, Tulsa City-County Library System, Tulsa, Oklahoma to the author in 1974.

31. Norman Cousins, "Save the Libraries," in his *Present Tense* (New York: McGraw, 1967), pp. 157–61.

32. "Let's Have It," *Akron Beacon-Journal* (Jan. 14, 1976).

33. Benjamin, p. 487.

34. Marilyn Salazar, minority recruitment specialist in ALA's Office for Library Personnel Resources, to the author, September 6, 1974. She provided information and materials designed to create career visibility.

35. Isaacs, p. 8.

36. Oscar Handlin, "Libraries and Learning," *Atlantic* 213:105 (Apr. 1964).

37. U.S. Bureau of Education, *Public Libraries in the United States of America* (Washington, D.C.: Govt. Print. Off., 1876), p. xi.

17
Services to Library Life Abroad

VIVIAN D. HEWITT
Carnegie Endowment for International Peace

In September 1877 thirteen U.S. librarians boarded the steamship, *Devonia*, as it prepared to leave New York on the return passage of its maiden voyage from Great Britain. This group was also engaged in a maiden effort for it was the first official delegation of the newly formed American Library Association to an international meeting of librarians. Heading the delegation and first up the gangplank was Justin Winsor, ALA's first president, 1876–85, librarian of the Boston Public Library, 1868–77, and librarian of Harvard University, 1877–97.

Second in command of these "seafaring librarians" was William Frederick Poole, a founder and the vice-president of ALA, also well-known as the compiler of an author/title index to periodical articles, which by manipulating titles furnished considerable "subject" access.

The third ranking member of the delegation was Lloyd Pearsall Smith, librarian of Benjamin Franklin's famous Library Company of Philadelphia.

Next were two librarians of equal prominence: Charles Ammi Cutter, whose two great advocacies, the card catalog and the dictionary arrangement, were being widely discussed in both Great Britain and America; and Melvil Dewey, who had devised a scheme of subject classification based on the metric system, was managing editor of the *American Library Journal*, first issued in September 1876, and was also a prime mover in the organization of the American Library Association.

In addition to those already introduced, delegates aboard the *Devonia* included: Charles Evans of the Indianapolis Public Library; **Annie R.**

Godfrey, Wellesley College Library; Samuel Swett Green, librarian of the Public Library of Worcester, Massachusetts; Reuben Aldridge Guild, Brown University librarian; Frederick Jackson, Public Library, Newton, Massachusetts; Cornelia B. Olmstead, Wadsworth Library, Geneseo, New York; P. T. W. Rogers, Fletcher Library, Burlington, Vermont; and J. Tingley, Allegheny College, Meadville, Pennsylvania. This outstanding group was joined in London by three other distinguished librarians, W. L. Ropes of Andover Theological Seminary Library, Alexander Sands of Cincinnati, Ohio, and the Rev. Thomas Vickers, librarian of the Cincinnati Public Library, making a total of sixteen American representatives.[1]

On Tuesday morning, October 2, 1877, after assembling in the lecture hall of the London Institute, the Conference of Librarians organized itself first by electing officers. The slate reflected the international character of the meeting: John Winter Jones, librarian of the British Museum, was elected president. Three of the ten vice-presidencies went to U.S. librarians: Justin Winsor, William F. Poole, and Lloyd P. Smith. The other vice-presidencies went to representatives of the United Kingdom (three), France (two), Belgium (one), and Italy (one). Six from the United States, Cutter, Dewey, Evans, Green, Guild, and Jackson, were elected to the twenty-one-member council, the others being British (twelve) and French (three). Thus nine of the sixteen U.S. delegates were chosen for official positions. As Budd Gambee has remarked, John Winter Jones lost no time in paying tribute to his transatlantic colleagues. In the very first paragraph of his opening address to the assembled group, he graciously declared that the "idea of holding a Conference of Librarians originated in America—in that country of energy and activity. . . ."[2]

More importantly, however, the conference provided the opportunity for librarians to compare the growing library systems in Great Britain, France, Italy, Belgium, and the United States, and for Dewey and Cutter to present their cataloging methods. Although the delegates argued about whether or not works of fiction ought to be included in public library collections and about library design and construction, all present seemed to recognize that library services bore many similarities no matter where they are located. Professional cooperation, the delegates agreed, should disregard national boundaries. The British librarians volunteered to help with *Poole's Index to Periodical Literature*. U.S. librarians, in turn, helped their British confreres to organize the Library Association of the United Kingdom. The *American Library Journal* dropped the limiting word *American* from its name and also became the organ of the Library Association. E. B. Nicholson, the librarian of the London Institution and the person who had called the conference, became the English corresponding editor; H. R. Teddler, librarian of the Athenaeum Club, London, became the general European editor.[3]

Although it was not officially designated as an "international" conference, the 1877 meeting was a landmark in the history of international library relations and only the first of many in which U.S. librarians played an influential role. Less than a year old at the time of the meeting, ALA had already begun to accept an international responsibility. In the years since then, librarians from the United States have advocated abroad several concepts that they believe to be crucial: libraries for the use of every class of readers, as distinct from libraries for the intellectual elite. They have argued for libraries for the public-at-large and for the freedom of access to the library's holdings. They have promoted open-shelf collections allowing the user to browse and to choose for himself. They have urged the abolition of fees for readers and borrowers alike, and the taking of books to readers by multiplication of branches in urban communities. Most recently U.S. librarians have demonstrated to colleagues abroad how bookmobiles can carry the benefits of learning to people in rural sections in many parts of the world. Their efforts have had an impact for both change and improvement from 1877 until today.[4]

Reciprocally, U.S. libraries and librarianship from their very inception have benefited a great deal from librarians' experiences overseas. Justin Winsor, Melvil Dewey, Charles A. Cutter, and others traveled to Europe and were keenly aware of what could be borrowed, adapted, and utilized from their observations of the libraries they visited.

Justin Winsor visited France in 1893 and came back impressed with French administrative techniques. In an article for the *Atlantic Monthly* he argued for centralized administration of libraries based on the model of the Franklin Society of Paris.[5]

> There can be no question, from the experience of the Société Franklin, that judicious paternal supervision over a large circle of dependent libraries, as scattered as they are in the French provinces, can yield many advantages, both financial and administrative, to each library in the circle . . . and subject primarily to its central discipline. The many small libraries scattered through the length and breadth of France are its absolute creatures.[6]

Winsor looked to the accomplishments of the Franklin Society both in the saving of money and in the perfection of methods to assess the advantages, both possible and likely.

> A central station of control amasses experience . . . far beyond what is possible in a single small library.
>
> Such a station can furnish material appliances for library service, made on approved patterns, and, being manufactured or bought in large quantities, at less cost.
>
> The same chance for better advantages would accrue in the purchase of books in large quantities.

> The cataloguing of such books, once done, would suffice for all libraries in the circle, and the same printed lists would serve equally well in all, each library inserting its own shelf-marks where it has the books.[7]

Winsor saw no reason why central control could not be effectively applied to U.S. libraries. Pointing out the difficulty of deciding upon the proportion of expenditure to be maintained between reference and other expensive books, and those of "a low cost and merely pastime character," he saw no reason why a central agency should not amass a collection of more costly books, to be sent to one library or another on loan, as occasion might require.[8]

The Franklin Society of Paris, whose central administration so impressed Justin Winsor, developed as effective an "operation out-reach" program as is known today. It had been started in 1862 by M. Girard, a French printer who had risen from poverty to a position of sufficient leisure and means to be able to attend courses of the Conservatory of Arts and Trades. Girard educated himself at the lectures and thought so highly of the privilege that he wanted to extend it throughout France by establishing a conservatory in every city. That idea was impractical. The professors would not leave Paris to teach in the hinterlands. But their books could travel. Thus, Girard decided that the way to spread knowledge among the common people was to establish a system of popular libraries throughout France like the library company organized by Benjamin Franklin in Philadelphia. He therefore organized the Société Franklin pour la Propagation des Bibliothèques Populaires to raise funds and implement his dream with some of its libraries sustained by subscriptions of one cent a month from school children.

The Franklin Society spent its money well. It published a catalog of books of moderate price suited to the reading of children and workmen to facilitate selection by the country school teachers, often unpaid librarians, who could neither choose well from booksellers' catalogs nor afford a journey to Paris. The society sponsored book talks once or twice a week. Excerpts from interesting books would be selected and read to audiences in society libraries. The reader was not to finish the story but to leave the listeners with their curiosities awakened and unsatisfied and eager to take the book from the library.[9] This invention of the Franklin Society program may have been a source of "book talks" as they are known in the United States and elsewhere today.

Despite all of its good points, the model of the Franklin Society of Paris became a source of debate among librarians in the United States. Following the Franklin Society example, Charles Ammi Cutter, originator of the card catalog system, hoped that the United States would not be backward in providing collections of books by which education received in its public schools would be confirmed and continued. At the same time, however, Cutter was well aware that autocratic control from a central headquarters was in many ways undesirable in a U.S. community accustomed to local autonomy.[10]

In the years that followed, other U.S. librarians visited Europe, bringing back suggestions on how both U.S. and foreign libraries could be strengthened and improved. Notable among these observers of the foreign scene were Professor E. C. Mitchell, librarian of the Chicago Theological Seminary, and, of course, Melvil Dewey.

Professor Mitchell wrote:

> It has been my privilege to visit most of the principal libraries of the old world; my object in doing so was chiefly to see what they contain in the department of biblical literature and criticism. At the same time, it was natural for a practical librarian to take some notice of the appliances for convenience and the methods of management, and to look for hints in regard to the details of library work.[11]

He lamented the limited, incomplete catalogs in many libraries he visited, and, in the case of the Vatican Library at Rome, no catalog, and "the visitor sees no books, nothing but cases, access to which is about as difficult as it is to the cave of Machpelah at Hebron." He found the University of Athens in Greece one of the best libraries in Europe in terms of quality of books, arrangement, and classification. As a result of his visit, he yearned for some cooperative plan to be devised for cataloging manuscript collections which would be descriptive and accurate, which would tell the world of scholars in what libraries they could be found, and what they contained.[12]

In 1889 Melvil Dewey, accompanied by W. S. Biscoe of the New York State Library, visited libraries in Scotland, England, and France as well as Great Britain. Dewey noted that "at Heidelberg the great University Library was clearly chiefly used for the storage of books little used. . . . An earnest university man, who had worked faithfully in his special field for some years, confessed that, till he accompanied us, he had never been inside the University Library."[13] Dewey also observed that the Amsterdam Library, although the youngest of those visited, had outstripped its older sisters and was better organized and administered. He noted that "the card catalog was made by mounting on cards titles clipped from the sheets. Each of the Dutch universities sends to the libraries of the others printed sheets of its additions, thus cooperating as we should do in America."[14]

The second international conference of librarians met in London in 1897, twenty years after the first one. Attended by well over 600 delegates, a fifth of whom represented libraries in the United States, there were representatives of twenty-one countries including France, Italy, Belgium, Denmark, Japan, and Australia, whose Library Association had only been organized the previous year (April 1896).[15]

326 / Environment

The ALA speakers included Justin Winsor, Melvil Dewey, Charles Ammi Cutter, R. R. Bowker, John Cotton Dana, Caroline Hewins, Herbert Putnam, and C. W. Andrews.[16]

Aside from the tours of local libraries, two highlights of the meeting were the exhibition of new library equipment and reports of the worldwide growth of the public library movement. Great Britain, for example, reported 350 public libraries with 5 million volumes. Australia had 844 public libraries with 1.4 million volumes. The 1896 statistics, the latest available, showed the United States as having 4,026 public libraries and 33 million volumes.[17] Herbert Putnam was so inspired by his international experience that he was prompted to say in his presidential address to ALA the next year:

> The community that we each serve may be local; but the work that we do for this community inevitably takes us abroad. . . . This service discountenances geographical and political barriers. It is necessarily international. We are inconceivable in isolation.[18]

In the decades between the turn of the century and World War I, international cooperation among librarians was most vigorous in matters pertaining to bibliographic problems. U.S. librarians supported such projects as the *International Catalogue of Scientific Literature* (London, 1902–19), the Concilium Bibliographicum (Zurich, 1890), and the "Repertoire Bibliographique Universal" (Brussels, 1896). U.S. librarians attended the 1910 Congress of Archivists and Librarians in Brussels. Sessions were devoted to the training of librarians, international interlibrary loans and exchanges, library design and construction, special libraries such as those for the blind, and decimal classification. C. W. Andrews of the John Crerar Library was elected a vice-president of the conference, and spoke about ALA and the Library of Congress cards that were then available.[19]

During the years of World War I, U.S. librarians were concerned about the fate of their European colleagues as well as their own access to European journals. The Committee on International Relations at the 1916 ALA Conference reported correspondence with French and Belgian groups regarding reconstruction plans after the war and the possible establishment of a model American library in Paris.[20] Herbert Putnam, who chaired the committee, cautioned against giving the impression that the ALA would be able to do a great deal, but indeed the American Library in Paris was founded in 1918 by the American Library Association as an extension of its work with the men of the American Expeditionary Force. In 1920 the book collections and library equipment, together with a contribution of $25,000 toward endowment, were presented by the ALA to the library to make it a permanent institution.

The American Library has actually become a cultural center for a large community of U.S. expatriates, including Ernest Hemingway,

Gertrude Stein, Thornton Wilder, and Stephen Vincent Benet, who lived in Paris between the two world wars. There had been hopes that it would also become a sort of cultural embassy to spread U.S. ideals abroad.[21]

Today, a portion of the library's income is from special gifts from patrons and life members. Families can join for $35 a year; students pay $12. At the end of 1974 the library had more than 2,000 members, of whom some 1,100 were U.S. citizens and 900 French.

Currently, it serves a growing number of French students (an estimated 500) and professors (250) who are involved in formal American studies courses. In addition, another 372 U.S. students from the American College in Paris, a private institution, use the American Library.[22]

The extension service is one of the most interesting phases of the work. Any book about the United States will be loaned to anyone in Europe without charge. The American Library still maintains five extension libraries at universities in Toulouse, Grenoble, Montpellier, and Nantes, plus one in a public library in Nancy serving about 4,000 students.[23]

During the World War I years, there were ALA committees on the importation of books, on promotion and cooperation in the development of printed catalog cards in accordance with international agreements, and also those dealing with other facets of the international relations picture. The ALA War Service Committee, chaired by James I. Wyer with Herbert Putnam as general director, was chiefly concerned with the problem of providing suitable reading matter to U.S. servicemen in camp, trench, and hospital. ALA administered large donations and sent librarians overseas to handle the distribution of sizable collections of books. Those who served abroad made friends wherever they went and public recognition of the services rendered was gratefully acknowledged.[24]

One of the U.S. librarians contributing substantially to the international aspects of librarianship in the years between World War I and II was Harry M. Lydenberg; as chairman of the Books for Europe Committee, he solicited funds from foundations and individuals to help restock devastated European libraries and rebuild some, including that of the University of Louvain, as well as the earthquake-destroyed University of Tokyo Library.[25] Another was Sarah C. N. Bogle, who developed library work with children at Pittsburgh and whose efforts to raise professional standards and to guide library schools made her nationally influential; she was director of the Paris Library School under ALA, 1924–29. Notable too was Arthur E. Bostwick, who as chief of circulation, New York Public Library, made the immigrant and foreign population welcome in the library. At the invitation of the Chinese National Association for the Advancement of Education, ALA sent him as a delegate to survey libraries and to advise on library development in mainland China.[26]

Certainly no discussion of international librarianship could be complete without mention of the distinguished, scholarly William Warner Bishop, associated with the University of Michigan Library and later reference librarian at Princeton University. Bishop wrote the *Practical Handbook of Modern Library Cataloging*, which first appeared in 1914 and was revised in 1924. It had a continuing influence not only in the United States and the other English-speaking countries, but also in Chinese and Russian translation. Even today the book is useful as a training and reference tool for catalogers.

Bishop joined the staff of the Library of Congress in 1907, where, as superintendent of the reading room, he had, among other duties, supervision of the tours for distinguished visitors, many from other countries.

A member of ALA since 1896, he was elected to the presidency in 1918, but his contribution to international librarianship began as early as 1898 when he first went to Europe as a student. His scholarly abilities were formally recognized in 1898 when he was offered one of three fellowships at the American School of Classical Studies in Rome. Much of his time was spent in the Vatican Library, because he was working on a project involving early Greek and Latin manuscripts. During this period, while carrying on his research work, he began his acquaintanceship with the Vatican Library. He also visited many other libraries and cataloged the book collection of the American School Library. Many of his later activities derive directly from his work with the Vatican Library, his first important contribution to international library cooperation.

In 1927 the Carnegie Endowment for International Peace selected Bishop to head the project for the recataloging and reorganizing of the Vatican Library in Rome. This assignment continued from 1927 to 1935. His earlier use of the library enabled him to provide unusual guidance to the entire project.[27]

Cardinal Tisserant, who became one of his admirers, wrote:

> The progress of the Vatican index is slow but it is continuous, and among the many undertakings to which Dr. Bishop gave beginning and impulse, none perhaps will have a wider repercussion than this one, in which the trustees of the Carnegie Endowment for International Peace manifested their wish to cooperate with the Church in its great task of promoting education, international understanding and international peace.[28]

Bishop's opinions were eagerly sought by many individual librarians from other countries. His varied experience abroad, as well as his knowledge of U.S. libraries and librarianship, enabled him to serve as a truly international librarian.[29]

In the twenties, thirties, and forties important boards and committees came into being in the American Library Association. Committees on adult education, library extension, education for librarianship, and international relations took on new meaning under the aggressive leadership of Carl H. Milam, who became executive secretary in 1920, a position he held for twenty-eight years. He became well known to many organizations and philanthropic foundations; the American Library Association became known all over the world. In 1926, when ALA met in Atlantic City to celebrate its fiftieth anniversary, there were sixty-three delegates from fifteen foreign countries. Financial assistance from foundations and other groups helped with the foreign visitors' expenses. Some twenty-five papers by librarians from abroad made the meeting truly international in character. From that meeting on, the ALA and its executive secretary were more and more involved in library progress on an international scale, and the prestige of the association grew accordingly.[30]

The first formal invitation to establish what is now the International Federation of Library Associations (IFLA) was issued at ALA's fiftieth anniversary Conference in 1926. The theme that year was international librarianship.

Since IFLA's founding, a number of distinguished U.S. and Canadian librarians have regularly attended its meetings. They have served on committees, participated in working groups as appropriate, and presented papers on a variety of aspects of librarianship. William Warner Bishop served as president of the Madrid Congress in 1935; Milton Lord and Douglas Bryant were vice-presidents. Two of the current vice-presidents are Robert Vosper, University of California at Los Angeles and H. C. Campbell, chief librarian, Toronto Public Libraries, Toronto, Ontario. David Clift, Foster Mohrhardt, Emerson Greenaway, Jean Lowrie have represented ALA while Frank E. McKenna, Donald Wasson, Karl Baer, Herbert White, and Erik Spicer and Gilles Frappier—both Canadian—have attended IFLA in behalf of the Special Libraries Association. The United States has always been represented on the governing board of IFLA, but since the federation has always maintained a European headquarters, responsibility for its day-to-day direction has for the most part remained in European hands. The IFLA General Council met in Chicago in 1933.[31] IFLA met in Canada in 1967, and there has been considerable Canadian university library participation in the work of the IFLA Committee on the Exchange of Publications, especially on the exchange of dissertations.[32]

More recently, the Canadian International Development Agency made a grant to IFLA's Working Group on Developing Countries to assist it in setting up a secretariat in Kuala Lumpur (Malaysia) and to undertake projects to benefit library and information work in developing countries.[33]

How appropriate that the second IFLA meeting to be held in the United States, convened in Washington, D.C. in November 1974, should have had as its theme "National and International Library Planning."

In an address to the opening plenary session of the 1974 meeting, Robert Vosper pointed to stepped-up international cooperation among universities as one indication of progress. As paraphrased by *Library Journal*, he explained that "the current trend in interlibrary cooperation involves getting national governments (Canada, Great Britain, and Germany) to support, participate, and even direct international library initiatives." He also called for "worldwide support for Universal Bibliographic Control, an international data base expected to be fully operative by 1984."[34]

IFLA in recent years has taken a number of steps or has cooperated with other organizations concerning Universal Bibliographic Control: in 1961 Paris meeting on Cataloguing Principles, its sequel in Copenhagen in 1969, seminars on the problems of the international use of magnetic bibliographic tapes, and various meetings on international standards for library statistics. For over a century, statistical data collection for librarianship on the international level had been planned and discussed, but only since the mid-sixties has substantial advance been made. Because of the close cooperation of UNESCO, IFLA, and ISO Technical Committee 46, the drafting of the UNESCO International Library Statistics Standard was completed in May 1970. Cooperation came about because IFLA's Committee on Statistics and Standards had forcefully emphasized the need for such a standard for nearly forty years. The 1974 Washington IFLA Conference was preceded by a three-day session of the Committee hosted by the College of Library and Information Services of the University of Maryland. Committee members and invited experts had the opportunity to explore subjects of major concern.[35]

To the Council on Library Resources goes particular credit for fostering the steady march toward international standards for cataloging ever since the Paris Conference of 1961 and the planning for that landmark meeting. A recent CLR grant, for example, to the Library of Congress, will enable LC to join with the national libraries of Australia, Canada, France, and Great Britain in funding an international bibliographic network study.[36]

In 1969 an International Meeting of Cataloguing Experts Working Party of IFLA was established to develop a standard for the descriptive portion of a bibliographic record and to adopt this standard for use in catalogs, listings, and bibliographies (including national bibliographies). The Library of Congress was represented on this committee by a member of its staff. The IFLA permanent Cataloguing Secretariat, housed in the British Museum, is maintained by a grant of the Council on Library Resources.[37]

The progress in the development of a standard machine format for bibliographic records has coincided with the development of a unique numbering system for books, the International Standard Book Number

(ISBN) and serials, the International Standard Serial Number (ISSN). IFLA, for its part, tries to contribute to these standardization programs, by making its expertise available. The IFLA Committee on Serial Publications has been active in the drafting of standards comparable to those it helped draft on cataloguing.[38]

U.S. librarians have been a continuing force in education for international librarianship from the first meeting of the ALA to the present day. The first library school in the United States, established by Melvil Dewey at Columbia University in 1887, was open to foreign students, and others followed suit. The Albany Library School graduated sixty-seven foreign students in one year and thirty-eight of these were Norwegians.[39] In an effort to meet the need for training in another way, shortly after World War I, a school of library service was organized within the American Library in Paris. The American Committee for Devastated France gave $50,000 as a starter, and contributions from various organizations made possible some scholarships. Mary P. Parsons was the resident director of the school which lasted for five years then unfortunately closed for lack of funds.[40]

Since the termination of this abortive effort, foreign students have continued to come to study at various U.S. and Canadian library schools. Most recently, there has been an influx of students from Africa, Asia, South America, and the Middle East. Although the exact number and distribution of foreign students studying librarianship in the United States and Canada today is not known, it can be said that the total professional influence of library school faculties on the training of librarians from other countries has been substantial.

Canadian involvement in the international aspects of librarianship found early expression in the activities leading to the establishment of the Canadian Library Association. One of the proposals in the *Report of the Activities Committee of the Proposed Canadian Library Association* (1946) was "(3) Library Exchanges within and beyond Canada of staff, material, etc."[41] Visits of librarians between Canada and Great Britain were formalized in 1951 in the Toronto Public Libraries' intern scheme for overseas librarians. Four or five British librarians were accepted into the Toronto public library system each year to provide them with an opportunity to see public librarianship in a Commonwealth country. The scheme was enlarged to include librarians from other Commonwealth countries, and in 1959 the Toronto Public Library Board began to cooperate in the Colombo Plan to aid countries in Asia and the Far East. Librarians from India and the Philippines came as interns, and, in 1960 the scheme was further extended when European libraries were invited to serve on the staff of the Toronto Public Library's Foreign Literature Centre.[42]

In keeping with International Cooperation Year (1965) special international undertakings were organized by Canadian librarians. A

Swedish-Canadian library conference was held in Norrbotten, Sweden, five Canadian librarians visited the USSR, seven Canadian librarians attended the IFLA meeting in Helsinki, an international issue of *Canadian Library Journal* was published, and Canadian librarians attended the International Conference of Music Library Associations at Dijon.[43] A return visit to Canada by fifteen Swedish librarians to observe library work of all kinds in Ontario and western Quebec followed in 1967.[44]

Government assistance was made available to further Canadian ties with the international library scene. In 1970–71 the Canadian International Development Agency supported a research project proposed by the Canadian Library Association on the "Development of Library Service in Africa: Identification of Needs and Available Resources in West Africa," coordinated by Don Forgie at the University of Toronto School of Library Science.[45] In 1972 the International Development Research Centre, a Canadian government agency, provided funds for representatives from developing countries to attend an INTAMEL conference (International Association of Metropolitan City Libraries) and to further INTAMEL's research projects on metropolitan libraries in developing countries.[46]

Much of the international cooperation that has evolved since the historic London conference in 1877 would not have been possible without the assistance of U.S. foundations. The contributions of the big three of the foundations, Carnegie Corporation, Ford, and Rockefeller, have been among the forces which have contributed immeasurably to the influence of American librarianship abroad. Historically speaking, Carnegie has been the most powerful name in library philanthropy.

The American Library Association received its initial endowment, $100,000, from Andrew Carnegie in 1902. The Carnegie Corporation, established in 1911, inherited its interest in libraries from its founder. Between 1924 and 1926 the corporation provided $549,500 towards ALA's general support, and in 1926 the corporation trustees approved gifts of $2 million toward ALA's endowment. The corporation relied heavily on the recommendations of Carl H. Milam, executive secretary of ALA, throughout his tenure, in distributing funds for the development of libraries and librarianship.

Of the 2,509 libraries that Andrew Carnegie financed himself, only 1,681 were built in the United States. The others were distributed around the English-speaking world: Great Britain, Canada, Australia, New Zealand, the West Indies, and elsewhere. Later the Carnegie Corporation provided grants for a number of overseas projects: to ALA to help to establish the Canadian Library Council, forerunner of the Canadian Library Association; to ALA to help Canadian librarians attend ALA meetings; to the New Zealand and Australian Library associations for support of their activities; to the Central Library in Trinidad so that the Eastern Caribbean Regional Library could be established. The Carnegie Corporation also provided fellowships which enabled foreign librarians to receive professional training and to participate in demonstration projects and area studies such as those conducted in Ghana and Nigeria. Between 1911 and 1961 the corporation distributed more than $5 million in grants for public library buildings and library programs in many areas of the world, including Australia, Bechuanaland, British Honduras, Gambia, Ghana, Hong Kong, Kenya, Malaya, Nigeria, Rhodesia, Sierra Leone, Tanganyika, and Uganda.[47]

Substantial Rockefeller Foundation grants to libraries have been made since the early 1920s. Among the enterprises benefited were the League of Nations Library building in Geneva; the reconstruction of the Tokyo University Library after the earthquake of 1923; new facilities at the Bodleian Library at Oxford; aid to the National Central Library and a library training center, both in London; three extensive cataloging projects at the British Museum, the Bibliothèque Nationale, and the Prussian State Library; forty-eight fellowships in library administration on an international scale, embracing nineteen countries in Europe, Latin America, and the Far East. The Rockefeller Foundation supported the International Relations Office of the American Library Association and the library collections of agricultural research institutions overseas.[48]

The Ford Foundation began operating relatively late, in 1936. Although the foundation's early interest in higher education and international affairs may have benefited libraries directly or indirectly, it was not until the early 1950s that Ford conducted a broad inquiry into the problems which resulted in the establishment of the Council on Library Resources in 1956. The council was given an initial grant of $5 million to be expended over a five-year period "(1) to develop the resources and services of libraries and (2) to improve relations between American [i.e., U.S.] and foreign libraries and archives."[49] In 1960, in 1967, and again in 1971 the Ford Foundation approved new grants totaling $18 million to enable the council to carry forward its programs of research and demonstration toward the solution of library problems here and abroad.

Although the Ford Foundation's principal contribution to libraries has been through the Council on Library Resources, it is nonetheless a major donor to libraries independently of the council.

The 1960s were years of great interest in international programs of all kinds in the United States. Many of them affected libraries. For international projects thirty foundations made 231 grants totaling $27,370,206.

Inspired at least in part by the early major contributors to libraries, Carnegie and Rockefeller, other foundations entered the field: Moody Foundation, the Andrew W. Mellon Foundation, and the Old Dominion Foundation. Far and away the largest donors to international library projects were Ford (71 grants, $13.4 million), Rockefeller (72 grants,

334 / Environment

$5.9 million), and the W. K. Kellogg Foundation (16 grants, $2.7 million). The Commonwealth Fund gave nearly a million dollars in 4 grants, and the China Medical Board of New York about $750,000 (12 grants). Twenty-four other foundations gave smaller amounts starting at $10,000 and running to $355,000; the Council on Library Resources was one of these, awarding 8 grants totaling $353,495.[50]

Of the 50 grant recipients receiving the most money from U.S. foundations, 30 (60 percent) were located in the developing countries in Asia, Africa, or Latin America. Others represented are Japan, Israel, Canada, Greece, Switzerland, Ireland, and England. At the head of the list are the University of Delhi, the University of the Philippines, and the American Library Association. About half of the recipients were universities, and the others research institutes, governments, and various nongovernmental organizations.

Of the 168 international grants identified by type of library, the college and university group came first, with 85; medical libraries were second, 31; special and independent research libraries received 28; agricultural, 20, and law, 4.

Funding by type of activity included 96 international grants, first, for buildings and equipment, then acquisition, cataloging, and bibliography. Microfilm, library education, and circulation and reference activities received fewer dollars. Categories notably absent were computerization, endowment funds, and undergraduate programs.[51]

Direct aid to foreign libraries during and after World War II was generally confined to donated book programs for war-ravaged libraries, cooperation with library associations, and consultations on problems relating to classification and cataloging, much of which was institutionalized through the American Library Association.[52] The collection of books and library school supplies has been an important Canadian activity through that country's Overseas Book Centre. By 1965 more than half a million books had been donated to forty countries.[53]

No complete roster of voluntary, private agencies for book and periodical donations appears to exist. A conference sponsored by the International Relations Office of ALA in October 1967 in Washington, D.C. was followed by the publication of its proceedings, which listed about thirty or more organizations actively engaged in assisting libraries in Africa, Asia, the Middle East, and Latin America. It included information on the Asia Foundation (with its Books for Asian Students program), the U.S. Book Exchange (the sleeping giant of international book exchange), the Peace Corps, the Library of Congress, UNESCO, U.S. Information Agency, and the professional library associations such as law and medicine.[54] A later publication, "Gift Book Programs for Libraries," assembled by ALA's International Relations Office, supplemented and updated the former publication.[55]

In the January 1972 issue of *Library Trends* Paul Bixler discussed extensively the rationale of book donations to individual and institutional recipients, the appropriateness of gift books for educational, informational, and social purposes. Indeed, the entire issue, whose special editor was Cecil K. Byrd, is "an analysis of the fairly large-scale overseas book and library assistance programs in which the American library profession has participated during the last twenty-five years."[56]

A striking phenomenon of the postwar period was the rapid development of the various agencies for the preparation of librarians. The older, well-developed countries engaged in significant remodeling operations of their educational systems. The newly developing countries emerged from a period when all their trained personnel had to be educated abroad and began to organize their own training programs. UNESCO, various technical aid programs, including the International Cooperation Administration, and the more affluent foundations were concerned with the education of librarians and the improvement of libraries and librarianship in the countries of Asia, Africa, the Middle East, and Latin America and in assisting in the development of training programs. The American Library Association, through its advisory and headquarters services, was a medium for carrying forward certain of these professional education programs and recruited personnel to implement them.

During the summer of 1942 a school was conducted in Bogota, Colombia, under ALA auspices with Rockefeller Foundation funds; and an ALA-sponsored school was established in 1951 at Keio University in Tokyo, also Rockefeller-supported. The Turkish Library School at the University of Ankara was aided by Ford Foundation funds in 1954, while in 1956 the Inter-American Library School at the University of Antioquia (Medellin) received money from the Rockefeller Foundation.[57] The support of U.S. foundations and other agencies in furthering the growth of library education in many parts of the world will no doubt exert a profound and lasting influence for years to come. Since World War II, the services of many U.S. librarians with experience to teach, to survey, to lecture, and to observe cannot be measured.

Observers of the international library scene in the late fifties and sixties could not fail to note a growing discussion of and activity in the area of national planning for library and documentation services. This did not come as a great surprise in view of the intense interest which both international organizations and governments of newly developing countries had shown since World War II in long-range planning for socio-economic development. Through UNESCO's Department of Documentation, Libraries and Archives requests to the American Library Association for technical assistance overseas were increasingly in the area of planning library services on a nationwide basis and for consultants to work in what the host country identified as key problem areas in major sectors of library development and educational planning. "Since 1951 more than twenty U.S. nationals have served as technical experts by helping member states carry out such recommended UNESCO programs as: Organizing documentation centers in Argentina, India, and Mexico; planning or organizing schools of librarianship in Israel, Greece, and Jamaica; organizing archival services in Tanzania; developing public library services in Colombia, Madagascar, and Israel; establishing library service in rural areas of Thailand; and developing university library service in Turkey and Thailand."[58]

During World War II, ALA staff involvement in international relations programs reached an all time high, the association itself assisting in the administration of various assistance programs.

The staff of the International Relations Office (established in 1956) worked closely with the members of the association, the executive secretaries, committee chairmen, and others who had expertise in the geographical area in which a project was in operation. The office, with a limited staff, was more of a catalyst, an initiator, or coordinator of projects rather than an operating entity, and sought to identify those library developmental needs and find funds for those opportunities consistent with association goals by establishing and maintaining contracts with individuals and organizations within the United States and abroad, and by visits to other countries as seemed appropriate and timely.[59]

Working very closely with the IRO office and personnel, the International Relations Committee of ALA reported to the Council at the Dallas Annual Conference (1971) the following goals:

> 1. Through meetings of the committee to: (a) study and examine international aspects of librarianship that are of concern to the association as a whole or to its units; (b) advise the executive director, the staff of the IRO, and, as appropriate, other staff, projects and membership units, and coordinate courses of action. . . . (c) recommend policy to the Executive Board and to the Council.
>
> 2. To provide for representation of the association at meetings relating to the international relations of the association, including the International Federation of Library Associations, the International Federation of Documentation, the International Association of Metropolitan Libraries, UNESCO, and the United Nations. . . .
>
> 3. To promote the exchange of librarians and professional information, ideas, and literature between this and other countries.
>
> 4. To testify before appropriate government libraries on matters relating to the international interests of the committee.
>
> 5. To inform the membership of the association on appropriate matters concerning international relations.[60]

The philosophy and direction of the IRO were determined by the terms of the financial grants which provided for its operation. As the ten-year limit for Rockefeller Foundation funds came to a close, ALA began to put a significant portion of its own money into its international program.[61]

The reliance of the IRO on ALA funds coincided with a time when Association funds were extremely limited. The ACONDA report asked that ALA redirect itself—and reallocate its budget accordingly—to six priorities, without specifying an order among them: social responsibilities; manpower; intellectual freedom; legislation; planning, research, and development; democratization and reorganization.[62] "Explaining and defending an international program is never an easy task. When the program competes with others more visible to the membership, the explanation and defense become heavy burdens indeed . . . the outcome of this period when ALA membership activities and attention have been drawn toward more limited organizational interests" was the curtailment in 1972 of the International Relations Office.[63] The report of the ALA Ad Hoc Committee to Study International Responsibilities, "International Organizational Activity, Bibliographic and Technological Activity, Education for International Librarianship, and Personal Involvement in Librarianship Abroad," published in 1974, pointed out that, despite its name, ALA is an international association and recommended the appointment of a full-time Coordinator of International Relations, to work directly under the Executive Director in Chicago. The current fiscal outlook for international activities in ALA was described as bleak, and the Committee focused on a survival program.[64] This recommendation of the appointment of a Coordinator of International Relations was endorsed by the ALA International Relations Committee in 1975, and a budget request presented for it.[65] Subsequently, Jane Wilson was appointed International Relations Officer of the American Library Association and began her new duties January 15, 1976. In her position she will serve as a coordinator for international relations within the ALA, and with other national, regional, and local library associations.[66]

Broader aspects of international cooperation in librarianship, however, were considered by Jean E. Lowrie, ALA president, in 1973. In her inaugural address she drew attention to some of the problems that remain to be resolved:

> In the field of international relations, international study and understanding, librarianship must reevaluate its priorities. . . . We have been guilty as a society in general, of attempting to impose upon other cultures, other societies our particular beliefs, more particularly our library image. . . . Although one type of library education may be highly significant and workable in one part of the world, a similar type of library education should not be superimposed on other countries. We need to devise new methods for sharing. A greater awareness of the development

of school and public library services applicable to society in other countries should be demonstrated. We need to look again at the patterns of international relationships which can be developed by professional associations.[67]

As the world grows smaller and smaller, aided by the twin twentieth-century phenomena, instant communication and rapid transportation, the need to reevaluate priorities, to explore new channels, and to share information in all fields of endeavor will become more and more crucial to our continued existence as human beings. If U.S. and Canadian librarians and library associations remain true to their historic tradition of international cooperation, they will continue to be interested in and seriously responsible for future library development not only at home but in foreign nations as well.

NOTES

1. Budd Gambee, "The Great Junket: American Participation in the Conference of Librarians, London, 1877," *Journal of Library History* 2:9–44 (Jan. 1967).
2. Quoted in ibid., p. 21.
3. R. R. Bowker, "The Library Journal and Library Organization: A Twenty Years' Retrospect," *Library Journal* 21:5 (Jan. 1896).
4. Albert Predeek, *A History of Libraries in Great Britain and North America* (Chicago: American Library Assn., 1947), pp. 98–113 passim.
5. Justin Winsor, "The Future of Local Libraries," *Atlantic Monthly* 71:815–18 (June 1893).
6. Ibid., pp. 815–16.
7. Ibid., p. 816.
8. Ibid., p. 817.
9. Charles A. Cutter, "The Franklin Society of Paris," *American Library Journal* 1:3–5 (Sept. 30, 1876).
10. Ibid.
11. E. C. Mitchell, "European Libraries," *Library Journal* 2:12 (Sept. 1877).
12. Ibid.
13. Melvil Dewey, "Notes on Some Continental Libraries," *Library Journal* 17:121–22 (Apr. 1892).
14. Ibid.
15. "Library Association of Australia," *Library Journal* 23:241 (June 1898).
16. "The Second International Library Conference, London, July 13–16, 1897," *Library Journal* 22:407–8 (Aug. 1897).
17. Ibid., 391.
18. As reproduced in *Library Journal* 23:4 (Aug. 1898).
19. Flora B. Ludington, "The American Contribution to Foreign Library Establishment and Rehabilitation," in Leon Carnovsky, ed., *International Aspects of Librarianship* (Chicago: Univ. of Chicago Pr., 1954), p. 116.
20. "French and Belgian Reconstruction Plans," *ALA Bulletin* 10:393 (July 1916).
21. Marjorie Griesser, "The American Library in Paris," *Wilson Library Bulletin* 4:250–51 (Dec. 1960).
22. Christopher Wright, "April—and the American Library in Paris," *American Libraries*, 6:226–27 (Apr. 1975).
23. Ibid.
24. Ludington, p. 117.

25. Ibid., p. 118.
26. "A Library Hall of Fame Compiled for the 75th Anniversary of the American Library Association, 1876–1951," *Library Journal* 76:466–72 (Mar. 15, 1951).
27. Foster E. Mohrhardt, "Dr. William Warner Bishop: Our First International Librarian," *Wilson Library Bulletin* 32:207–15 passim (Nov. 1957).
28. Eugene, Cardinal Tisserant, "The Preparation of a Main Index for the Vatican Library," in Harry M. Lydenberg and Andrew Keogh, *William Warner Bishop: A Tribute* (New Haven, Conn.: Yale Univ. Pr., 1941), p. 185.
29. Mohrhardt, passim.
30. Emily Miller Danton, "Mr. ALA: Carl Hastings Milam," *ALA Bulletin* 53:752–62 (Oct. 1959).
31. Ludington, p. 119.
32. Hilda Gifford, "Canadian Participation in IFLA: Its Growth and Problems," *Canadian Library Journal* 32:128 (Apr. 1975).
33. Ibid., p. 130.
34. "International Library Planning Explored at IFLA Meet," *Library Journal* 100:354 (Feb. 15, 1975).
35. Frank L. Schick, "International Library Statistics Activities" in *The Bowker Annual of Library and Book Trade Information* (20th ed. New York: Bowker, 1975), p. 338.
36. *College & Research Libraries News* Mar. 1976, p. 60.
37. Margreet Wijinstroom, *The International Federation of Library Associations* (18th ed. New York: Bowker, 1973), p. 230.
38. Ibid., pp. 229–32.
39. Ludington, pp. 11–14.
40. Ibid., p. 117.
41. *Librarianship in Canada, 1946 to 1967: Essays in Honour of Elizabeth Homer Morton,* ed. by Bruce Peel (Ottawa: Canadian Library Assn., 1968), p. 27.
42. H. C. Campbell. "Toronto's Overseas Interne Scheme: 10 Years After," *Journal of Education for Librarianship* 2:158–61 (Winter 1962).
43. "These Years of CLA-ACB, 1960–1966: Report of the Directors of the Corporation," *Canadian Library* 23:493 (May 1967).
44. "This Year of CLA-ACB: Report of the Directors of the Corporation," *Canadian Library* 24:569 (May 1968).
45. "CLA 1970–1971: Report of the Directors of the Corporation," *Canadian Library Journal* 28:198 (May 1971).
46. Gifford, p. 130.
47. Florence Anderson, *Carnegie Corporation: Library Program 1911–1961* (New York: Carnegie, 1963) p. 25 passim.
48. Thomas B. Buckman, Judith B. Margolin, and Richard Serota, "American Foundations and Their Grants to Libraries," mimeographed (New York: Foundation Center, [1973]).
49. Ibid.
50. Ibid.
51. Ibid.
52. Cecil K. Byrd, ed., "The Influence of American Librarianship Abroad," *Library Trends* 20:3 (Jan. 1972).
53. J. Roby Kidd, "The Peoples Are You Waiting," *Canadian Library* 22:133–38 (Nov. 1965).
54. "Gift Book Programs for Libraries," *Libraries in International Development* no. 19:1–5 (Feb. 1970).
55. *Who Is Doing What in International Book and Library Programs,* Proceedings of a conference sponsored by the International Relations Office, American Library Association, October 9, 1967 (Washington, D.C.: American Library Assn., [1967]).

56. Byrd, p. 475.

57. Alice Lohrer and William Vernon Jackson, "Education and Training of Librarians in Asia, the Near East, and Latin America," *Library Trends* 8:243–77 (Oct. 1959), esp. pp. 261, 264.

58. David G. Donovan, "Library Development and the U.S. Consultant Overseas," *Library Trends* 20:506–14 passim (Jan. 1972).

59. Emerson Greenaway, "Progress in International Librarianship," *American Libraries* 3:803–6 (July–Aug. 1972).

60. As presented in ibid., p. 806.

61. Peggy Sullivan, "The International Relations Program of the American Library Association," *Library Trends*, 20:577–90 (Jan. 1972), esp. pp. 588–91.

62. *Library Journal* 95:16 (Sept. 15, 1970), p. 2968.

63. Sullivan, p. 577.

64. *Library of Congress Information Bulletin* 33:A-45 (Feb. 15, 1974).

65. *Library of Congress Information Bulletin* 34:A-49 (Feb. 14, 1975).

66. *Leads* 18, no. 1:8 (Mar. 1976).

67. Jean E. Lowrie, "Inaugural Address: What Is Librarianship?" *American Libraries* 4:563–64 (Oct. 1973).

18
Research

SIDNEY L. JACKSON
Kent State University

On January 1, 1876 operating libraries in the United States and Canada had for nearly a century faced problems and solved some of them. At hand was not only a shelf of significant contributions from abroad, but a modest published literature of domestic origin. Besides library catalogs, journal articles, biographical materials, and at least one solid history,[1] there were two attempts at retrospective and current research: Charles C. Jewett's assemblage of facts and figures of 1849, the celebrated *Notices of Public Libraries in the United States*, released in 1851 by his employer, the Smithsonian Institution; and the effort by Smithsonian clerk W. J. Rhees to supplement what librarian Jewett had done, which appeared in 1859 as *Manual of Public Libraries, Institutions, and Societies in the United States and British Provinces of North America*, sponsored by Lippincott. The impact of Rhees's labors was not quite like that of Darwin's *Origin of Species by Natural Selection*, also an 1859 imprint, but Rhees had done much more than was originally planned, and his product was soon of great benefit to the federal Bureau of Education.

Although library publication between 1876 and 1930 included some materials valuable for writing history, the value tended to lie in the

---

This paper was prepared with the assistance of Greg Byerly, Hans Bynagle, Edgar Jones, Pamela Keirstead, Richard Rubin, Nancy Stewart, Andras Jablonkay, and David Zavortink.

342 / Environment

authors' ability to call on their personal experience in libraries rather than in systematic scholarly research.[2] Publication of a research character was largely confined to current fact-gathering.

One purpose of the U.S. Bureau of Education, founded in 1867, was to collect statistics. It began publishing statistics relating to libraries in 1870, when the commissioner's annual report contained a list of 161 principal libraries (not including colleges). In 1872 utilizing data gathered in the U.S. census of 1870, the commissioner reported 1,080 libraries (other than private) of 1,000 volumes or more, but only 213 librarians; also the number and circulation of various types of periodicals in states and territories were reported. Soon afterward, the commissioner's staff began to gather monographs as well as statistics for the Centennial Exhibition in Philadelphia in 1876. Their success inspired an attempt at maximum impact by means of a single large volume. (The practice of dispensing such enlightenment in individual circulars of information was a later development.) Aware that education was constitutionally a state rather than a federal function, the editors protected their flank with a long vigorous paragraph emphasizing the services already rendered by the "General Government" in this sphere and ignoring the constitutional question. The outcome was the two-part Special Report, *Public Libraries in the United States of America: Their History, Condition, and Management* (1876), of which the 89-page part 2 was Charles Cutter's *Rules for a Printed Dictionary Catalogue*.

Part 1 presented in 1,187 pages 39 chapters with remarkably broad coverage. Chapter topics included "Public Libraries a Hundred Years Ago," by Horace E. Scudder; "The Organization and Management of Public Libraries," by William F. Poole; "Library Catalogs," by Charles A. Cutter, which included statistics on the cost of printing book catalogs and a list of all printed catalogs; "Catalogs and Cataloging," by Melvil Dewey, S. B. Noyes, Jacob Schwartz, and John J. Bailey; "Works of Reference for Libraries," by A. R. Spofford; "Public Libraries of Ten Principal Cities" (Boston, Baltimore, Chicago, Cincinnati, New York City, Brooklyn, San Francisco, Charleston, St. Louis, and Philadelphia); and "General Statistics of All Public Libraries in the U.S." There was also a list of librarians.

The facts were drawn by the contributors, mainly librarians, from their own experience and knowledge, with considerable aid from the Jewett and Rhees reports. Although women were already a visible element in libraries, the bureau report paid very little attention to them as such. Not surprisingly, there was still less about children and school libraries, and nothing whatever about Negroes and Indians.

If the search for facts stimulated thoughts about research method now and then, grappling with statistics put methodology and standards center stage. Having presented and discussed quantitative data about libraries in the 257 pages of chapters 37 and 39, with numerous additional tables in earlier chapters, the editors felt bound to point out in their preface that circumstances were not favorable. Many libraries kept records poorly, the response to the surveyors varied greatly, and even the most cooperative applied the basic terms differentially. The reader was assured that the figures offered were "the most trustworthy evidence procurable," but that it was plain that serious studies would require standardization of nomenclature as to what could be called a library, for instance, and other improvements.[3]

How many read the 1876 report we do not know. Fifty years later, however, the commissioner referred to it as fundamental,[4] and one doubts that there was any disagreement. It was reprinted several times.[5]

For more than two decades after 1876, the commissioner's annual report furnished updated statistics, which presumably helped standardize terms like *Free or Subscription* by means of repetition, although they were not defined. How consistent they were, not to speak of how reliable, remains a matter for investigation. Likewise awaiting study is the question of parallel efforts in the several states.

The commissioner's report for 1892–93, taking advantage of the publicity attending the Columbian Exposition in Chicago in 1893, once more offered not only statistics but several essays, based mainly on experience. It was the last bureau general survey of libraries, the next document of that sort being the semicentennial survey undertaken in 1926 by ALA itself. Even if the arts of surveying and reporting were not advanced thus, it might be argued nevertheless that research methodology was benefiting potentially from the comparisons made possible by the numerous analyses of European education in the bureau reports.

Although no actual methodological advance can be identified in them, the research shelf did include new editions of Poole's index and additional reference tools. These represent that interest sometimes called research whose aim is to make accessible library materials. In 1882 Stephen B. Griswold of the New York State Library added periodical reference to a subject index to law books; enrichments followed in supplements of 1893 and 1903. In 1888 Judge Leonard A. Jones published an index to materials in legal periodicals of Anglo-America, pertinent literary reviews, and papers of bar association meetings; there was a supplement in 1899, but a proposed second supplement approved in principle was left hanging in 1907 for lack of funds. Besides, the 1907 ALA Conference heard that the Library of Congress had just published the *ALA Index to Portraits*, 1,700 pages assembled after ten years' work; that the Carnegie Institution of Washington had changed its mind about Adelaide Hasse's indexes to economic materials in state documents and would handle them itself rather than turning them over to the ALA Publishing Board; and that the Committee on Architecture had collected the floor plans of more than 100 library buildings, to be accompanied by explanations and criticisms.[6]

344 / *Environment*

During the years just reviewed, librarians were accumulating experience with questionnaire-based surveys, the results of which were often revealed at ALA conferences, and either on that basis or some other, appeared in *Library Journal*. Perhaps the earliest of weight was E. C. Richardson's 1885 report on 115 theology libraries, not all of which were among the Bureau of Education's respondents.[7] Two years later H. C. Carr analyzed data for 16 libraries involving population served, volumes in circulation, total registration, and the ratio of circulation to registration; it was a pioneer effort at seeking patterns among variables.[8] Pioneering not in research method but in focusing attention on what called for research, Salomé C. Fairchild illuminated the Library Section of the International Congress of Arts and Sciences (St. Louis, 1904) with data on the sexual composition, responsibilities, pay, of library staffs as indicated by the ninety-four libraries which had answered her questionnaire; the presentation in *Library Journal* included comment and paraphrase of comment on the status of women.[9]

In partial contrast with these and other isolated studies was a sequence of investigations of children's reading and library services to children which seems to have begun in 1882 with the modest mail query to twenty-five leading libraries by Caroline M. Hewins: "What are you doing to encourage a love of good reading in boys and girls?"[10] The crudity of that approach was gradually chipped away as larger and larger undertakings were mounted. In 1897 Electra C. Doren's remarks about school children's reading were reportedly based on direct observation, interviews with teachers, and written replies to her questions from 3,192 Dayton pupils.[11]

Doren's and other related papers in the notable April 1897 issue of *Library Journal* also appeared in chapter 15 of the 1897–98 report of the commissioner of education. His *Report . . . for the Year 1899–1900* presented among other things a National Education Association committee report on "The Relations of Public Libraries to Public Schools," several essays devoted primarily to persuasion but including some evaluation of reports received, from state normal schools and (very incompletely) from school libraries in rural schools and villages of less than 2,500 inhabitants. Without dismissing the valuable remarks about book selection and child psychology, it may be noted that, from the viewpoint of research, the most significant observations were the following contribution from John Cotton Dana:

> In recent years a good many elaborate investigations have been made by teachers, psychologists, and others, of the reading of children; what books and papers they read; what kind they most enjoy; what books furnish them with good ideals; what ones seem most to influence their lives. The replies to these questions have led to little in the way of definite conclusions. Few people can so frame a set of inquiries as to make the answers to them of value, even if those answers are clear and

honest. Few teachers—and most of the inquiries have been made by teachers—can put a set of questions to their pupils in such a way as to get from them straightforward, unprejudiced replies.[12]

Dana went on to consider the few facts established and concluded simply that "books can have and do have a greater influence for good or ill, on the lives of most people, by affecting them when they are young, than we had supposed." He acknowledged that that was not really new, but emphasized its great importance to librarians. The remainder of his comments was devoted to the librarian, the teacher, and the children, with wisdom and grace seldom matched by later generations.

Many more statistics were gathered and issued by federal and state agencies and library associations in the next generation. The initial efforts owed much to the League of Library Commissions (1904–   ) and the state federations of women's clubs; the fruits, when properly identified through research not yet done, will probably include enhancement of professional consciousness. Despite the labor and thinking expended up to that point, George R. Winchester submitted in 1913 "Suggestions for an ALA Statistical Handbook"; one of his concerns was to stress the desirability of categorizing public libraries by size of population served, whereas holdings were more suited to academic library grouping.[13] Nor had the situation changed much a decade later: ALA's own survey in 1926 testified to the severe shortage of sophistication in research methods as well as of dollars. Yet, a new foundation was being laid for the research to come. In *Training for Librarianship* (1923), Charles C. Williamson's Carnegie-backed analysis of library education programs, the emphatic stress on scholarship in a university context raised the curtain on a new era.

The foundation of the Graduate Library School at the University of Chicago in 1928 with $1 million of Carnegie endowment, opened a new epoch. Within three years the research style customary in the academic and professional world was unveiled to those in librarianship unfamiliar with it, and to those who may have been familiar with it but did not associate it with librarianship. Setting the new pace was Douglas Waples and Ralph W. Tyler's *What People Want to Read About*, the first of a number of studies destined to color librarianship heavily with the methods and insights of the social scientist. Clearly indicating one road ahead was the financing of the Waples-Tyler research: first by "the Carnegie Corporation at the instance of the American Association for Adult Education and the American Library Association through their joint Committee on the Reading Interests and Habits of Adults"; later "by the Graduate Library School of the University of Chicago, by the American Historical Association's Commission on the teaching of the social studies, and by the National Survey of the Education of Teachers."[14]

346 / Environment

What Waples and Tyler did that differed from earlier "research" was to begin by focusing on "methods whereby the reading interests of various adult groups might be reliably determined." When the report of "the first two years' work" was released they noted that "most time has been spent on the technical problems involved in developing trustworthy methods of investigation." They considered the findings shown "mainly useful in explaining the methods and in defining the problems for further study."[15] They expected their work to benefit "those in a position to make practical use of the findings (librarians, teachers, and the like)"; students of library science, education, and the social sciences wishing to pursue the data in detail; and researchers in the field of reading.[16] Their vision of the future included studies of the relationships between reading interests and actual reading; the data had already been secured with regard to three "populations . . . college students, the teaching profession, and graduates of state universities grouped according to vocation."[17]

Chapter 7 of *What People Want to Read About* was devoted to "Technical Questions." The student was invited to ponder the "adequacy, validity, and reliability" of the findings and the methods used to obtain them. The librarian in the making, among others, was presented with a case study in scientific investigation as understood by statisticians and other social scientists. Answers were given to such question as "How were the topics in the list selected?" "Do the ratings given by persons checking the list express their real interests?" and "How valid is the method of computing group scores?" The statistical devices were explained.[18] The forms used and the mathematics of the principal formulas were supplied in exhibits in the Appendix. Not only this sophistication, but its application to librarian interest in readers, was new to librarianship.

The next few years saw several more such studies. Contributions by Waples himself, and numerous others, were acknowledged in the text and footnotes of his *People and Print* in 1937. Sober scholarship also reached out in other directions, notably in Carlton Joeckel's *Government of the American Public Library* (1935), Louis R. Wilson's *County Library Service in the South* (1935) and *The Geography of Reading* (1938), and Glwadys Spencer's *The Chicago Public Library: Origins and Background* (1943). Joeckel's labors brought to bear careful analysis of statutes and other documents of local government, Spencer's the entire range of resources traditionally exploited by professional historiography; Wilson introduced meticulous analysis of federal census returns and the literature being produced by state extension agencies. Furthermore, rich survey experience both preceded and followed McDiarmid's *The Library Survey* (1940). Much of the research pursued in Chicago was concerned with learning whether public library practice was properly organized for achieving library goals.

Meanwhile, the *Library Quarterly* was launched in January 1931, to encourage research and publish a selection of the research available. Its first issue was headed by C. C. Williamson's Founder's Day address at the Western Reserve library school, delivered the preceding June 30. The impact was powerful not simply because Williamson had written a famous report calling for library science education at the graduate level in an academic setting, or because his audience was a promising link between Williamson and the Carnegie Corporation on the one hand, and the journal's sponsor, the University of Chicago, on the other. Most important was the title, "The Place of Research in Library Service," and Williamson's straight talk about what was needed to justify the phrase *library science*.[19]

What was then lacking, he detailed unmercifully: organized or cooperative plans, money specifically for research in library service, staff assigned to study problems of library service, research fellowships, research professorships, a single book or pamphlet on the subject, a journal in which to publish such materials. Happily, the Carnegie Corporation had lately appropriated $25,000 to help start a journal to be edited and published at the new Chicago Graduate Library School. As much as dollars, however, true research required individuals who would not be content to shape their actions solely on the basis of experience but would master scientific methods. Surely there was enough to be learned to occupy a good student the three years associated with earning a Ph.D.! Williamson went on to discuss briefly various implications for both curriculum and spirit. Solid and sensible as his ideas were, however, the presentation of the "scientific" never touched on theory that could shape action. Training in scientific method meant to him, as to many others, learning how to "observe, infer, and make generalizations about phenomena."[20] Comprehension of the laws of change was not yet on the agenda; not even, as the depression-era monographs mentioned above attest, those of dramatic social change.

The same issue listed "some problems under investigation" at the Chicago school, 1928–30. The great majority were practical, presumably infusing "scientific methods" into topics either familiar to librarians or on their way to that status. None directly addressed any problem of the philosophy of librarianship.[21] Indeed, illustrating what might be expected of the research genre were two articles based on survey techniques. One dealt with "the service loads of library-school faculties," seventeen of them; the data had been condensed from a report rendered in December 1929, doubtless from facts of earlier vintage.[22] The other analyzed "what can the foreigner find to read in the public library?" on the basis of data of 1926 published in two volumes of 1927.[23] Application of scientific criteria to community surveys was brought to bear, critically, in Douglas Waples's review of F. K. W. Drury's *Book Selection* (1930).[24] Philosophical issues emerged for a brief moment in Pierce Butler's review of *The Organization of Knowledge and the System of the Sciences*, by Henry E. Bliss (1929).[25]

The second number, dated April 1931, picked up steam. It was led by the first portion of Joeckel's classic study of public libraries from the governmental point of view. The next item was an early attempt, possibly the earliest, to relate school children's book borrowing at the public library to the same children's characteristics as revealed by educational tests and measurements (in the Los Angeles city schools). Following that was a report on "the voluntary reading of our children and the agencies that provide them with reading matter."[26] The analysts were the Committee on Reading of the White House Conference on Child Health and Protection: children's librarians and other child specialists, under the leadership of ALA Secretary Carl H. Milam. The material they worked with chiefly, "statistical information on reading facilities and on the publication and distribution of juvenile reading matter and of matter suitable for juvenile and adolescent reading,"[27] was so meager that the question of "what children actually have to read was no where satisfactorily answered."[28] Also at their disposal were about ninety studies limited to particular groups or particular reading problems; "altogether too many" seemed defective methodologically. Drawn on additionally was a substantial fund of records of experience, which drew critical attention to the fact that enthusiasm and informality were encouraged by the nature of children's work beyond a sound balance with objectivity, vitiating the usefulness to science of what those closest to the work had said.

Also furnished in this issue was an advance summary of Douglas Waples's *What People Want to Read About*. Waples introduced it with this statement:

> To make the account as clear as possible all technical matters have been omitted. Only those items are mentioned which librarians and others directly concerned with the selection and distribution of reading matter are likely to find significant.[29]

It might have been argued, on the contrary, that the book ought to be shaped for wide appeal, leaving technical matters for this, the learned journal. Obviously, either Waples or the editors or both did not think the would-be learned journal's readers so inclined.

Leading off the review department, Theodore Norton described concern for professional status as "once rather widespread." As for the book being judged, he submitted that the "inconclusive" treatment of "forty-odd subjects" barried it from being considered "a genuine contribution to librarianship"; the philosophical issues attached to establishing the "conclusive" were left faintly implied.[30] A bit more explicitly philosophical was J. C. M. Hanson's evaluation of Ernest C. Richardson's *Classification, Theoretical and Practical*, then in its third edition

(1930): the Decimal Classification, declared Hanson, "must prove an intolerable straight-jacket" in the larger and scholarly libraries "as new subjects come up, or new phases or developments in old subjects demand expansion and further subdivision"; he charged the protagonists of the DC with neglect of that point.[31]

Philosophy of service was addressed in Leon Carnovsky's remarks about James I. Wyer's *Reference Work* (1930). The sphere of library awareness of the community was dissected with care; it was urged that reference departments undertake "to collect the questions that are *not* asked of it, but are asked of others" (travel, income tax, etc.),[32] and deduce from there what the library's collection and information files ought to look like. A similarly broad view emerges from Helen L. Butler's comments on Effie L. Power's *Library Service for Children* (1930) that sophisticated techniques for judging the "difficulty and age levels" of children's books had not been mentioned, and "vague criteria" predominated.[33] Also planned for behavior-stretching were reviews of the *Social Work Year Book, 1929*, volume 1 of *A Systematic Source Book in Rural Sociology* (1930), and Abraham Flexner's *Universities: American, English, German* (1930).

The third number of this first volume offered an essay on the history of printing, the fourth, a biographical monograph. Thus was the basic pattern set for what *Library Quarterly* would contribute for many years, usually at a high level. An additional feature most helpful to the advance of scholarship appeared first in volume 3 (1933), a list of the graduate theses accepted by U.S. library schools in the preceding period. The first list covered four years; the second, published in volume 4, covered two. Presentation by broad subject covered became the main characteristic of these reports, which occasionally offered supplementary analysis. By 1953 the papers read at the annual conferences of the Graduate Library School were being published both in *Library Quarterly* and separately; these papers were frequently research reports.

In December 1939, alluding to the crisis in higher education and Branscomb's discouraging evidence about student use of college libraries in *Teaching with Books*, the Association of College and Reference Libraries began its own publication, *College and Research Libraries*. As a professional periodical, it was thought obligated to "seek to stimulate research and experimentation," but that was the seventh and last of its stated purposes; the first six concerned disseminating organizational and operational information. That practitioners would pay less attention than educators to research was doubtless predictable; harmonizing therewith was the record of "Carnegie Grants for Academic Libraries" published in the same issue, a total of $4,330,146 with a meager $92,000 for "bibliographical-research experiments." *College and Research Libraries* soon became useful to its constituents, but it was not expected to be notable for research.

Close reporting upon developments in photographic, mechanical, and other technical areas was the business of ALA's *Journal of Documentary Reproduction*, begun in 1938 but abandoned in 1943.

On the other hand, the war years facilitated drawing renewed attention to public libraries, and in 1946, at the urging of ALA, the Social Science Research Council declared an inquiry on that subject to be important, and appropriate for its own sponsorship.[34] Carnegie money was soon obtained, and by the end of the forties a number of volumes began to appear (certain others were never published), in some cases based on research. The Public Library Inquiry had however been confided to more nonlibrarian than librarian hands. This tacit rebuke seems likely to have influenced the birth of *Library Trends*, which the University of Illinois Library School organized in 1952 with inspiration credited to "the Annals of the American Academy, the Review of Educational Research, and the Law Forum."[35] Despite the labors of individual scholars and the publication possibilities represented by twenty years of *Library Quarterly* and ten of *College and Research Libraries*, it was clear that "the surface of studies needed has barely been stretched."[36] *Library Trends* adopted from the outset the one-broad-topic-per-issue plan already appreciated in some other fields of study. Its focus on "current trends" in this or that sphere proved to have the great advantage of flexibility and implied practical benefits; it also allowed a very modest role to historical perspective. Its state-of-the-art character naturally militated against publishing much research, as distinct from essays surveying research. Research reports did play a part in the Illinois-sponsored Allerton House conferences which began in 1954.

The year 1946 is also a landmark for the foundation of the Canadian Library Association, an achievement soon followed by steady progress in the research in library holdings required to organize various means of national bibliographic control.

There were by this time numerous research monographs emanating from Chicago and the other doctoral schools, some of which were published. The Ford Foundation was moved to set up the Council on Library Resources in September 1956; grants were announced nine months later. In October 1957, however, when *Library Trends* looked long and hard at research for the first time, no great satisfaction could be reported. Not all that was labeled research really merited the label, noted Carnovsky; frequently uncertain were project aims and the validity of the devices used to pursue them.[37] Sweeping still wider horizons, Shera declared that "the past record of research in documentation and librarianship is not one to inspire confidence in an early solution to the many vexing problems"; he demanded of it "much more than mere fact-finding."[38]

The library survey continued to be respected, partly because some were done very well, partly also no doubt because several (1950–)

involved the expensive services of the new-style professional management consultants. E. W. Erickson's *College and University Library Surveys 1938–1952* (1961) explored the fate of many surveyors' recommendations. He reported a great many implemented. Meanwhile, M. F. Tauber submitted a "Survey of Surveys," disseminated by *Library Journal* among others, which indicated lessons learned from some 500 libraries, 300 of them public.[39] Distinctly pioneering was the 1956 assemblage of data on how 5,500 library patrons actually used catalogs at 39 libraries of different sorts and sizes; the basic tool was a behavior-at-the-catalog checklist.[40]

The sophistication so often brought by money, sometimes only by money, appeared at the same time, not surprisingly, in the offices of the scientists close to industrial and military matters. In 1950 resuming the labors of the defunct *Journal of Documentary Reproduction* and projecting much greater breadth of interest, *American Documentation* was undertaken by the institute of the same name, with an editorial board led by Vernon D. Tate, librarian of the Massachusetts Institute of Technology. Its scope was announced as "documentation," defined by the International Federation for Documentation as "the creation, transmission, collection, classification, and use of 'documents' . . . recorded knowledge in any format."[41] The quarterly offerings proved to be mainly descriptions of devices and processes, analyses of technical reports, book reviews, and proposals for new techniques, with some discussion of aims and policies. Occasional papers were partly of research character.

A qualitative leap in commitment occurred in 1958 when the National Science Foundation established the Office of Science Information Service, and the Department of Defense organized cognate units five years later.[42] Research and development in information processing received a great lift; the resources of the latest technology were henceforth to be called upon with money as well as dedication. During the five years (1959–64) in which the U.S. Office of Education published *Library Research in Progress*, the total support reported was $8,730,036. Half of that was credited to the federal government, the principal agencies granting funds being the National Science Foundation and the USOE.[43]

A qualitative leap in performance was recorded with the preliminary 1961 report (refined in 1969) on *Patterns in the Use of Books in Large Research Libraries*, by Herman H. Fussler and Julian L. Simon. The major purpose of the Council on Library Resources-funded study was to answer the question, "Will any kind of statistical procedure predict with reasonable accuracy the frequencies with which groups of books with defined characteristics are likely to be used in a research library?" Chapter 1 discussed the "random model of book use," the "development of a measure of the 'value' or 'usefulness' of books," the "definition of sampling units," "determination of subject area size," "choice of subject areas to study," "requirements of monograph sampling plan," and the "sample size" correct statistically. Judgment entered into the procedures not only in particulars within the statistical constructions but as an independent test of the statistical indexes of recorded use. The concluding remark referred to the investigation as "essentially exploratory," with the hope that other investigators would undertake to "verify, qualify, or extend our conclusions."[44]

The USOE had meanwhile been developing new statistics gathering and reporting, thanks in part to the establishment in 1937 of the Library Services Unit. Public library activities serving populations of 100,000 and more were reported annually, and more elaborate surveys every five to seven years also included academic and school libraries. (Badly needed improvement for the latter was finally provided by the National Defense Education Act of 1958; in 1963 it became possible to assign a staff member to reporting on special libraries. These developments were partially interrupted in 1965 by the shift of personnel to the National Center for Educational Statistics and the shift of emphasis to evaluation of grant proposals.) But the mounting concern over comparability of the statistics gathered led successfully to a 1946 conference aimed at formulating a program, increased attention to the subject by ALA leading bodies, enlistment of Council on Library Resources interest,[45] and a national conference in 1966, which promoted statistical standardization and in particular the newly published *Library Statistics: A Handbook of Concepts, Definitions, and Terminology*.

In 1970 Kenneth Beasley identified the outstanding weaknesses as follows:

> 1. . . . the confusion by many librarians of descriptive statistics, standards, and qualitative evaluations . . .
>
> 2. . . . [difficulty in achieving] clear definition of [library] functions . . .
>
> 3. . . . not understanding that there are two levels or types of statistics which overlap in some instances but still have clear identities . . . those which are the basis for a qualitative measurement and setting of standards . . . [and] a lower order . . . concerned with operations.
>
> 4. [the absence of] a data bank.[46]

Although World War II and the years immediately after it had directed many more dollars to library research than had been available before, the service orientation was bound to emphasize empirical investigation unless philosophical postulates and objectives were brought to bear. That had been begun at Chicago, but the same war dispersed the advocates, and the next generation dollars were granted mainly where statistics were promised. As Shera noted in 1964, objectivity was still confused with counting; true research was by definition challenging, therefore disquieting.[47] He urged broad conceptualizing and hailed the new "team" research. By 1970 money, machines, and thinking enriched the "documentation" field to the point where "information science" burst forth as a major activity, led in the United States by a broadened and deepened *American Documentation*, now called the *Journal of the American Society for Information Science*. Also an important sponsor of research study was the private Association for Library Automation Research Communications (LARC), which in early 1976 merged into World Information Systems Exchange (WISE).

Among the trail-blazers in research publication of the more familiar sort were the Festschrift for Elizabeth Homer Morton, *Librarianship in Canada, 1946 to 1967*, issued by the Canadian Library Association in 1968; and *Library and Information Service Needs of the Nation* (1974), notable among other things for serious investigation of the reading "interests" alleged to be cherished by specific groups of non-library users in the Los Angeles area.[48]

Altogether, as one looks back one hundred years, research publication has gained in financing and sophistication, but the defects may well owe something to uncertainty philosophically. If the purpose and direction of our libraries and librarianship were clearer, we might at least have what we presently lack, "a service . . . which identifies research in progress in the field of library and information science."[49] Solving that problem would greatly facilitate shaping the research we all need.

NOTES

1. Such materials had been produced since colonial days. The outstanding historical work was Josiah Quincy's *History of the Boston Athenaeum* (Cambridge, Mass.: Metcalf, 1851).
2. See the critical summary by Jesse Shera in "Literature of American Library History," *Library Quarterly* 15:1–24 (Jan. 1945).
3. U.S. Bureau of Education, *Public Libraries in the United States of America*, (Washington, D.C.: Govt. Print. Off., 1876), pp. ix, xvii, xxxv. See also summary in Sidney L. Jackson, *Libraries and Librarianship in the West* (New York: McGraw-Hill, 1974), pp. 348–52 passim.
4. U.S. Office of Education, *Annual Report of the Commissioner for the Fiscal Year Ending June 30, 1926* (Washington, D.C.: Govt. Print. Off., 1926), p. 13.
5. For dates see *List of Publications of the Bureau of Education, 1867–1910* (Washington, D.C.: Govt. Print. Off., 1940).
6. *ALA Bulletin* 1:9 (Jan. 1907); ibid., pp. 54, 58, 119–20, 252–54 (July 1907).
7. "First Yearly Report on Theological Libraries," *Library Journal* 10:269–76 (Oct. 1885).
8. "Registration of Book Borrowers," *Library Journal* 12:340–44 (Sept.–Oct. 1887).
9. *Library Journal* 29:157–62 (1904).
10. Caroline M. Hewins, "Yearly Report on Boys' and Girls' Reading," *Library Journal* 7:182–90 (July–Aug. 1882).
11. *Library Journal* 22:190–93 (Apr. 1897).
12. U.S. Bureau of Education, *Report of the Commissioner for the Year 1899–1900*, pt. 1 (Washington, D.C.: Govt. Print. Off., 1900), p. 710.
13. George F. Winchester, "Suggestions for an ALA Statistical Handbook," *Library Journal* 38:556–58 (Oct. 1913).

354 / Environment

14. Douglas Waples and Ralph W. Tyler, *What People Want to Read About* (Chicago: American Library Assn. and Univ. of Chicago Pr., 1931), p. vii.
15. Ibid.
16. Ibid., p. viii–ix.
17. Ibid., p. x.
18. Ibid., pp. 148, 173–86 passim.
19. C. C. Williamson, "The Place of Research in Library Service," *Library Quarterly* 1:5 (Jan. 1931).
20. Ibid., p. 16.
21. "Some Problems under Investigation," ibid., pp. 34–36.
22. Ernest J. Reece, "The Service-Loads of Library School Faculties," ibid., pp. 37–56 passim.
23. William M. Randall, "What Can the Foreigner Find to Read in the Public Library?" ibid., pp. 79–88 passim.
24. *Library Quarterly*, pp. 95–97.
25. Ibid., pp. 92–94.
26. A. H. Starke, "Children's Reading," ibid., p. 175.
27. Ibid., pp. 175–76.
28. Ibid., p. 180.
29. Douglas Waples, "What Subjects Appeal to the General Reader?" ibid., p. 189.
30. Theodore Norton, review of *University Librarianship* by George Herbert Bushnell, ibid., p. 215.
31. J. C. M. Hanson, review of *Classification . . .* by Ernest C. Richardson, ibid., pp. 217–18.
32. Leon Carnovsky, review of *Reference Work* by James I. Wyer, ibid., p. 220.
33. Helen L. Butler, review of *Library Service for Children* by Effie L. Power, ibid., pp. 224–25.
34. "The Public Library Inquiry," *Library Journal* 72:698 (May 1, 1947).
35. Robert B. Downs, "Introduction," *Library Trends* 1:3 (July 1952).
36. Ibid., p. 6.
37. Leon Carnovsky, "Methodology in Research and Applications," *Library Trends* 6:234–46 passim.
38. Jesse L. Shera, ibid., pp. 187, 188.
39. M. F. Tauber, "Survey of Surveys," *Library Journal* 86:1351–57 (Apr. 1, 1961).
40. Sidney L. Jackson, *Catalog Use Study* (Chicago: American Library Assn., 1958).
41. Vernon D. Tate, special notice to subscribers of the *Journal of Documentary Reproduction*, *American Documentation* 1:2 (Jan. 1950).
42. Paul C. Janacke, "Federally Funded Research in Librarianship," *Library Trends* 24:104 (July 1975).
43. Ibid., pp. 108–9.
44. Herman H. Fussler and Julian L. Simon, *Patterns in the Use of Books in Large Research Libraries* (Chicago: Univ. of Chicago Pr., 1969), pp. 5–13 passim, 147, 148.
45. *Planning for a Nation Wide System of Library Statistics*, David C. Palmer, ALA project director and general ed. (Washington, D.C.: Dept. of Health, Education, and Welfare, 1970), pp. 31–33.
46. *Planning . . .* , pp. 54–56.
47. Jesse L. Shera, "Darwin, Bacon, and Research in Librarianship," *Library Trends* 13:145–48 (July 1964).
48. Washington, D.C.: Government Printing Office, 1974. In particular Donald V. Black's "Library Needs of the Disadvantaged," pp. 281–314 passim, esp. table A–16, p. 306.
49. Janacke, p. 109.